# RSF: The Russell Sage Foundation Journal of the Social Sciences

*The Fiftieth Anniversary of the Kerner Commission Report*

**VOLUME 4, NUMBER 6, SEPTEMBER 2018**

**RSF: The Russell Sage Foundation Journal of the Social Sciences**   ISSN 2377-8261

## The Russell Sage Foundation

The Russell Sage Foundation, one of the oldest of America's general purpose foundations, was established in 1907 by Mrs. Margaret Olivia Sage for "the improvement of social and living conditions in the United States." The foundation seeks to fulfill this mandate by fostering the development and dissemination of knowledge about the country's political, social, and economic problems. While the foundation endeavors to assure the accuracy and objectivity of each book it publishes, the conclusions and interpretations in Russell Sage Foundation publications are those of the authors and not of the foundation, its trustees, or its staff. Publication by Russell Sage, therefore, does not imply foundation endorsement.

## Board of Trustees

Claude M. Steele, *Chair*

Larry M. Bartels
Karen S. Cook
Sheldon H. Danziger
Kathryn Edin
Michael Jones-Correa
Lawrence F. Katz
David Laibson

Nicholas Lemann
Sara S. McLanahan
Martha Minow
Peter R. Orszag
Mario Luis Small
Shelley E. Taylor
Hirokazu Yoshikawa

## Mission Statement

*RSF: The Russell Sage Foundation Journal of the Social Sciences* is a peer-reviewed, open-access journal of original empirical research articles by both established and emerging scholars. It is designed to promote cross-disciplinary collaborations on timely issues of interest to academics, policymakers, and the public at large. Each issue is thematic in nature and focuses on a specific research question or area of interest. The introduction to each issue will include an accessible, broad, and synthetic overview of the research question under consideration and the current thinking from the various social sciences.

## RSF Journal Editorial Board

Elizabeth O. Ananat, Duke University
Sheldon H. Danziger, Russell Sage Foundation
Mesmin Destin, Northwestern University
Shigeo Hirano, Columbia University
Maria Krysan, University of Illinois, Chicago
Michal Kurlaender, University of California, Davis
Helen Levy, University of Michigan
Martha Minow, Harvard University
Mary E. Pattillo, Northwestern University
Becky Pettit, University of Texas at Austin
Miguel S. Urquiola, Columbia University

Copyright © 2018 by Russell Sage Foundation. All rights reserved. Printed in the United States of America. No part of this publication may be reproduced, stored in a retrieval system, or transmitted in any form or by any means, electronic, mechanical, photocopying, recording, or otherwise, without the prior written permission of the publisher. Reproduction by the United States Government in whole or in part is permitted for any purpose.

Opinions expressed in this journal are not necessarily those of the editors, editorial board, trustees, or the Russell Sage Foundation.

We invite scholars to submit proposals for potential issues through the *RSF* application portal: https://rsfjournal.onlineapplicationportal.com/. Submissions should be addressed to Suzanne Nichols, Director of Publications.

To view the complete text and additional features online please go to **www.rsfjournal.org**.

## Open Access Policy

*RSF: The Russell Sage Foundation Journal of the Social Sciences* is an open access journal. It is published under a Creative Commons Attribution-NonCommercial-No Derivs 3.0 Unported License.

**Russell Sage Foundation**
112 East 64th Street
New York, NY 10065

**ISSN (print):** 2377-8253
**ISSN (electronic):** 2377-8261
**ISBN:** 978-0-87154-447-6

RSF: The Russell Sage Foundation
Journal of the Social Sciences

VOLUME 4, NUMBER 6,
SEPTEMBER 2018

# The Fiftieth Anniversary of the Kerner Commission Report

ISSUE EDITORS
Susan T. Gooden, Virginia Commonwealth University
Samuel L. Myers Jr., University of Minnesota

## CONTENTS

The Kerner Commission Report Fifty Years Later: Revisiting the American Dream  1
*Susan T. Gooden and Samuel L. Myers Jr.*

### Part I. The Kerner Commission in Context

How Does It Feel to Be a Problem? The Missing Kerner Commission Report  20
*Keisha L. Bentley-Edwards, Malik Chaka Edwards, Cynthia Neal Spence, William A. Darity Jr., Darrick Hamilton, and Jasson Perez*

From Bakke to Fisher: African American Students in U.S. Higher Education over Forty Years  41
*Walter R. Allen, Channel McLewis, Chantal Jones, and Daniel Harris*

Whither Whiteness? The Racial Logics of the Kerner Report and Modern White Space  73
*Matthew W. Hughey*

Measuring the Distance: The Legacy of the Kerner Report  99
*Rick Loessberg and John Koskinen*

### Part II. Policing, Law, and Communities

Changes in the Policing of Civil Disorders Since the Kerner Report: The Police Response to Ferguson, August 2014, and Some Implications for the Twenty-First Century  122
*Patrick F. Gillham and Gary T. Marx*

The Effects of the Neighborhood Legal Services Program on Riots and the Wealth of African Americans  144
*Jamein P. Cunningham and Rob Gillezeau*

### Part III. Urban Cities in Focus

Fifty Years After the Kerner Commission Report: Place, Housing, and Racial Wealth Inequality in Los Angeles  160
*Melany De La Cruz-Viesca, Paul M. Ong, Andre Comandon, William A. Darity Jr., and Darrick Hamilton*

The Evolution of Black Neighborhoods Since Kerner  185
*Marcus D. Casey and Bradley L. Hardy*

Detroit Fifty Years After the Kerner Report: What Has Changed, What Has Not, and Why?  206
*Reynolds Farley*

# The Kerner Commission Report Fifty Years Later: Revisiting the American Dream

SUSAN T. GOODEN AND SAMUEL L. MYERS JR.

The 1968 account of the 1967 race riots, authored by the National Advisory Commission on Civil Disorders (the Kerner Commission, thus the Kerner report), directly called into question the fundamental premise of the American Dream. "The idea of the American dream has been attached to everything from religious freedom to a home in the suburbs, and it has inspired emotions ranging from deep satisfaction to disillusioned fury. Nevertheless, the phrase elicits for most Americans some variant of Locke's fantasy—a new world where anything can happen and good things might" (Hochschild 1995, 17). The premise of the American Dream rests on three fundamental tenets: the equal opportunity to participate and the ability to start over, a reasonable anticipation of success, and the notion that success is under one's control (Hochschild 1995). The basis of each of these tenets is strongly refuted in the report first released on February 29, 1968 (commonly referred to as the Kerner Commission report in reference to the commission chairman, Otto Kerner).

Understanding the shortcomings of American society in implementing its democratic ideals relative to African Americans was advanced long before the Kerner report. Writings by W. E. B. DuBois (1903), Franklin Frazier (1940), Gunnar Myrdal (1944), Kenneth Clark (1965), and Gary Marx (1967), for example, expose a deep-seated disconnect between philosophy and practice. In his 1890 commencement address at Harvard University, DuBois reflected on a "nation [that] was founded on the loftiest ideals, and who many times forgot those ideals with a strange forgetfulness" (1903, 19).

## OVERVIEW OF THE KERNER REPORT: WHAT IS IT AND WHY IS IT IMPORTANT?

The Kerner report was the final report of a commission appointed by the U.S. President Lyndon B. Johnson on July 28, 1967, as a response to preceding and ongoing racial riots across many urban cities, including Los Angeles, Chicago, Detroit, and Newark. These riots largely took place in African American neighborhoods, then commonly called ghettos. On February 29, 1968, seven months after the commission was formed, it issued its final report. The report

---

**Susan T. Gooden** is interim dean and professor of public administration and policy at the L. Douglas Wilder School of Government and Public Affairs at Virginia Commonwealth University. **Samuel L. Myers Jr.** is Roy Wilkins Professor of Human Relations and Social Justice and directs the Roy Wilkins Center for Human Relations and Social Justice at the University of Minnesota.

© 2018 Russell Sage Foundation. Gooden, Susan T., and Samuel L. Myers Jr. 2018. "The Kerner Commission Report Fifty Years Later: Revisiting the American Dream." *RSF: The Russell Sage Foundation Journal of the Social Sciences* 4(6): 1–17. DOI: 10.7758/RSF.2018.4.6.01. Direct correspondence to: Susan T. Gooden at stgooden @vcu.edu, 923 W. Franklin St., Richmond, VA 23284.

Open Access Policy: *RSF: The Russell Sage Foundation Journal of the Social Sciences* is an open access journal. This article is published under a Creative Commons Attribution-NonCommercial-NoDerivs 3.0 Unported License.

was an instant success, selling more than two million copies.

The pathbreaking nature of the Kerner report is not based so much on what was said, but on who said it. A White House commission, responding to Executive Order 11365, issued by then President Lyndon B. Johnson, explicitly identified white racism as the principal cause of the civil disorder evidenced across hundreds of U.S. cities in which riots occurred: "What white Americans have never fully understood—but what the Negro can never forget—is that white society is deeply implicated in the ghetto. White institutions created it, white institutions maintain it, and white society condones it" (Kerner Report 1968, 2). The report directly acknowledged the gripping role of white racism in U.S. society. A report commissioned by a U.S. president powerfully introduced institutional racism into the political mainstream.

Fifty years have passed since the release of the Kerner report. President Johnson tasked the commission with three central questions following four summers of urban racial disorders and violence in several major cities: What happened? Why did it happen? What can be done to prevent it from happening again? After conducting a comprehensive investigation, visiting cities affected by riots, and consulting with scores of experts and witnesses, the Kerner report attributed the cause of urban violence to white racism, and the neglect and isolation it produced for African Americans. The basic conclusion was this: "Our nation is moving toward two societies, one black, one white—separate and unequal."

The Kerner report outlined core recommendations for a National Plan of Action, the goal of which was moving toward "a single society and a single American identity." It called for the substantial investment of federal funds to assist African American communities and prevent further racial polarization and violence. The main recommendations were in the areas of education, employment, housing, police-community relations, and welfare. Although he commissioned the report, President Johnson never accepted or acted on its findings. Shortly after it was released, the nation was shaken by the assassination of the Reverend Dr. Martin Luther King Jr. Riots and violence broke out in many cities across the country.

The Kerner report documents 164 civil disorders that occurred in 128 cities across the forty-eight continental states and the District of Columbia in 1967 (1968, 65). Other reports indicate a total of 957 riots in 133 cities from 1963 until 1968, a particular explosion of violence following the assassination of King in April 1968 (Olzak 2015). Estimates of the number of persons who died during these riots vary. The Kerner report, however, puts the number at eighty-three, citing 1,897 injuries in the study of seventy-five disturbances by the Permanent Subcommittee on Investigations of the Senate Committee on Government Operations (1968, 66).

The fiftieth anniversary of the Kerner Commission report provides a critical opportunity to revisit the report, its findings, and its recommendations in light of contemporary political realities, social structures, and policy debates. This is the purpose of this issue of *RSF: The Russell Sage Foundation Journal of the Social Sciences*, which includes nine essays from thought-leaders in a range of social science disciplines including economics, sociology, public policy, and public administration.

This introductory essay provides historical context on the Kerner Commission, as well as its importance and relevancy today. Additionally, it examines measures of inequality from 1963 to 2016 in income, education, poverty, and unemployment. We demonstrate that some areas—educational attainment and poverty—show relative improvement but other areas—family income and unemployment disparities—show little change. By multiple measures, the relevancy of the Kerner report is ever increasing.

Emblematic of this, just as contributing authors prepared drafts of their manuscripts for this volume during the summer of 2017, violence erupted in Emancipation Park in the City of Charlottesville, Virginia. The August 12 uprising occurred when white nationalists gathered for a march that ended in violence. The result was the tragic killing of Heather Heyer, who died when a car plowed into the crowd of protesters. Revisiting the Kerner report on its fiftieth anniversary is not a symbolic opportunity to reflect on its critical importance, but

**Table 1.** Timeline Highlights from the 1960s

| | |
|---|---|
| February 1, 1960 | Greensboro, NC, lunch counter sit-ins |
| November 8, 1960 | John F. Kennedy elected president |
| May 3, 1963 | Bull Conner uses fire hoses and police dogs on protestors |
| August 28, 1963 | Civil rights march on Washington (Dr. Martin Luther King Jr.'s "I Have a Dream" speech) |
| September 15, 1963 | Birmingham Church bombings |
| November 23, 1963 | President Kennedy assassination |
| January 8, 1964 | President Lyndon B. Johnson declares War on Poverty |
| May 22, 1964 | President Johnson proclaims the "Great Society" |
| Summer 1964 | Freedom Summer |
| July 2, 1964 | Civil Rights Act of 1964 signed |
| December 10, 1964 | Dr. Martin Luther King Jr. receives Nobel Prize |
| February 21, 1965 | Malcolm X assassination |
| March 7, 1965 | Selma-Montgomery March—"Bloody Sunday" |
| July 30, 1965 | Creation of Medicare and Medicaid |
| August 6, 1965 | Voting Rights Act of 1965 signed |
| August 11–16, 1965 | Watts riots |
| September 24, 1965 | Johnson Executive Order 11246 enforcing affirmative action |
| July 1967 | Riots in several U.S. cities, including Newark and Detroit |
| July 28, 1967 | President Johnson appoints Kerner Commission in response to riots |
| October 2, 1967 | Thurgood Marshall sworn in as Supreme Court justice |
| February 29, 1968 | Kerner Commission report released |
| March 31, 1968 | President Johnson announces he will not seek reelection |
| April 4, 1968 | Dr. Martin Luther King Jr. assassination |
| April 11, 1968 | Civil Rights Act of 1968 signed prohibiting housing discrimination |
| November 5, 1968 | Richard Nixon elected president |

*Source:* Authors' tabulation.

an acute need to provide acumen for America's future.

## THE KERNER COMMISSION IN CONTEXT

It is important to highlight three characteristics of the Kerner report: the commission operated within a turbulent political environment, a primary data source for the report included images and voices of those directly affected by the urban riots, and the report recommendations were never implemented. We consider each of these in turn.

### The Commission's Turbulent Political Environment

President Johnson formed the commission well after establishing his legacy Great Society programs designed to combat poverty and racial injustice. Such programs included the Job Corps, Head Start, and Upward Bound, as well as an expansion of Social Security and Food Stamps. They also included signature and controversial civil rights legislation, namely, the Civil Rights Act of 1964 and the Voting Rights Act of 1965. Johnson's Fair Housing Act, the third pillar of his civil rights agenda, was passed after the urban riots, the Kerner report, and the assassination of Dr. King in 1968. As table 1 highlights, the Kerner Commission was formed toward the end of the 1960s, a decade in U.S. history squarely focused on civil rights. As Julian Zelizer explains,

> Civil rights leaders, including Martin Luther King Jr., had been making housing discrimination in northern cities a central issue of their campaign.... Among the many issues raised by civil rights and black power advocates, housing triggered an especially sharp backlash. Urban landlords, white eth-

**Table 2.** Members of the National Advisory Commission on Civil Disorders (Kerner Commission)

Otto Kerner (chairman), governor of Illinois
John V. Lindsay (vice chairman), mayor of New York City
Fred R. Harris, United States senator, Oklahoma
I.W. Abel, president, United Steelworkers of America (AFL-CIO)
Edward W. Brooke, United States senator, Massachusetts
Charles B. Thornton, chairman of the board and chief executive officer, Litton Industries, Inc.
James C. Corman, United States representative, 22nd District of California
Roy Wilkins, executive director, National Association for the Advancement of Colored People
William M. McCulloch, United States representative, 4th District of Ohio
Katherine Graham Peden, commissioner of commerce, state of Kentucky (1963–1967)
Herbert Jenkins, chief of police, Atlanta, Georgia

*Source:* Authors' tabulation.

nic votes, and other Americans remained fretful over declining property values in the nation's suburbs. The tensions over the housing bill had played out in the midterm campaigns, with Republicans in many states riding white discontent into gubernatorial and congressional seats. . . . As the political situation around Johnson continued to deteriorate in July 1967, he then confronted some of the most difficult weeks of his presidency. In July, two major riots devastated the cities of Newark, New Jersey and Detroit, Michigan. These were the worst of 163 riots that broke out that summer. . . . On July 12, rioting started in Newark after rumors that the police mistreated an African American cab driver whom they were arresting. . . . [The riots occurred during at a time when] Johnson, northern Democrats, and the Great Society were already on the defensive. (2016, xiv, xv)

The Kerner Commission was formed rather hastily out of Johnson's desperation to do something in response to the riots. Members of Johnson's cabinet cautioned that the Commission's report could turn into a political nightmare. "The President tried to avert this problem by stacking the commission with established political figures who were moderate and committed to the existing economic and political system . . . He wanted commissioners who would demonstrate that the administration took the problem seriously, but he also remained intent on appointments that would ensure a final report that praised his Great Society programs. Furthermore, he resisted giving the commission sufficient funding, thus guaranteeing that they would be handcuffed from the start" (Zelizer 2016, xvii). Table 2 provides a listing of the members of the commission. The eleven members of the Kerner Commission included two African Americans, Republican Edward Brooke, a new senator from Massachusetts, and Roy Wilkins, the iconic civil rights leader and former president of the NAACP (National Association for the Advancement of Colored People).

Wilkins was a strong Johnson supporter who respected the president's pro-government approach to promoting civil rights. As Wilkins explained in an oral history interview at the time,

> I don't think anyone even now pretends to know precisely what to do. But he [Johnson] knew that opportunity had to be provided for some of the people who had never had opportunity in their lives. And he knew also that the traditional political machinery had not worked. . . . So he conceived the federal government's role to be that to provide an opportunity for the inner-cities. . . . I think it was a daring assault by a man of Mr. Johnson's background to come to that conclusion and to actually authorize the machinery. (Baker 1969, 9)

In 1969, Senator Brooke described the rioters as everyday citizens frustrated with deeply entrenched racial inequality in the United States.

> The people who rioted during the summer of 1967 were, for the most part, neither social misfits nor habitual criminals. They were not alcoholics or drug addicts. They were not Communists, and they were not inspired by Communists. And they were not part of an organized conspiracy designed to bring down the United States by attacking its great urban centers. Rather, they were men and women who were driven by the fear and frustration which accompanies continuing second-class citizenship in a country dedicated to the principle of equality. (Brooke 1969, 25)

### The Kerner Report, Social Scientists, and Field Research

The Kerner report was grounded in empirical social science research, which included a team of social scientists with a deep understanding of structural racism. As Zelizer explains,

> During the investigative phase, the staff, as well as some commissioners, traveled in teams of six to twenty-three cities where there had been urban unrest so they could interview local citizens and activists.... In Milwaukee, Senator Fred Harris [(D-Oklahoma) the sole living member of the Kerner Commission] spent most of his day in a black barbershop, where he learned from customers about how segregation was far worse in Wisconsin than in the South. (2016, xxiv)

The data collection process that formed the basis of the Kerner report included direct engagement by members of the Kerner Commission with members of the affected communities. Members of the commission traveled to rioted cities and had conversations with inner-city residents within their community space. These involved firsthand, up-front, and personal conversations that allowed commissioners to hear, see, and understand the realities of deeply entrenched structural racial inequalities. One of their fundamental conclusions was that though variation across cities was considerable, there was "a complex relationship between the series of incidents and the underlying grievances.... When grievance-related incidents recurred and rising tensions were not satisfactorily resolved, a cumulative process took place in which prior incidents were readily recalled and grievances reinforced. At some point in the mounting tension, a further incident—in itself often routine or even trivial—became the breaking point, and the tension spilled over into violence" (Kerner Report 1968, 108).

Although not explicitly stated in the report, this intensive, firsthand engagement with inner-city African Americans provided an eye-opening, transformational experience that narrowed the social distance between the *us* and *them* worlds of members of the commission and inner city residents. As Kerner Commissioner former senator Fred Harris (D-Oklahoma) explained during a 2017 National Public Radio interview, "We held about 20 days of hearings, and then we divided up into teams and visited the cities where riots had occurred. And what we found was that there'd been a huge influx since World War II of African Americans from Southern states coming from criminally inferior schools, looking for jobs about the time that jobs were disappearing. They didn't have any transportation. Housing was awful. The schools were inferior. And there'd been all sorts of conflicts with the police so that there was enormous hostility between the people and the police in those cities" (NPR 2017).

Personal interactions are powerful. For example, when natural disasters strike communities, one of the most important actions elected officials can take is to travel to the affected communities, interact with residents, listen to their concerns, and witness firsthand the experiences of the affected. This creates an important emotional connection: empathy. The data collection process of the Kerner Commission offers an important roadmap for elected officials, academics, and practitioners alike in understanding the perspectives of individuals in urban and poor communities. Further, it offers a direct observation of these individuals' experiences vis-à-vis the core principles of the American Dream.

## Lack of Implementation of Kerner Commission Report Recommendations

The core recommendation of the Kerner report included the following objectives for national action:

- Opening up all opportunities for those who are restricted by racial segregation and discrimination, and eliminating all barriers to their choice of jobs, education, and housing.
- Removing the frustration of powerlessness among the disadvantaged by providing the means to deal with the problems that affect their own lives and by increasing the capacity of our public and private institutions to respond to those problems.
- Increasing communication across racial lines to destroy stereotypes, halt polarization, end distrust, and hostility, and create common ground for efforts toward common goals of public order and social justice. (Kerner Report 1968, 413)

President Johnson was enormously displeased with the report, which in his view grossly ignored his Great Society efforts. The report also received considerable backlash from many whites and conservatives for its identification of attitudes and racism of whites as a cause of the riots. "So Johnson ignored the report. He refused to formally receive the publication in front of reporters. He didn't talk about the Kerner Commission report when asked by the media," and he refused to sign thank-you letters for the commissioners (Zelizer 2016, xxxii–xxxiii).

Kerner Commission member Roy Wilkins was profoundly disappointed in President Johnson's response.

> I was disappointed . . . now the report did not say that white racism . . . is behind every single act that's committed—or every single Machiavellian scheme that's hatched. . . . It didn't say that. It simply said that the creation of the climate, which has brought about our present tension, has been because, to use the words of the report, "of the attitude of white Americans towards black Americans." . . . It is perfectly in line with his actions as President and with the accomplishments of his Administration. I think probably, maybe the word racism, white racism, frightened him. He didn't want to go down in history as the President who had pointed his finger at his own people. (Baker 1969, 12)

Unfortunately, the fundamental recommendation of the Kerner report, a call for unity was virtually ignored. As the commissioners wrote, "This deepening racial division is not inevitable. The movement apart can still be reversed. . . . The alternative is not blind repression or capitulation to lawlessness. It is the realization of common opportunities for all within a single society. . . . From every American it will require new attitudes, new understanding, and above all, new will" (Kerner Report 1968, 1).

## CRITICISMS OF THE KERNER COMMISSION REPORT

The Kerner Commission report was a best seller, millions of copies sold across the country and devoured by a generation of intellectuals, activists, community organizers, and politicians. Not surprisingly, early critics of the report were numerous. Given the central role *white racism* played as the defining cause of the riots, much of the attacks on the Right and the Left concerned the significance of white racism in contributing to the civil disorders across the country.

Two years after the production of the Kerner Commission's final report, the University of Illinois hosted a retrospective analysis of the report, bringing together top Illinois politicians, business leaders, media executives, and academics. The commentary captured what had emerged as an enduring refrain about the shortcomings of the report. The most prominent concern, echoed by other writers over the years was the focus on white racism:

> [The Report's] basic finding that "white racism" was the fundamental cause of racial disorders and the emphasis placed upon that finding by the mass media have given the erroneous impression that the guilt of white

society is simply a matter of prejudicial attitudes. The Kerner Commission Report failed to specify exactly what was meant by white racism and largely ignored the problem of institutional racism—the less overt, more subtle acts that sustain and perpetuate racist policies in virtually every American institution.... Thus, the Report placed too much emphasis on changing white attitudes and underplayed the importance of changing white behavior and the basic structure of such institutions as schools, labor unions, and political parties. (Meranto 1970, 3)

The notion that the report fails to examine deeply institutional racism nor propose solutions that will remedy the problems rooted in institutional racism was recognized early among reviewers. For example, as Michael Parenti writes,

The Kerner Report demands no changes in the way power and wealth are distributed among the classes; it never gets beyond its indictment of "white racism" to specify the forces in the political economy which brought the black man to riot; it treats the obviously abominable ghetto living conditions as "cause" of disturbance but never really inquires into the causes of the "causes," viz., the ruthless enclosure of Southern sharecroppers by big corporate farming interests, the subsequent mistreatment of the black migrant by Northern rent-gorging landlords, price-gorging merchants, urban "redevelopers," discriminating employers, insufficient schools, hospitals and welfare, brutal police, hostile political machines and state legislators, and finally the whole system of values, material interests and public power distributions from the state to the federal Capitols which gives greater priority to "haves" than to "have-nots," servicing and subsidizing the bloated interests of private corporations while neglecting the often desperate needs of the municipalities. The Kerner Report reflects the ideological cast of its sponsors, the Johnson Administration, and in that sense is no better than the interests it served.... To treat the symptoms of social dislocation (e.g., slum conditions) as the causes of social ills is an inversion not peculiar to the Kerner Report. Unable or unwilling to pursue the implications of our own data, we tend to see the effects of a problem as the problem itself. The victims, rather than the victimizers, are defined as "the poverty problem." It is a little like blaming the corpse for the murder. (1970, 145–46)

Related, and relevant to the current rise of working-class whites who view programs in support of immigrants and racial minority group members as depriving them of economic benefits, is the criticism that the report fails to adequately identify the beneficiaries of alleged white racism. As famed black political scientist Mack Jones, former chair of Atlanta University's Department of Political Science, writes,

[An] important failing of the Report was that it failed to put white racism in a systems context so that we can see who benefits directly and materially from American racism. I am talking about the economics of racism. Such analysis, it seems to me, must by definition precede any attempt to devise even the most tentative prescription for change. However, from the Kerner Report one could infer that either all whites benefit equally or that they all suffer equally from racism in this country. The truth is that white racism has a highly differentiated impact in the white community. Only a small number of the white majority realize immediate material gains while the remainder must content themselves with psychic payoffs for their racism. (1970, 156)

A second line of criticism comes from the failure to acknowledge the significance of emerging black nationalism and the roles of the Black Panthers, the Nation of Islam and black self-help organizations in producing successful remedies to problems of economic distress in urban neighborhoods. Mack Jones, once again, provides powerful insights:

The Commission discussed what it entitled "Black Power" in little more than two pages. The major thrust of this part of the Report was the argument that the new mood in the black community was really old wine in new bottles, and that therefore it represented a retreat from integration and confrontation with racism. This may have been the greatest disservice of the entire Report, because while black power may be old wine in new bottles, the Commission had both the wrong wine and the wrong bottles. The new mood in the black community is a function of the intensification of the old argument between nationalists and integrationists which has been going on in the black community since the days of Frederick Douglass and Martin Delany. These two currents have always been present in the black community. Historically, those blacks espousing integrationism as an ideology have allied themselves with forces in the white community, and as a result the black liberation struggle has always been controlled in varying degrees by whites. Meanwhile, those who accept nationalism as the optimum sustaining ideology for the black struggle have always constituted an isolated and relatively impotent minority with little or no standing in their communities. The new mood which the Commission tried to deal with its "wine-bottle" analogy is really an indication that the followers of integrationism as an ideology are losing out to the nationalists. Although this development is more pronounced among the young, it is taking hold in every sector of the black community. (1970, 159)

Other notable criticisms of the report include the concern that there was little connection between the policy recommendations and the problem definition (Briggs 1968) and that the premise that the riots themselves were irrationally and randomly determined was unsupported by the evidence presented in the report. Michael Lipsky and David Olson questioned the extent to which riot commissions generally can be effective given the larger political landscape in which they operate (1969). A recurring theme among conservative critics of the report, moreover, was that the report misstated the degree of deterioration of the economic conditions of blacks and ignored improvements in relative earnings and incomes in the years before the riots (Thernstrom, Siegel, and Woodson 1998).

Modern social science researchers studying racial and ethnic economic inequality will note three types of omissions from the Kerner report. The first is that little attention is paid to the causal impacts of the riots in differentiating between outcomes among riot cities and nonriot cities. The interviews and data collection focus almost exclusively on riot cities, making it a bit more difficult to draw the conclusion that riots were "caused" by the frustrations and blocked opportunities faced by blacks living in cities that experienced riots. If riots were caused by these factors, then one would need to show that the pathways to economic outcomes differed between riot cities and nonriot cities. The descriptive evidence we provide in the next section of this essay is motivated by an attempt to address this issue of causality.

A second social science concern is that the report largely ignores the issue of wealth inequality, focusing instead on measures of income and poverty. Modern social science researchers note that black-white wealth inequality is far greater than black-white income inequality, even within common income quartiles. Recognition of the huge gap in home ownership and in ownership of other assets and the role of the federal government in contributing to and perpetuating wealth disparities would have prompted policy recommendations from the commission that spoke to such issues as antidiscrimination legislation in mortgage lending and compensation for government culpability in creating and sustaining racial disparities in ownership of property.

A third omission, surprising in retrospect, is an analysis of the role of the Federal Bureau of Investigation and law enforcement agencies in collecting information on dissident groups and their leadership. This role, coupled with the heavy investment by the federal government thwarting challenges to contemporary militarism and industrial capitalism, may have created an atmosphere ripe for revolutionary change. Although the report takes great pains to discount and discredit such a state role in contributing to the riots, it is surprising that little or no mention is made of the now infamous COINTELPRO operations. These covert efforts designed to discredit black organizations may have contributed to the heightened violence in urban areas in America by infiltrating black political organizations and contributing to distrust and hostility towards the police. It is not known whether the COINTELPRO activities blocked efforts of the commission or whether the commission's efforts purposefully avoided confronting evidence of the infiltration of black organizations. What is known is that shortly after the release of the commission's report, King was assassinated. Nowhere in the report does the commission investigate Dr. King's contention that "racism, economic exploitation, and militarism" are the triple evils of American society and that these evils are caused by capitalism. So, the commission ignored King's contention that ending racism requires a "revolution of American values" along with "fundamental structural transformation" of American society.

## THE STATE OF INEQUALITY: FIFTY YEARS AFTER KERNER

We are motivated to explore the trajectory of social-economic outcomes in riot cities and nonriot cities, before, during and after the riots by questions raised in the criticisms to the Kerner report. The report has implications for several areas of inequality within public policy, including education, employment, housing, police-community relations, and welfare. In the 1960s, the U.S. educational system was largely segregated, and blacks had far fewer educational opportunities than whites. Today, although high school completion rates are higher, classrooms within schools are perplexingly segregated, blacks struggling in basic classrooms with high rates of suspension and whites often enjoying the benefits of gifted and talented programs, sometimes within the same physical school. Although college attendance rates have soared, college completion rates remain widely disparate. By many accounts, housing segregation is as deeply rooted today as it was fifty years ago, particularly for low-income blacks.

Many racial disparities persist, particularly among minority youth in urban areas. Housing segregation, often viewed as one of the causes of black-white disparities in quality of education and access to jobs, appears to be as acute today as it was in the 1960s. Job markets, wages, and earnings all indicate significant racial differentials. In addition, those with criminal records often have very few labor market options. Housing policies have a significant impact on asset accumulation and economic well-being. The Kerner report highlighted specific public policy areas where changes were needed to reduce segregation and discrimination. Notable public policies on home ownership, rental housing and public housing, and lending all emerged after the Kerner report. A core component of the report focused on racial violence and its relationship to police behavior. Recent reports from the Department of Justice confirm that significant areas of concern remain regarding the relationship between law enforcement and the African American community. Finally, welfare policies have played a core role in the post–Kerner Commission era. Antipoverty measures were a primary focus of the War on Poverty. However, welfare policy has been largely shaped by conceptualizations of the deserving versus the undeserving poor. Since the Kerner report, the politics and public policy in approaches to welfare policy have gravitated toward efforts to dismantle the social safety net.

### Violent Protests Before and After the Kerner Commission

If anything, the Kerner Commission sought to quell the rise of violent protest. Figure 1, drawn from the work of Susan Olzak and various online sources, shows estimates of the number of racial riots from 1954 to 1992 and from 1993 to 2016 (Olzak 2015).[1] Although the methodologies differ between the two sources, the patterns displayed confirm a well-established historical record: that throughout the civil rights era of the late 1950s and throughout the 1960s, race riots were frequent across virtually hundreds of cities, peaking before the Kerner Commission and declining thereafter. Upticks in 1980, 1987, and 1992 and more recently in 2016

---

1. For a list of incidents of civil unrest in the United States since the Revolution, see https://en.wikipedia.org/wiki/List_of_incidents_of_civil_unrest_in_the_United_States#2000.E2.80.932009 (accessed May 14, 2018).

**Figure 1.** Urban Race Riots, 1954–2016

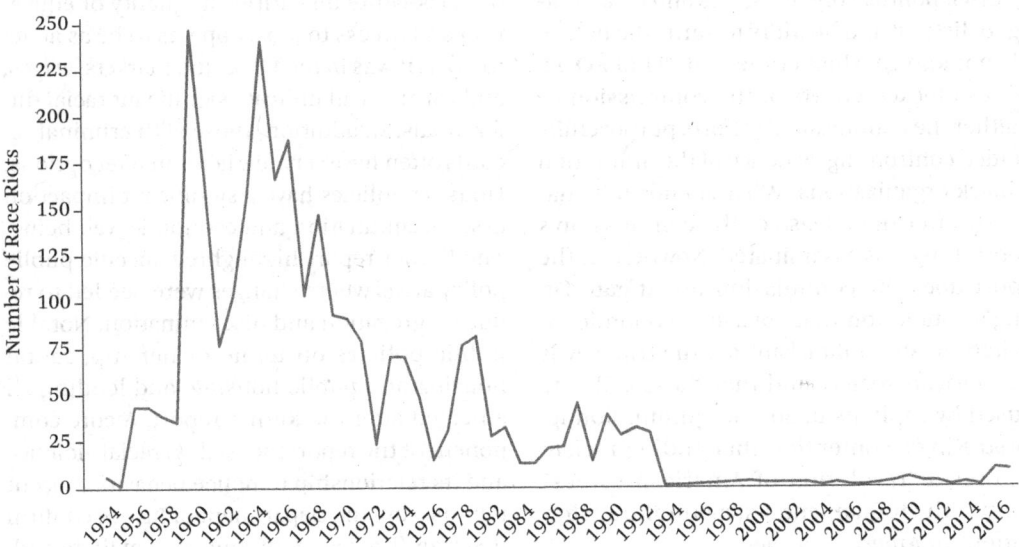

*Source:* Authors' compilation based on Olzak 2015 and "List of Ethnic Riots," Wikipedia, https://en.wikipedia.org/wiki/List_of_ethnic_riots (accessed September 5, 2017).

seem minor relative to the massive civil disorders of the 1960s.

Arguably, the incidence of race riots in urban areas declined after the turbulent 1960s. The reasons for the quelling of urban unrest are the subject of a copious literature. But, for the purposes of this essay, we focus on several key economic indicators that putatively describe the underlying causes of the conditions that led to the riots.

Of the major criticisms of the Kerner report, the easiest to confront is the one concerning causality. The report failed to include in its analysis interviews from nonriot cities. Because only riot cities are examined, it is impossible to know whether the determining factors highlighted in the report are different from conditions in nonrioting cities. Four major economic indicators painted a dire portrait of the black-white divide in America in the Kerner report. Blacks had lower incomes, higher poverty rates, higher unemployment rates, and lower educational attainment than whites. One might ask: Were conditions worse in the riot cities than in the nonrioting cities? Further, did the riot cities experience trajectories of these economic indicators that differed from those of the nonrioting cities?

### Trajectories of Riot Cities and Nonriot Cities

To answer these questions, we have compiled information from the March Supplements of the Current Population Surveys from 1963 until 2016 and plotted the ratios of black to white family incomes, unemployment rates, high school graduate rates, and poverty rates.[2]

Figure 2 shows the pattern of black-white family incomes from 1964 until 2016 for riot cities and nonrioting cities. Rioting cities, located disproportionately in the Northeast, Midwest, and West, maintained higher ratios of black to white family incomes than all other

---

2. All the analysis on CPS used the March Supplement. The data source is IPUMS-CPS. Person weights were used for unemployment and education disparities; household weights were used for family income and poverty rates. Unemployment rate excludes persons not in Universe for labor market status, not in labor force, or missing in employment status. High school graduates excludes people with missing education variable and includes high school equivalents (GED degree).

**Figure 2.** Mean Family Incomes, Black-White Ratio

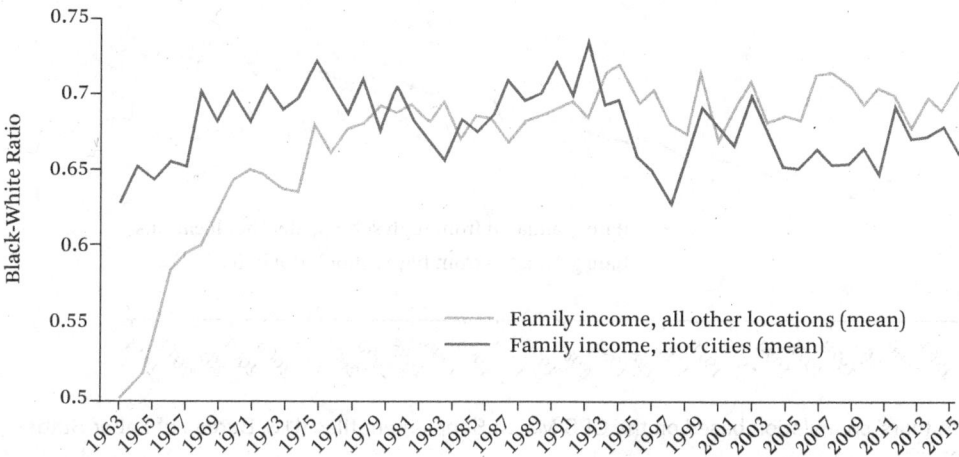

*Source:* Authors' compilation based on the CPS March Supplement files (U.S. Bureau of Labor Statistics 2018).

**Figure 3.** Unemployment Rates, Black-White Ratio

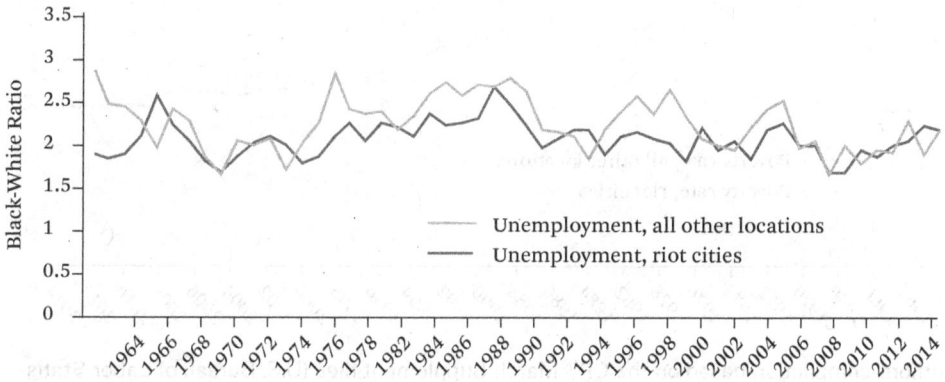

*Source:* Authors' compilation based on the CPS March Supplement files (U.S. Bureau of Labor Statistics 2018).

parts of the country before the major riots. In the year of the passage of the Civil Rights Act of 1964, black family income was about half of white family income in nonrioting cities and 63 percent in rioting cities. By the time Ronald Reagan was elected president in 1980, the racial gap in family incomes had narrowed in both series, and the black-white family income ratio converged to 0.68 and 0.69 in nonriot and riot cities respectively. By 1998, the ratio had fallen to 0.63 in the riot cities but hovered at 0.68 in the nonriot areas. Throughout most of the 2000s, the black-white family income ratio was higher in the nonriot areas than the riot cities, perhaps signaling the impacts of gentrification and out-flight of the black middle class. Gentrification in riot cities meant higher white incomes and lower ratios of black to white incomes. Out-flight of the black middle class in the riot cities meant lower ratios of black to white incomes relative to nonriot cities. Figure 3 shows the pattern of black-white unemployment rates from 1964 to 2016 in riot and nonriot cities. Rioting cities showed higher ratios of

**Figure 4.** High School Graduate Rates, Black-White Ratio

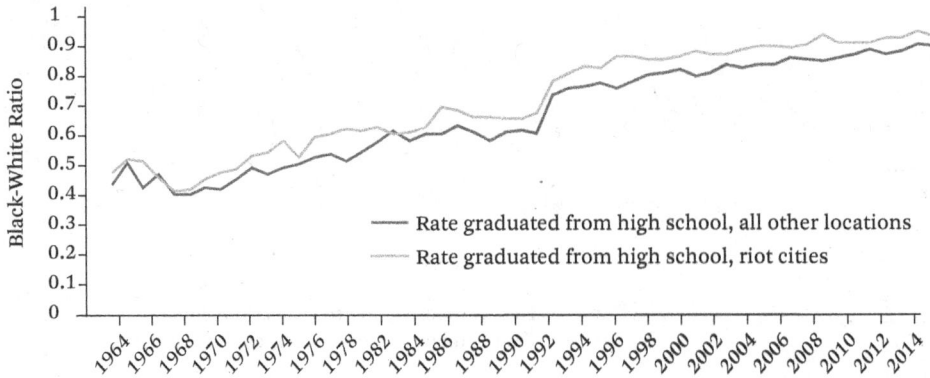

*Source:* Authors' compilation based on the CPS March Supplement files (U.S. Bureau of Labor Statistics 2018).

**Figure 5.** Poverty Rates, Black-White Ratios

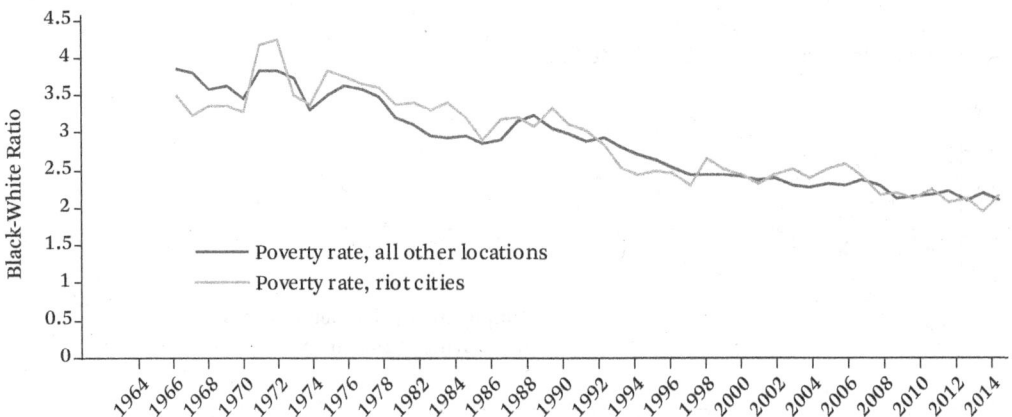

*Source:* Authors' compilation based on the CPS March Supplement files (U.S. Bureau of Labor Statistics 2018).

black to white unemployment rates than other locations before the riots. Black unemployment in the riot cities was three times that of white unemployment rates in 1964. Both series converged to about 2:1 to 2.5:1 throughout the rest of the century, the riot cities having slightly higher ratios than the nonriot cities until about 2007, when the two series became virtually identical.

Figure 4 reports the ratio of black to white individuals who are high school graduates (among those over sixteen) for riot and nonriot cities. The two series are nearly identical, though the riot cities have a slight edge. The ratio rose from around 0.40 the year of the major riots prompting the creation of the Kerner Commission to 0.93 and 0.89 in the riot and nonriot locations.

Figure 5 reports the ratio of black to white poverty rates for family householders in the riot and nonriot cities. At the time of the Kerner report, the ratio hovered around 3.5:1 to 3.8:1 in both riot and nonriot locations. It jumped up to 4.2:1 for riot cities in 1973 but declined for both series thereafter reaching the current level of a little over 2:1 in 2016.

This evidence points to a possible flaw in the Kerner Commission's report. Although the evidence clearly points to a divided America—a divide that continues today—the trajectories of the riot cities and the nonriot cities are remarkably similar. Thus, it is a bit more difficult to embrace the conclusion that this racial divide was the cause of the riots given that the racial divide was evident in both riot cities and nonriot cities and perhaps was even more pronounced in the nonriot cities than in the riot cities before the riots.

Fifty years later, it is worth revisiting these issues and also exploring whether successful policies designed to reduce the racial divide have emerged. The articles in this volume collectively address the questions of how far we have come, what worked and what did not work, and what the implications are for the twenty-first century.

## OVERVIEW

The articles in this volume are interdisciplinary. Contributing authors bring to their essays diverse backgrounds in economics, sociology, law, medicine, history, public policy, and real world practice. The authors discuss the blackness and whiteness of the racial identity, the police-community relationship, and various aspects of racial inequalities in education, housing, and wealth at both the national level and the local level.

In "How Does It Feel to Be a Problem? The Missing Kerner Commission Report," Keisha Bentley-Edwards and her co-authors offer a critique of the Kerner report's positioning of black rage as deviant. By protracting the history of white race riots back to 1877, the authors find that white race riots, which resulted in the loss of black lives, black-owned property, and constitutional rights, have been perceived as maintaining social order. However, black riots, marked by the loss of white-owned property but few white lives, were what prompted the formation of a national commission to investigate the events. The authors also show the influence of the Moynihan report in 1965, which identified "Negro family social disorganization" as the source of a culture of poverty that impedes black social and economic progress, on the Kerner report in 1968 (Geary 2015). Besides positioning black rage as the problem, the Kerner report is also criticized for ignoring the intersectionality of race and gender. This article points out that the face of civil unrest described in the Kerner Commission's report was predominately male, and that the lived experiences of inequality of black females were absent. Juxtaposing the President's Task Force on the 21st Century Policing in 2015 with the Kerner report, Bentley-Edwards and her co-authors show that little has changed in terms of problematizing black rage and the invisibility of the black female over the past fifty years.

In "From Bakke to Fisher: African American Students in U.S. Higher Education over Forty Years," Walter Allen and his co-authors focus on racial inequality in higher education, which was, as they point out, "strangely minimal within the Kerner Commission report." The article connects higher education to the wider society with arguments that unrest did occur on college campuses in the 1960s, that campus unrest reflects persistent racial inequality across the society, and that higher education systematically reproduces society's racial hierarchies. Referring to critical race theory, the authors study black student patterns and trends in public higher education since the Kerner report. They use the Integrated Postsecondary Education Data System data from 1976 to 2015 to analyze national patterns and trends in black college enrollment, degree completion, and gender differences in the twenty states with the largest proportion black populations, by types of institutions including the state flagship university, the most prominent historically black colleges and universities, and the most prominent black-serving institutions. They conclude with broad strokes regarding the three questions raised in this volume.

In "Whither Whiteness? The Racial Logics of the Kerner Report and Modern White Space," Matthew Hughey studies another overlooked aspect of whiteness in the Kerner report: how whites functioned in the racial regime. Hughey conducts content analysis of the full text of the Kerner report in 1986 and ethnographic study among six all-white organizations to answer two questions: How did the Kerner report describe the intersection of whites with employment, education, housing, and police-community relations? How do whites today make meaning of their intersection with these same four areas? Hughey's analyses also reveal little progress since the Kerner report. Taken together, the content analyses and ethnographic analyses demonstrate that the shared racial logics of white identity are stable and robust over both space (varied all-white locales) and time (1968 to 2018). Hughey further argues that these logics are often marshaled to promote a specific, or ideal form of white racial identity known as hegemonic whiteness.

In "Measuring the Distance: The Legacy of the Kerner Report," Rick Loessberg and John Koskinen, as a practitioner and a former Kerner Commission staff member respectively, provide insights into the legacy of the Kerner report, tapping their direct knowledge of the report and a review of the report's recommendations. Referring to various data sources and literature, Loessberg and Koskinen show that since the Kerner report, some areas, such as the incidence of poverty, have noticeably improved, whereas in others, such as black unemployment, virtually nothing has changed. Unlike many other studies that criticize the underimplementation of the Kerner report's recommendations, Loessberg and Koskinen demonstrate that some form of action was taken on many of the report's National Action recommendations, much of it occurring within the first five years, and that many recommendations of lesser scale have been implemented at the local levels. Along the same line, the authors argue that the Kerner report was and continues to be influential because it can educate, inform, and persuade America, and serves as the reference point of the discourse about racial inequality in the United States.

In "Changes in the Policing of Civil Disorders Since the Kerner Report: The Police Response to Ferguson, August 2014, and Some Implications for the Twenty-First Century," Patrick Gillham and Gary Marx focus on the changes in the police-protester relationship since the Kerner report. The authors argue that the relatively more sane, humane, and effective responses to the policing of disorders and protest is one of the most significant factors contributing to the absence of the large-scale, destructive, and spiraling riots since the 1960s. Gillham and Marx take a closer look at the changes in police disorder management during the 2014 Ferguson uprising, using the recommendations in the Kerner report as their analytical framework. The Kerner report identifies causes of policy mismanagement that include weakness in the command and control structure for policing disorders, lack of information or intelligence available to police, and inadequate self-protection equipment for the police. Drawing on media reports, police and activist accounts, after-action reports, and field observations of the 2014 uprising in Ferguson, Gillham and Marx find dramatic changes in the operational planning and equipment for policing disorders. The authors conclude with broader discussions about racial discrimination and inequality, police power, and justice in democratic societies.

In "The Effects of the Neighborhood Legal Services Program on Riots and the Wealth of African Americans," Jamein Cunningham and Rob Gillezeau evaluate the impact of Neighborhood Legal Services Program (NLSP), one of the many policy responses to the uprisings in the 1960s, on civil disorders and resulting changes in property values in African American communities. After brief reviews of the history of the legal service program and its relation to the War on Poverty, and to civil disorders, the authors hypothesize that the NLSP directly (through legal consultation) or indirectly (through reduction of riot propensities and severities) has a positive impact on wealth through property appreciation. Drawing on data from National Archives Community Action Program, Census City and County Data Books, and various other secondary datasets, the authors adopt continuous difference-in-difference analysis to determine the effectiveness of the NLSP as an antiriot policy, controlling for observable demographic characteristics as well as fixed effects to capture unobserved heterogeneity. The authors also use the age of the oldest nearby law school as an instrumental variable to deal with endogeneity related to the timing, location, and intensity of the NLSP as the treatment. Empirical analyses confirm the NLSP's effectiveness in combating civil disorders and in increasing property values. The authors conclude with broader discussions about the lessons and progress since the Kerner report as well as implications for the twenty-first century.

In "Fifty Years After the Kerner Commission Report: Place, Housing, and Racial Wealth Inequality in Los Angeles," Melany De La Cruz-Viesca and her co-authors focus on wealth disparity, an ignored dimension of inequalities in both the Kerner Commission's report and California's McCone Commission report on the 1965 Watts riots in Los Angeles. The authors examine how place intersects with housing policy, racial discrimination, immigration, and globalization in Los Angeles, which contextualizes data analysis of wealth disparities through the lens of home ownership. Using data from sources including the U.S. Census Bureau public-use micro samples, the American Community Survey sample, and the American Housing Survey, this article studies the case of Los Angeles from 1960 to 1990 and then to 2015. Data analyses reveal that the black and Hispanic residents are disadvantaged in both homeownership rate and property value. The authors criticize the two reports' housing policy recommendations for focusing only on the rental sector, preventing asset building through homeownership and perpetuating wealth disparities. The two reports, according to the authors, also failed to foresee the significant demographic changes in Los Angeles. In terms of implications for the twenty-first century, the authors point out the necessity and importance of studying racial wealth inequality.

In "The Evolution of Black Neighborhoods Since Kerner," Marcus Casey and Bradley Hardy study the evolution of African American neighborhoods since the Kerner report. The authors match riot locations with tract-level census data to compare neighborhoods directly affected by the riots in the 1960s with those not affected in Detroit, Newark, Los Angeles, and Washington, D.C. The authors also expand the scope of the analysis nationally to study how black neighborhoods fared relative to nonblack neighborhoods from 1970 to 2010. The analytical results show that disparities identified as policy priorities by the Kerner report—primarily income, poverty, and unemployment—persist over the observation period despite declines in extreme segregation and increased suburbanization of blacks. Neighborhoods directly affected by riots in the four cities remain among the most economically disadvantaged today. And socioeconomic gaps continue to persist between black and nonblack neighborhoods regardless of the history of rioting. The authors conclude that fifty years after the Kerner Commission's report, pathways for black individuals to achieve economic mobility—through better education attainment and better access to elite employment, income, and wealth—have improved greatly, but that black neighborhoods remain economically stagnant.

In "Detroit Fifty Years After the Kerner Report: What Has Changed, What Has Not, and Why?," Reynolds Farley analyzes the racial changes in metropolitan Detroit in focus areas identified by the Kerner report. Drawing on the history of Detroit and data about the city from the Census Bureau's American Community Survey and Current Population Survey, the article shows progress since the 1960s in residential integration, indicated by the suburban ring being open to African Americans, and in social integration, indicated by increased interracial marriage and increased proportion of African Americans in the prestigious occupations. However, Farley also finds that African Americans in the metropolitan Detroit area are today further behind whites than they were in 1967 when it comes to key economic measures. Farley attributes the lack of progress to the dramatic changes in Detroit's labor market and the failure of the educational system to provide the trainings needed for jobs in the new economy to African Americans.

## CONCLUSION

Fifty years ago, in the midst of violent protests and unprecedented urban riots, the Kerner Commission concluded that the United States had drifted into a wide racial divide: one white and one black. This volume and the articles in it underscore the theme that in many respects the racial divide persists into the twenty-first century. Although patterns of improvement—lower poverty rates, fewer instances of violent protest, and improved education for some segments of the population—are clear, the racial divide persists.

Given the renewed national attention to the

problems of race relations in the United States, the fiftieth anniversary of the Kerner report provides an opportunity to revisit the report, its findings, and recommendations in light of contemporary political realities, social structures, and policy debates. Each chapter included in this volume considers the following:

- How far have we come?
- What worked and what did not work?
- What are the implications for the twenty-first century?

The Kerner report exposed cracks in the premises of the American Dream. The challenge of living up to the ideals of the American Dream remains a very real one today—characterized by a continuous gulf between the democratic principle of equality and its actual practice. Confronting structural racial inequities is a "nervous area of government." "It has a pervading emotional and historical context that can make avoidance and minimization appear attractive options . . . addressing a nervous area of government requires active and sustained attention" (Gooden 2014, 196).

In his *Richmond Times-Dispatch* commentary published two weeks after the Charlottesville violence in August 2017, former Virginia governor L. Douglas Wilder poignantly discussed the American Dream and a contemporary challenge in a Richmond city elementary school struggling for basic funding. As Governor Wilder, the first elected African American governor since Reconstruction, stated, "It might be difficult in some quarters to imagine how that made parents and students feel about their status in the community—about their grasp of the American Dream. This is going on more than 150 years after Emancipation, and more than 50 years after the country got serious about protecting the civil rights to vote and hold office" (2017). This thought-provoking volume of essays offers a critical examination and analysis of the Kerner Commission fifty years later through the lens of American society today and highlights the continuing legacy of racial inequality documented fifty years ago.

# REFERENCES

Allen, Walter R., Channel McLewis, Chantal Jones, and Daniel Harris. 2018. "From Bakke to Fisher: African American Students in U.S. Higher Education over Forty Years." *RSF: The Russell Sage Foundation Journal of the Social Sciences* 4(6): 41–72. DOI: 10.7758/RSF.2018.4.6.03.

Baker, Thomas H. 1969. Roy Wilkins Oral History Interview I (transcript). Austin, Tex.: Lyndon Baines Johnson Library.

Bentley-Edwards, Keisha L., Malik Chaka Edwards, Cynthia Neal Spence, William A. Darity Jr., Darrick Hamilton, and Jasson Perez. 2018. "How Does It Feel to Be a Problem? The Missing Kerner Commission Report." *RSF: The Russell Sage Foundation Journal of the Social Sciences* 4(6): 20–40. DOI: 10.7758/RSF.2018.4.6.02.

Briggs, Vernon M., Jr. 1968. "Report of the National Advisory Commission on Civil Disorders: A Review Article." Ithaca, N.Y.: Cornell University ILR School. Accessed May 14, 2018. http://digitalcommons.ilr.cornell.edu/cgi/viewcontent.cgi?article=1047&context=hrpubs.

Brooke, Edward W. 1969. "Interview to *Social Education*." Edward William Brooke papers, 1956–1988. Box 557, Folder Interviews with Press, Published Interviews 1967–1975. Manuscript Division. Washington: Library of Congress.

Casey, Marcus D., and Bradley L. Hardy. 2018. "The Evolution of Black Neighborhoods Since Kerner." *RSF: The Russell Sage Foundation Journal of the Social Sciences* 4(6): 185–205. DOI: 10.7758/RSF.2018.4.6.09.

Clark, Kenneth B. 1965. *The Dark Ghetto: Dilemmas of Social Power*. New York: Harper and Row.

Cunningham, Jamein P., and Rob Gillezeau. 2018. "The Effects of the Neighborhood Legal Services Program on Riots and the Wealth of African Americans." *RSF: The Russell Sage Foundation Journal of the Social Sciences* 4(6): 144–57. DOI: 10.7758/RSF.2018.4.6.07.

De La Cruz-Viesca, Melany, Paul M. Ong, Andre Comandon, William A. Darity Jr., and Darrick Hamilton. 2018. "Fifty Years After the Kerner Commission Report: Place, Housing, and Racial Wealth Inequality in Los Angeles." *RSF: The Russell Sage Foundation Journal of the Social Sciences* 4(6): 160–84. DOI: 10.7758/RSF.2018.4.6.08.

DuBois, W. E. B. 1903. *The Souls of Black Folk*. Chicago: A. C. McClug and Co.

Farley, Reynolds. 2018. "Detroit Fifty Years After the Kerner Report: What Has Changed, What Has Not, and Why?" *RSF: The Russell Sage Foundation Journal of the Social Sciences* 4(6): 206–41. DOI: 10.7758/RSF.2018.4.6.10.

Frazier, Franklin E. 1940. "The Negro Family and Negro Youth." *Journal of Negro Education* 9(3): 290–99.

Geary, Daniel. 2015. "The Moynihan Report: An Annotated Edition." *The Atlantic*, September 14. Accessed May 14, 2018. https://www.theatlantic.com/politics/archive/2015/09/the-moynihan-report-an-annotated-edition/404632/.

Gillham, Patrick F., and Gary T. Marx. 2018. "Changes in the Policing of Civil Disorders Since the Kerner Report: The Police Response to Ferguson, August 2014, and Some Implications for the Twenty-First Century." *RSF: The Russell Sage Foundation Journal of the Social Sciences* 4(6): 122–44. DOI: 10.7758/RSF.2018.4.6.06.

Gooden, Susan T. 2014. *Race and Social Equity: A Nervous Area of Government*. New York: Routledge.

Hochschild, Jennifer L. 1995. *Facing Up to the American Dream: Race, Class and the Soul of the Nation*. Princeton, N.J.: Princeton University Press.

Hughey, Matthew W. 2018. "Whither Whiteness? The Racial Logics of the Kerner Report and Modern White Space." *RSF: The Russell Sage Foundation Journal of the Social Sciences* 4(6): 73–98. DOI: 10.7758/RSF.2018.4.6.04.

Jones, Mack H. 1970. "The Kerner Commission: Errors and Omissions." In *The Kerner Report Revisited,* edited by Philip Meranto. Urbana-Champaign: The Institute of Government and Public Affairs, University of Illinois.

Kerner Commission. 1968. *Report of the National Advisory Commission on Civil Disorders*. Washington: Government Printing Office.

Lipsky, Michael, and David J. Olson. 1969. "Riot Commission Politics." *Trans-action* July/August: 9–21.

Loessberg, Rick, and John Koskinen. 2018. "Measuring the Distance: The Legacy of the Kerner Report." *RSF: The Russell Sage Foundation Journal of the Social Sciences* 4(6): 99–119. DOI: 10.7758/RSF.2018.4.6.05.

Marx, Gary T. 1967. *Protest and Prejudice: A Study of Belief in the Black Community*. New York: Harper & Row.

Meranto, Philip. 1970. *The Kerner Report Revisited*. Urbana-Champaign: The Institute of Government and Public Affairs, University of Illinois. Accessed May 14, 2018. https://archive.org/stream/kernerreportrevi00asse/kernerreportrevi00asse_djvu.txt.

Myrdal, Gunnar. 1944. *An American Dilemma: The Negro Problem and Modern Democracy*. New York: Harper & Row.

NPR News. 2017. "50 Years On, Sen. Fred Harris Remembers Great Hostility During 1967 Race Riots." July 20. Accessed May 14, 2018. http://www.npr.org/2017/07/20/538370689/50-years-on-sen-fred-harris-remembers-great-hostility-during-1967-race-riots.

Olzak, Susan. 2015. *Ethnic Collective Action in Contemporary Urban United States: Data on Conflicts and Protests, 1954-1992*. ICPSR34341-v1. Ann Arbor, Mich.: Inter-university Consortium for Political and Social Research [distributor]. DOI: 10.3886/ICPSR34341.v1.

Parenti, Michael. 1970. "The Possibilities for Political Change." In *The Kerner Report Revisited*, edited by Philip Meranto. Urbana-Champaign: The Institute of Government and Public Affairs, University of Illinois.

Thernstrom, Stephan, Fred Siegel, and Robert Woodson. 1998. "The Kerner Commission Report and the Failed Legacy of Liberal Social Policy." Heritage Lecture No. 619. Washington, D.C.: The Heritage Foundation.

U.S. Bureau of Labor Statistics. 2018. "Labor Force Statistics from the Current Population Survey." March Supplement. Washington: Government Printing Office. Accessed May 14, 2018. http://www.bls.gov/cps/.

Wilder, L. Douglas. 2017. "Conversation on Monuments Must Delve Deep into America's Racial History and Prompt Action." *Richmond Times Dispatch*, August 26. Accessed August 30, 2017. http://www.richmond.com/opinion/their-opinion/guest-columnists/l-douglas-wilder-conversation-on-monuments-must-delve-deep-into/article_3f4f572a-0411-58ae-b054-c9cbe9b1cb8f.html.

Zelizer, Julian E. 2016. "Introduction to the 2016 Edition." In *The Kerner Report: The National Advisory Commission on Civil Disorders*, edited by Sean Wilenz. Princeton, N.J.: Princeton University Press.

# PART I
# The Kerner Commission in Context

# How Does It Feel to Be a Problem? The Missing Kerner Commission Report

KEISHA L. BENTLEY-EDWARDS, MALIK CHAKA EDWARDS,
CYNTHIA NEAL SPENCE, WILLIAM A. DARITY JR.,
DARRICK HAMILTON, AND JASSON PEREZ

*Using an intersectional lens of race and gender, this article offers a critique of the Kerner Commission report and fills the gap of the missing analysis of white rage and of black women. A protracted history of white race riots resulted in the loss of black lives, black-owned property, and constitutional rights. However, only black riots, marked by the loss of white-owned property but few white lives, was the issue that prompted the formation of a national commission to investigate the events. Then and now, the privileging of white property rights over black life and liberty explains why black revolts result in presidential commissions, but white terror campaigns have never led to any comparable study.*

**Keywords:** race riots, civil disorders, Kerner Commission report, white terror campaigns, racial and gender violence, National Advisory Commission on Civil Disorders

In 1903, W. E. B. Du Bois wrote of the implicit awareness and curiosity of his white counterparts that he, as an African American man in America, was viewed as a problem. Even at that time, he remarked that it would be considered "indelicate" to state outright that black people are a problem, even if it was believed to be true.[1] Sixty-five years later, President Lyndon Johnson formed the National Advisory Commission on Civil Disorders (1968), better known as the Kerner Commission, to help understand and control the surge of black urban uprisings that

**Keisha L. Bentley-Edwards** is associate director of research at the Samuel DuBois Cook Center on Social Equity and assistant professor of general internal medicine at Duke University. **Malik Chaka Edwards** is associate professor at North Carolina Central University School of Law. **Cynthia Neal Spence** is director of the Social Justice Program and associate professor of sociology at Spelman College and director of the UNCF/Mellon Programs. **William A. Darity Jr.** is founding director of the Samuel DuBois Cook Center on Social Equity and Samuel DuBois Cook Professor of Public Policy, African and African American Studies, and Economics at Duke University. **Darrick Hamilton** is professor of economics and public and urban policy at the New School in New York. **Jasson Perez** is an economics student at the University of Illinois at Chicago and an activist fighting police misconduct.

© 2018 Russell Sage Foundation. Bentley-Edwards, Keisha L., Malik Chaka Edwards, Cynthia Neal Spence, William A. Darity Jr., Darrick Hamilton, and Jasson Perez. 2018. "How Does It Feel to Be a Problem? The Missing Kerner Commission Report." *RSF: The Russell Sage Foundation Journal of the Social Sciences* 4(6): 20–40. DOI: 10.7758/RSF.2018.4.6.02. Direct correspondence to: Keisha L. Bentley-Edwards at keisha.bentley.edwards@duke.edu, Samuel DuBois Cook Center on Social Equity, Duke University, 2024 W. Main St., Durham, NC 22705.
Open Access Policy: *RSF: The Russell Sage Foundation Journal of the Social Sciences* is an open access journal. This article is published under a Creative Commons Attribution-NonCommercial-NoDerivs 3.0 Unported License.

1. In *The Souls of Black Folk*, Du Bois discusses how when his white counterparts ask him about other black men or about "Southern outrages" that their underlying question is in fact "How does it feel to be a problem?"

occurred in 1967. In other words, to understand the problem with black people.

According to the Kerner Commission report (thus the Kerner report), white racism is the impetus, but the so-called race problem in America is characterized as a black people problem. The onus for resolving these problems rested primarily on black people's ability to conform to white cultural norms, rather than to allow America to become two societies, one white and one black.

In this article, we examine how the Kerner report interprets black rage or social circumstances but provides little or no acknowledgment of or analysis on white rage and its manifestations. Rather than seeing racial uprisings by black people as a normal response to incessant oppression and degradation, racial discontent and uprisings are seen through the lens of black deficiency. The police atrocities that triggered the black uprisings in 1967 were the result of state violence.[2] On the other hand, white riots were state sanctioned and occurred with police participation or complicity. In negating a balanced inquiry on black and white civil disorders in America, we find ourselves in a constant loop of rage, disenfranchisement, and destruction. This article provides the missing analyses on the causes and consequences of white rage and expands the original analysis by engaging an intersectional framework that acknowledges gender, race, and class as organizing constructs when discussing state-sanctioned violence.

Although the theoretical concept known as *intersectionality* was coined by Kimberlé Crenshaw in 1989, black women existed within an axis of race and sex-based discrimination at the time of and prior to the writing of the Kerner Commission report. Sojourner Truth asserted, "Ain't I a Woman?" in 1851. Somewhat later, in their speeches and writings, Anna Julia Cooper and Ida B. Wells-Barnett in the late nineteenth and early twentieth centuries, acknowledged the unique experiences and multiplicative social burdens that black women in America face (Collins 2000). Specific considerations of black women in the context of racial and gender strife was thus not a new concept, and should have been included in the Kerner report, but was largely ignored. Therefore we discuss the perils of excluding the experience of black women from investigations of state-sanctioned violence.

Whether it is during the white race riots in 1917, the long, hot summer of 1967, or police brutality in 2017, the invisibility of black women in reports and initiatives does not guarantee their safety from racial violence. Black women as well as men were victims of lynching, and targeted in white riots and continue to be victimized by police brutality.[3] In addition, rape was often used as a weapon to control and harm black women and to demean black men in the post-reconstruction and civil rights era (Feimster 2009; McGuire 2010). These unprovoked actions against black women have not been characterized as emblematic of white pathology or rage. According to Danielle McGuire, sexual and racial violence against black people was used to "control, coerce and harass" throughout the nineteenth and twentieth centuries (2010). Black women's experiences and harm remain an afterthought in how the Black Lives Matter movement is commonly perceived as a fight to save black men from police brutality.

In light of contemporary racial tensions, we examine the President's Task Force on 21st Century Policing (2015) juxtaposed against the Kerner report. These reports overlap in their focus on the causes, consequences, and solutions for *managing* black rage. Just as notes of the Moynihan report (1965) are interwoven throughout the Kerner report, the influence of the My Brother's Keeper Initiative (White

---

2. In this article, we use the terms *state sanctioned* and *state violence*. State violence (in America) is defined as violence authorized by the U.S. government, state, and local agencies that can include police violence, economic exploitation, and the destruction of property. State-sanctioned violence may or may not be committed with police or government agency participation, but includes a passive approach to preventing violence or holding perpetrators accountable (Clarke 1998).

3. According to a report by the NAACP, between 1889 and 1922, eighty-three women were known victims of lynching, sixty-six of whom were "colored" and seventeen were white (1922).

House 2014) is apparent in the report of the President's Task Force on 21st Century Policing.[4] Furthermore, the influence of the Moynihan report and the My Brother's Keeper Initiative, on the Kerner report and the President's Task Force report, respectively, can be seen through the enduring depiction of angry, problematic black men and emasculating or invisible black women (Crenshaw 2014)—an enduring narrative of black pathology. Although the triggers were white rage and police violence directed against blacks, black rage and riots prompted both the Kerner report and the 21st Century Policing Task Force report. This leaves open the question why no comparable report has been produced on white rage and riots.

### PROBLEMATIZING BLACK RAGE AND NORMALIZING WHITE RAGE

Until the early 1960s, the concept of a race riot was equated, ubiquitously, with white terror campaigns against black people.[5] This dynamic changed in 1963, most notably in Birmingham, Alabama. The Children's Crusade, a peaceful march of schoolchildren, was met by police with sprays from firehoses, vicious attack dogs, and arrests. The culmination of these attacks, were bombings that occurred throughout the city, including the 16th Street Baptist Church and the home of A. D. King, the brother of Rev. Dr. Martin Luther King Jr.

Outraged by these assaults as well as by the oppressive conditions that provoked the march in the first place, community members protested and some began to destroy white-owned businesses in black neighborhoods (Eskew 1997). By the summer of 1967, black-initiated race riots erupted in more than one hundred cities across the country. President Lyndon Johnson ordered the formation of the Kerner Commission to investigate and report on civil disorders. The Kerner report purportedly is on civil disorders, not black riots or black civil disorders. Yet black-initiated riots are explored at length, and white-initiated riots receive little analysis. We provide a sociohistorical and multitextured interrogation, not addressed in the Kerner report, of the precursors to black-initiated race riots for the Kerner report that includes the history of white terror campaigns, which typically have provided the underlying context for black-initiated riots and is missing from analysis. We posit that this analysis better contextualizes the oppressive conditions that stimulated community protests. In addition, this analysis expands the focus to examine the impact of oppressive conditions on black men and women.

### THE MISSING ANALYSIS: WHITE CIVIL UNREST

It can be argued that slavery in and of itself was a white terror campaign, but we begin our analysis in 1877, the year that Reconstruction and thus the federal protections of black people (the formerly enslaved and free coloreds) officially ended. The Kerner report acknowledges that the post-reconstruction era was a vicious turning point in white racial violence and black disenfranchisement (1968, 218), but it fails to connect them directly to the uprising of the 1960s.

Part 2 of the Kerner report focused on "Why Did it Happen?" in reference to the causes of the 1967 urban civil disorders (that is, black riots). We focus your attention to chapter 5, interestingly titled "Rejection and Protest: An Historical Sketch," which introduces a historical framework of black subjugation in America by stating that

> The events of the summer of 1967 are in large part the culmination of 300 years of racial prejudice. Most Americans know little of the origins of the racial schism separating our white and Negro citizens. Few appreciate how central the problem of the Negro has been to our social policy. Fewer still understand that today's problems can be solved only if white Americans comprehend the rigid social, economic and educational barriers that have prevented Negroes from participating in the

---

4. *The Negro Family: The Case for National Action* is commonly known as the Moynihan report.

5. The Harlem race riots of 1935 and 1943 were black-initiated riots, triggered by a mistaken report of police brutality directed against a black child and the accurate report of police brutality directed against a black soldier defending a black woman, respectively. No comparable riot occurred until 1963.

mainstream of American life. (Kerner Report 1968, 211)

This opening paragraph is followed by an accounting of social norms, policy, and legal barriers to freedom from the colonial period, the U.S. Constitution, through to the Civil War. This chapter also provides a glimpse of the Reconstruction era white riots in Memphis, Tennessee, and in Colfax and Coushatta, Louisiana, to demonstrate white intolerance of black political, economic, and social progress (Kerner Report 1968, 217). The analysis of the massacres that occurred during and after Reconstruction until the call for the Kerner report (from 1877 through 1967) are covered in two pages, and would lead you to believe that no large-scale white riots occured after 1870, or that riots were isolated to the South—neither is true. Conspicuously missing are major riots, including the Wilmington massacre of 1898, the Atlanta riot of 1906, the Tulsa riot of 1921, and the Detroit riot of 1943. Even though the Kerner report is about the causes and consequences of civil unrest, white-initiated civil unrest is missing. To be clear, there is no fundamental accounting and analysis of white riots and aggression—despite an acknowledgement that the oppressive conditions that prompted the long, hot summer of 1967 had roots in white terror campaigns; for example, "Negroes who voted or held office were refused jobs or punished by the Ku Klux Klan" (Kerner Report 1968, 217). To understand civil unrest in America, white riots and mobs should have been interrogated in the Kerner report, and we offer that missing analysis in this article.

Even acts of white terrorism that were contemporary to the writing of the report, such as the attacks on Freedom Riders in Alabama and Mississippi in 1961, are absent. White terror campaigns are not scrutinized for their causes, their triggers, or their costs in terms of life, liberties, and property (see table 1). Perhaps it is due to an assumption that white racial violence is well understood. White rage may have been seen as an obvious and normal response to perceived black progress and increased proximity (hence, the chapter 5 title of "Rejection and Protest"). Perhaps that is why the violent period between 1917 and 1921, which included riots in more than thirty cities during the Red Summer of 1919, did not prompt a full federal investigation—although it should have. In response to the Chicago Riot of 1919, the governor of Illinois ordered the formation of the Chicago Commission on Race Relations (1922), which offered some insight on the context of white racial violence. However, a statewide commission on the Tulsa race riots in 1921 was not assembled until 1997.

A key point that makes the interpretation of white terror campaigns difficult is the ambiguity in making distinctions between the abundant occurrence of lynchings, terrorist acts, sexual assaults, and post-reconstruction race riots and massacres.[6] Although both lynchings and race riots involve the enactment of white rage through mob violence, the former typically focuses on a specific person or people, whereas the latter is violence broadly and indiscriminately applied. Terrorist acts, such as the fifty bombings that occurred between 1947 and 1965 in black communities in Birmingham that resulted in death, injury, and property damage—the same types of destruction associated with race riots—further complicate precise characterization of the types of manifestations of white rage.

Lynchings and race riots often overlapped with underlying contexts in being related to perceptions of increasing black prosperity or political power, greater competition for employment, and the potential loss of white power and privilege. The violent backlash often has involved the use of white women as both props and participants to justify and initiate white terror campaigns (Kirshenbaum 1998; Feimster 2009). For example, under the guise of protecting white women from black male sexual predators, the Wilmington race riot of 1898 was in fact about resentment of a blossoming black

---

6. Between 1882 and 1968, 3,446 African Americans were lynched. For a comprehensive account of white riots, see Rucker and Upton's *Encyclopedia of American Race Riots* (2007); for an in-depth analysis of how sexual assault was used as weapon against black women and their communities during the civil rights movement, see Danielle McGuire's *At the Dark End of the Street* (2010).

*(Text continues on p. 29.)*

**Table 1.** Summary of the Context, Casualties, and Aftermath of U.S. Race Riots, 1883–1967

| Year | Location | Context | Injuries | Deaths | Aftermath | Estimated Cost At the Time | Estimated Cost 2017 |
|---|---|---|---|---|---|---|---|
| 1883 | Danville, VA | Danville riots TR: black men failed to give way to let a white man pass UC: rise in black political power and prosperity | 2 blacks 2 whites | 4 blacks 1 white | Black disenfranchisement | ** | ** |
| 1898 | Wilmington, DE | Wilmington race riot TR: black newspaper anti-lynching article claiming that black men were no more predators than white men UC: rise in black political power and prosperity; organized by NC Democratic Party | ** | 14 to 250 | 1,500 blacks left Wilmington; blacks no longer the majority; black city employees fired; black newspaper destroyed; prosperous blacks and politicians run out of town; black disenfranchisement | ** | ** |
| 1900 | New Orleans, LA | Robert Charles riots TR: murder of a white policeman by Robert Charles | 50 to 70 | 28 | Black city school destroyed | ** | ** |
| 1906 | Atlanta, GA | Atlanta race riot TR: unsubstantiated newspaper reports of rapes of white women by black men UC: black prosperity | ** | 10 to 100 blacks 2 whites | ** | ** | ** |
| 1908 | Springfield, IL | Springfield riots TR: white mob angered by the arrest and transport of 2 black men charged of raping a white woman UC: black prosperity and political gains | ** | 2 blacks 5 whites | 2,000 blacks left town; 35 black-owned business damaged; black neighborhoods destroyed by fire | $200,000 | $5 million |
| 1910 | Sixteen cities across the United States | TR: blacks celebrate Jack Johnson's prize fight defeat of Jeff Jeffries; white attack | 106 | 11 to 26 | ** | ** | ** |

| Year | Location | Description | | Deaths | Other outcomes | | |
|---|---|---|---|---|---|---|---|
| 1917 | East St. Louis, IL | TR: labor dispute of black strikebreakers<br>UC: increase in black population | ** | 40 to 200 blacks<br>9 whites | 6,000 blacks homeless; 244 to 312 businesses and homes destroyed | $373,000–1 million | $7–19 million |
| 1917 | Houston, TX | Houston Mutiny of 1917<br>TR: police brutality of a black woman and black soldiers; black World War I vets demand respect | 19 | 4 blacks<br>16 whites<br>1 Mexican American | 118 soldiers court-martialed; 63 life sentences; 18 condemned to death | ** | ** |
| 1919 | Charleston, SC | Red Summer riots<br>TR: white sailors claim to be cheated by bootlegger, begin harassing other blacks | 18 blacks<br>8 whites | 4 blacks | 49 arrested; 8 fined $50; 1 fined $100; 3 sailors court martialed; 2 sentenced to 1 year in prison | ** | ** |
| 1919 | Chicago, IL | Red Summer riots; Chicago riot of 1919<br>TR: breach of segregated beach<br>UC: Great Migration–related tensions | 537 | 23 blacks<br>13 whites | 1,000 homes destroyed; Chicago Commission on Race Relations | ** | ** |
| 1919 | Knoxville, TN | Red Summer riots; Knoxville riot of 1919<br>TR: black man accused of murdering a white woman<br>UC: rising black political power | 14+ | 25 to 100+ | White prisoners freed by mob | ** | ** |
| 1919 | Omaha, NE | Red Summer riots<br>TR: alleged assault of a white woman by a black man<br>UC: black migration; black political gains; black strikebreakers | 50 | 3 | 2,000 blacks left Omaha | ** | ** |
| 1919 | Washington, D.C. | Red Summer riots<br>TR: alleged sexual assault of white woman by a black man | 150 | 39 blacks<br>5 whites | ** | ** | ** |

*(continued)*

Table 1. (continued)

| Year | Location | Context | Injuries | Deaths | Aftermath | Estimated Cost At the Time | Estimated Cost 2017 |
|------|----------|---------|----------|--------|-----------|----------------------------|---------------------|
| 1921 | Tulsa, OK | Tulsa riots of 1921; black Wall Street riots<br>TR: shooting of a police officer while freeing a black prisoner who was to be lynched<br>UC: black prosperity, pride, and self-protection/arms | 800 | ~300 | 35 blocks in the black community (Greenwood) were destroyed | ** | ** |
| 1923 | Rosewood, FL | Rosewood massacre<br>TR: white woman claims assault by a black man; rise of black working class; black independence | ** | 6 to 150 | Town destroyed; black residents displaced | ** | ** |
| 1935 | New York, NY | Harlem race riot<br>TR: mistaken report of police brutality of a teenager<br>UC: poverty/Great Depression | 64 | 1 to 3 | Ending Harlem Renaissance; 600 windows smashed, businesses looted and vandalized; Mayor's Commission | $147,000 | $2.6 million |
| 1943 | Mobile, AL | Mobile race riot<br>TR: black shipyard promotions<br>UC: jobs and black empowerment | 50 | 0 | Segregated shipyards | ** | ** |
| 1943 | Beaumont, TX | Beaumont race riots<br>TR: alleged rape of a white woman by a black man<br>UC: population increase; resource shortages | 50 | 3 blacks<br>1 white | Black-owned structures looted and burned | ** | ** |
| 1943 | Detroit, MI | Detroit race riot<br>TR: unsubstantiated rumors of assaults on black and white women and babies<br>UC: conflict between immigrant Eastern Europeans and black migrants from the South | 760 | 34<br>Includes 16 shot by police | ** | $2 million | $28 million |

| Year | Location | Event | Injuries | Deaths | Notes | Property Damage | (Adjusted) |
|------|----------|-------|----------|--------|-------|-----------------|------------|
| 1943 | Los Angeles, CA | Zoot Suit riots<br>TR: attack and disrobing of Mexican American men wearing zoot suits during World War II rationing<br>UC: xenophobia | ** | 0 | ** | ** | ** |
| 1943 | New York, NY | Harlem riot of 1943<br>TR: police brutality of black soldier defending a black woman; reaction to racism, police brutality, housing discrimination | 40 police officers | 6 blacks | 500 to 1,000 arrested | ** | ** |
| 1961 | Anniston, Montgomery, and Birmingham, AL<br>Jackson, MS | Freedom Rides riot<br>TR: white anger over integrated public transportation<br>UC: black social gains; civil rights movement | 300 | 0 | Freedom Riders in Mississippi sentenced to 30 days in jail; federal protection required | ** | ** |
| 1963 | Birmingham, AL | Birmingham riot<br>TR: police brutality at Children's Crusade March; bombings<br>UC: desegregation in schools, bombings in black neighborhoods; enduring poverty | 6 | 2 | White-owned buildings in black communities destroyed | | |
| 1964 | Jersey City, NJ | Jersey City race riot<br>TR: arrest of a black woman<br>UC: housing segregation | 46 | 0 | 52 arrested; 71 businesses damaged | | |
| 1964 | New York, NY | Harlem race riot<br>TR: police brutality | 118 to 500 | 1 | 465 arrested | $500,000 to $1 million | $4 to $8 million |
| 1964 | Philadelphia, PA | 1964 North Philadelphia riot–Columbia Avenue riot<br>TR: police confrontation and arrest of a black woman (along with rumor of beating or killing of a pregnant woman); response to Civil Rights Act; rise of Black Power Movement | 339 | 1 | 800 people arrested; 220 businesses damaged or destroyed; accelerated white flight; population drop; blighting of neighborhood | $3 million | $23 million |

*(continued)*

**Table 1.** (*continued*)

| Year | Location | Context | Injuries | Deaths | Aftermath | Estimated Cost At the Time | Estimated Cost 2017 |
|---|---|---|---|---|---|---|---|
| 1964 | Rochester, NY | Rochester race riot TR: police brutality; segregated housing and education; employment discrimination | 350 | 4 | 1,000 arrested; 204 stores looted or damaged; black social empowerment | $1 million | $8 million |
| 1965 | Watts, CA | Watts riot; Watts rebellion TR: police confrontation during traffic stop | 1,000+ | 34 | 4,000 arrested; 600 buildings burned or looted; Watts community blighted | $44 million | $322 million |
| 1966 | Chicago, IL | Division Street riots TR: police brutality at Puerto Rican Week Parade | 16 Puerto Ricans | ** | 49 arrested; 50 buildings damaged | ** | ** |
| 1966 | Cleveland, OH | Hough riots TR: racism and poverty or black nationalist-communist | 50 | 4 | 275 arrested | $1 to $2 million | $7 to $14 million |
| 1967 | Detroit, MI | Detroit riot TR: police raid on an unlicensed bar; working class blacks fighting police, national guard, and U.S. army | 1,189 | 43 | 7,000 arrested | $42 million | $307 million |
| 1967 | Newark, NJ | Newark riot TR: police brutality, poverty, low political power | 725 | 26 | 1,500 arrested; Central Ward blighted | $115 million | $110 million |

*Source:* Authors' tabulations based on *Chicago Tribune* 2014; Perl 1999; Hamilton and Darity 2006; Kirshenbaum 1998; Rucker and Upton 2007; Chicago Commission on Race Relations 1922; Danville Committee of Forty 1883; Dailey 1997; Smith and Wynn 2009; Merritt 2008; Rehagen 2017; Haynes 1973; McWhirter 2011.

*Note:* TR = triggering incident; UC = underlying circumstances; **not reported or unavailable.

middle class and black gains in politics. As table 1 shows, this massacre resulted in the displacement of at least 1,500 African Americans. To gain an idea of the massacre's enduring impact, black people have not been a racial majority in Wilmington since the 1898 riot (Hamilton and Darity 2006).[7]

In his 1944 analysis of race in America, Gunnar Myrdal posited that white rage was expressed as lynchings in the South and race riots in the North (1996). This is not the case. Lynchings were more frequent in the South, but they occurred throughout the country. Although not an exhaustive list of race riots, table 1 demonstrates that race (white) riots also were a national phenomenon. This article focuses on white rage manifested specifically through race riots because the civil unrest of urban riots is the focus of the Kerner Commission's report.

### Triggers and Underlying Circumstances

E. M. Beck and Stewart Tolnay posit that white racial violence is characterized by the interactive and multiplicative result of violence potential and a threshold event (1995). Violence potential includes the underlying circumstances that create racial tension in a community. Violence potential is the product of racist ideology, permissiveness of the state, and competition of resources. As these underlying circumstances build and interact with one another, the threshold event serves as a trigger to racial violence (Beck and Tolnay 1995). Depending on the sociohistorical context and underlying circumstances, the trigger can be a dramatic incident, such as the death of a white deputy, as in the 1919 riots in Elaine, Arkansas, or as seemingly innocuous an event as a black teenager floating to the white side of a segregated beach, such as in the Chicago riots of 1919 (Williams 1972).

In both the North and the South, the pattern of triggering incidents involved police confrontations, jobs, and most often, alleged assaults on white women (Rucker and Upton 2007; Kirshenbaum 1998; Merritt 2008; Feimster 2009). Common underlying circumstances across regions included the enforcement of black social inferiority, competition over housing and political power, and flare-ups in response to black prosperity, and, during times of war, returning black soldiers asserting equal status (Haynes 1973; Merritt 2008; Dailey 1997; Perl 1999).

The oppressive conditions of the South, as well as black displacement due to white riots, served as motivating factors for the Great Migration of African Americans (Reich 2014; Wilkerson 2010). However, black newcomers found that racism was pervasive in their new home as well and created unique underlying circumstances to race riots in the North. For instance, in places such as Chicago and East St. Louis, resistance to black population growth and integration, black migrant and Eastern European immigrant conflicts at the workplace and in housing were an undercurrent to race riots (Rucker and Upton 2007; McWhirter 2011; Williams 1972; Rehagen 2017).

### Casualties and Aftermath

The driving motivation for white race riots is the preservation of white supremacy and the benefits and privileges that it affords. It also can be argued that preserving white supremacy is the source of complacency in investigating these riots and their consequences. For example, although President Woodrow Wilson publicly admonished the East St. Louis riots of 1917, he did not initiate a federal investigation.[8] The aftermath of white-initiated riots can be characterized by an enormous loss of black life, de-

---

7. According to the City of Wilmington, its 2014 racial-ethnic demographics are 75.3 percent white, 19.8 percent African American, and 5.6 percent Hispanic.

8. Congress launched an investigative committee on the East St. Louis riots of 1917 when President Wilson refused to do so (1917). From the investigation, Representative Leonidas C. Dyer (MO) reported on the savage nature of the riot and the complicity of law enforcement. Although the triggering incident of the East St. Louis riot is typically reported as conflicts with black strikebreakers, Dyer noted that immigrants working in the packing houses had been on strike for two years and that black workers (and not strikebreakers) had taken their place shortly thereafter. When pressed by the committee to take action, President Wilson wrote, "The Attorney General and I have been giving a great deal of thought to the situation in East St. Louis, and the United States district attorney there, as well as special agents of the Department of Justice, have been at work gathering information

struction of black-owned properties, mass displacement, and the loss of constitutional rights—specifically, voting rights, due process, equal protection of the law, free speech, the right to assemble, freedom of the press, and the right to bear arms. Further, Lisa Cook argues that a direct relationship can be found between white terror campaigns and policies and the fall (or rise) of black patents—an indication of the quality of black economic growth and intellectual output (2014). In contrast to numerous accountings of the costs of black-initiated riots (*Chicago Tribune* 2014; Collins and Margo 2007; Iris 1983), very little is written or verifiable on the cost and casualties of white-initiated riots (Hamilton and Darity 2006). The violent and sexual assaults, as well as deaths of black women, during these riots are further unacknowledged.

As shown in table 1, the estimated loss of black lives is often wildly disparate, yet the recording of white deaths is exact, for example, Atlanta in 1906 and East St. Louis in 1917. Injuries are typically assumed to be massive but typically have no estimates. In her book on the New Orleans riot of 1900, the anti-lynching activist Ida B. Wells-Barnett wrote, "How many colored men and women were abused and injured is not known, for those who escaped were glad to make a place of refuge and took no time to publish their troubles" (1900, 29).[9] Hospitals, churches, and schools that served black people were among the properties destroyed in race riots, which further exacerbates the ability to count the dead, injured, and displaced—particularly women and children.

The disparity in casualties typically depends on who is doing the reporting, such as the local government versus activists such as Wells-Barnett or organizations such as the NAACP (National Association for the Advancement of Colored People) and the Red Cross (Danville Committee of Forty 1883; Wells-Barnett 1917; Gruening and Du Bois 1917). Government accounts from the police, coronors, and city officials invariably report smaller numbers of black casualties, whereas activists and relief organizations report larger numbers (Rucker and Upton 2007; Brophy 2003; McWhirter 2011; Merritt 2008; Wicentowski 2017). It is difficult to verify which estimates were more accurate, but given the disregard for black lives, as well as the complicity of local government in riot activities, data gathered from activists and relief organization are likely to be more precise.

A similar lack of records can be found in documenting the value of black-owned properties lost in race riots. In several instances, entire black communities or towns were decimated in race riots without a record of the financial burden. A complicating factor is that these accounts are typically done through claims fulfilled by insurance companies. Purchasing insurance on property was not always available to black people during the peak of white race riots. As was the case in the 1921 Tulsa riots, the insurance companies cited a "riot exclusion clause" to deny property claims (Brophy 2003). Estimating the loss of black-owned property would then be left to complicitous local government officials.

### Black Rage

The Kerner report makes the argument that blacks have legitimate concerns that contributed to the 1967 uprisings and were prompted by white racism. The report also concludes that the riots were not coordinated nor a product of

---

to enable us to determine whether any Federal statute has been violated. Up to this time I am bound in candor to say that no facts have been presented to us which would justify Federal action." However, it should be brought into context that President Wilson expanded racial segregation to the federal government and enthusiastically endorsed the Ku Klux Klan propaganda film *Birth of a Nation*, describing it as "history written in lightening." Thus, a presidential commission on this or the numerous other race riots that occurred during his presidency (1913–1921) was highly unlikely.

9. Families often hid in swamps, woods or cemeteries during the chaos of a race riot to escape ravenous mobs; some never returned. Ida B. Wells-Barnett was among a group of women called the Anti-Lynching Crusaders, a spin-off organization from the NAACP that investigated and reported the causes and aftermath of lynchings and race riots. She was known for her meticulous notes and interviews of community members and victims of white terror campaigns.

an anarchistic conspiracy, and that the typical uprising was triggered by the perception of police physical abuse and abuse of power. These can be viewed as positive aspects of the report.

However, the Kerner report has a pattern of explaining systemic barriers to positive social, health, economic, and education outcomes, quickly followed by assertions of black pathology. The report does not conclude that it is absolutely logical to find oppression intolerable and that some type of action should be expected, or an apathy toward political and educational systems would be a rational response to these barriers (Utsey, Bolden, and Brown 2001; Fanon 1961). The Kerner report's framework is thus shaped by a view of black violence as a product of a pernicious social deviance, influenced by "broken" family structures led by black women—a clear reference to the findings of the Moynihan report (Moynihan 1965, chapter 7).

For centuries, campaigns of white violence have been perceived as maintaining social order, whereas black-initiated riots have been perceived as disrupting the social order and as revolutionary behavior to overturn the status quo. If whites generally like the status quo, then they will be considerably less bothered by white terror campaigns or police killings of blacks. Indeed, white violence is not seen as dangerous for whites but black violence is perceived as untamed/illogical, something that may spill out of the ghetto and therefore must be understood and stopped.

The Kerner report briefly acknowledges violence by "white racists" in Birmingham and "white segregationists" in Saint Augustine Florida (1968, 37, 38). In its phrasing, the report evaluates these incidents as a problem with racists rather than racism.[10] Failing to acknowledge white supremacy leads to an attempt to problematize black behavior. This is captured most eloquently by Kwame Ture and Charles Hamilton:

> When white terrorists bomb a black church and kill five black children, the act is deemed individual racism, widely deplored by most segments of the society. But when in that same city—Birmingham, Alabama—five hundred black babies die each year because of the lack of proper food, shelter, and medical facilities, and thousands more are destroyed and maimed physically, emotionally, and intellectually because of conditions of poverty and discrimination in the black community, it is deemed a function of institutional racism. (Ture and Hamilton 1967, 4)

The triggering incident in black riots could be perceived as an individual racist encounter, like the police brutality that triggered almost every uprising (see table 1). If that were the case, black rage would be directed at individuals rather than the police force. The black riots that prompted the Kerner report were in fact initiated by the underlying circumstance of enduring institutional racism in policing and housing policies. From this perspective, targeting law enforcement and white-owned properties, including those with exploitive credit or lending and rental practices, were a cogent outlet of black rage (Baradaran 2017). Although white passersby and drivers may have had bricks or bottles thrown at them or their cars, they were not hunted down and attacked in their communities, something that occurred frequently in white riots directed against black people.

Whether due to ignorance of the incident or a sense of privilege-based safety, the white people endangered in these situations were driving through black communities at the time of a race riot and were targets of convenience. The chaos of the Bloody Summer of 1967 is therefore not analogous to the indiscriminate violence of the Red Summer of 1919.

## MISSING ANALYSIS: GENDER AND THE KERNER REPORT

How does one begin to integrate a discussion of gender into the volumes of scholarly and activists' work attempting to explain the complex web of relationships between the police, courts,

---

10. In contemporary times, this is the "few bad eggs" notion used to defend the police. Thus, police brutality, poor teaching or even micro-aggressions, are problems with bad (or ignorant) whites, not all whites or whiteness itself (Berard 2012).

corrections, and the African American community? The Kerner Commission's report certainly attempted to uncover the very complex nature of race relations in response to the riots of the 1960s. Its conclusions and recommendations were considered by some to be a radical departure from the status quo assessments of the race problem. One might assert that the commission shared what Carol Anderson refers to as "the unspoken truth about our racial divide" (2016, 5).

The conclusions of the Kerner Commission affirmed the prophetic words of W. E. B. Du Bois in 1903 when he observed that the presence of black skin on the body of a male in the United States was perceived as intrinsically problematic. Du Bois's classic theoretical analysis was incomplete. He failed to acknowledge the vulnerable positionality of the black female. She too was considered a problem by those in power. The very nature of one's skin tone on black male bodies has historically evoked and evinced emotional and structural responses fueled by malignant history and ideological dogma. The black male body has been rendered a serious safety threat, and the black female body has also experienced a precarious fate due to state-sanctioned social control.

The eloquence and insights of Du Bois and many other thought leaders must not be diminished within the canons of classic intellectual thought, but the historical invisibility of the plight of black women must be engaged as we reflect on the state-sanctioned violence that the African American community experiences. Gender and class must be included in any analysis that acknowledges the otherness of blackness— especially when their inclusion can account for aggravating and mitigating factors in the context of criminal justice policies and procedures.

The face of civil unrest described in the Kerner report characterizes the 1967 riots in urban centers including Newark and Paterson, New Jersey, and Detroit, Michigan, as events involving black males who were considered the most vulnerable to the legacy of racist governmental policies and practices (Kerner Report 1968, 7).

The report references findings from surveys designed to measure community attitudes toward the police that proved valuable to assessing the climate of communities and supported recommendations to improve police-community relations.[11] The researchers, however, solicited and reported on the responses of black adult males and black male youth only (Kerner Report 1968, 302–04). The analysis disregarded the reality that black women's stories, along with those of black males, would have provided a more accurate assessment of the nature and scope of police-sanctioned violence in the black community. Then, as now, black males were considered the primary protagonists in narratives about civil disorder that position them as the most visible victims of state-sanctioned violence. This analysis asserts that the experiences of black females with the police were not a priority for the Kerner Commission. Black male attitudes controlled the deliberations of what to do about police-community relationships. These narratives ignored the reality of state-sanctioned violence against black women.

Black males are treated as most vulnerable to racist social and legal policies in historical and journalistic accounts of the impact of state-sanctioned racist practices, from the period of enslavement to the present. Much of the national response focused on what to do about the problem of black male violence. Inherent in even the most liberal responses were calls to rectify some of the attendant consequences of poverty to develop more "orderly" communities. A specific focus on the role of well-

---

11. In the summary, the Kerner report provides results from "24 disorders in the 23 cities surveyed." Among its key findings is a description of black rioters: "The typical rioter was a teenager or young adult, a life-long resident of the city in which he rioted, a high school dropout; he was, nevertheless, somewhat better educated than his nonrioting Negro neighbor, and was usually underemployed or employed in a menial job. He was proud of his race, extremely hostile to both whites and middle-class Negroes and, although informed about politics, highly distrustful of the political system" (1968, 7). Although most black rioters are noted as being male, how many and under what circumstances black women were engaged in the riots is not assessed. It appears that a social demographic profile of black women rioters was apparently not deemed necessary.

behaved black males as a stabilizing force in the African American community has been central to the enduring narrative of what to do about urban civil unrest.

## TASK FORCE ON TWENTY-FIRST CENTURY POLICING

Like the Bloody Summer of 1967 that initiated the Kerner report, police brutality is at the core of contemporary urban riots: 1992 in Los Angeles, 2014 in Ferguson and Oakland, and 2015 in Baltimore. The confluence of riots and high-profile police shootings of unarmed black people precipitated President Barack Obama's Task Force on 21st Century Policing (2015). The task force was charged with "identifying best practices and offering recommendations on how policing practices can promote effective crime reduction while building public trust" (1). Interestingly, neither the shootings nor the riots that initiated the assembling of the task force are discussed directly in the final report. It would seem that a painstaking effort was made to exclude the phrases "police brutality" and "unarmed shooting" from it.

Whereas the Kerner report talks explicitly about race, and to a lesser degree, racism, the task force report is inundated with discussions of implicit or unconscious bias versus explicit bias or racial discrimination. Although making the distinction between unintentional and intentional discrimination provides a frame of reference for police interactions with the community, the result of unarmed shootings of black people remains. The institutionalized racism that supports implicit and explicit bias continues to be unaddressed. Further, this process individualizes police brutality and white terror campaigns, rather than examining them as cultural or systemic. Police brutality, regardless of its pervasiveness, is thus seen as a problem of bad-apple police officers, not as endemic of police and American culture (Lersch and Mieczkowski 2005).

The similarities in recommendations of the 21st Century Policing and Kerner reports are startling. The most striking is the recommendation for police to find "alternatives to deadly force" in the Kerner report and the development of "less than lethal technology" in the task force report. The former recommended increasing the use of chemical weapons such as mace, and the latter the use of conductive energy devices (stun guns). Each report warned of current abuse of these alternative strategies and that appropriate use of force policies were needed for these nonlethal tools.

## THE INFLUENCE OF THE MOYNIHAN REPORT AND MY BROTHER'S KEEPER

Presidents Obama and Johnson created antipoverty commissions that resulted in a focus or development of initiatives to better support black males, particularly in terms of employment. In the Johnson-initiated Moynihan report, "Negro family social disorganization" is identified as the source of a culture of poverty that impedes black social and economic progress.[12]

The influence of the Moynihan report can be seen directly in the Kerner report in chapter 7, "Unemployment, Family Structure, and Social Disorganization." This chapter is included in the section on causes of civil unrest. They point to the proportion of black women in the labor force as an indicator of black male absence or underemployment; in 1966, 55 percent for nonwhite women in comparison to 38 percent for white women. Taking a page from the Moynihan report, the Kerner report cites the prevalence of female headed households as a systemic problem in the black community that leads to "social disorganization" and the lack of "solid citizens" in the ghetto (1968, 261).

---

12. Moynihan begins chapter 2 of the report with "At the heart of the deterioration of the fabric of Negro society is the deterioration of the Negro family" (1965, 5). He notes that this is evidenced by the trend of urban and lower class black families lacking a nuclear family structure. He points to illegitimate births (babies born to unwed mothers) and female-headed households (due to father absence and unemployment and domineering black wives) as the sources of social disorganization and reliance on public welfare. He also states that centuries of injustice, particularly slavery, contributed to the familial and therefore structural pathologies found in black communities. The phrasing "Negro family social disorganization" was based on E. Franklin Frazier's *The Negro Family in the United States* (1951), which declares the harm of family disorganization for African Americans.

Besides pointing to the poor parenting skills of single or working mothers, black women are largely absent in the Kerner report. Even though mistreatment of black women by the police was often the trigger for race riots (see table 1), no deeper inquiry was undertaken into the root causes for this vigilance. Black women and girls were also subjected to the horrors of white terror campaigns and police brutality, with the added trauma of sexual assault (McGuire 2010; Feimster 2009).[13]

In 2014, President Obama kicked off the My Brother's Keeper Initiative in response to the plight of black men. Whereas the Moynihan report painted black women as emasculating single mothers, black women are remarkably absent from the My Brother's Keeper Initiative—as they largely are in the 21st Century Policing report. The need for initiatives that support black men and boys should not be minimized, but the absence of similar efforts designed to respond to the circumstances of black girls and women cannot be denied.

## THE CONTINUING INVISIBILITY OF BLACK WOMEN AND GIRLS

Numerous scholars and activists bring attention to the invisibility of black girls and women's experiences as victims of state violence (Cohen and Jackson 2016; Collins 2000; Crenshaw 2014; Davis 2016; Jackson 2016; Richie 2012). Ashley Smith asserts that "when action is taken to bring awareness to structural injustices based on race, Black women, girls, and their experiences are left in the background" (2016, 261).

It is instructive to examine the work of Crenshaw, executive director of the African American Policy Forum and the #SayHerName campaign launched in 2015, to bring attention to and honor the lives of women and girls who have been victimized by police violence. According to a position paper produced by the African American Policy Forum, "black women who are profiled, beaten, sexually assaulted, and killed by law enforcement officials are conspicuously absent" from racial justice movements (2015, 3).

According to the position paper, black women experience racial profiling while driving, have been casualties of the war on drugs through association, have disproportionately suffered injuries and assaults while in the custody of law enforcement, and have been doubly victimized when seeking help from domestic violence situations where the intervention by law enforcement has ended in the use of deadly force against the victim. The #SayHerName campaign brings attention to the circumstances of countless women, girls, and members of the LGBTQ community who have been wrongly arrested, prosecuted, punished, and victimized by police use of excessive and deadly force.

The absence of public narratives and outcry about legally sanctioned violence against diverse communities of women and men when protesting systemic racialized police violence is problematized by the #SayHerName movement. Ironically, this absence is even evident in social justice advocacy groups, which have adopted the Black Lives Matter call for social justice, without emphasizing the disproportionate representation of women, girls, and members of the LGBTQ community who have been victimized by state-sanctioned violence (Amnesty International USA 2005).

It is ironic that the Black Lives Matter movement was created and inspired by the social justice advocacy of queer females, Patrisse Cullors, Opal Tometi, and Alicia Garza. The Black Lives Matter movement has received more public support and media attention when the victims of police brutality and the unlawful use of deadly force have been black males. This was certainly not the intention of the founders of the movement.

---

13. In the Kerner report is a discussion of the build-up to an uprising in Tampa, Florida, triggered by a police shooting of a nineteen-year-old black man. This accounting demonstrates a missed opportunity to further analyze the position of black women and girls in the context of urban civil unrest, "As they began to mill about and discuss the shooting, old grievances, both real and imagined, were resurrected: discriminatory practices of local stores, advantages taken by white men of Negro girls" (Kerner Report 1968, 44). To further complicate this documentation, it is not clear which grievances were real and which were "imagined"—including assertions that black girls were being victimized by white men.

As Peniel Joseph writes, "few grassroots uprisings have done as much, in such a short period of time, to focus attention on long-neglected issues of racial justice, gender and economic inequality" (2017, 18). The absence of social justice advocacy group and media attention to the experiences of black women and girls and members of the LGBTQ community being subjected to police brutality and deadly force has been at best minimized and at worst ignored. This is disturbing as one reflects on the faces of the movements often being black mothers.[14] Their presence as grieving subjects is not juxtaposed with their vulnerability as likely victims of the police use of violence and deadly force.

The Black Lives Matter movement creates a space for broadening the discussion of the impact of state-sanctioned violence to include the experiences of diverse marginalized communities. The intersectional analytical framework offered by the founders of the Black Lives Matter movement complicates Du Bois's notion of what it means to be a problem by focusing on how multiple and intersecting identities compound and engender stereotypes that result in legalized repression and punishment of not only black males, but also other marginalized groups whose identities and presence are seen as threats, especially when they embody blackness. Patricia Hill Collins asserts that intersectional frameworks "add additional layers of complexity to understandings of social inequality, recognizing that social inequality is rarely caused by a single factor" (2000, 26). Racialized gender tropes yield particular responses from those in power.

For instance, the Georgetown Law report "Girlhood Interrupted" points to perceptions of black girls as being considered less innocent than white girls. In comparison with their white and Latina counterparts, black girls are the most likely to be disciplined in schools, receive in-school suspensions, and be referred to juvenile authorities. According to the report,

> black girls are 20 percent more likely to be charged with a crime than white girls,
>
> black girls are 20 percent more likely than white girls to be detained, and
>
> black girls are less likely to benefit from prosecutorial discretion.

The study finds that prosecutors dismissed only 30 percent of cases against black girls, but 70 percent of those against their white counterparts (Epstein, Blake, and González 2017).

The desire for greater social control of black males and females has historically been evident throughout the administration of criminal justice (Anderson 2016; Davis 2003; Du Bois 2009; Foner 1988; Ransby 2015; Alexander 2010). This intentionality around close monitoring and surveillance of African American communities has created tense relationships between the police and the community, as the Kerner report notes.

Melissa Harris-Perry, in describing the vulnerability of black women, notes that "because of their history as chattel slaves, their labor market participation as domestic workers and their role as dependents in a punitive modern welfare state, black women in America live under heightened scrutiny by the state" (2011, 39). It is clear that this heightened scrutiny can be aggravated and mitigated by numerous factors, including socioeconomic class, gender performance that is nonconforming to heteropatriarchal norms, and neighborhood, to name a few.

### Neo-Capitalist Punishment Ideology

Smith's introduction of a neo-capitalist punishment ideological framework provides a helpful lens to examine the injustices black women and girls are subjected to by law enforcement (2016). According to Smith, "neo-capitalist punishment ideology highlights the ways in which governmentality validates the use of severe discipline and punishment tactics against targeted bodies through its method of control over marginalized people" (263).

It is important to note that neo-capitalist punishment ideology is an extension of Michel

---

14. A group of seven mothers has become known as the Mothers of the Movement. Each has lost a son or daughter to gun violence, mostly at the hands of the police. They have become activists fighting police brutality and gun violence.

Foucault's theorizing about how the state exercises control over marginalized populations (1977). His analysis is particularly useful because it situates the relationship between the state and the marginalized body and introduces us to a particular architecture of what he refers to as the very intentional coerciveness of the carceral state (293–308). Notably, Smith introduces components of this ideological framework that are applicable to recent instances of excessive force used against black girls and women.

Public punishment is one component intended to achieve the goal of general deterrence as a way to diffuse "bad girl behavior." This public punishment component recently was enacted in an incident involving a disturbance at a June 2015 teen pool party in McKinney, Texas, where a "noncompliant" black girl was the victim of the use of excessive physical force by a police officer who chose to shove the fifteen-year-old face down to the ground and pressed his knee into her back, ostensibly to subdue her while other teens were held at gunpoint. His behavior was subsequently ruled "indefensible" by his police chief. When a suspect is seen as a threat, even when that suspect is a young black girl, it is assumed by law enforcement that public punishment is an acceptable response to perceived disruptive behavior.

Invisibility is the next component of the neo-capitalist punishment ideology that Smith cites, which speaks to the fact that "over the past three years, more than 70 Black women and girls have been murdered due to state violence (Khaleeli 2016)" (Smith 2016, 264). The lack of media attention, as well as selective social justice movement attention, is problematic. The devaluation of the lives of women and girls is evidenced within both public and private spheres. This devaluation of the lives of women and girls privileges narrative accounts of males as the sole victims of state-sanctioned violence.

The intersectional realities of black women and girls' lives are not considered when examining their engagement with law enforcement. Smith asserts that the instances of state-sanctioned violence black women and girls and men and boys experience are "directly linked to their intersectional identities" (2016, 265). Although it is apparent that blackness, regardless of class, presages a potential threat, particularly in the form of a male body, perceived economic status does matter.

The Kerner Commission's focus on inner-city, economically insecure urban communities as hotbeds for civil unrest recognizes that the attendant consequences of structural inequality nurture a volatile community context that requires study and analysis. The confluence of race, class, and gender, though not specifically interrogated in the Kerner report, yields recommendations that definitely acknowledge socioeconomic class as an aggravating factor in structural inequality.

The neo-capitalist punishment ideology also advances the expectation that marginalized populations must be docile in the face of law enforcement. The Kerner Commission cites "deep hostility between police and ghetto communities as a primary cause of the disorders" (Kerner Report 1968, 299). This hostility is emblematic of a distrust between community members and law enforcement. In the 21st Century Policing report, law enforcement witnesses lament the lack of respect they receive from people they are charged with protecting.

In some cases, when law enforcement officers believed that the subjects of their authority were not respectful (that is, docile) enough, they perceived them as threats (Greene 2000). Because of this, if a law enforcement officer's authority is challenged, it can result in the use of deadly force regardless of whether the perception is based on reality. Stereotypes about black women and girls often do not suggest docility (Collins 2000; Harris-Perry 2011).

The prevalence of technology further complicates the relationship between law enforcement and the community, because in spite of what Smith describes as the "hyper-visibility" of incidents against members of the black community, including women and girls, the justice system continues to often ignore this evidence as indictable against law enforcement officers (2016, 266). Ignoring photographic or video evidence of brutality against black people was true in the height of white racial terror campaigns, and remains true contemporarily, as in the cases of Rodney King, Sandra Bland, Tamir Rice, and Philando Castille (see Wells-Barnett 1900; see also postcard depictions of lynches).

## CONCLUSION

Four presidential commissions with an overall theme of addressing the race problem have been assembled without identifying the context of the problem. Therefore we must ask ourselves how far have we come, what worked, and how does this inform twenty-first-century realities?

### How Far Have We Come?

Black rage and riots in response to state violence prompted both the Kerner Commission and the 21st Century Policing Task Force. Because no comparable report has been produced on white rage and riots, one must question how far America can or has progressed in race relations. Essentially, without a dual reflection of race, how can the causes and consequences of civil unrest be fully understood?

Regardless of the race initiating riots, black people are the majority of deaths and injuries and bear the burden of decimated property in predominantly black communities. A distinction can be made in ownership of these properties. In white race riots, black people were hunted and the black-owned properties were targeted based on proprietorship and location in the black community. Law enforcement and white-owned properties in black communities were targeted in black riots. How these outcomes are valued sheds light on why black riots result in presidential commissions and white terror campaigns do not.

One must question whether the failure to fully examine white protest is that far too often they were de facto or de jure state sanctioned. James Garland, using Alabama as an example, documents state support of white terrorism: "Sorting out government influence on 'private' racially-motivated violence in Alabama is often a daunting task. Indeed, the fusion of public and private prejudice for much of Alabama history has been so complete that 'law' and lawlessness in the state have often been one and the same" (2001, 26).

### What Worked and What Did Not Work?

Identifying white racism as "essentially responsible" for the civil unrest of 1967 is the Kerner report's greatest strength. At the same time, racism is identified as the profoundly influential but politically inexpedient culprit of the uprisings. As a result, prevention efforts initiated to eliminate the population-level racial disparities in education, employment, wealth, and health that were the underlying cause of the urban riots focused on individual-level interventions rather than on dismantling institutional-level racism (that is, the underlying cause of the disparities). This strategy reinforces the narrative that racial problems in America are in fact problems of black people and their communities. As a result, whites are relegated to the roles of saviors of black people, and bystanders to addressing systemic racism's repercussions.

Each of these executive actions suffers from a failure to address intersectionality. The Kerner report's findings that the country is divided by race places a singular focus on race that fails to interrogate the many ways black women and girls are marginalized and disenfranchised in U.S. society. When reports and or public policies do not include the experiences and voices of women and girls in a nation divided, they forfeit the ability to provide comprehensive programmatic initiatives. Violence against black women, from enslavement to the contemporary moment, must be included in discussions focusing on civil unrest, the perils of police brutality, and the unauthorized use of deadly force on black bodies. The use of legalized violence to control the "black community" historically has been justified by racist and sexist ideologies that dehumanize black people—both male and female.

### What Are the Implications for the Twenty-First Century?

A study of the racial divide must examine both the strength and virulence of enduring racial stereotypes attributed to black people and their communities and how they are employed to legitimize racism. Just as the Kerner report acknowledges that many (white) Americans do not know the historical and institutional structures that cause and support racial disparities, the same dynamics are illustrated today.[15] In 2018, just as in 1968, the United States is a nation divided by race.[16]

Urban uprisings continue to be triggered by excessive use of police force, even though the Kerner Commission and the 21st Century Policing Task Force both recommend the widespread use of nonlethal police methods. As the United States moves forward as a nation, presidential commissions such as the Kerner Commission must move from identifying problems and making recommendations that fail to address a comprehensive response to the impact of police-sanctioned violence against the entire black community. It is impossible to reform any systemic problems resulting from a history of racist and sexist practices until the truth about how systems informed by racism and sexism is revealed. The truth must be sought before any form of reformation and reconciliation can occur. This analysis has attempted to expand the analysis of police-community relationships to reveal the sometimes unspoken truths about state-sanctioned violence against the black community by members of the white community. Once these truths are unveiled, commissions can seek to organize citizen groups that represent a cross-section of members of the black community to share their experiences and recommendations about ways to improve police-community relationships. The impact of police-sanctioned violence on black females and members of the LGBTQ community must be included in discussions about how to improve police-community relationships. The commission's recommendations must reflect an intersectional lens as a way to focus on the most effective methods for engaging diverse black voices.

## REFERENCES

African American Policy Forum. 2015. "Say Her Name: Resisting Police Brutality Against Black Women." New York: Center for Intersectionality and Social Policy Studies. Accessed May 3, 2018. http://www.aapf.org/publications/.

Alexander, Michelle. 2010. *The New Jim Crow: Mass Incarceration in the Age of Colorblindness*. New York: The New Press.

Amnesty International USA. 2005. *Stonewalled: Police Abuse and Misconduct Against Lesbian, Gay, Bisexual and Transgender People in the U.S*. New York: Amnessty International USA.

Anderson, Carol. 2016. *White Rage: The Unspoken Truth of the Racial Divide*. New York: Bloomsbury Press.

Baradaran, Mehrsa. 2017. *The Color of Money: Black Banks and the Racial Wealth Gap*. Cambridge, Mass.: Harvard University Press.

Beck, E. M., and Stewart E. Tolnay. 1995. "Violence Toward African Americans in the Era of the White Lynch Mob." In *Ethnicity, Race, and Crime: Perspectives Across Time and Place*, edited by Darnell Felix Hawkins. Albany: State University of New York Press.

Berard, Tim J. 2012. "Collective Action, Collective Reaction: Inspecting Bad Apples in Accounts for Organizational Deviance & Discrimination." *Interaction and Everyday Life: Phenomenological and Ethnomethodological Essays in Honor of George Psathas*: 261–77.

Brophy, Alfred L. 2003. *Reconstructing the Dreamland: The Tulsa Riot of 1921: Race, Reparations, and Reconciliation*. New York: Oxford University Press.

Chicago Commission on Race Relations. 1922. *The Negro in Chicago: A Study of Race Relations and a Race Riot*. Chicago: University of Chicago Press.

Chicago Tribune. 2014. "The 10 Most-Costly Riots in the U.S." November 26. Accessed May 3, 2018. http://www.chicagotribune.com/chi-insurance-civil-unrest-riots-bix-gfx-20141126-htmlstory.html.

---

15. In a 2018 poll conducted by The Economist/YouGov, 56 percent of whites either agreed or strongly agreed that "Irish, Italian, Jewish, and many other minorities overcame prejudice and worked their way up. Blacks should do the same without any special favors." (Table 26B, "Racial Resentment," April 1–3, https://d25d2506sfb94s.cloudfront.net/cumulus_uploads/document/maf7idof71/econTabReport.pdf, accessed May 21, 2018.)

16. In a 2016 Gallup Poll, only 49 percent of blacks and 55 percent of whites perceived black-white relations in the United States to be somewhat or very good. (Frank Newport, "Majority in U.S. Still Hopeful for Solution to Race Problems," http://news.gallup.com/poll/193682/majority-hopeful-solution-race-problems.aspx, accessed May 21, 2018.)

Clarke, James W. 1998. *The Lineaments of Wrath: Race, Violent Crime, and American Culture.* Piscataway, N.J.: Transaction Publishers.

Cohen, Cathy J., and Sarah J. Jackson. 2016. "Ask a Feminist: A Conversation with Cathy J. Cohen on Black Lives Matter, Feminism, and Contemporary Activism." *Signs: Journal of Women in Culture and Society* 41(4): 775–92.

Collins, Patricia Hill. 2000. "Gender, Black Feminism, and Black Political Economy." *ANNALS of the American Academy of Political and Social Science* 568(1): 41–53.

Collins, William J., and Robert A. Margo. 2007. "The Economic Aftermath of the 1960s Riots in American Cities: Evidence from Property Values." *Journal of Economic History* 67(4): 849–83. DOI: 10.1017/S0022050707000423.

Cook, Lisa. 2014. "Violence and Economic Activity: Evidence from African American Patents, 1870–1940." *Journal of Economic Growth* 19(2): 221–57.

Crenshaw, Kimberlé. 1989. "Demarginalizing the Intersection of Race and Sex: A Black Feminist Critique of Antidiscrimination Doctrine, Feminist Theory and Antiracist Politics." *University of Chicago Legal Forum* 1989(1): 139–67.

———. 2014. "The Girls Obama Forgot, My Brother's Keeper Ignores Young Black Women." *New York Times*, July 29.

Dailey, Jane. 1997. "Deference and Violence in the Postbellum Urban South: Manners and Massacres in Danville, Virginia." *Journal of Southern History* 63(3): 553–90.

Danville Committee of Forty. 1883. *Danville Riot, November 3, 1883: Report of Committee of Forty: With Sworn Testimony of Thirty-Seven Witnesses*, edited by John Hope Franklin Research Center. Reprint, Richmond, Va.: Johns & Goolsby.

Davis, Angela. 2003. *Are Prisons Obsolete?* New York: Seven Stories Press.

———. 2016. *Freedom Is a Constant Struggle: Ferguson, Palestine, and the Foundations of a Movement.* Chicago: Haymarket Books.

Du Bois, W. E. B. 2009. *The Souls of Black Folk*, edited by Nathan Irvin Huggins and John Edgar Wideman. New York: Library of America.

Epstein, Rebecca, Jamilia J. Blake, and Thalia González. 2017. "Girl Interrupted: The Erasure of Black Girlhood." Washington, D.C.: Georgetown Law School, Center on Poverty and Inequality.

Eskew, Glenn T. 1997. "'Bombingham': Black Protest in Postwar Birmingham, Alabama." *Historian* 59(2): 371–90.

Fanon, Frantz. 1961. *The Wretched of the Earth, damnés de la terre. English.* New York: Grove Press.

Feimster, Crystal Nicole. 2009. *Southern Horrors: Women and the Politics of Rape and Lynching.* Cambridge, Mass.: Harvard University Press.

Foner, Eric. 1988. *Reconstruction: America's Unfinished Revolution, 1863–1877.* New York. Harper Perennial.

Foucault, Michel. 1977. *Discipline and Punish.* New York: Vintage Press.

Frazier, E. Franklin. 1951. *The Negro Family in the United States.* New York: Dryden Press.

Garland, James Allon. 2001. "The Low Road to Violence: Governmental Discrimination as a Catalyst for Pandemic Hate Crime." *Law & Sexuality: Rev. Lesbian, Gay, Bisexual & Transgender Legal Issues* 10(1): 1–91.

Greene, Helen Taylor. 2000. "Understanding the Connections Between Race and Police Violence." In *The System in Black and White: Exploring the Connections Between Race, Crime, and Justice.* Westport, Conn.: Praeger.

Gruening, Martha, and W. E. B. Du Bois. 1917. "The Massacre of East St. Louis." *The Crisis*, September, 219–38.

Hamilton, Tod G., and William Darity Jr. 2006. "An Interpretation of the Economic Impact of the Wilmington Riot of 1897 Summary of Preliminary Findings." In *1898 Wilmington Race Riot Report*, edited by LeRae Umfleet. Raleigh, N.C.: Wilmington Race Riot Commission.

Harris-Perry, Melissa. 2011. *Sister Citizen: Shame, Stereotypes, and Black Women in America.* New Haven, Conn.: Yale University Press.

Haynes, Robert V. 1973. "The Houston Mutiny and Riot of 1917." *The Southwestern Historical Quarterly* 76(4): 418–39.

Iris, Mark. 1983. "American Urban Riots Revisited." *American Behavioral Scientist* 26(3): 333–52.

Jackson, Sarah. J. 2016. "(Re)Imagining Intersectional Democracy from Black Feminism to Hashtag Activism." *Women's Studies in Communication* 39(4): 375–79.

Joseph, Peniel E. 2017. "Why Black Lives Matter Still Matters." *New Republic* 248(5): 16–19.

Kerner Commission. 1968. *Report of the National Advisory Commission on Civil Disorders.* Washington: Government Printing Office.

Khaleeli, Homa. 2016. "#SayHerName: Why Kimberle Chenshaw is Fighting for Forgotten Women." *The Guardian*, May 30, 12.

Kirshenbaum, Andrea Meryl. 1998. "The Vampire That Hovers over North Carolina: Gender, White Supremacy, and the Wilmington Race Riot of 1898." *Southern Cultures* 4(3): 6–30.

Lersch, Kim Michelle, and Tom Mieczkowski. 2005. "Violent Police Behavior: Past, Present, and Future Research Directions." *Aggression and Violent Behavior* 10(5): 552–68.

McGuire, Danielle L. 2010. *At the Dark End of the Street: Black Women, Rape, and Resistance—A New History of the Civil Rights Movement from Rosa Parks to the Rise of Black Power*. New York: Vintage.

McWhirter, Cameron. 2011. *Red Summer: The Summer of 1919 and the Awakening of Black America*. New York: Henry Holt.

Merritt, Carole. 2008. *Something So Horrible: The Springfield Riot of 1908*. Springfield, Ill.: Abraham Lincoln Presidential Library Foundation.

Moynihan, Daniel P. 1965. *The Negro Family: The Case for National Action*. Washington: U.S. Department of Labor.

Myrdal, Gunnar. (1944) 1996. *An American Dilemma: The Negro Problem and Modern Democracy*, introduction by Sissela Bok. Reprint, New Brunswick, N.J.: Transaction Publishers.

NAACP. 1922. "The Anti-Lynching Crusaders: The Lynching of Women." In *NAACP Papers, Part 7: The Anti-Lynching Campaign, 1912–1955*. Washington, D.C.: National Association for the Advancement of Colored People.

Perl, Peter. 1999. "Race Riot of 1919 Gave Glimpse of Future Struggles." *Washington Post*, March 1.

President's Task Force on 21st Century Policing. 2015. *Final Report of the President's Task Force on 21st Century Policing*. Washington, D.C.: Office of Community Oriented Policing Services.

Ransby, Barbara. 2015. "The Class Politics of Black Lives Matter." *Dissent* 62(4): 31–34. DOI: 10.1353/dss.2015.0071.

Rehagen, Tony. 2017. "Forgotten Lessons from the 1917 East St. Louis Race Riots." *St. Louis Magazine*. Accessed May 3, 2018. http://projects.stlmag.com/1917-stl-race-riots.

Reich, Steven A. 2014. *The Great Black Migration: A Historical Encyclopedia of the American Mosaic*. Santa Barbara, Calif.: Greenwood.

Richie, Beth. 2012. *Arrested Justice: Black Women, Violence and America's Prison Nation*. New York: New York University Press.

Rucker, Walter C., and James N. Upton. 2007. *Encyclopedia of American Race Riots: Greenwood Milestones in African American History*. Westport, Conn.: Greenwood Press.

Smith, Ashley. 2016. "#BlackWomenMatter: Neo-Capital Punishment Ideology in the Wake of State Violence." *Journal of Negro Education* 85(3): 261–73.

Smith, Jessie Carney, and Linda T. Wynn. 2009. *Freedom Facts and Firsts: 400 Years of the African American Civil Rights Experience*. Detroit: Visible Ink Press.

Ture, Kwame, and Charles V. Hamilton. 1967. *Black Power: The Politics of Liberation in America*, edited by Charles V. Hamilton. New York: Random House.

U.S. Congress. House of Representatives. 1917. House Committee on Rules. *Riot at East St. Louis, Illinois: Hearings before the Committee on Rules*. 65th Cong., 1st sess., on H.J. res. 118, August 3, 1917.

Utsey, Shawn O., Mark A. Bolden, and Andraé L. Brown. 2001. "Visions of Revolution from the Spirit of Frantz Fanon: A Psychology of Liberation for Counseling African Americans Confronting Societal Racism and Oppression." In *Handbook of Multicultural Counseling*, 2nd ed., edited by Casas Ponterotto and Alexander Suzuki. Thousand Oaks, Calif.: Sage.

Wells-Barnett, Ida B. 1900. *Mob Rule in New Orleans: Robert Charles and His Fight to Death, the Story of His Life, Burning Human Beings Alive, Other Lynching Statistics*. Chicago: Ida B. Wells.

———. 1917. *The East St. Louis Massacre: The Greatest Outrage of the Century*. Chicago: The Negro Fellowship Herald Press.

The White House. 2014. "Remarks by the President on 'My Brother's Keeper' Initiative." February 27. Washington: Office of the Press Secretary.

Wicentowski, Danny. 2017. "First-Hand Accounts Show the Horror of East St. Louis' 1917 Race Riot." *Riverfront Times*, June 28. Accessed May 3, 2018. https://www.riverfronttimes.com/newsblog/2017/06/28/first-hand-accounts-show-the-horror-of-east-louis-1917-race-riot.

Wilkerson, Isabel. 2010. *The Warmth of Other Suns: The Epic Story of America's Great Migration*. New York: Random House.

Williams, Lee E. 1972. *Anatomy of Four Race Riots: Racial Conflict in Knoxville, Elaine (Arkansas), Tulsa, and Chicago, 1919–1921*. Hattiesburg: University and College Press of Mississippi.

# From Bakke to Fisher: African American Students in U.S. Higher Education over Forty Years

WALTER R. ALLEN, CHANNEL MCLEWIS, CHANTAL JONES, AND DANIEL HARRIS

We consider how antiblack legal precedents constrain African American access and success in higher education. We employ critical race theory to assess status and trends for African American college, graduate, and professional students. Our forty-year analysis traces national patterns of African American student enrollment and degree completion at public, four-year institutions. Using the Integrated Postsecondary Education Data System, we find that higher education remains a site of intense racial struggle for African American students. Across institutions we see various trends: the number of African American students at flagships has declined, more students enroll and complete degrees at black-serving institutions, and historically black colleges and universities are more racially diverse.

**Keywords:** higher education, college access, racism, affirmative action, African American education

Black undergraduates are severely underrepresented at more selective four-year institutions. This situation has mostly remained unchanged, but in many cases markedly declined, with the adoption of anti–affirmative action policies and practices (Ashkenas, Park, and Pearce 2017). We explore how policies and practices since the 1968 report on the National Advisory Commission on Civil Disorders (the Kerner Commission and thus the Kerner report) have systematically created a separate and unequal system of higher education. Particularly, we extend the analysis by Walter Allen and his colleagues (2005) to examine how higher education enrollment and degree completion among African American students is affected by several court decisions. We conclude that antiblack sentiments are major drivers of inequality in enrollment and degree completion in higher education.

Between 1965 and 1972, African American college students across the nation confronted

---

**Walter R. Allen** is Allan Murray Cartter Professor of Higher Education and distinguished professor of education, sociology, and African American studies at the University of California, Los Angeles. **Channel McLewis** is a doctoral candidate in higher education at the University of California, Los Angeles. **Chantal Jones** is a doctoral candidate in higher education at the University of California, Los Angeles. **Daniel Harris** is a doctoral candidate in higher education at the University of California, Los Angeles.

© 2018 Russell Sage Foundation. Allen, Walter R., Channel McLewis, Chantal Jones, and Daniel Harris. 2018. "From Bakke to Fisher: African American Students in U.S. Higher Education over Forty Years." *RSF: The Russell Sage Foundation Journal of the Social Sciences* 4(6): 41–72. DOI: 10.7758/RSF.2018.4.6.03. Acknowledgments: University of California Libraries. Direct correspondence to: Walter R. Allen at wallen@ucla.edu, Moore Hall 3101A-1, 405 Hilgard Avenue, Los Angeles, CA 90095–1521; Channel McLewis at cmclewis@ucla.edu; Chantal Jones at chantalj@ucla.edu; and Daniel Harris at dph28@ucla.edu.

Open Access Policy: *RSF: The Russell Sage Foundation Journal of the Social Sciences* is an open access journal. This article is published under a Creative Commons Attribution-NonCommercial-NoDerivs 3.0 Unported License.

racism with organized protest, demanding institutional and societal change (Rogers 2012). More than two hundred campuses were rocked by a "dramatic explosion of militant activism [which] set in motion a period of conflict, crackdown, negotiation, and reform that profoundly transformed college life. At stake was the very mission of higher education" (Biondi 2012, 1). In 1967, the policies and practices of most historically white institutions (HWI) were implicitly—if not explicitly—committed to the segregation and subjugation of African Americans (Allen et al. 2007). At historically black colleges and universities (HBCUs), African American students protested traditional attitudes and conservative politics (Rogers 2012). However, African American student activism sometimes faced violent backlash. For example, in the 1968 Orangeburg massacre, police fired on unarmed African American college students at South Carolina State University, killing three and wounding twenty-seven. Widespread campus protests linked African American college students to civil unrest across the country. Whether on campuses or in ghettoes, African American communities rose up to resist racial oppression, racist attitudes and rampant antiblack violence.

In the fall of 2015, students protested across ninety campuses, drawing national attention to the hostile racial climates, ongoing racism, and glaring inequality that many African American students attending HWIs experienced (Kelley 2016). Mass and social media captured the Concerned Student 1950 movement at the University of Missouri on the national stage. Student activists at other institutions stood in solidarity to confront institutional racism and antiblackness (Ali 2016). African American college student-led protests and social movements resulted in the removal of several campus and administrative leaders who failed to address the deep history of campus racial hostility, exclusion, and discrimination (Tatum 2017).

African American college student activism, campus unrest, and broader progressive social movements, such as the #BlackLivesMatter movement, highlight how higher education systematically reproduces society's racial hierarchies. Thus, universities are neither neutral nor safe spaces for African American students (Smith et al. 2016). In fact, Daniel Solórzano and Octavio Villalpando conclude that "higher education reflects the structural and ideological contradictions that exist in the larger society" (1998, 220). Antiblack racism confronts African American college students with severe inequities in enrollment, retention, degree completion, hostile campus climates, unequal resources, and the dismal underrepresentation of African American faculty.

We use Integrated Postsecondary Education Data System (IPEDS) data to analyze national patterns and trends in African American college enrollment and degree completion in public higher education, in the twenty states with the largest proportion African American populations. We ask the broad question "What is the status and prospects for African American higher education?" and discuss its implications. In today's society, the baccalaureate degree is more essential for future economic viability than the high school diploma was during the late 1960s (Snyder, de Brey, and Dillow 2018a). We therefore focus on African Americans in higher education institutions to explore three central questions: How far have we come? What worked and did not work? What are the implications for the twenty-first century?

## THEORETICAL FRAMEWORK

The critical race theory (CRT) literature helps explain how race, racism, and power shape African American student trajectories in higher education (Ladson-Billings and Tate 1995). CRT challenges dominant frames that perpetuate white supremacy, maintains the centrality of race and racism as key components of U.S. society, seeks social justice, and recognizes higher education as both an oppressive and empowering space (Solórzano and Yosso 2002). Emerging from legal frameworks, CRT has informed critical higher education research (Harris 2015). Lori Patton Davis discusses higher education's deep connections to white supremacy; links higher education to "imperialistic and capitalistic efforts that fuel the intersections of race, property, and oppression"; and validates transmission and production of knowledge rooted in white supremacy (2016,

317). CRT also reveals how larger cultural, political, economic, social, and legal factors intersect to create, maintain and explain the stubborn persistence of African American student disadvantages in U.S. higher education and in wider society (Bell 2003).

### Antiblackness Framework

Michael Dumas and kihana ross argue "antiblackness is not simply racism against Black people. Rather antiblackness refers to a broader antagonistic relationship between blackness and (the possibility of) humanity" (2016, 429). Further, "antiblackness does not signify a mere racial conflict that might be resolved through organized political struggle and appeals to the state and to the citizenry for redress. Instead, antiblackness marks an irreconcilability between the Black and any sense of social or cultural regard. The aim of theorizing antiblackness is not to offer solutions to racial inequality, but to come to a deeper understanding of the Black condition within a context of utter contempt for, and acceptance of violence against the Black" (Dumas 2016, 13).

Dumas also argues that education policy has historically been a site of antiblackness, under which African American children suffer from "(mal)distribution of material resources," struggle against negative ideologies and representations, and "endure physical and psychic assaults" (2016, 16). Interrogating "antiBlackness in higher education means looking for more than explicit forms of oppression, as the structure and culture norms mask violence as normal" (Mustaffa 2017, 725).

Walter Allen argues that U.S. higher education has been content with the inequities in African American college student experiences and outcomes and committed to their perpetuation (1992). He links political, historical, social, and economic factors identified in the 1968 Kerner report to widespread racial disadvantages across higher education institutions. These disparities result from negative effects of racial hierarchy based on overlapping systems of racial oppression dating back to 1619. Higher education is deeply implicated in perpetuating white supremacy. Although colleges and universities have the expertise, power, and resources to eliminate racial inequities, they have lacked the will and commitment to implement enduring systematic change.

### AFRICAN AMERICAN STUDENTS IN HIGHER EDUCATION

Higher education is believed to be "a special, deeply political, almost sacred, civic activity" (Bowen and Bok 1998, xxii). We expect higher education to produce benefits for society, "through knowledge production, leadership development, a literate electorate, and cultural and economic development, to name a few" possibilities (Kezar, Chambers, and Burkhardt 2005, xiv). We highlight the importance of higher education for African American people and overview the landscape of African American participation in U.S. public universities.

The pursuit of a college education is influenced by the anticipated returns on investment (Sissoko and Shaiu 2005), including wealth accumulation (Shapiro 2017), better employment prospects (Bishop 1977), improved lifestyle and well-being (Mirowsky and Ross 1998), and enhanced civic engagement (Baum, Ma, and Payea 2013). The reality that higher education can be a site of antiblackness, however, is antithetical to these ideals (Dumas and ross 2016; Mustaffa 2017).

According to the U.S. Department of Education, African Americans students make up 13 percent of current college students; in 1976, they constituted 9 percent (Snyder, de Brey, and Dillow 2018b). This suggests improvements; however, on closer examination we see that African American students concentrate in particular segments of higher education. African American college students represent 14 percent of total enrollment at public two-year institutions; more than 50 percent of all African American college students are enrolled in community colleges, and only 40 percent of whites attend these institutions. African American students are also overrepresented in for-profit institutions, where students pay higher tuition, more frequently default on student loans, and graduate less often (Iloh and Toldson 2013).

Increased numbers of African American college students indicates some progress, but the growing number of African American college students concentrated at community colleges and for-profits is problematic. It is not clear "whether these colleges offer long-term strategies to ameliorate educational and economic inequities, or ineffective bandages for racism that is entrenched in the economic and educational structure of the U.S." (Iloh and Toldson 2013, 209). The concentration of African American students in community colleges and in for-profit institutions, relative to their underrepresentation in baccalaureate degree-granting institutions, symbolizes a separate and unequal system of higher education.

Compared with African American men, African American women are more likely to be enrolled in higher education (Allen et al. 2005). However, in 2012, 23 percent of all African American undergraduate women and 19 percent of all African American undergraduate men attended for-profit institutions (Baum 2013). Tressie McMillan Cottom cautions that though college attendance is increasing for African American women, they tend to be concentrated in lower prestige programs with lower postgraduate employment and earnings returns (2017).

Overall, African American college students make up only 11 percent of the public and 16 percent of the private total four-year sectors (Snyder, de Brey, and Dillow 2018b). Notably, as of 2015, although HBCUs are approximately 2 percent of the higher education landscape, they award 14 percent of baccalaureate degrees to African American students (Snyder, de Brey, and Dillow 2018c, 2018d, 2018e). The pivotal contributions of HBCUs to increasing African American college attendance and graduation is well documented (Allen 1992). Although we affirm the central importance of examining African American student enrollment and degree completion across all sectors and institutional types, our attention is on public, four-year institutions. Since 2015, public four-year degree-granting institutions were the largest higher education sector, enrolling approximately 8.4 million students, 917,000 of whom were African American (Snyder, de Brey, and Dillow 2018b).

## The Courts and African American Access to Higher Education

Despite the clear benefits of higher education, the U.S. legal and judicial system has systematically limited African American attendance at public institutions (Harper, Patton, and Wooden 2009). HBCUs, established under the Morrill Land Grant Act, gave African American students the opportunity to attend college despite being denied entry to HWIs. Because "separate but equal" was overturned in federal courts, the majority of African American college students now attend HWIs (Allen et al. 2007). However, despite expanded access to HWIs, African American student college opportunities continue to be limited by structural disadvantages and systematic racism. Moreover, legal incrementalism and failures to adequately implement and enforce equity-based policies have limited the participation of African Americans in higher education (Harper, Patton, and Wooden 2009).

In 1973, *Adams v. Richardson* concluded that Louisiana, Mississippi, Oklahoma, North Carolina, Florida, Arkansas, Pennsylvania, Georgia, Maryland, and Virginia continued to operate segregated systems of higher education.[1] Although the district court ordered these states to submit desegregation plans, many ignored the order or presented unacceptable plans, yet faced few consequences.[2]

Supreme Court decisions in *Regents of the University of California v. Bakke*, *Gratz v. Bollinger*, *Grutter v. Bollinger*, and *Fisher v. University of Texas at Austin* narrowly tailor or eliminate the use of race to achieve equality within higher education.[3] Legislation such as Proposition 209 in California and Proposal 2 in Michigan validated the language of "color blindness" or "reverse racism" and decreased campus di-

---

1. *Kenneth Adams et al. v. Elliot L. Richardson, Individually, and as Secretary of the Department of Health, Education and Welfare, et al.*, 356 F. Supp. 92 (D.D.C. 1973).

2. Ibid., Declaratory Judgment and Injunction Order (John H. Pratt), https://law.justia.com/cases/federal/district-courts/FSupp/356/92/1892620 (accessed May 7, 2018).

3. *Regents of the University of California v. Bakke*, 438 U.S. 265 (1978); *Grutter v. Bollinger*, 539 U.S. 306 (2003); *Fisher v. University of Texas at Austin* 570 U.S. _ (2013), 579 U.S. _ (2016).

versity (Vue, Haslerig, and Allen 2017). As a result, African American higher education participation has declined and been severely challenged (Harper, Patton, and Wooden 2009). In the aftermath of continued bans of affirmative action and *Fisher v. University of Texas at Austin* it is important to assess African American educational progress. We examine African American student college enrollment and degree completion in public universities since the Kerner report to better understand past, present, and future patterns. The answers will also provide a lens onto the current status of African Americans in America.

## DATA AND METHODS

We use Integrated Postsecondary Education Data System and other data from the Department of Education to examine racial patterns and trends in public higher education since the Kerner report. IPEDS provides key descriptive, longitudinal information about students attending U.S. higher education institutions. We examine higher education enrollment and completion trends for African American college students across four-year, public universities in the twenty states with the largest numerical African American populations (table 1). In each state, we focus on selected public, four-year institutions, including the state flagship university, most prominent black-serving institution (BSI), and the most prominent HBCU (where present). Flagships have designated leadership roles and emphasis in state public higher education systems. BSIs—traditionally white institutions with a high representation of African American students, such as Georgia State University and Chicago State University—are prominent in the production of African American college graduates. Finally, HBCUs such as Morgan State University or Savannah State University, once legally segregated by race, continue to play significant roles in contemporary African American higher education.

Our sample also includes states that received national attention for desegregation cases (for example, *Adams v. Richardson*, *United States v. Fordice*, and *Ayers v. Fordice*) and challenges to affirmative action (for example, *Regents of the University of California v. Bakke*, *Grutter v. Bollinger*, and *Fisher v. University of Texas at Austin*).[4] Forces in all these states mobilized to actively resist and subtly undercut African American progress toward equity in higher education. It is therefore imperative to now ask, "What is the status of African American students in public higher education institutions in these states?"

Our race definition includes people who identify as African American or as African American in combination with other races. Although this operational decision can essentialize racial identity, we acknowledge the wealth of diversity within the African American community. The simple fact is that we are bound by earlier government and university decisions regarding the statistical classification of race. Limitations aside, these data provide the best, most comprehensive, empirical overview available on African American student participation in U.S. higher education.

We use 1976–2015 enrollment and completion data for African American undergraduate and graduate full-time students. This reflects the fact that until the mid-1970s, the majority of African American college student enrollment and degree completion was at HBCUs (Lambert 1979). Our analyses focus on full-time enrollment and completion (total number of degrees conferred each year) in baccalaureate, graduate, and professional programs by race and gender at public, four-year universities. For undergraduates, we look at all full-time students seeking baccalaureate degrees; for completion, we only select baccalaureate degrees. We also note the majority of undergraduates in degree-granting postsecondary institutions are full-time students (McFarland et al. 2016). Results from our forty-year longitudinal view compare only the years 1976 to 2015 in the text. However, for those who seek more detailed comparisons, data are also compared at five-year intervals between 1976 and 2015 (see online appendix, tables 3 and 4).[5]

---

4. *United States v. Fordice*, 505 U.S. 717 (1992); *Ayers v. Fordice*, 40 F. Supp. 2d 382 (1999).

5. The online appendix is available at: https://www.rsfjournal.org/doi/suppl/10.7758/RSF.2018.4.6.03.

**Table 1.** Largest African American Population by State: List of States, Institution Names, and Institution Type

| State | Number and Percent of State Total | | Institution Name | Institution Type |
|---|---|---|---|---|
| Florida | 3,401,179 | 17.3 | University of Florida | Flagship |
| | | | Florida A&M University | HBCU |
| | | | Florida Atlantic University | BSI |
| Texas | 3,390,604 | 12.8 | University of Texas at Austin | Flagship |
| | | | Texas Southern University | HBCU |
| | | | University of Houston, Downtown | BSI |
| New York | 3,344,602 | 17 | SUNY, Albany | Flagship |
| | | | CUNY, Medgar Evers College | BSI |
| | | | CUNY, City College | BSI |
| Georgia | 3,212,824 | 32.1 | University of Georgia | Flagship |
| | | | Savannah State University | HBCU |
| | | | Georgia State University | BSI |
| California | 2,710,216 | 7.1 | University of California, Berkeley | Flagship |
| | | | University of California, Los Angeles | Flagship |
| | | | California State University, Dominguez Hills | BSI |
| North Carolina | 2,241,952 | 22.8 | University of North Carolina at Chapel Hill | Flagship |
| | | | North Carolina A&T State University | HBCU |
| | | | University of North Carolina at Charlotte | BSI |
| Illinois | 1,972,360 | 15.3 | University of Illinois Urbana-Champaign | Flagship |
| | | | Chicago State University | BSI |
| | | | Southern Illinois University, Carbondale | BSI |
| Maryland | 1,848,257 | 31.2 | University of Maryland, College Park | Flagship |
| | | | Morgan State University | HBCU |
| | | | University of Maryland, Baltimore County | BSI |
| Virginia | 1,717,174 | 20.8 | University of Virginia | Flagship |
| | | | Norfolk State University | HBCU |
| | | | Old Dominion University | BSI |
| Ohio | 1,585,347 | 13.7 | The Ohio State University | Flagship |
| | | | Central State University | HBCU |
| | | | Cleveland State University | BSI |
| Pennsylvania | 1,561,343 | 12.2 | Pennsylvania State College, University Park | Flagship |
| | | | Lincoln University | HBCU |
| | | | Temple University | BSI |
| Louisiana | 1,528,695 | 33.1 | Louisiana State University | Flagship |
| | | | Southern University and A&M College | HBCU |
| | | | Northwestern State University of Louisiana | BSI |

**Table 1.** (continued)

| State | Number and Percent of State Total | | Institution Name | Institution Type |
|---|---|---|---|---|
| Michigan | 1,509,779 | 15.2 | University of Michigan, Ann Arbor | Flagship |
| | | | Michigan State Uni. | BSI |
| | | | Wayne State University | BSI |
| South Carolina | 1,367,604 | 28.6 | University of South Carolina, Columbia | Flagship |
| | | | South Carolina State University | HBCU |
| | | | Francis Marion University | BSI |
| New Jersey | 1,314,132 | 14.8 | Rutgers University, New Brunswick | Flagship |
| | | | Kean University | BSI |
| | | | Rutgers University, Newark | BSI |
| Alabama | 1,312,584 | 27.2 | University of Alabama | Flagship |
| | | | Alabama State University | HBCU |
| | | | University of Alabama Birmingham | BSI |
| Tennessee | 1,150,035 | 17.7 | University of Tennessee | Flagship |
| | | | Tennessee State University | HBCU |
| | | | Middle Tennessee State University | BSI |
| Mississippi | 1,136,159 | 38 | University of Mississippi | Flagship |
| | | | Jackson State University | HBCU |
| | | | University of Southern Mississippi | BSI |
| Missouri | 764,195 | 12.6 | University of Missouri | Flagship |
| | | | Lincoln University | HBCU |
| | | | University of Missouri St. Louis | BSI |
| Indiana | 678,881 | 10.3 | Indiana University Bloomington | Flagship |
| | | | Indiana State University | BSI |
| | | | Indiana University Purdue University Indianapolis | BSI |

*Source:* Authors' calculations based on U.S. Census Bureau 2015.
*Note:* HBCU: historically black college and university; BSI: black-serving institution.

## Limitations

Viewed over time, IPEDS offers a reliable summary of patterns and trends across higher education institutions. IPEDS data provide a standardized snapshot of key institutional characteristics for U.S. colleges and universities. However, a key limitation of IPEDS data is the restricted range of information and variables reported. Also, because the data are self-compiled and self-reported, institutional errors are possible. Finally, IPEDS collects only aggregate, institutional data; therefore rich, detailed information about individual student factors such as backgrounds, values, experiences, and outcomes is lacking.

## FINDINGS

We examined African American student enrollment and completion patterns and trends at public, four-year institutions to investigate African American student access and success in higher education from 1976 to 2015. Our comparisons and analyses are presented across three distinct types of institutions: flagship universities, black-serving institutions, and historically black colleges and universities.

### Enrollment: Flagships

The overall proportion of African American undergraduates enrolled at public flagship institutions has remained persistently low over

**Figure 1.** Mississippi Percent African American Enrollment, 1976–2015

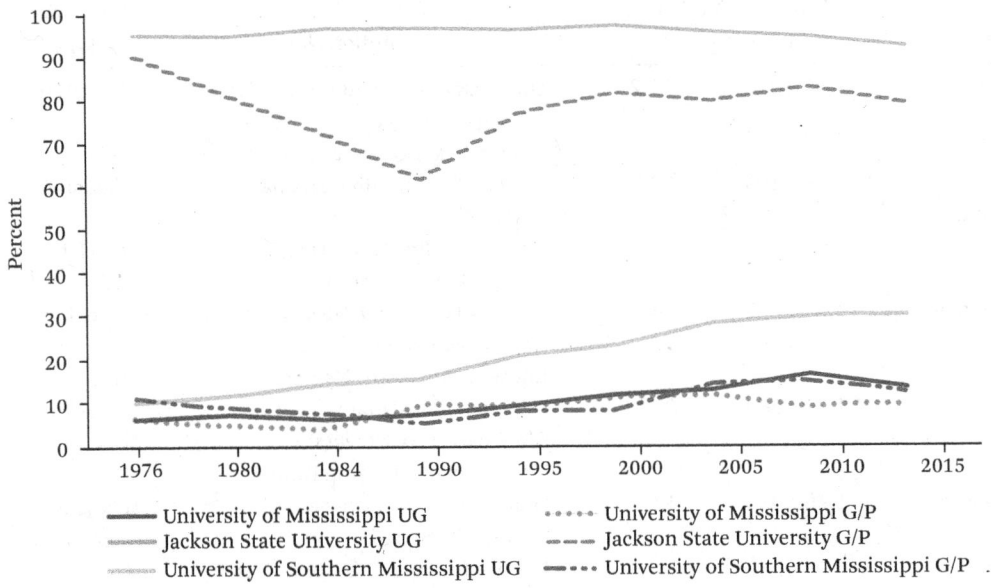

*Source:* Authors' calculations based on National Center for Education Statistics; U.S. Department of Health, Education, and Welfare 1978a.
*Note:* UG: undergraduate; G/P: graduate and professional.

forty years. Given the overall number of African American undergraduates attending public four-year institutions has increased, we would expect comparable enrollment increases at public flagship institutions. But this is not the case. Further, when we consider the African American proportion of the overall state population, African American undergraduate enrollment at flagship institutions (generally less than 4 percent) is significantly below the representation of African Americans in the state (tables 1 and 2). The most striking example is Mississippi. In 2015, the African American population in the state was nearly 40 percent, however, African American undergraduate enrollment at the University of Mississippi was only 13.4 percent (tables 1 and 2, figure 1). This pattern confirms Hechinger report data showing that more than a third of U.S. states had a least a 10-point gap, including eight with a 20-point gap, between the percentage of public high school graduates who are African American and the percentage of their flagships' freshman class who are African American (Kolodner 2018, para. 2).

African American undergraduate enrollment has remained significantly lower than the African American proportion of state population where affirmative action faced court challenges. For example, African American undergraduate enrollment at the University of California, Berkeley; University of California, Los Angeles; University of Michigan, Ann Arbor; and University of Texas, Austin was approximately 4.5 percent or lower in 2015 (table 2). This, despite the fact that the African American population is 7.1 percent in California, 15.2 percent in Michigan, and 12.8 percent in Texas (table 1). Striking declines in African American undergraduate enrollments in California and Michigan were not surprising given the strong anti–affirmative action sentiments expressed in bans passed by voters in both states (Proposition 209 in California and Proposal 2 in Michigan).

By contrast, African American undergraduate enrollment was typically higher at institutions not directly named in affirmative action litigation. Still, 2015 African American undergraduate enrollment only reached double digits at five institutions: University of Alabama,

(*Text continues on p. 56.*)

**Table 2.** Percent African American Enrollment and Completion by Gender, 1976 and 2015

| | Enrollment | | | | | | | | Completion | | | | | | | |
|---|---|---|---|---|---|---|---|---|---|---|---|---|---|---|---|---|
| | 1976 | | | | 2015 | | | | 1976 | | | | 2015 | | | |
| | 1 | 2 | 3 | 4 | 1 | 2 | 3 | 4 | 1 | 2 | 3 | 4 | 1 | 2 | 3 | 4 |
| **Alabama** | | | | | | | | | | | | | | | | |
| University of Alabama | | | | | | | | | | | | | | | | |
| UG | 12,835 | 8.5 | 5.0 | 3.5 | 28,447 | 10.5 | 6.6 | 3.9 | 2,329 | 5.0 | 3.3 | 1.7 | 5,662 | 10.7 | 7.3 | 3.3 |
| G/P | 3,618 | 7.6 | 4.8 | 2.7 | 3,321 | 11.1 | 8.5 | 2.6 | 1,392 | 6.3 | 4.7 | 1.6 | 2,195 | 12.4 | 9.6 | 2.8 |
| Alabama State University | | | | | | | | | | | | | | | | |
| UG | 3,209 | 99.7 | 56.2 | 43.5 | 4,377 | 92.4 | 57.5 | 34.8 | 451 | 99.8 | 67.6 | 32.2 | 529 | 92.2 | 59.9 | 32.3 |
| G/P | 891 | 99.3 | 69.4 | 30.0 | 291 | 55.3 | 40.2 | 15.1 | 405 | 100.0 | 75.1 | 24.9 | 177 | 63.3 | 47.5 | 15.8 |
| University of Alabama Birmingham | | | | | | | | | | | | | | | | |
| UG | 7,788 | 20.7 | 14.2 | 6.5 | 8,259 | 25.4 | 16.9 | 8.5 | 1,041 | 10.2 | 6.8 | 3.4 | 2165 | 23.0 | 16.0 | 6.9 |
| G/P | 3,059 | 11.7 | 7.7 | 4.0 | 3,515 | 9.4 | 7.1 | 2.4 | 1,103 | 12.7 | 11.4 | 1.3 | 2,248 | 12.9 | 10.1 | 2.8 |
| **California** | | | | | | | | | | | | | | | | |
| University of California-Berkeley | | | | | | | | | | | | | | | | |
| UG | 19,837 | 4.0 | 2.1 | 1.9 | 26,622 | 2.1 | 1.1 | 0.9 | 5,713 | 3.4 | 1.6 | 1.8 | 7,647 | 1.9 | 1.1 | 0.8 |
| G/P | 9,425 | 4.1 | 2.1 | 2.1 | 9,338 | 3.0 | 1.8 | 1.2 | 3,346 | 4.0 | 1.6 | 2.4 | 3,551 | 2.9 | 1.5 | 1.4 |
| University of California-Los Angeles | | | | | | | | | | | | | | | | |
| UG | 20,588 | 5.3 | 3.1 | 2.2 | 29,000 | 3.0 | 1.8 | 1.1 | 4,733 | 5.3 | 2.9 | 2.5 | 7,977 | 2.3 | 1.5 | 0.8 |
| G/P | 10,303 | 5.1 | 2.5 | 2.6 | 11,493 | 3.5 | 2.3 | 1.2 | 3,020 | 5.1 | 2.9 | 2.2 | 4,376 | 3.0 | 2.0 | 1.0 |
| California State University Dominguez Hills | | | | | | | | | | | | | | | | |
| UG | 5,202 | 33.8 | 16.2 | 17.6 | 9,173 | 12.4 | 8.2 | 4.2 | 904 | 30.0 | 13.8 | 16.2 | 2,581 | 16.3 | 11.6 | 4.7 |
| G/P | 768 | 23.2 | 14.1 | 9.1 | 1,049 | 11.4 | 8.7 | 2.8 | 365 | 27.1 | 11.2 | 15.9 | 771 | 14.8 | 10.5 | 4.3 |
| **Florida** | | | | | | | | | | | | | | | | |
| University of Florida | | | | | | | | | | | | | | | | |
| UG | 20,852 | 4.8 | 2.6 | 2.2 | 29,862 | 6.3 | 4.1 | 2.2 | 4,998 | 2.5 | 1.5 | 1.0 | 8,393 | 7.3 | 4.9 | 2.5 |
| G/P | 6,206 | 3.4 | 1.5 | 2.0 | 12,479 | 4.7 | 2.8 | 2.0 | 2,359 | 4.3 | 1.8 | 2.5 | 5,520 | 4.6 | 2.9 | 1.7 |
| Florida A&M University | | | | | | | | | | | | | | | | |
| UG | 4,896 | 89.4 | 46.2 | 43.1 | 6,943 | 91.2 | 59.0 | 32.3 | 612 | 91.2 | 46.7 | 44.4 | 1,507 | 95.0 | 59.6 | 35.4 |
| G/P | 140 | 75.0 | 49.3 | 25.7 | 1,523 | 72.0 | 49.8 | 22.3 | 217 | 88.9 | 59.9 | 29.0 | 584 | 79.8 | 55.3 | 24.5 |
| Florida Atlantic University | | | | | | | | | | | | | | | | |
| UG | 4,425 | 5.5 | 4.0 | 1.5 | 15,670 | 18.3 | 11.1 | 7.2 | 1,419 | 4.8 | 3.4 | 1.4 | 5,473 | 11.7 | 7.8 | 3.9 |
| G/P | 1,017 | 6.2 | 4.2 | 2.0 | 2,014 | 13.9 | 9.8 | 4.0 | 542 | 8.1 | 4.8 | 3.3 | 1,559 | 6.9 | 4.8 | 2.1 |

*(continued)*

Table 2. (continued)

| | Enrollment | | | | | | | | Completion | | | | | | | |
|---|---|---|---|---|---|---|---|---|---|---|---|---|---|---|---|---|
| | 1976 | | | | 2015 | | | | 1976 | | | | 2015 | | | |
| | 1 | 2 | 3 | 4 | 1 | 2 | 3 | 4 | 1 | 2 | 3 | 4 | 1 | 2 | 3 | 4 |
| **Georgia** | | | | | | | | | | | | | | | | |
| University of Georgia | | | | | | | | | | | | | | | | |
| UG | 16,759 | 8.5 | 2.0 | 1.6 | 25,737 | 7.6 | 4.8 | 2.8 | 3,777 | 2.1 | 1.3 | 0.7 | 6,935 | 7.2 | 5.2 | 2.0 |
| G/P | 4,178 | 2.6 | 1.3 | 1.3 | 6,640 | 7.3 | 5.6 | 1.7 | 2,308 | 4.5 | 2.8 | 1.7 | 2,490 | 8.9 | 6.4 | 2.5 |
| Savannah State University | | | | | | | | | | | | | | | | |
| UG | 2,458 | 89.3 | 54.2 | 35.1 | 4,030 | 83.5 | 49.6 | 33.8 | 259 | 97.7 | 61.4 | 36.3 | 492 | 86.8 | 53.9 | 32.9 |
| G/P | 389 | 33.9 | 23.4 | 10.5 | 104 | 64.4 | 51.9 | 12.5 | — | — | — | — | 71 | 64.8 | 50.7 | 14.1 |
| Georgia State University | | | | | | | | | | | | | | | | |
| UG | 13,278 | 15.5 | 9.3 | 6.1 | 18,652 | 40.9 | 27.2 | 13.8 | 1,911 | 11.0 | 4.9 | 6.1 | 4,771 | 36.4 | 25.1 | 11.3 |
| G/P | 7,005 | 13.6 | 9.9 | 3.7 | 5,075 | 18.1 | 12.5 | 5.6 | 2,303 | 13.6 | 8.6 | 5.0 | 2,561 | 19.6 | 13.0 | 6.6 |
| **Illinois** | | | | | | | | | | | | | | | | |
| University of Illinois Urbana-Champaign | | | | | | | | | | | | | | | | |
| UG | 24,435 | 3.9 | 2.2 | 1.7 | 31,552 | 5.5 | 3.2 | 2.3 | 5,903 | 2.2 | 1.1 | 1.2 | 8,024 | 5.0 | 3.0 | 2.1 |
| G/P | 8,565 | 3.2 | 1.4 | 1.8 | 9,767 | 3.4 | 2.1 | 1.3 | 3,685 | 3.9 | 2.0 | 1.9 | 4,390 | 3.8 | 2.2 | 1.6 |
| Chicago State University | | | | | | | | | | | | | | | | |
| UG | 4,361 | 76.1 | 48.8 | 27.4 | 2,259 | 73.1 | 53.7 | 19.4 | 1,037 | 67.5 | 46.0 | 21.5 | 661 | 78.1 | 57.5 | 20.6 |
| G/P | 841 | 47.1 | 34.2 | 12.8 | 736 | 42.0 | 28.5 | 13.5 | 327 | 48.0 | 32.1 | 15.9 | 286 | 48.3 | 38.1 | 10.1 |
| Southern Illinois University, Carbondale | | | | | | | | | | | | | | | | |
| UG | 18,282 | 9.1 | 4.4 | 4.7 | 11,255 | 19.6 | 11.2 | 8.4 | 3,128 | 5.7 | 2.7 | 3.0 | 3,259 | 16.0 | 8.6 | 7.4 |
| G/P | 3,769 | 5.5 | 2.8 | 2.8 | 2,589 | 10.9 | 7.1 | 3.8 | 1,040 | 5.4 | 3.1 | 2.3 | 1,512 | 8.7 | 5.4 | 3.3 |
| **Indiana** | | | | | | | | | | | | | | | | |
| Indiana University Bloomington | | | | | | | | | | | | | | | | |
| UG | 23,233 | 4.8 | 2.6 | 2.3 | 31,559 | 4.2 | 2.4 | 1.8 | 4,077 | 2.7 | 1.5 | 1.2 | 7,339 | 3.6 | 2.2 | 1.4 |
| G/P | 8,612 | 2.9 | 1.4 | 1.5 | 6,275 | 3.2 | 1.5 | 1.8 | 3,077 | 3.1 | 1.7 | 1.4 | 3,280 | 3.4 | 1.9 | 1.5 |
| Indiana State University | | | | | | | | | | | | | | | | |
| UG | 9,175 | 10.0 | 5.3 | 4.7 | 9,623 | 19.5 | 11.2 | 8.4 | 1,661 | 5.8 | 3.4 | 2.4 | 1,784 | 11.7 | 7.7 | 4.0 |
| G/P | 2,339 | 2.1 | 0.8 | 1.3 | 991 | 9.3 | 6.0 | 3.3 | 978 | 1.0 | 0.5 | 0.5 | 613 | 7.7 | 5.5 | 2.1 |
| Indiana University Purdue University Indianapolis | | | | | | | | | | | | | | | | |
| UG | 12,427 | 10.9 | 6.7 | 4.2 | 16,932 | 9.2 | 6.0 | 3.1 | 1,258 | 4.8 | 2.8 | 2.0 | 3,922 | 8.1 | 5.6 | 2.5 |
| G/P | 6,379 | 5.2 | 3.1 | 2.1 | 4,575 | 7.4 | 5.0 | 2.4 | 1,273 | 4.2 | 1.3 | 2.8 | 2,367 | 5.8 | 4.2 | 1.6 |

**Louisiana**

Louisiana State University

|  | | | | | | | | | | | | | | | | |
|---|---|---|---|---|---|---|---|---|---|---|---|---|---|---|---|---|
| UG | 18,781 | 8.5 | 2.1 | 1.4 | 23,450 | 12.1 | 7.5 | 4.6 | 2,892 | 2.0 | 1.3 | 0.7 | 4,649 | 9.6 | 6.0 | 3.6 |
| G/P | 5,008 | 4.2 | 2.6 | 1.6 | 4,236 | 8.6 | 5.7 | 2.9 | 1,386 | 4.3 | 2.9 | 1.4 | 1,734 | 9.6 | 6.3 | 3.2 |

Southern University and A&M College

|  | | | | | | | | | | | | | | | | |
|---|---|---|---|---|---|---|---|---|---|---|---|---|---|---|---|---|
| UG | 7,646 | 96.3 | 53.2 | 43.2 | 4,631 | 93.5 | 59.9 | 33.6 | 1,251 | 98.8 | 62.1 | 36.7 | 652 | 94.5 | 61.2 | 33.3 |
| G/P | 1,187 | 93.3 | 61.3 | 31.9 | 632 | 71.2 | 52.1 | 19.1 | 425 | 97.2 | 67.8 | 29.4 | 307 | 83.7 | 57.0 | 26.7 |

Northwestern State University of Louisiana

|  | | | | | | | | | | | | | | | | |
|---|---|---|---|---|---|---|---|---|---|---|---|---|---|---|---|---|
| UG | 5,230 | 13.8 | 7.5 | 6.3 | 5,016 | 30.4 | 20.0 | 10.5 | 787 | 69.1 | 37.4 | 31.8 | 1,069 | 26.6 | 19.7 | 6.8 |
| G/P | 1,121 | 11.8 | 8.7 | 3.1 | 193 | 19.7 | 11.9 | 7.8 | 564 | 19.9 | 6.9 | 12.9 | 252 | 17.1 | 13.9 | 3.2 |

**Maryland**

University of Maryland, College Park

|  | | | | | | | | | | | | | | | | |
|---|---|---|---|---|---|---|---|---|---|---|---|---|---|---|---|---|
| UG | 25,895 | 7.8 | 4.6 | 3.2 | 25,272 | 12.7 | 7.1 | 5.6 | 5,058 | 4.3 | 2.7 | 1.5 | 7,166 | 11.2 | 6.7 | 4.5 |
| G/P | 7,141 | 5.5 | 3.4 | 2.1 | 8,091 | 6.1 | 3.7 | 2.5 | 1,842 | 4.3 | 2.9 | 1.5 | 3,255 | 6.5 | 3.5 | 3.0 |

Morgan State University

|  | | | | | | | | | | | | | | | | |
|---|---|---|---|---|---|---|---|---|---|---|---|---|---|---|---|---|
| UG | 4,750 | 95.6 | 54.0 | 41.6 | 5,589 | 82.4 | 46.6 | 35.8 | 658 | 88.6 | 55.3 | 33.3 | 931 | 87.3 | 52.1 | 35.2 |
| G/P | 900 | 61.0 | 29.9 | 31.1 | 1,003 | 61.0 | 41.1 | 19.9 | 255 | 58.8 | 32.9 | 25.9 | 292 | 78.8 | 48.3 | 30.5 |

University of Maryland, Baltimore County

|  | | | | | | | | | | | | | | | | |
|---|---|---|---|---|---|---|---|---|---|---|---|---|---|---|---|---|
| UG | 5,135 | 19.9 | 13.5 | 6.4 | 9,577 | 17.1 | 9.2 | 7.9 | 625 | 7.8 | 5.3 | 2.6 | 2,432 | 16.9 | 9.8 | 7.0 |
| G/P | 207 | 8.7 | 5.3 | 3.4 | 1,160 | 9.1 | 4.8 | 4.2 | 15 | 0.0 | 0.0 | 0.0 | 794 | 13.9 | 7.8 | 6.0 |

**Michigan**

University of Michigan, Ann Arbor

|  | | | | | | | | | | | | | | | | |
|---|---|---|---|---|---|---|---|---|---|---|---|---|---|---|---|---|
| UG | 22,120 | 6.9 | 3.9 | 3.1 | 27,161 | 4.3 | 2.6 | 1.8 | 4,839 | 5.4 | 3.2 | 2.2 | 7,091 | 4.0 | 2.7 | 1.3 |
| G/P | 14,743 | 8.4 | 4.4 | 4.0 | 13,856 | 3.9 | 2.3 | 1.6 | 4,989 | 7.7 | 4.3 | 3.3 | 5,902 | 4.0 | 2.5 | 1.5 |

Michigan State University

|  | | | | | | | | | | | | | | | | |
|---|---|---|---|---|---|---|---|---|---|---|---|---|---|---|---|---|
| UG | 35,561 | 5.8 | 3.4 | 2.3 | 35,425 | 7.2 | 4.5 | 2.7 | 7,343 | 5.4 | 3.2 | 2.2 | 8,299 | 5.6 | 3.7 | 1.9 |
| G/P | 12,235 | 5.3 | 2.9 | 2.4 | 8,381 | 4.6 | 2.9 | 1.6 | 3,464 | 5.5 | 2.2 | 3.2 | 3,342 | 4.5 | 2.8 | 1.7 |

Wayne State University

|  | | | | | | | | | | | | | | | | |
|---|---|---|---|---|---|---|---|---|---|---|---|---|---|---|---|---|
| UG | 23,410 | 27.7 | 15.3 | 12.4 | 11,617 | 15.8 | 10.2 | 5.5 | 3,288 | 19.9 | 11.9 | 8.0 | 3,180 | 15.4 | 10.8 | 4.6 |
| G/P | 9,574 | 13.3 | 8.3 | 5.0 | 6,066 | 7.6 | 5.7 | 1.9 | 2,917 | 15.2 | 10.7 | 4.5 | 2,856 | 10.9 | 8.5 | 2.3 |

*(continued)*

Table 2. (continued)

| | Enrollment | | | | | | | | Completion | | | | | | | |
|---|---|---|---|---|---|---|---|---|---|---|---|---|---|---|---|---|
| | 1976 | | | | 2015 | | | | 1976 | | | | 2015 | | | |
| | 1 | 2 | 3 | 4 | 1 | 2 | 3 | 4 | 1 | 2 | 3 | 4 | 1 | 2 | 3 | 4 |
| **Mississippi** | | | | | | | | | | | | | | | | |
| University of Mississippi | | | | | | | | | | | | | | | | |
| UG | 6,973 | 8.5 | 3.5 | 2.7 | 17,120 | 13.4 | 8.6 | 4.7 | 1,352 | 3.6 | 2.1 | 1.4 | 3,659 | 13.8 | 10.1 | 3.7 |
| G/P | 1,505 | 5.9 | 2.7 | 3.2 | 3,270 | 9.6 | 6.7 | 2.8 | 778 | 6.8 | 4.4 | 2.4 | 1,478 | 13.4 | 10.2 | 3.2 |
| Jackson State University | | | | | | | | | | | | | | | | |
| UG | 6,203 | 95.4 | 48.5 | 46.9 | 6676 | 91.5 | 58.1 | 33.4 | 669 | 95.5 | 54.9 | 40.7 | 989 | 88.5 | 58.6 | 29.8 |
| G/P | 1,135 | 91.5 | 55.6 | 35.9 | 870 | 79.3 | 58.0 | 21.3 | 393 | 91.1 | 62.8 | 28.2 | 504 | 82.9 | 61.9 | 19.8 |
| University of Southern Mississippi | | | | | | | | | | | | | | | | |
| UG | 9,069 | 10.0 | 6.5 | 3.5 | 10,297 | 30.3 | 20.7 | 9.6 | 1,974 | 5.8 | 3.7 | 2.1 | 2,352 | 23.4 | 16.7 | 6.7 |
| G/P | 2,569 | 10.5 | 6.5 | 4.0 | 1,435 | 12.2 | 9.1 | 3.1 | 854 | 8.1 | 4.8 | 3.3 | 943 | 10.5 | 8.7 | 1.8 |
| **Missouri** | | | | | | | | | | | | | | | | |
| University of Missouri | | | | | | | | | | | | | | | | |
| UG | 17,704 | 2.9 | 1.6 | 1.3 | 25,909 | 8.2 | 5.0 | 3.2 | 3,398 | 1.2 | 0.6 | 0.6 | 5,995 | 6.6 | 4.2 | 2.4 |
| G/P | 6,153 | 2.2 | 0.9 | 1.2 | 4,963 | 3.3 | 1.9 | 1.5 | 1,741 | 1.6 | 0.7 | 0.9 | 2,352 | 2.8 | 1.4 | 1.4 |
| Lincoln University of Missouri | | | | | | | | | | | | | | | | |
| UG | 2,098 | 39.1 | 19.1 | 20.0 | 1,911 | 57.5 | 28.7 | 28.8 | 329 | 39.2 | 17.9 | 21.3 | 287 | 33.1 | 19.5 | 13.6 |
| G/P | 243 | 18.1 | 8.2 | 9.9 | 53 | 22.6 | 11.3 | 11.3 | 84 | 17.9 | 8.3 | 9.5 | 35 | 20.0 | 17.1 | 2.9 |
| University of Missouri St. Louis | | | | | | | | | | | | | | | | |
| UG | 10,187 | 12.6 | 6.6 | 6.1 | 5,541 | 15.6 | 11.0 | 4.6 | 1,499 | 4.2 | 1.8 | 2.4 | 2246 | 15.3 | 11.4 | 4.0 |
| G/P | 1,419 | 8.8 | 6.2 | 2.6 | 1,001 | 9.3 | 7.0 | 2.3 | 372 | 3.2 | 2.4 | 0.8 | 886 | 11.4 | 9.0 | 2.4 |
| **New Jersey** | | | | | | | | | | | | | | | | |
| Rutgers University–New Brunswick | | | | | | | | | | | | | | | | |
| UG | 17,883 | 8.2 | 4.9 | 3.3 | 33,294 | 7.3 | 4.5 | 2.8 | 3,832 | 9.3 | 5.0 | 4.3 | 7,569 | 7.6 | 4.8 | 2.8 |
| G/P | 9,056 | 6.9 | 4.3 | 2.6 | 8,737 | 7.9 | 6.0 | 2.0 | 1,804 | 8.8 | 4.9 | 3.9 | 4,033 | 9.0 | 7.0 | 2.0 |
| Kean University | | | | | | | | | | | | | | | | |
| UG | 8,734 | 13.6 | 8.6 | 5.1 | 9,191 | 19.9 | 12.0 | 7.9 | 1,554 | 8.6 | 6.6 | 2.1 | 2,712 | 17.3 | 11.3 | 6.0 |
| G/P | 1,355 | 7.7 | 5.9 | 1.8 | 853 | 20.0 | 14.8 | 5.3 | 508 | 9.6 | 6.7 | 3.0 | 621 | 18.4 | 12.9 | 5.5 |
| Rutgers University-Newark | | | | | | | | | | | | | | | | |
| UG | 3,754 | 13.7 | 8.8 | 5.0 | 6,206 | 18.5 | 11.2 | 7.2 | 1,095 | 17.3 | 9.8 | 7.5 | 1,544 | 17.9 | 10.2 | 7.6 |
| G/P | 2,849 | 8.9 | 3.8 | 5.1 | 1,805 | 10.0 | 5.8 | 4.2 | 778 | 8.4 | 2.1 | 6.3 | 1,317 | 12.1 | 6.5 | 5.5 |

### New York

**SUNY Albany**

| | | | | | | | | | | | | | | | | |
|---|---|---|---|---|---|---|---|---|---|---|---|---|---|---|---|---|
| UG | 9,321 | 8.5 | 2.2 | 2.1 | 12,151 | 16.6 | 9.6 | 7.0 | 2,154 | 1.8 | 0.9 | 0.9 | 2,875 | 13.8 | 8.5 | 5.3 |
| G/P | 3,458 | 2.3 | 0.9 | 1.4 | 2,218 | 6.7 | 5.2 | 1.5 | 1,401 | 2.4 | 1.6 | 0.9 | 1,435 | 5.2 | 3.0 | 2.2 |

**CUNY, Medgar Evers College**

| | | | | | | | | | | | | | | | | |
|---|---|---|---|---|---|---|---|---|---|---|---|---|---|---|---|---|
| UG | 2,806 | 82.9 | 60.9 | 22.0 | 4,366 | 78.0 | 55.7 | 22.4 | 120 | 86.7 | 44.2 | 42.5 | 472 | 82.8 | 62.9 | 19.9 |
| G/P | — | — | — | — | — | — | — | — | — | — | — | — | — | — | — | — |

**CUNY, City College**

| | | | | | | | | | | | | | | | | |
|---|---|---|---|---|---|---|---|---|---|---|---|---|---|---|---|---|
| UG | 11,918 | 32.7 | 17.0 | 15.7 | 9,636 | 15.3 | 8.7 | 6.6 | 2,278 | 23.6 | 12.6 | 11.1 | 2,156 | 21.8 | 13.1 | 8.7 |
| G/P | 1,663 | 22.5 | 15.6 | 6.9 | 376 | 17.3 | 8.2 | 9.0 | 956 | 16.9 | 11.4 | 5.5 | 861 | 17.1 | 10.9 | 6.2 |

### North Carolina

**University of North Carolina at Chapel Hill**

| | | | | | | | | | | | | | | | | |
|---|---|---|---|---|---|---|---|---|---|---|---|---|---|---|---|---|
| UG | 13,170 | 6.1 | 3.4 | 2.7 | 17,606 | 7.8 | 5.1 | 2.7 | 3,078 | 4.6 | 2.5 | 2.1 | 4,624 | 8.9 | 6.0 | 2.9 |
| G/P | 5,534 | 6.4 | 3.1 | 3.3 | 6,425 | 7.0 | 4.8 | 2.1 | 1,909 | 4.6 | 2.3 | 2.4 | 3,360 | 6.5 | 4.6 | 1.9 |

**North Carolina A&T State University**

| | | | | | | | | | | | | | | | | |
|---|---|---|---|---|---|---|---|---|---|---|---|---|---|---|---|---|
| UG | 4,754 | 95.1 | 47.6 | 47.5 | 8,376 | 85.1 | 47.6 | 37.5 | 769 | 97.0 | 45.4 | 51.6 | 1,293 | 86.6 | 50.0 | 36.7 |
| G/P | 671 | 69.6 | 37.3 | 32.3 | 907 | 56.7 | 35.9 | 20.7 | 285 | 65.3 | 33.7 | 31.6 | 473 | 62.6 | 38.9 | 23.7 |

**University of North Carolina at Charlotte**

| | | | | | | | | | | | | | | | | |
|---|---|---|---|---|---|---|---|---|---|---|---|---|---|---|---|---|
| UG | 5,909 | 5.7 | 3.0 | 2.6 | 19,745 | 16.5 | 9.3 | 7.2 | 1,177 | 3.6 | 1.4 | 2.2 | 4,513 | 14.4 | 9.7 | 4.6 |
| G/P | 1,225 | 15.0 | 11.1 | 3.9 | 2,419 | 8.8 | 6.7 | 2.1 | 257 | 14.4 | 7.4 | 7.0 | 1,467 | 7.9 | 5.5 | 2.5 |

### Ohio

**The Ohio State University**

| | | | | | | | | | | | | | | | | |
|---|---|---|---|---|---|---|---|---|---|---|---|---|---|---|---|---|
| UG | 38,408 | 6.3 | 3.6 | 2.7 | 40,898 | 5.2 | 2.9 | 2.4 | 6,418 | 2.8 | 1.6 | 1.2 | 10,414 | 5.8 | 3.4 | 2.5 |
| G/P | 11,574 | 4.5 | 2.7 | 1.9 | 9,861 | 4.1 | 2.7 | 1.5 | 3,841 | 4.2 | 2.5 | 1.7 | 4,400 | 4.0 | 2.5 | 1.6 |

**Central State University**

| | | | | | | | | | | | | | | | | |
|---|---|---|---|---|---|---|---|---|---|---|---|---|---|---|---|---|
| UG | 1,849 | 91.9 | 43.2 | 48.7 | 1,649 | 95.3 | 52.8 | 42.5 | 339 | 84.4 | 47.2 | 37.2 | 287 | 95.5 | 51.9 | 43.6 |
| G/P | — | — | — | — | — | — | — | — | — | — | — | — | 4 | 100.0 | 50.0 | 50.0 |

**Cleveland State University**

| | | | | | | | | | | | | | | | | |
|---|---|---|---|---|---|---|---|---|---|---|---|---|---|---|---|---|
| UG | 12,446 | 12.2 | 7.1 | 5.1 | 9,046 | 15.4 | 10.1 | 5.3 | 1,794 | 7.9 | 4.2 | 3.6 | 2,317 | 14.4 | 9.9 | 4.5 |
| G/P | 3,914 | 11.4 | 6.0 | 5.4 | 2,269 | 10.1 | 7.7 | 2.4 | 786 | 8.9 | 5.9 | 3.1 | 1,666 | 11.1 | 7.7 | 3.4 |

*(continued)*

Table 2. (continued)

| | Enrollment | | | | | | | | Completion | | | | | | | |
|---|---|---|---|---|---|---|---|---|---|---|---|---|---|---|---|---|
| | 1976 | | | | 2015 | | | | 1976 | | | | 2015 | | | |
| | 1 | 2 | 3 | 4 | 1 | 2 | 3 | 4 | 1 | 2 | 3 | 4 | 1 | 2 | 3 | 4 |
| **Pennsylvania** | | | | | | | | | | | | | | | | |
| Pennsylvania State College, University Park | | | | | | | | | | | | | | | | |
| UG | 26,037 | 8.5 | 1.0 | 0.8 | 39,294 | 4.2 | 2.3 | 1.8 | 7,562 | 1.5 | 1.0 | 0.6 | 10,876 | 4.7 | 3.0 | 1.8 |
| G/P | 4,797 | 2.1 | 0.9 | 1.3 | 5,890 | 3.0 | 1.7 | 1.3 | 1,747 | 1.6 | 0.9 | 0.7 | 2,015 | 3.5 | 2.0 | 1.4 |
| Lincoln University | | | | | | | | | | | | | | | | |
| UG | 1,090 | 95.6 | 47.5 | 48.1 | 1,546 | 86.0 | 54.6 | 31.4 | 191 | 91.6 | 52.9 | 38.7 | 265 | 74.3 | 46.8 | 27.5 |
| G/P | — | — | — | — | 139 | 95.0 | 64.0 | 30.9 | — | — | — | — | 99 | 92.9 | 56.6 | 36.4 |
| Temple University | | | | | | | | | | | | | | | | |
| UG | 18,078 | 18.7 | 11.9 | 6.8 | 25,128 | 12.2 | 7.8 | 4.4 | 3,090 | 12.7 | 7.8 | 4.9 | 6,024 | 12.8 | 8.1 | 4.6 |
| G/P | 8,563 | 8.6 | 5.2 | 3.5 | 6,979 | 6.7 | 4.2 | 2.5 | 2,350 | 10.3 | 5.9 | 4.3 | 2,638 | 8.0 | 5.4 | 2.5 |
| **South Carolina** | | | | | | | | | | | | | | | | |
| University of South Carolina, Columbia | | | | | | | | | | | | | | | | |
| UG | 16,079 | 10.8 | 6.4 | 4.5 | 23,328 | 9.0 | 5.3 | 3.7 | 3,138 | 5.4 | 3.1 | 2.3 | 5,412 | 10.2 | 6.6 | 3.6 |
| G/P | 7,261 | 9.7 | 6.0 | 3.5 | 5,828 | 10.2 | 7.9 | 2.3 | 2,165 | 9.8 | 7.0 | 2.8 | 2,374 | 12.3 | 9.1 | 3.2 |
| South Carolina State University | | | | | | | | | | | | | | | | |
| UG | 2,931 | 98.7 | 55.1 | 43.6 | 2,223 | 96.2 | 48.4 | 47.8 | 448 | 98.2 | 59.4 | 38.8 | 486 | 93.6 | 53.1 | 40.5 |
| G/P | 502 | 85.3 | 55.4 | 29.9 | 200 | 87.0 | 63.5 | 23.5 | 232 | 83.2 | 56.0 | 27.2 | 131 | 84.0 | 61.8 | 22.1 |
| Francis Marion University | | | | | | | | | | | | | | | | |
| UG | 2,237 | 12.8 | 7.3 | 5.5 | 3,106 | 47.1 | 36.1 | 11.0 | 293 | 9.6 | 5.5 | 4.1 | 569 | 38.7 | 30.8 | 7.9 |
| G/P | 374 | 26.7 | 22.7 | 4.0 | 102 | 15.7 | 13.7 | 2.0 | 72 | 13.9 | 9.7 | 4.2 | 93 | 15.1 | 11.8 | 3.2 |
| **Tennessee** | | | | | | | | | | | | | | | | |
| University of Tennessee | | | | | | | | | | | | | | | | |
| UG | 22,494 | 5.0 | 2.8 | 2.2 | 20,467 | 7.0 | 3.8 | 3.2 | 3,751 | 2.4 | 1.5 | 0.9 | 4,445 | 6.1 | 3.6 | 2.5 |
| G/P | 5,947 | 4.0 | 2.5 | 1.5 | 3,894 | 5.4 | 3.7 | 1.7 | 1,938 | 3.8 | 2.4 | 1.4 | 2,133 | 4.8 | 3.0 | 1.8 |
| Tennessee State University | | | | | | | | | | | | | | | | |
| UG | 4,462 | 91.7 | 49.5 | 42.2 | 5966 | 72.0 | 46.1 | 25.9 | 563 | 92.0 | 51.2 | 40.9 | 872 | 73.4 | 48.4 | 25.0 |
| G/P | 869 | 43.4 | 27.5 | 15.9 | 830 | 29.4 | 19.3 | 10.1 | 283 | 83.7 | 51.2 | 32.5 | 462 | 36.4 | 26.4 | 10.0 |

| Institution | 1 | 2 | 3 | 4 | 1 | 2 | 3 | 4 | 1 | 2 | 3 | 4 | 1 | 2 | 3 | 4 |
|---|---|---|---|---|---|---|---|---|---|---|---|---|---|---|---|---|
| **Middle Tennessee State University** | | | | | | | | | | | | | | | | |
| UG | 8,660 | 7.3 | 3.8 | 3.5 | 16,141 | 22.3 | 13.7 | 8.6 | 1,433 | 4.5 | 2.1 | 2.4 | 4,051 | 15.7 | 10.0 | 5.6 |
| G/P | 997 | 3.1 | 1.0 | 2.1 | 794 | 9.4 | 6.3 | 3.1 | 647 | 4.6 | 2.5 | 2.2 | 821 | 9.1 | 5.7 | 3.4 |
| **Texas** | | | | | | | | | | | | | | | | |
| *University of Texas at Austin* | | | | | | | | | | | | | | | | |
| UG | 32,415 | 8.5 | 1.2 | 1.0 | 36,357 | 4.2 | 2.6 | 1.6 | 7,126 | 1.0 | 0.5 | 0.5 | 9,503 | 3.9 | 2.3 | 1.6 |
| G/P | 8,972 | 1.5 | 0.6 | 0.9 | 10,442 | 2.9 | 1.9 | 1.0 | 2,464 | 1.1 | 0.3 | 0.8 | 4,567 | 2.9 | 1.8 | 1.1 |
| *Texas Southern University* | | | | | | | | | | | | | | | | |
| UG | 7,754 | 84.4 | 43.5 | 40.9 | 5,884 | 80.1 | 47.8 | 32.3 | 571 | 92.6 | 53.2 | 39.4 | 927 | 77.3 | 48.8 | 28.6 |
| G/P | 1,616 | 75.8 | 44.2 | 31.6 | 1,650 | 59.9 | 37.9 | 22.1 | 404 | 82.4 | 41.6 | 40.8 | 622 | 67.5 | 43.2 | 24.3 |
| *University of Houston-Downtown* | | | | | | | | | | | | | | | | |
| UG | — | — | — | — | 6,640 | 20.0 | 12.8 | 7.2 | — | — | — | — | 2,338 | 23.2 | 16.6 | 6.5 |
| G/P | — | — | — | — | 45 | 28.9 | 20.0 | 8.9 | — | — | — | — | 97 | 29.9 | 18.6 | 11.3 |
| **Virginia** | | | | | | | | | | | | | | | | |
| *University of Virginia* | | | | | | | | | | | | | | | | |
| UG | 10,070 | 3.9 | 2.0 | 2.0 | 15,218 | 6.1 | 3.7 | 2.5 | 2,275 | 2.5 | 1.4 | 1.2 | 3,836 | 6.5 | 4.0 | 2.5 |
| G/P | 5,067 | 2.9 | 1.2 | 1.7 | 5,940 | 4.2 | 2.3 | 1.9 | 2,024 | 3.1 | 1.2 | 1.9 | 2,651 | 4.6 | 2.6 | 2.0 |
| *Norfolk State University* | | | | | | | | | | | | | | | | |
| UG | 6,599 | 95.9 | 56.1 | 39.8 | 3,738 | 84.5 | 51.7 | 32.9 | 762 | 94.1 | 54.1 | 40.0 | 992 | 80.2 | 55.6 | 24.6 |
| G/P | 292 | 68.8 | 51.0 | 17.8 | 385 | 75.6 | 58.4 | 17.1 | 12 | 91.7 | 58.3 | 33.3 | 199 | 72.9 | 52.8 | 20.1 |
| *Old Dominion University* | | | | | | | | | | | | | | | | |
| UG | 8,280 | 4.2 | 2.3 | 1.8 | 15,319 | 29.0 | 17.2 | 11.8 | 1,512 | 1.7 | 0.9 | 0.8 | 3,858 | 21.0 | 14.2 | 6.7 |
| G/P | 1,641 | 6.6 | 4.0 | 2.6 | 1,604 | 10.5 | 7.5 | 2.9 | 481 | 5.4 | 3.3 | 2.1 | 1,335 | 9.9 | 7.2 | 2.7 |

*Source:* Authors' calculations based on National Center for Education Statistics; U.S. Department of Health, Education, and Welfare 1978a, 1978b.

*Note:* UG: undergraduate; G/P: graduate and professional; 1: grand total; 2: percent African American total; 3: percent African American women; 4: percent African American men.

**Figure 2.** Alabama Percent African American Enrollment, 1976–2015

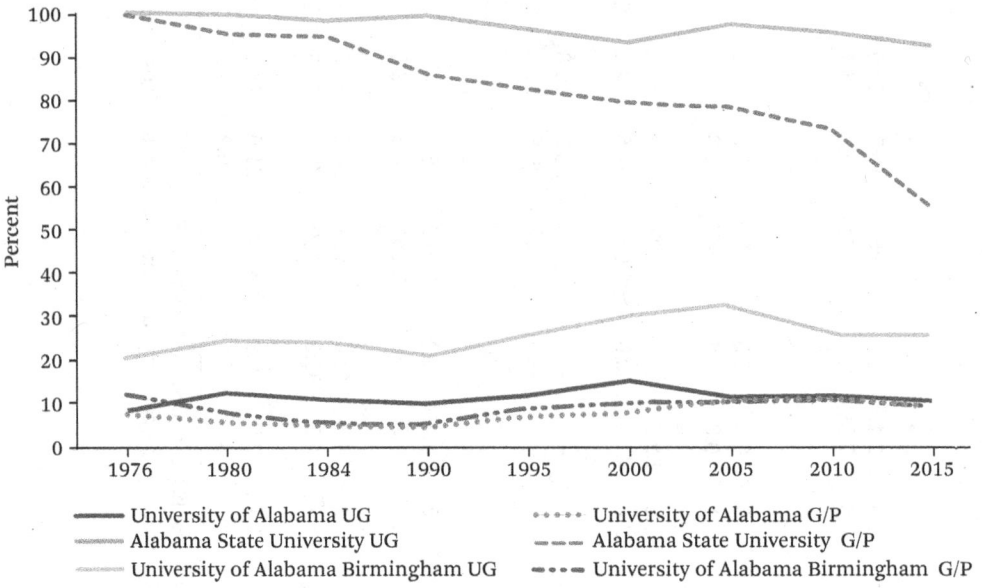

*Source:* Authors' calculations based on National Center for Education Statistics; U.S. Department of Health, Education, and Welfare 1978a.
*Note:* UG: undergraduate; G/P: graduate and professional.

10.5 percent; Louisiana State University, 12.1 percent; University of Maryland, College Park, 12.7 percent; University of Mississippi, 13.4 percent; and State University of New York at Albany, 16.6 percent (table 2, figures 1 and 2).

Patterns were similar for African American professional and graduate students at public flagship campuses. In states where affirmative action cases reached the Supreme Court, African American graduate enrollment at public flagships dropped below already-abysmal levels. For example, in 1976 African American graduate enrollment at the University of Michigan–Ann Arbor; the University of California, Berkeley; and University of California, Los Angeles was 8.4 percent, 4.1 percent, and 5.1 percent respectively (table 2, figure 3). Following increases, African American graduate enrollment at these institutions peaked and then sharply declined after states adopted anti–affirmative action policies.

At other flagships, African American graduate and professional enrollment either held steady or declined. For example, African American graduate and professional enrollment at the Ohio State University was 4.5 percent in 1976 and 4.1 percent in 2015 (table 2). This pattern is repeated for University of Alabama, University of Missouri, and University of Georgia (table 2, figure 2). Overall, these findings confirm that African American undergraduate and graduate enrollment at flagships has not approached African American representation in the state. We would logically expect African American enrollment at flagship institutions to be higher given that increasing numbers of African American students are entering higher education. Yet we see continued declines in African American undergraduate and graduate enrollment in states where anti–affirmative action litigation, policies, and practices were adopted.

### Enrollment: Black-Serving Institutions

There were pronounced and variable changes in African American undergraduate enrollment between 1976 and 2015 across BSIs (table 2). The University of Maryland, Baltimore County experienced relatively small declines in African American student enrollment, less than 3 percent. However, for many BSIs, African American undergraduate student enrollments in-

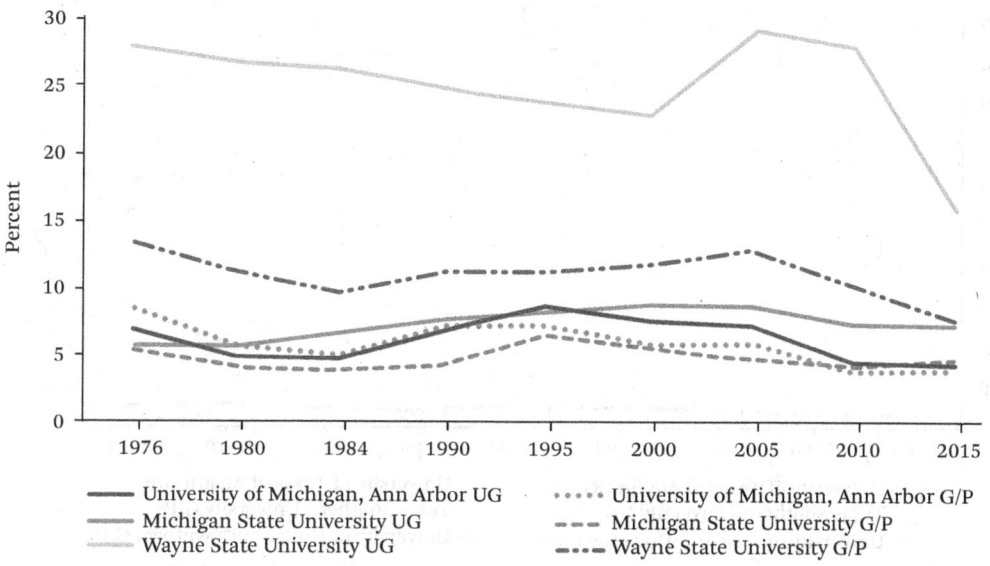

**Figure 3.** Michigan Percent African American Enrollment, 1976–2015

*Source:* Authors' calculations based on National Center for Education Statistics; U.S. Department of Health, Education, and Welfare 1978a.
*Note:* UG: undergraduate; G/P: graduate and professional.

creased between 1976 and 2015. It is striking that in states where the proportion of African American undergraduate students at public flagship universities declined, total African American undergraduate enrollment at BSIs generally increased. For example, in South Carolina, African American undergraduate enrollment at Francis Marion University grew from 12.8 percent in 1976 to 47.1 percent in 2015. At the University of South Carolina, Columbia, however, it declined from 10.8 percent in 1976 to 9 percent in 2015. Similar patterns were evident in New Jersey at Kean University and Rutgers University, New Brunswick. Some states—such as Florida, Louisiana, and Georgia—saw increases at both BSIs and flagships from 1976 to 2015, but much larger gains at BSIs. Interestingly, African American undergraduate enrollment at Georgia State University grew exponentially, from 15.5 to 40.9 percent, but African American enrollment fluctuated at the University of Georgia (table 2).

Over the period, substantial gains at many BSIs reinforced their prominent roles in educating African American college students. At face value, this seems to support anti–affirmative action arguments that African American students excluded from flagships will simply cascade down to lower-ranked institutions, better suited to their academic qualifications. In fact, this pattern of displacement represents substantial overall net losses in African American undergraduate enrollment. For example, not only was African American enrollment in California down at University of California flagships Berkeley (4 percent in 1976 to 2.1 percent in 2015) and Los Angeles (5.3 to 3 percent), it also declined at the BSI California State University, Dominguez Hills (33.8 to 12.4 percent). It also dropped on several other BSI campuses: from 27.7 percent in 1976 to 15.8 percent in 2015 at Wayne State University; from 32.7 to 15.3 percent at City University of New York, City College; and from 18.7 to 12.2 percent at Temple University (table 2).

Turning to African American graduate and professional student enrollment, we see many similarities to patterns and trends in African American undergraduate enrollment. Since 1976, the proportion of African American graduate enrollment at BSIs has significantly increased. For example, close to a third (28.9 per-

**Figure 4.** Texas Percent African American Enrollment, 1976–2015

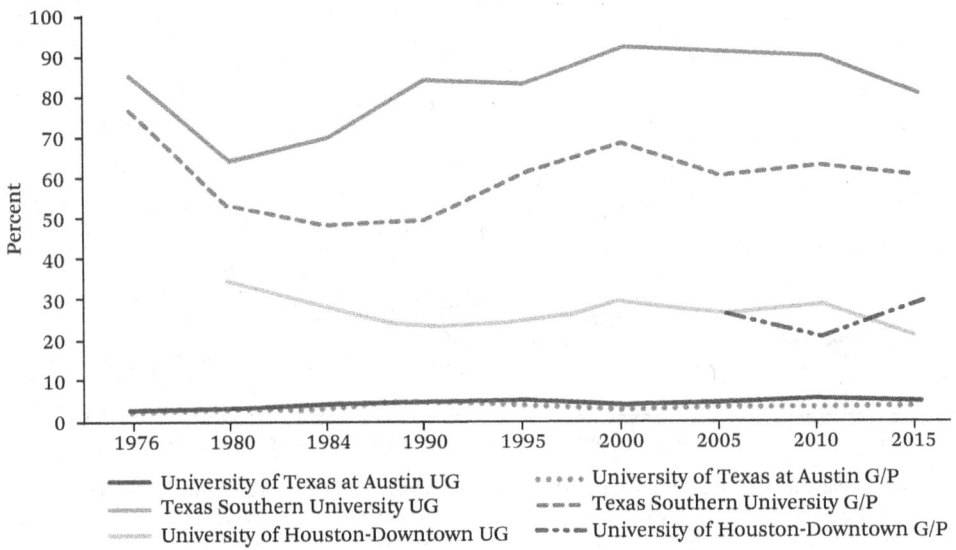

Source: Authors' calculations based on National Center for Education Statistics; U.S. Department of Health, Education, and Welfare 1978a.
Note: UG: undergraduate; G/P: graduate and professional.

cent) of University of Houston–Downtown graduate students were African American, as were 18.1 percent at Georgia State University and 19.7 percent at Northwestern Louisiana State University (table 2, figure 4). Overall, compared with flagship institutions, BSIs are now enrolling most African American graduate and professional degree seekers.

### Enrollment: Historically Black Colleges and Universities

Since 1976, although the African American proportion of total institutional enrollment grew at several HBCUs (for example, Florida A&M University, Lincoln University of Missouri, and Central State University), the majority of HBCUs (eleven of fourteen) saw undergraduate decreases between 2.5 percent and 20 percent (table 2). This trend is distinct from the large increases reported for most other public institutions. Disproportionate growth between BSIs and HBCUs from 1976 to 2015 was particularly pronounced in certain states. Savannah State University's proportion African American undergraduate enrollment dropped nearly 6 percent, 89.3 in 1976 to 83.5 percent in 2015, relative to a 25 percent increase at Georgia State University, 15.5 to 40.9 percent. This symbolizes how "separate and unequal" policies, practices, and funding have penalized public HBCUs and greatly restricted their capacity to serve more students (Minor 2008).

Many HBCUs increased the percentage of African American graduate and professional students enrolled by 2015. Among these are Savannah State University, from 33.9 to 64.4 percent, and Norfolk State University, from 68.8 to 75.6 percent (table 2). HBCUs also enroll higher proportions of African American students overall than flagships. It is important that for both undergraduate and graduate or professional enrollment at HBCUs, the proportion of white and nonblack students is increasing; for example, graduate and professional students at: Morgan State University, 39 percent; North Carolina A&T, 43 percent; and Texas Southern, 40 percent. The racial diversity of HBCU graduate and professional student enrollments shows their power and promise as tools to help desegregate public higher education in states that previously operated de jure or de facto racially segregated systems (Conrad, Brier, and Braxton 1997).

## Enrollment: Gender Differences

In general, African American women outnumber African American men in undergraduate and graduate-professional degree enrollment across all institutional types (table 2). Although in comparison, African American women enrollments are higher, when "raced," or viewed through a critical race lens, the gender differences are negligible at select public flagship institutions. For example, in 2015 at University of California flagships Berkeley and Los Angeles, African American women represented 1.1 percent and 1.8 percent to 0.9 percent and 1.1 percent for African American men. Similarly, at the University of Michigan, only 2.6 percent were African American women and 1.8 percent were African American men. At the end of the day, African American enrollment on these campuses is alarmingly low—for both African American women and African American men.

The percent enrollment for undergraduate and graduate-professional African American women at BSIs rose between 1976 and 2015. For example, at the University of Southern Mississippi, undergraduate African American women increased from 6.5 to 20.7 percent, and among graduate or professional students, from 6.5 to 9.1 percent (table 2, figure 1). By contrast, declines occurred at City University of New York, City College, from 17 to 8.7 percent, and 15.6 to 8.2 percent, respectively. Many BSIs saw increased enrollment for undergraduate and graduate-professional school African American men, including Florida Atlantic University, from 1.5 to 7.2 percent, and 2 to 4 percent. As well, we find instances of significant enrollment declines, for example, California State University–Dominguez Hills, from 17.6 to 4.2 percent, and 9.1 to 2.8 percent, respectively.

We also observe increases and decreases in undergraduate and graduate-professional enrollment across HBCUs between 1976 and 2015. At Jackson State University, African American women undergraduates increased from 48.5 to 58.1 percent; at Alabama State University, however, graduate or professional students decreased from 69.4 to 40.2 percent (table 2, figures 1 and 2). In addition, marked declines in enrollment of undergraduate and graduate-professional African American men are visible across the majority of HBCUs. For example, African American male enrollment at Jackson State University declined from 46.9 to 33.4 percent and 35.9 to 21.3 percent, respectively, and Southern University and A&M College, from 43.2 to 33.6 percent and 31.9 to 19.1 percent.

## Completion: Flagships

Given enrollment patterns and trends, African American student degree completion at flagships is predictably discouraging. Among several public flagship institutions explored in this study, African American degree completion declined from already low levels in 1976 (table 2). For example, African American undergraduate degree completion at the University of California, Berkeley dropped from 3.4 percent in 1976 to 1.9 percent in 2015. Similarly, at the University of California, Los Angeles degree completion dropped from 5.3 percent in 1976 to 2.3 percent in 2015. At the University of Michigan, Ann Arbor it was 5.4 percent in 1976 and 4 percent in 2015 (table 2, figure 5). Significantly, at these institutions, African American completed degrees peaked between 1990 and 2000 and then declined (online appendix table 4).

By comparison, the proportion of African American undergraduates earning baccalaureate degrees actually increased at several other state flagships between 1976 and 2015: University of Mississippi, from 3.6 to 13.8 percent; University of Maryland, from 4.3 to 11.2 percent; University of Alabama, from 5 to 10.7 percent); University of Georgia, from 2.1 to 7.2 percent; and University of Texas at Austin, from 1 to 3.9 percent (table 2, figures 6, 7, and 8). These findings suggest that, particularly at so-called Public Ivy state flagships, African American students are less likely to be represented among the graduates. Even when institutions increased the proportion of African American undergraduate degree completion, the proportion of African Americans graduating is still notably lower than the proportion enrolled.

In terms of African American graduate and professional degree completion, we find graduation at public flagship institutions has kept pace with enrollment. These trends indicate African American graduate and professional degree earners complete degrees at rates more closely proportional to their enrollment at public flagship institutions. Despite this encourag-

**Figure 5.** Michigan Percent African American Degree Completion, 1976–2015

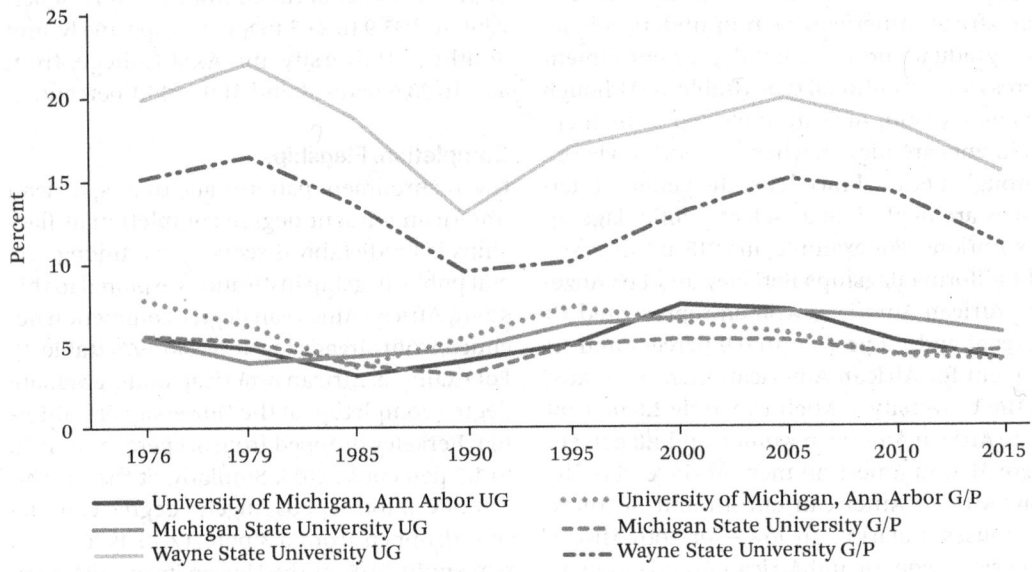

*Source:* Authors' calculations based on National Center for Education Statistics; U.S. Department of Health, Education, and Welfare 1978b, 1981.
*Note:* UG: undergraduate; G/P: graduate and professional.

**Figure 6.** Mississippi Percent African American Degree Completion, 1976–2015

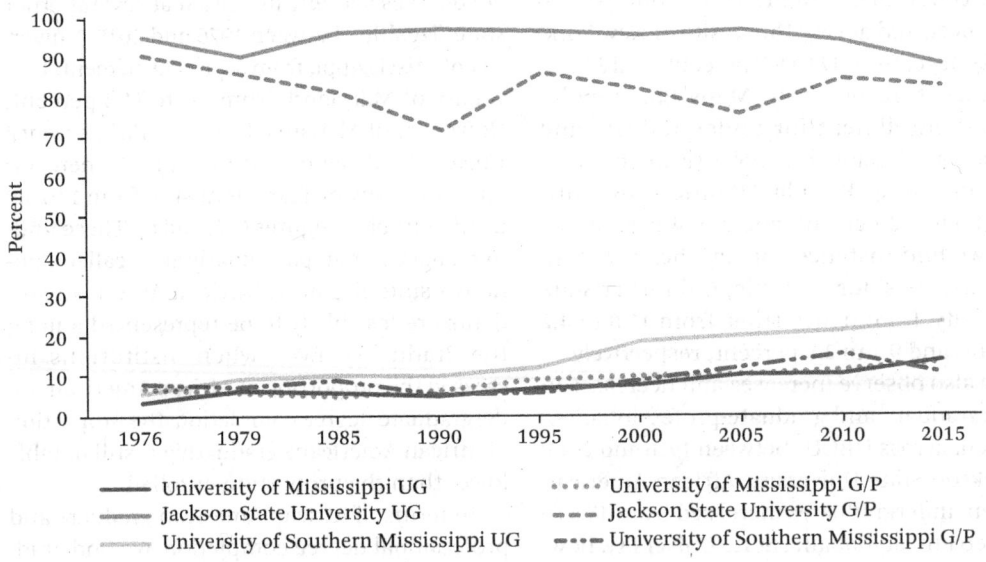

*Source:* Authors' calculations based on National Center for Education Statistics; U.S. Department of Health, Education, and Welfare 1978b, 1981.
*Note:* UG: undergraduate; G/P: graduate and professional.

**Figure 7.** Alabama Percent African American Degree Completion, 1976–2015

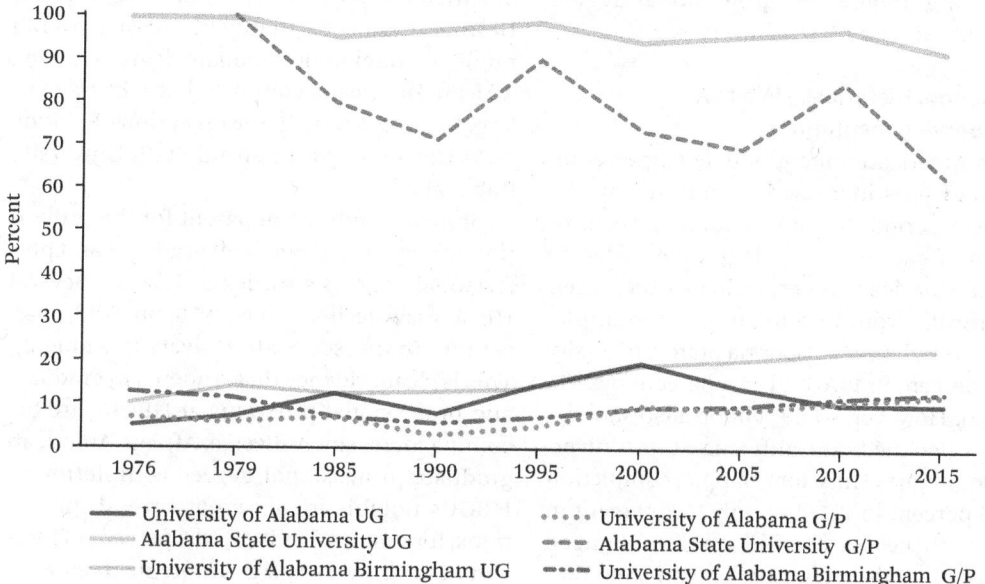

—— University of Alabama UG  ····· University of Alabama G/P
—— Alabama State University UG  ---- Alabama State University G/P
—— University of Alabama Birmingham UG  --·-- University of Alabama Birmingham G/P

*Source:* Authors' calculations based on National Center for Education Statistics; U.S. Department of Health, Education, and Welfare 1978b, 1981.
*Note:* UG: undergraduate; G/P: graduate and professional.

**Figure 8.** Texas Percent African American Degree Completion, 1976–2015

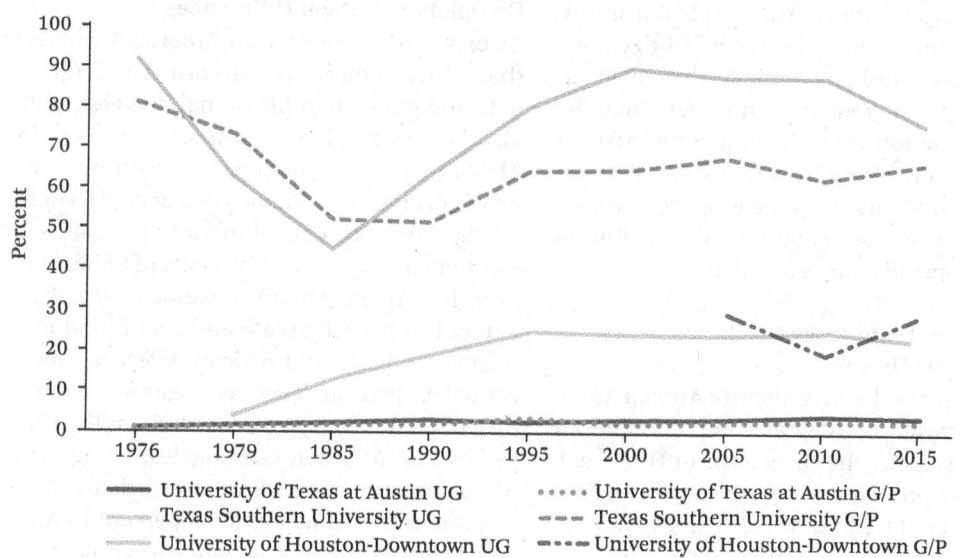

—— University of Texas at Austin UG  ····· University of Texas at Austin G/P
—— Texas Southern University UG  ---- Texas Southern University G/P
—— University of Houston-Downtown UG  --·-- University of Houston-Downtown G/P

*Source:* Authors' calculations based on National Center for Education Statistics; U.S. Department of Health, Education, and Welfare 1978b, 1981.
*Note:* UG: undergraduate; G/P: graduate and professional.

ing sign, there has been little growth in African American graduate and professional degree representation on these campuses.

## Completion: Historically White, Black-Serving Institutions

African American undergraduate degree completion at BSIs increased overall during the forty-year period. In some instances, the proportion of baccalaureate degrees awarded to African American undergraduates increased dramatically from 1976 to 2015. For example, degree completion at Georgia State University was 11 percent in 1976 and 36.4 percent by 2015 (table 2). However, some schools also saw significant declines. At California State University–Dominguez Hills, for example, completion was 30 percent in 1976 but only 16.3 percent in 2015. In other cases, completion rates changed little over four decades. At Michigan State University, completion essentially held steady: 5.4 percent in 1976 and 5.6 percent in 2015 (table 2, figure 5).

Overall, African American graduate and professional degree completion at BSIs increased during the observed period. Several BSIs recorded impressive gains: Georgia State University and University of Maryland, Baltimore County. Others, however, recorded declines: Wayne State University. Notably, since 1995, African American graduate and professional degree completion trend has mirrored African American enrollment, suggesting African American students are graduating BSIs proportionate to their representation at the institution (online appendix tables 3 and 4).

## Completion: Historically Black Colleges and Universities

HBCUs represent a large share of African American undergraduate degree completion in our data set. To place the sheer scale of HBCU college degree production in perspective, consider the number of baccalaureate degrees awarded to African American undergraduates in 2015: Florida A&M University (1,432), North Carolina A&T State University (1,120), Morgan State University (813), Norfolk State University (796), and Texas Southern University (717). Relative to both flagships and BSIs that have as many as ten times more students enrolled and earning degrees, HBCUs claim a disproportionate share of African American undergraduate degrees. Despite these consistently impressive overall numbers, total undergraduate degrees among African Americans completed at HBCUs have largely decreased, with the exception of Florida A&M University and Central State University (table 2).

Similar trends are apparent for the proportion African American of all graduate and professional degrees awarded at HBCUs. Several HBCUs saw declines since 1976, up to 47.4 percent at Tennessee State University (table 2). This is clear evidence that students in graduate and professional programs at HBCUs are becoming increasingly diverse. African American graduate-professional degree completion at HBCUs notably increased at several institutions; for example, in 1976, 58.8 percent of Morgan State University's graduate degrees were awarded to African American students, compared to 78.8 percent in 2015. African American graduate-professional degree completion also grew at HBCUs including Lincoln University of Missouri (17.9 to 20 percent) and South Carolina State University (83.2 to 84 percent).

## Completion: Gender Differences

As expected more African American women than African American men earned undergraduate and graduate-professional degrees (table 2). Like with enrollment, gender differences in African American degree completion rates nearly disappear at Public Ivy flagships, where African American enrollment is persistently low. Remarkably, at the University of California, Berkeley African American women earned 1.1 percent of baccalaureate and 1.5 of graduate degrees in 2015, and African American men earned 0.8 percent of baccalaureate and 1.4 percent of graduate degrees. Similarly, at the University of California, Los Angeles, 1.5 percent of baccalaureate degrees were awarded to African American women and 0.8 percent to African American men; graduate earned degrees were 2 percent and 1 percent respectively.

African American women had higher completion rates than African American men on many flagship campuses, similar to the gender difference for other racial-ethnic groups. Although African American women completed degrees at higher rates than African American men, both had alarmingly low rates overall. At the University of Georgia, African American undergraduate degree completion was 5.2 percent for African American women and 2 percent for African American men (total African American completion was only 7.2 percent) (table 2).

The gender gap between African American women and African American men in degree completion widens for BSIs. For example, at California State University–Dominguez Hills, the number of African American women earning baccalaureate degrees was twice that for African American men in 2015, 11.6 percent versus 4.7 percent of total degrees conferred (table 2). The gender disparity in earned degrees even persisted for schools where both African American men and African American women had double-digit baccalaureate degree completion rates: Chicago State University (African American women earned 57.5 percent of total degrees and African American men 20.6 percent) and Georgia State University (25.1 and 11.3 percent. African American women were also twice as likely to earn African American graduate and professional degrees at many BSIs. For instance, in 2015, African American–earned degrees at the University of Alabama at Birmingham were 10.1 percent for women and 2.8 percent for men; at Georgia State University, to 13 and 6.6 percent; and at California State University–Dominguez Hills, to 10.5 and 4.3 percent. However, the gender disparity in earned degrees was negligible at several BSIs, including the University of Maryland–Baltimore County (7.8 and 6 percent) and Rutgers University–Newark (6.5 and 5.5 percent).

Both African American women and men graduated HBCUs with baccalaureate degrees at double digit rates (table 2, figures 6 and 7). However, African American women were roughly twice as likely to graduate at several HBCUs in 2015: at Alabama State University, 59.9 percent were African American women and 32.3 percent were African American men; at Jackson State University, 58.6 and 29.8 percent; and at Morgan State University, 52.1 percent and 35.2 percent. In 2015, the proportion of African American women was also higher among African American–earned graduate and professional degrees at HBCUs. The gender difference was nearly triple at Savannah State University: 50.7 percent African American women and 14.1 percent African American men. Although African American women are more likely than their male counterparts to attend and graduate from public universities, the representation of all African American students at Public Ivy and other flagships remains distressingly low.

## DISCUSSION

African American students confront systemic barriers that continue to hinder their access and success in higher education. African Americans attend a variety of higher education institutions—community colleges, for-profit institutions, small private colleges, and HBCUs (Iloh and Toldson 2013). We focus on four-year public universities because as a public good, they *should* benefit all the nation's students (Harper, Patton, and Wooden 2009). This societal ideal warrants closer empirical examination to determine whether public universities equitably serve African American undergraduate, graduate, and professional students.

African American student access to highly selective, public institutions has been greatly limited. These institutions are sites of fierce contests over whether consideration of race in college admissions is constitutional. Legislation such as Proposition 209 and Proposal 2 and judicial decisions such as *Regents of the University of California v. Bakke, Hopwood v. The University of Texas Law School, Gratz v. Bollinger,* and *Grutter v. Bollinger* drove the retreat from race-conscious admission policies and procedures.[6] As a result, African American student enrollment and completion has suffered at these institutions (Solórzano and Yosso 2002). The focus has shifted from racial remedies to eradicate inequality and discrimination to concerns about the benefits of diversity for white people (Gurin et al. 2002). This paradigm shift requires critical examination in the context of political, historical, and socioeconomic factors routinely mobilized to block African American

---

6. *Hopwood v. The University of Texas Law School*, 78 F.3d 932 (5th Cir. 1996); *Gratz v. Bollinger*, 539 U.S. 244 (2003).

educational gains. Anti–affirmative action legal challenges, state referendums, and attitudes are evidence of persistent antiblackness ideology. CRT helps frame and better understand societal obstacles to the African American struggle for equitable education.

### Flagship Institutions

African American students continue to be largely excluded from the pursuit of degrees at prestigious, public, flagship institutions. The alarming few changes in the presence of African American students over time at these universities clearly demonstrates the persistence of racial inequities. Skeptics attempt to explain the continued underrepresentation as the result of demographic shifts and changing diversity. However, despite our laser focus on states with the largest African American populations, we found that consistently across the country African American participation in higher education was unreasonably low and not at all reflective of African American "critical mass." For example, African American students make up 32 percent of Georgia's population, yet represent only 7.6 percent of undergraduate students and 7.3 percent of graduate and professional students at the flagship campus. Our analyses revealed that while African American students increasingly attended lower-tier BSIs, African American rates of enrollment at public flagship institutions remained stagnant or declined. This necessitates careful recognition and systematic interrogation of the underlying social, economic, political, and historical factors persistently blocking African American opportunities in higher education.

The systematic exclusion of African American students from the most selective, public institutions confirms the reality of institutionalized racism, white supremacy, and antiblackness (Anderson 2015, 1988; Mustaffa 2017). Hostile campus climates characterized by racial micro- and macro-aggressions, hypersurveillance, stereotyping, invisibility, and gendered racism continue to marginalize African American students (Patton et al. 2016; Smith et al. 2016).

Efforts to overcome oppressive restrictions on African American students in higher education have been driven in part by a long history of court cases. Several states faced lawsuits after refusing to desegregate their higher education systems: *Adams v. Richardson*, *Geier v. University of Tennessee*, *Ayers v. Fordice*, and *Knight v. Alabama*.[7]

Following the Civil Rights Act of 1964, affirmative action programs attempted to rectify the history of systemic inequitable access to higher education, contracts, and employment opportunities for African Americans and other disadvantaged groups. Affirmative action policies produced dramatic gains in African American college access and success. For instance, the University of California, Los Angeles's School of Medicine enrolled its first African American student in 1967; by 1969, African American students made up 5.6 percent of the student population (Karabel 1999). Despite the progress during the 1960s and early 1970s, however, the advances were short lived. The proportion of first-time, full-time freshmen enrollments peaked by the mid-1970s, and African American student enrollment in medical schools began to decline (Astin 1982). In short, efforts to redress past wrongs met massive, systematic and effective opposition calculated to preserve the status quo of African American exclusion.

Opponents of affirmative action relied on the narrative of reverse racism to argue it was unconstitutional discrimination against white people (Tatum 2017). A key point in the struggle over affirmative action was the Supreme Court's *Bakke* decision that race could only be used as a "plus factor" in admission decisions, and the use of quotas was prohibited. The *Bakke* decision weakened affirmative action because it restricted the intentional use of race in admission practices.

The ongoing resistance against affirmative action confirms a fundamental tenet of CRT, that racism—and its intersection with multiple forms of subordination—is a central component of American society, in law, policy, practice, and everyday experiences (Delgado and Stefancic 2012). The gains of the civil rights movement have warped into illusions of equal

---

7. *Geier v. University of Tennessee*, 597 F. 2d 1056 (1979); *Knight v. Alabama*, 469 F. Supp. 2d 1016 (2006).

opportunity in a purported postracist society. Alan Bakke's appeal to the Supreme Court was grounded in the false premise that he was more qualified than other applicants . . . or most certainly all applicants of color. His position exemplifies broader dominant narratives that frame individualism and meritocracy as neutral and colorblind measures of a person's worth and illustrates how these dominant narratives are in fact mechanisms used to defend persistent inequities (Crenshaw 2006).

High school grade point averages, standardized test scores, and course requirements are routinely used as race-neutral criteria for admissions decisions at public institutions, particularly flagships. However, research shows how racial inequities in K–12 schooling have a negative impact on African American students' academic trajectories (Ladson-Billings 1998), their performance on standardized tests (Steele and Aronson 1995), and their overall educational opportunities (Tatum 2017). Eduardo Bonilla-Silva argues that the ideology of colorblindness maintains racial hierarchies and "serves today as the ideological armor for a covert and institutionalized system in the post–civil rights era" (2018, 3). The colorblindness frame of abstract liberalism, where "whites can appear 'reasonable' and even 'moral,' while opposing almost all practical approaches to deal with de facto racial inequality" is a fearsome weapon in defense of the status quo (Bonilla-Silva 2018, 56). Plaintiffs, masked in the dominant narratives of "colorblindness," "neutrality," and "meritocracy," defend "the absolute right to exclude," through institutional policies and legislation enacting and protecting white supremacy through the law (Harris 1993, 1736; Omi and Winant 2014). We continue to see threads of these perspectives woven throughout cases such as *Gratz v. Bollinger*, *Grutter v. Bollinger*, and *Fisher v. University of Texas at Austin*. Colorblind ideology restricts how race is discussed and understood in higher education, even in states without current anti–affirmative action bans (Vue, Haslerig, and Allen 2017) and undermines the possibility of racial justice (Bonilla-Silva 2018).

The tepid efforts to desegregate higher education institutions are a form of antiblack racism in higher education. Nearly three decades ago, Derrick Bell described how "whites may agree in the abstract that blacks are citizens and are entitled to constitutional protection against racial discrimination, but few are willing to recognize that racial segregation is much more than a series of quaint customs that can be remedied effectively without altering the status of whites" (1980, 522). Abigail Fisher's petition to the Supreme Court represented entrenched resistance to African American students having greater access to flagship institutions, because there would necessarily be fewer guaranteed seats for white people. Hence, support for expanded African American access to flagship institutions depends on a convergence of interests (Bell 1980)—which ultimately privileges white interests. A contemporary example is the diversity rationale in higher education. In *Grutter v. Bollinger*, the Court accepted the argument that diversity was important for society (Gurin et al. 2002). Although a strategic compromise by proponents of affirmative action, the diversity rationale does little to ensure racial justice for African Americans and instead centers the benefits of diversity for whites (Bell 2003; McPherson 2015; Harris 1993). Undergirding critiques of the diversity paradigm is the question of cui bono (who benefits?).

## Black-Serving Institutions

Although African American students are mostly denied admission into the ivory gates of flagship institutions, some institutions offer African American and other underrepresented students opportunities to attend and complete college. HBCUs, BSIs, and minority-serving institutions (MSIs) have demonstrated commitments to serve students from underrepresented racial and ethnic groups. In 2011, MSIs enrolled 3.6 million undergraduates, one-quarter of all U.S. undergraduates (Gasman and Conrad 2015). Advocates of MSIs highlight how these institutions offer alternatives for underrepresented students and contribute to the institutional diversity in the U.S. higher education system. For many students, the appeal of HBCUs and MSIs is their unique missions, supportive campus environments, faculty and staff diversity, and the richness of the culturally relevant curricula and offerings

(Allen 1992; Gasman, Nguyen, and Conrad 2015).

Many institutions in our sample serve students who are academically underprepared, first-generation, and low-income; for example, two-thirds to three-quarters of students at HBCUs are Pell Grant eligible. On average, 49 percent of the student population for BSIs are Pell Grant recipients. More specifically, Pell Grant awardees constituted 81 percent of full-time, first-time degree-seeking students at CUNY (City University of New York) Medgar Evers, 84 percent at Chicago State University, and 86 percent at CUNY City College. However, instruction at BSIs is disproportionately conducted by less-credentialed, non-tenure track faculty and these institutions tend to have lower graduation rates than at more selective institutions (Ehrenberg and Zhang 2005). For example, the rates for the 2009 cohort for full-time, first-time degree, and certificate-seeking undergraduates was 35 percent and 29 percent for African American undergraduates at California State University–Dominguez Hills. More startling were the African American rates of 16 percent at Cleveland State University, 12 percent at Wayne State University, 12 percent at Kean University, 11 percent at Chicago State University, 11 percent at CUNY Medgar Evers College, and 10 percent at the University of Houston–Downtown. Previous research reveals such dismal outcomes result from BSIs trying to do and serve more underprepared students, yet being provided fewer resources than the flagship institutions (Shapiro 2017). Negative racial climate is also a contributing factor.

Under existing tax codes, more selective, better-endowed institutions reap maximum benefits from taxpayers, but enroll and graduate the fewest number and lowest percentage of low-income students (Klor de Alva and Schneider 2015). Relative to research-intensive institutions that receive per student funding, ranging from $8,881 to $46,817, our sample of BSIs received a range of $5,567 to $19,630.[8] Although funding may seem racially neutral and merely context-bound, CRT's critiques of liberalism and multicultural and diversity paradigms highlight political contradictions (Dumas and ross 2016; Ladson-Billings and Tate 1995). On one hand, the commitment of African American and minority-serving institutions to serve underrepresented students is celebrated and honored. On the other hand, the economic and material conditions of black-serving institutions vividly illustrate the state's disinvestment or refusal to invest in the education of African American people and other underserved communities. It is perplexing that these public institutions must struggle for fiscal support, resources, or survival when society claims to value diversity and equal opportunity (Griffin and Hurtado 2011). Gloria Ladson-Billings critiques the failures of liberalism, which benefits white interests and resists sweeping changes because of reliance on incrementalism (1998). Michael Omi and Howard Winant further confirm that this has been the brilliance and agility of the continually shifting historical "project" that maintains white supremacy (2014).

### Historically Black Colleges and Universities

Originating as normal schools to train African American teachers to educate African American children in the South, HBCUs morphed into "separate but equal" colleges and universities that "legally" segregated African American students from southern public institutions viewed as the province of whites (Anderson 2015, 1988). The history of HBCUs is complex because white missionaries, the Freedmen's Bureau, African American missionaries, white industrial philanthropists, and of course African American communities each played significant roles in establishing African American colleges (Anderson 2015, 1988). CRT's interest convergence theory explains white missionary involvement in HBCUs less as misguided altruism, and more as determined efforts to maintain financial and organizational power over African American institutions (Bell 1980; Harper, Patton, and Wooden 2009). Rampant white paternalism jus-

---

8. Core revenues per FTE enrollment, by source, for fiscal year 2015. The lowest for research-intensive institutions was $8,881 at Pennsylvania State University. However, state and local appropriations were not available, so this number may actually be higher.

tified their "God-given task to both 'civilize and educate'" African American people through a curriculum rooted in whiteness, emphasizing manual training and attempting to imbue "appropriate"—that is, white, middle class American—values of dress, speech, and activity (Allen and Jewell 2002, 243). The emphasis on vocational education promoted the labor market interests of white industrialists and farmers (Harper, Patton, and Wooden 2009), was rooted in white supremacists' notions of African American inferiority (Mustaffa 2017), and further underscored the centrality of racism. In the realm of higher education, both Northern (missionaries and philanthropists, for example) and Southern whites (such as government officials) sought to exclude African Americans from white institutions and to limit African American control over their own institutions (Harper, Patton, and Wooden 2009).

Desegregation pressures can threaten the missions of HBCUs, and from 1976 to 2015 we saw striking decreases in the percentage of African American students enrolling in HBCUs (Allen et al. 2007). Many feared that cases like *Adams v. Richardson* and *United States v. Fordice* would pressure HBCUs to change their missions, especially after K–12 public school desegregation closed so many African American schools and caused massive displacement of African American educators (Harper, Patton, and Wooden 2009; Anderson 1988).

HBCUs continue to enroll and graduate large numbers of African American students. These institutions "punch above their weight," representing only 3 percent of U.S. higher education institutions but graduating approximately 20 to 25 percent of African American baccalaureates in any given year (Allen and Jewell 2002). However, HBCUs are more often in precarious positions due to reduced federal funding and desegregation efforts that undermine their original mission (Harper, Patton, and Wooden 2009). Several HBCUs have closed and others are threatened by financial exigencies and racial stigmas that erode their viability. Given severely inequitable funding, James Minor argues that federal support could more accurately be described as "financial aid for HBCUs rather than purposeful investment" (2008, 32). HBCUs are routinely disadvantaged relative to HWIs in the same state system of public higher education; for example, in North Carolina, HWIs received nearly double the funding allocated to HBCUs on a per student basis (Minor 2008). To avoid further declines in overall African American college access and success, states must expand the capacity of HBCUs to help serve growing demand and diversity in higher education.

HBCUs pursue the uncertain path of supplementing budgets and funding shortfalls with tuition, grants, corporate partnerships, and private donations (Richardson and Harris 2004). This is tricky, however, because the increased influence of private interests may erode their mission (Giroux 2002). Heavy reliance on philanthropy also potentially opens the door to increased white control over them (Gasman and Tudico 2008). Disparities in federal and state funding signal undervaluing, or even targeted attacks on public HBCUs. HBCUs are spaces that center African American people, history, and knowledge in direct challenge to white supremacy. These institutions emerged from a complex, contradictory history to become an "engine in producing Black scholars, leaders for the Civil Rights movement, and research to highlight racist issues," as well as a place for black life-making (Mustaffa 2017, 719).

CRT legal scholars point to the perseverance of white supremacy and pervasive anti-black racism to explain why, despite the legal equality, African Americans have been able to realize only relatively modest gains (Harris 2015). African American students' low enrollment and completion rates at public, four-year universities drives home the harsh realities of racism. Systemic racism runs deep and wide in the DNA of higher education, forming symbiotic relationships with other institutions in U.S. society. For instance, the soaring mass incarceration rates for African American men and declines in the numbers of African American men college graduates are inextricably linked (Alexander 2012). Given these permanent, mutually reinforcing racial hierarchies, it is difficult to foresee a future when resistance to full African American participation in public higher education is eliminated (Bell 1992).

## HOW FAR HAVE WE COME? BROAD STROKES

Our inquiry into African American student enrollment and completion at select public higher education institutions since the Kerner report centers three questions: How far have we come? What worked and did not work? What are the implications for the twenty-first century? Despite the report's call for expanded African American educational opportunity, college enrollments for both African American women and men have been persistently disadvantaged. Regarding the Public Ivies and flagships, African American enrollments have mostly remained stagnant, hovering near the same, very low levels apparent in 1976. African American enrollments on these prestigious campuses dropped precipitously after affirmative action programs were attacked and rolled back.

However, bright spots were also evident: African American student enrollment grew at several public flagships, several BSIs expanded the numbers of African American students, and HBCUs continued to produce a disproportionate share of the nation's African American college graduates. Nevertheless, the absence of significant, sustained growth in African American student enrollment and completion at public four-year universities that account for a significant proportion of U.S. college graduates is disturbing. Although public universities grew exponentially, and despite substantial growth in the numbers of African American high school graduates, no commensurate, overall increase in African Americans on these campuses followed.

### What Has Worked?: Looking to the Courts

The question of what has worked defies a simple answer. The insidious perpetuation of antiblackness excludes "the very possibility of overcoming racism through discursive structures" (Harris 2015, 266). Backlash against affirmative action policies and a rash of court challenges retards progress. Efforts to destabilize and defeat affirmative action rely on the false narratives of colorblindness and liberalism (Tatum 2017). Beverly Tatum confirms the devastating consequences of Proposition 209 and Proposal 2 for African American enrollment at Public Ivy flagships in California and Michigan and points to the unsteady ground on which affirmative action stands (2017). Court challenges to affirmative action have already targeted Harvard University and the University of North Carolina at Chapel Hill for the next round of attacks on African American educational opportunity. True to form, these cases are falsely framed as equal justice investigations of "intentional race-based discrimination in college and university admissions" (Savage 2017, para. 2).

### The Future: Implications for the Twenty-First Century

African American student enrollment, college degree attainment, and economic advancement continue to be undermined by antiblack perspectives, institutional biases, racial discrimination, and white privilege. A complex set of factors—institutional and individual, historical and contemporary, brutal and silky smooth, governmental and civil society, intentional and unconscious, economic and cultural, mysterious and predictable—combine to create and maintain African American student disadvantages in U.S. higher education. Beyond coincidence, these factors intersect by design to ultimately preserve and reinforce white supremacy and racial hierarchy.

Moving forward, antiblackness must be forcefully contested in higher education and across society. Lionel McPherson positions higher education as "deeply implicated in the history and legacy of antiblack racial injustice. This is the basis of the distinctive moral responsibility these institutions have to be concerned about substantive equality of opportunity with respect to blacks in particular" (2015, 125–26). Higher education is a space of both opportunity and oppression (Solórzano and Yosso 2002), requiring resistance, as with campus activism; and where we also find "Black life-making" (Mustaffa 2017).

Higher education and racial inequality intersect with wealth; African Americans are three times more likely than whites to be low income and twice as likely to be under or unemployed and to hold significantly less wealth. Prohibitively high college costs (Sissoko and Shiau 2005), especially at public four-year institutions (Ma et al. 2017), the declining purchase power of Pell Grants (King and Bannon 2002), and limited federal subsidies combine to disproportionately restrict African American student college enrollment and graduation. Racial inequality in wealth, health, and higher education is no mystery. Instead, "It is the result of the same historical, political, economic, social, cultural, and psychological patterns that have perpetuated Black subjugation and oppression since Blacks arrived on these shores in 1619" (Allen 1992, 41–42).

Beyond higher education policies and practices that force African Americans into the lowest-tier institutions, restrict college access, impede college success, and limit returns from earned degrees, is a larger antiblack social, political, economic, historical, and cultural context. The surveillance and disgraceful mass incarceration of African Americans is clear evidence of antiblackness and systematic efforts to dominate and control African Americans. These attitudes and practices are reflected over the long time line of slavery, Jim Crow segregation, "Southern Political Strategies," and the "War on Drugs" (Alexander 2012; Browne 2015; Tatum 2017). Education is directly implicated in African American subjugation, and the logic in the madness that grafts discriminatory educational policy and practices onto the socioeconomic and political-historical disempowerment of African American communities is indisputable. The ultimate result—if not goal—is to inexorably divert African Americans from the higher education pipeline.

The American Dream ethos touts education as the great equalizer, a way for African American students to break the vicious cycle of poverty and achieve success in life. We reject this narrative for its failures to contend with racism, intersectional oppression, and colorblind rhetoric (Bonilla-Silva 2018; Patton 2016). Patton further debunks this myth as a source of meritocratic discourse which "attaches nobility to higher education without examining its contributions to the inequality it purports to disrupt" (2016, 318). Instead African American students continue to be denied educational opportunities and to be forced down pathways leading to poverty, drugs, prison, premature death, and defeat. Unless and until these changes are made, the United States will continue to be a society described in the Kerner report as "separate and unequal."

## REFERENCES

Alexander, Michelle. 2012. *The New Jim Crow: Mass Incarceration in the Age of Colorblindness*. New York: The New Press.

Ali, Fadumo. 2016. "Top 10 Black Student Activism Stories of the Year." *Huffington Post*, April 20.

Allen, Walter R. 1992. "The Color of Success: African American College Student Outcomes at Predominantly White and Historically Black Public Colleges and Universities." *Harvard Educational Review* 62(1): 26–44.

Allen, Walter R., Uma Jayakumar, Kimberly Griffin, William Korn, and Sylvia Hurtado. 2005. "Black Undergraduates from Bakke to Grutter: Freshman Status, Trends, and Prospects, 1917–2004." Los Angeles: University of California, Higher Education Research Institute.

Allen, Walter R., and Joseph O. Jewell. 2002. "A Backward Glance Forward: Present, and Future Perspectives on Historically Black Colleges and Universities." *The Review of Higher Education* 25(3): 241–61.

Allen, Walter R., Joseph O. Jewell, Kimberly A. Griffin, and De'Sha S. Wolf. 2007. "Historically Black Colleges and Universities: Honoring the Past, Engaging the Present, Touching the Future." *Journal of Negro Education* 76(3): 263–80.

Anderson, James D. 1988. *The Education of Blacks in the South, 1860–1935*. Chapel Hill: University of North Carolina Press.

———. 2015. "Eleventh Annual Brown Lecture in Education Research, A Long Shadow: The American Pursuit of Political Justice and Education Equality." *Educational Researcher* 44(6): 319–35.

Ashkenas, Jeremy, Haeyoun Park, and Adam Pearce. 2017. "Even with Affirmative Action, Blacks and Hispanics Are More Underrepresented at Top Colleges Than 35 Years Ago." *New York Times*, August 24.

Astin, Alexander W. 1982. *Minorities in American Higher Education: Recent Trends, Current Prospects, and Recommendations*." San Francisco, Calif.: Jossey-Bass.

Baum, Sandy. 2013. "Where Do African American Students Go to College?" *Urban Wire*, August 22.

Baum, Sandy, Jennifer Ma, and Kathleen Payea. 2013. "Education Pays, 2013: The Benefits of

Higher Education for Individuals and Society." New York: College Board.

Bell, Derrick. 1980. "Brown v. Board of Education and the Interest-Convergence Dilemma." *Harvard Law Review* 93(3): 518–33.

———. 1992. "Racial Realism." *Connecticut Law Review* 24(2): 363–79.

———. 2003. "Diversity's Distractions." *Columbia Law Review* 103(6): 1622–33.

Biondi, Martha. 2012. *The Black Revolution on Campus*. Berkeley: University of California Press.

Bishop, John. 1977. "The Effect of Public Policies on the Demand for Higher Education." *Journal of Human Resources* 12(3): 285–307.

Bonilla-Silva, Eduardo. 2018. *Racism Without Racists: Color-Blind Racism and the Persistence of Racial Inequality in America*, 5th ed. Lanham, Md.: Rowman & Littlefield.

Bowen, William G., and Derek Bok. 1998. *The Shape of the River: Long-Term Consequences of Considering Race in College and University Admissions*. Princeton, N.J.: Princeton University Press.

Browne, Simone B. 2015. *Dark Matters: On the Surveillance of Blackness*. Durham, N.C.: Duke University Press.

Conrad, Clifton F., Ellen M. Brier, and John M. Braxton. 1997. "Factors Contributing to the Matriculation of White Students in Public HBCUs." *Journal for a Just and Caring Education* 3(1): 37–62.

Crenshaw, Kimberlé W. 2006. "Framing Affirmative Action." *Michigan Law Review First Impressions* 105(1): 123–33. Accessed May 7, 2018. https://repository.law.umich.edu/mlr_fi/vol105/iss1/4.

Delgado, Richard, and Jean Stefancic. 2012. *Critical Race Theory: An Introduction*, 2nd ed. New York: New York University Press.

Dumas, Michael J. 2016. "Against the Dark: Antiblackness in Education Policy and Discourse." *Theory into Practice* 55(1): 11–19.

Dumas, Michael J., and kihana miraya ross. 2016. "Be Real Black for Me: Imagining BlackCrit in Education." *Urban Education,* 51(4): 415–42.

Ehrenberg, Ronald G., and Liang Zhang. 2005. "Do Tenured and Tenure-Track Faculty Matter?" *Journal of Human Resources* 40(3): 647–59.

Gasman, Marybeth, and Clifton Conrad. 2015. *Educating a Diverse Nation: Lessons from Minority-Serving Institutions*. Cambridge, Mass.: Harvard University Press.

Gasman, Marybeth, and Christopher L. Tudico, ed. 2008. *Historically Black Colleges and Universities: Triumphs, Troubles, and Taboos*. New York: Palgrave Macmillan.

Gasman, Marybeth, Thai-Huy Nguyen, and Clifton F. Conrad. 2015. "Lives Intertwined: A Primer on the History and Emergence of Minority Serving Institutions." *Journal of Diversity in Higher Education* 8(2): 120–38.

Giroux, Henry A. 2002. "Neoliberalism, Corporate Culture, and the Promise of Higher Education: The University as a Democratic Public Sphere." *Harvard Educational Review* 72(4): 425–64.

Griffin, Kimberly A., and Sylvia Hurtado. 2011. "Institutional Variety in American Higher Education." In *Student Services: A Handbook for the Profession*, edited by John H. Schuh, Susan R. Jones, and Shaun R. Harper and Associates. San Francisco, Calif.: John Wiley & Sons.

Gurin, Patricia, Eric L. Dey, Sylvia Hurtado, and Gerald Gurin. 2002. "Diversity and Higher Education: Theory and Impact on Educational Outcomes." *Harvard Educational Review* 72(3): 330–66.

Harper, Shaun R., Lori D. Patton, and Ontario S. Wooden. 2009. "Access and Equity for African American Students in Higher Education: A Critical Race Historical Analysis of Policy Efforts." *Journal of Higher Education* 80(4): 389–414.

Harris, Angela P. 2015. "Critical Race Theory." In *International Encyclopedia of the Social and Behavioral Sciences*, edited by James D. Wright. Amsterdam: Elsevier.

Harris, Cheryl I. 1993. "Whiteness as Property." *Harvard Law Review* 106(8): 1707–91.

Iloh, Constance, and Ivory A. Toldson. 2013. "Black Students in 21st Century Higher Education: A Closer Look at For-Profit and Community Colleges (Editor's Commentary)." *Journal of Negro Education* 82(3): 205–12.

Karabel, Jerome. 1999. "The Rise and Fall of Affirmative Action at the University of California." *Journal of Black in Higher Education* (25): 109–12.

Kelley, Robin D.G. 2016. "Black Study, Black Struggle." *Boston Review*, March 7. Accessed May 7, 2018. https://bostonreview.net/forum/robin-d-g-kelley-black-study-black-struggle.

Kerner Commission. 1968. *Report of the National Advisory Commission on Civil Disorders*. Washington: Government Printing Office.

Kezar, Adrianna, J., Tony C. Chambers, and John C. Burkhardt. 2005. *Higher Education for the Public*

Good: Emerging Voices from a National Movement. San Francisco, Calif.: Jossey-Bass.

King, Tracey, and Ellynne Bannon. 2002. "The Burden of Borrowing: A Report on the Rising Rates of Student Loan Debt." Washington, D.C.: The State PIRGs' Higher Education Project.

Klor de Alva, J., and Mark Schneider. 2015. "Rich Schools, Poor Students: Tapping Large University Endowments to Improve Student Outcomes." San Francisco, Calif.: Nexus Research and Policy Center.

Kolodner, Meredith. 2018. "Many State Flagship Universities Leave Black and Latino Students Behind." *Hechinger Report*, January 29. Accessed May 7, 2018. http://hechingerreport.org/many-state-flagship-universities-leave-black-latino-students-behind/.

Ladson-Billings, Gloria. 1998. "Just What Is Critical Race Theory and What's It Doing in a Nice Field Like Education?" *International Journal of Qualitative Studies in Education* 11(1): 7–24.

Ladson-Billings, Gloria, and William F. Tate. 1995. "Towards a Critical Race Theory of Education." *Teachers College Record* 97(1): 47–68.

Lambert, Linda. 1979. "Access of Black Americans to Higher Education: How Open Is the Door?" Washington, D.C.: National Advisory Committee on Black Higher Education and Black Colleges and Universities.

Ma, Jennifer, Sandy Baum, Matea Pender, and Meredith Welch. 2017. *Trends in College Pricing*. New York: College Board. Accessed May 7, 2018. https://trends.collegeboard.org/college-pricing.

McFarland, Joel, Bill Hussar, Cristobal de Brey, Tom Snyder, Xiaolei Wang, Sidney Wilkinson-Flicker, Semhar Gebrekristos, et al. 2017. "Actual and Projected Undergraduate Enrollment in Degree-Granting Postsecondary Institutions, by Attendance Status: Fall 2000–2026." Figure 3 in *The Condition of Education 2017*. NCES 2017-144. Washington: U.S. Department of Education, National Center for Education Statistics. Accessed May 7, 2018. https://nces.ed.gov/pubsearch/pubsinfo.asp?pubid=2017144.

McMillan Cottom, Tressie M. 2017. *Lower Ed: The Troubling Rise of For-Profit Colleges in the New Economy*. New York: The New Press.

McPherson, Lionel K. 2015. "Righting Historical Injustice in Higher Education." In *The Aims of Higher Education: Problems of Morality and Justice*, edited by Harry Brighouse and Michael McPherson, Chicago: University of Chicago Press.

Minor, James T. 2008. "Contemporary HBCUs: Considering Institutional Capacity and State Priorities: A Research Report." East Lansing: Michigan State University College of Education, Department of Educational Administration.

Mirowsky, John, and Catherine E. Ross. 1998. "Education, Personal Control, Lifestyle and Health: A Human Capital Hypothesis." *Research on Aging* 20(4): 415–49.

Mustaffa, Jalil B. 2017. "Mapping Violence, Naming Life: A History of Anti-Black Oppression in the Higher Education System." *International Journal of Qualitative Studies* 30(8): 711–27.

National Center for Education Statistics. Integrated Postsecondary Education Database System, Fall Enrollment and Degree Completion by Race/Ethnicity and Gender. Washington: U.S. Department of Education.

Omi, Michael, and Howard Winant. 2014. *Racial Formation in the United States*, 3rd ed. New York: Routledge.

Patton Davis, Lori. 2016. "Disrupting Postsecondary Prose: Toward a Critical Race Theory of Higher Education." *Urban Education* 51(3): 315–42.

Patton Davis, Lori, Kimberlé Crenshaw, Chayla Haynes, and Terri N. Watson. 2016. "Why We Can't Wait: (Re)Examining the Opportunities and Challenges for Black Women and Girls in Education (Guest Editorial)." *Journal of Negro Education* 85(3): 194–98.

Richardson, Jeanita W., and J. John Harris III. 2004. "Brown and Historically Black Colleges and Universities (HBCUs): A Paradox of Desegregation Policy." *Journal of Negro Education* 73(3): 365–78.

Rogers, Ibram H. 2012. "The Black Campus Movement: Black Students and the Racial Reconstitution of Higher Education, 1965–1972." New York: Palgrave MacMillan.

Savage, Charlie. 2017. "Justice Dept. to Take On Affirmative Action in College Admissions." *New York Times*, August 1. Accessed May 7, 2018. https://www.nytimes.com/2017/08/01/us/politics/trump-affirmative-action-universities.html.

Shapiro, Thomas M. 2017. *Toxic Inequality: How America's Wealth Gap Destroys Mobility, Deepens the Racial Divide, and Threatens Our Future*. New York: Basic Books.

Sissoko, Macki, and Liang-Rong Shiau. 2005. "Minority Enrollment Demand for Higher Education at Historically Black Colleges and Universities from 1976 to 1998: An Empirical Analysis." *Journal of Higher Education* 76(2): 181–208.

Smith, William A., Jalil Bishop Mustaffa, Chantal M. Jones, Tommy J. Curry, and Walter R. Allen. 2016. "'You Make Me Wanna Holler and Throw Up Both My Hands!': Campus Culture, Black Misandric Microaggressions, and Racial Battle Fatigue." *International Journal of Qualitative Studies in Education* 29(9): 1189–209.

Snyder, Thomas, D., Cristobal de Brey, and Sally A. Dillow. 2018a. "Rates of High School Completion and Bachelor's Degree Attainment Among Persons Age 25 and Over, by Race/Ethnicity and Sex: Selected Years, 1910 Through 2016." Table 104.10 in *Digest of Education Statistics 2016*, 52nd ed., NCES 2017-094. Washington: U.S. Department of Education, National Center for Education Statistics. Accessed July 14, 2018. https://nces.ed.gov/pubs2017/2017094.pdf.

———. 2018b. "Total Fall Enrollment in Degree-Granting Postsecondary Institutions, by Level and Control of Institution and Race/Ethnicity of Student: Selected Years, 1976 Through 2015." Table 306.20 in *Digest of Education Statistics 2016*, 52nd ed., NCES 2017-094. Washington: U.S. Department of Education, National Center for Education Statistics.

———. 2018c. "Number of Educational Institutions, by Level and Control of Institution: Selected Years, 1980–81 Through 2014–15." Table 105.50 in *Digest of Education Statistics 2016*, 52nd ed., NCES 2017-094. Washington: U.S. Department of Education, National Center for Education Statistics.

———. 2018d. "Selected Statistics on Degree-Granting Historically Black Colleges and Universities, by Control and Level of Institution: Selected Years, 1990 Through 2015." Table 313.30 in *Digest of Education Statistics 2016*, 52nd ed., NCES 2017-094. Washington: U.S. Department of Education, National Center for Education Statistics.

———. 2018e. "Bachelor's Degrees Conferred by Postsecondary Institutions, by Race/Ethnicity and Sex of Student: Selected Years, 1976–77 Through 2014–15." Table 322.20 in *Digest of Education Statistics 2016*, 52nd ed., NCES 2017-094. Washington: U.S. Department of Education, National Center for Education Statistics.

Solórzano, Daniel G., and Octavio Villalpando. 1998. "Critical Race Theory, Marginality, and the Experience of Students of Color in Higher Education." In *Sociology of Education: Emerging Perspectives*, edited by Carlos Alberto Torres and Theodore R. Mitchell. Albany: State University of New York Press.

Solórzano, Daniel G., and Tara J. Yosso. 2002. "A Critical Race Counterstory of Race, Racism, and Affirmative Action." *Equity & Excellence in Education* 35(2): 155–68.

Steele, Claude M., and Joshua Aronson. 1995. "Stereotype Threat and the Intellectual Test Performance of African Americans." *Journal of Personality and Social Psychology* 69(5): 797–811.

Tatum, Beverly Daniel. 2017. *Why Are All the Black Kids Sitting Together in the Cafeteria? And Other Conversations About Race*. New York: Basic Books.

U.S. Census Bureau. 2015. "2011–2015 American Community Survey 5-Year Estimates; Black or African American Alone or in Combination with One or More Other Races and Comparative Demographic Estimates." Washington.

U.S. Department of Health, Education, and Welfare, Office for Civil Rights. 1978a. *Racial, Ethnic, and Sex Enrollment Data from Institutions of Higher Education: Fall 1976*. Washington.

———. 1978b. *Data and Earned Degrees Conferred from Institutions of Higher Education by Race, Ethnicity, and Sex, Academic Year 1975–1976*, vol. 1. Washington.

———. 1981. *Data and Earned Degrees Conferred from Institutions of Higher Education by Race, Ethnicity, and Sex, Academic Year 1978–1979*, vol. 1. Washington.

Vue, Rican, Siduri Jayaram Haslerig, and Walter R. Allen. 2017. "Affirming Race, Diversity, and Equity Through Black and Latinx Students' Lived Experiences." *American Educational Research Journal* 54(5): 868–903.

# Whither Whiteness? The Racial Logics of the Kerner Report and Modern White Space

MATTHEW W. HUGHEY

*The Kerner report was, and is, unrelenting in its appraisal of the deleterious effects of racial inequality but opaque as to how whites functioned in that regime. Fifty years later, and in a moment of renewed urban unrest and rioting, whites continue to benefit from racial inequality within key social structures: education, employment, housing, and policing. To understand both the evaluations of the Kerner report and contemporary white interpretations of the social order, I systemically analyze the report alongside six ethnographies in all-white organizations across the United States. The analysis opens a window on similar racial logics in the report and among contemporary whites. These logics assist in the reproduction of white interests, even under the supposed best of intentions, legal remedies, and policy recommendations.*

**Keywords:** identity, race, racism, riots, social structure, whiteness

Widely regarded as a biting inquiry into the causes of the 1967 race riots, the 1968 account from the National Advisory Commission on Civil Disorders (the Kerner Commission, thus the Kerner report) stands as a scathing appraisal of U.S. race relations. Distinguished by its blunt language, the Kerner report uses phrases such as "white society is deeply implicated in the ghetto. White institutions created it, white institutions maintain it, and white society condones it" (Kerner Report 1968, 1). The report is unrelenting in its appraisal of the deleterious effects of white dominance in four key areas: employment, education, housing, and police-community relations. Yet, it is simultaneously opaque as to how whites functioned—whether through anxiety, antipathy, or apathy—in that racial regime. Although the report makes frequent mention of whiteness, rarely is the cause of racial inequality and segregation à la whiteness and white people specified.

Fifty years later, when race riots and white dominance are still provocative issues, our racial realities beckon scholars to wrestle with

---

**Matthew W. Hughey** is associate professor of sociology at the University of Connecticut and a research associate in critical studies in higher education transformation at Nelson Mandela University in South Africa.

© 2018 Russell Sage Foundation. Hughey, Matthew W. 2018. "Whither Whiteness? The Racial Logics of the Kerner Report and Modern White Space." *RSF: The Russell Sage Foundation Journal of the Social Sciences* 4(6): 73–98. DOI: 10.7758/RSF.2018.4.6.04. I wish to express gratitude to the Russell Sage Foundation director of publications Suzanne Nichols, to issue editors Susan T. Gooden and Samuel L. Myers Jr., to the participants in the Russell Sage Foundation conference in October 2017 for their collective feedback, and to the anonymous reviewers for their helpful criticisms on prior drafts. Direct correspondence to: Matthew W. Hughey at matthew.hughey@uconn.edu, Department of Sociology, University of Connecticut, 344 Mansfield Road, Unit 1068, Storrs, CT, 06269, USA.

Open Access Policy: *RSF: The Russell Sage Foundation Journal of the Social Sciences* is an open access journal. This article is published under a Creative Commons Attribution-NonCommercial-NoDerivs 3.0 Unported License.

two related issues. On one hand are the authoritative state interpretations of white people's place in the social order. On the other hand are white people's interpretations of their own place in the social order. Hence, based on a content analysis of the Kerner report and ethnographic study among six all-white organizations, I ask the following questions: First, how did the report describe the intersection of whites with the four noted areas? Second, how do whites today, across geographic areas, political persuasions, and socioeconomic divides, make sense of their intersection with these four areas? The results provide insight on the racial logics that further white interests, even under the supposed best of intentions, legal remedies, and policy recommendations.

## BACKGROUND

The 1967 decision to formally investigate rioting—and to understand, in President Lyndon Johnson's words, "What happened? Why did it happen? What can be done to prevent it from happening again and again?"—was neither a new nor prosaic concern.[1] Still, the report's underscoring of "white racism" captured attention. For the lay public, thirty thousand copies of the Bantam Books edition of the report sold out in three days while another 1.6 million copies sold between March and June of 1968 (Lipsky and Olson 1977). For academics, the notes and comments to the June 1968 issue of the *Social Service Review* asserted, "Not only did it [the report] attribute the disorders of recent summers to what it called 'white racism,' but it also denounced the movement toward a policy of separation" (261). The article concluded optimistically: "we know that white racism will not disappear today or even tomorrow, we do know that change in action [referring to congressional feat] may bring change in attitude" (263).[2] Not all reviews were positive. In 1969, the *American Political Science Review* claimed the report's identification of "white racism" was overly abstract: "the report neglected to document (though ample documentation was available) precisely how white racism has engendered black grievances and frustration" (Fogelson, Black, and Lipsky 1969, 1270). Moreover, Gary T. Marx, himself a contributor to the report, deeply criticized the commission's use of "racism":

> While I think the focus on racism is correct on both strategic and intellectual grounds, it could have been better documented and treated in a conceptually more sophisticated way.... The concept of racism as used is too abstract and general. Because it accuses everyone, it accuses no one.... What is needed is, if not a report that names names, at least one that names institutions and contrasts varying manifestations of racism. One looks in vain for an adequate discussion of who specifically profits in what ways from having a large black underclass. Just which white institutions created, maintain, and condone the ghetto? (1970, 83)

By 1971, critiques of the Kerner report's vague use of the phrase "white racism" continued. For example, Michael Lipsky argues, "it is noteworthy that an assertion concerning the responsibility of 'white racism' may escape such scrutiny because of its diffuse applicability. On the other hand, allegations of specific

---

1. Johnson made the remarks on July 29, 1967 while signing the order establishing the President's Commission on Law Enforcement and the Administration of Justice. The commission shortly thereafter published *The Challenge of Crime in a Free Society* (1967). Two other commissions were then established: the National Commission on the Causes and Prevention of Violence, which published *To Establish Justice, to Insure Domestic Tranquility* (1969) and the President's Commission on Campus Unrest, which published the *Report of the President's Commission on Campus Unrest* (1970) (also known as the Scranton report).

2. Loessberg's interviews with key participants in the Kerner Commission illumines why white racism may be mentioned but never clearly defined in its systemic operation: "What the Commission was about to conclude was not only a major departure from convention, but it was doing so in a very powerful manner. [Commission member Fred] Harris recalls that when the Commission had earlier come to the conclusion that discrimination and racism were the cause of the problems that now threatened the nation, there was initially a hesitancy to use these words because of the harshness associated with them" (Loessberg 2017, 12).

racist behavior are subject to extremely high standards of proof, and are correspondingly absent from the Kerner Commission document" (1971, 79).

Despite these criticisms, the report became notable for its focus on racial inequality (concentrating on the black-white color line) across four major areas: employment, education, housing, and police-community relations. Chapter 17 under "Recommendations for National Action," directly addresses employment, education, and housing; and chapter 7 again highlights employment. The report calls attention to the intersection of race and policing throughout, with an additional focus in chapter 11, "The Police and the Community." Overall, the report identified these structures as contributing to the creation of a violent, segregated, and impoverished "racial ghetto" (1968, 1).

By 1992, both the twenty-fifth anniversary of the Kerner report and the Los Angeles riots made the report once again salient. However, the report's focus on whiteness and white people was not often present in the commemoratory discourse. For example, the *North Carolina Law Review* held a retrospective symposium, in which contributing authors emphasized the parallelism of the 1967 Detroit and 1992 Los Angeles riots (Johnson and Farrell 1992), naivety of the Kerner report on racial integration (Rosenbaum et al. 1992), and the erratic development of welfare programs (Stoesz 1992). Overall, most presented a sobering view on how the "social and economic diagnoses of the Kerner Commission remain pertinent" (Boger 1992, 1293). However, most articles failed to examine the place of white people in the orchestration of the color line. One exception was John Calmore, who critically analyzed the role of whites in both housing discrimination and white "solutions" for that discrimination, concluding that "the invidious nature of the discrimination stemmed not simply from individual perpetrators engaged in the disparate treatment of individual blacks, but from a white group disposition to dominate and exclude blacks. . . . The white desire to exercise this power remains strong today, especially when directed to poor, urban blacks" (1992, 1499).

Despite some resurgence in scholarship on the report after both the thirtieth and fortieth anniversary reports, most discussion was marked by political debates over racial trends since 1968. Now at the fiftieth anniversary, some attention turns once again toward whiteness. For example, Adolph Reed eviscerates the report for the "diagnosis that 'white racism' was the ultimate cause of the unrest [which] suggested at the same time that combating racism and its effects could be the necessary remedy" (2017, 35). He further argues that these recommendations were both misguided and neutered given that they were "separated from its specific policy recommendations" (35). In addition, I have elsewhere argued that the report's "failure to outline the specific sociological operation of white domination . . . beckon scholars to wrestle with how this state-issued report . . . both reflects and reproduces dominant assumptions about the 'race' concept, violence, and human nature" (Hughey 2018a).

This body of scholarship gestures toward a necessity to both engage in a systematic evaluation of the logics used in the Kerner report toward the place of white people within core social institutions and to compare—now a half-century removed—how whites today use similar logics to make meaning of those institutions and related policy and legal considerations.

## DATA AND METHODOLOGY

I undertook a three-tiered content analysis of 324 pages (approximately 250,000 words) of the Kerner report (all but the front matter, the appendices, and the index). First, I followed a deductive approach in which I searched for specific expressions and words related to as *white* (N = 966), education (N = 313), employment (N = 258), housing (N = 281), and police (N = 1222). Second, I inductively reexamined the Kerner report to identify "sensitizing concepts" related to these topics (Blumer 1954), which led to discovery and comparison of concepts that are neither "static and inflexible" nor quantitatively frequent, but qualitatively important (Altheide and Schneider 2013, 26). For instance, terms such as "white racism" (N = 4), "white repression" (N = 4), "white power" (N = 3), and "white terrorism" (N = 2) are only cursorily declared, yet their appearance denotes a principal focus within the report. Third, I organized the

**Table 1.** Frames, Themes, and Discourse from the Kerner Report

| Frame (N = 592) | Theme (N = 250) | Discourse (N = 208) | Frequency/Category Total (Code Instance Percentage) |
|---|---|---|---|
| Education | | | 134/592 (22.64%) |
| | White normativity in education | | 17/250 (6.8) |
| | | Deprivational harm | 8/208 (3.85) |
| | | White structural invisibility | 12/208 (5.77) |
| | Innocence of everyday white people | | 13/250 (5.2) |
| | | Exceptional white terrorists | 7/208 (3.37) |
| | | Noncausal systems | 9/208 (4.33) |
| | White ignorance and messianic import | | 37/250 (14.8) |
| | | Paradoxical white flight | 10/208 (4.81) |
| | | Imagined communities | 8/208 (3.85) |
| Employment | | | 165/592 (27.87) |
| | Blackness of the culture of poverty | | 37/250 (14.8) |
| | | Black family | 6/208 (2.88) |
| | | White immigrants from the past | 7/208 (3.37) |
| | | Invisible pathways to white affluence | 9/208 (4.33) |
| | White control of resources | | 28/250 (11.2) |
| | | Intertwining segregation and culture | 10/208 (4.81) |
| | | Self-fulfilling black perceptions | 16/208 (7.69) |
| Housing | | | 106/592 (17.91) |
| | Black underprivilege without white overprivilege | | 25/250 (10.0) |
| | | Missing mechanisms for uplift | 9/208 (4.33) |
| | Causality of white racist attitudes | | 29/250 (11.6) |
| | | Hiding hidden practices | 10/208 (4.81) |
| | | Promoting white assimilation | 12/208 (5.77) |
| Police-community relations | | | 187/592 (31.59) |
| | Condemning attitudes and excusing behavior | | 44/250 (17.6) |
| | | Police attitudes = white attitudes | 37/208 (17.79) |
| | | Administrative policy changes | 7/208 (3.37) |
| | | Police ignorance | 19/208 (9.13) |
| | | Lack of resources | 5/208 (2.40) |
| | Deracializing internal police white supremacy | | 21/250 (8.4) |
| | | Causality without measurement | 3/208 (1.44) |
| | | Double standards about double standards | 4/208 (1.92) |

*Source*: Author's compilation based on Kerner Report 1968.

deductively based and inductively refined coding schema into first-level frames, second-level themes, and third-level discourse. Frames are, as David Altheide and Christopher Schneider write, "the focus, a parameter or boundary, for discussing a particular event"; secondary themes are "the recurring typical theses"; and tertiary "discourses" are specific talking-points within themes (2013, 53) (see table 1).

Each page served as the unit of analysis. Many of these coded elements were intimately linked; in instances in which more than one code appeared on a page, each was acknowledged: each scored a 1 for coinciding categories (0 = no, 1 = yes). The total frequency distribution included 592 frame instances, 250 theme instances, and 208 discourse instances (a total of 1,050 coding instances drawn from 347 pages

**Table 2.** Intercoder Reliability Measures

| Frame (N = 592) | % Agreement | Scott's Pi | Cohen's Kappa | Krippendorff's Alpha (Nominal) | N Agree | N Disagree |
|---|---|---|---|---|---|---|
| Education (N = 130) | 93.8 | −0.032 | 0 | −0.028 | 122 | 8 |
| Employment (N = 137) | 89.8 | −0.054 | 0 | −0.05 | 123 | 14 |
| Housing (N = 157) | 90.4 | −0.05 | 0 | −0.047 | 142 | 15 |
| Police-community relations (N = 168) | 85.7 | −0.077 | 0 | −0.074 | 144 | 24 |

*Source:* Author's calculations based on Kerner Report 1968.

for an average of 3.03 codes per page). Intercoder reliability measures on the theme codings were conducted and reveal high levels of reliability (see table 2).

### Multisite Ethnography

For this segment, I draw on data collected as part of multisite ethnographies (N = 6) of all-white organizational spaces. I engaged in the first two ethnographies in the U.S. mid-Atlantic over 2006 and 2007: a majority-male, white nationalist organization I call National Equality for All (NEA) and a majority-male, white antiracist organization I call Whites for Racial Justice (WRJ). I conducted the next two in the U.S. Deep South over 2010 through 2012: an all-white, mixed-gender, young professionals group I call Mississippi Alabama Young Educated Professionals (MAYEP) and an all-white, mixed-gender, college alumni chapter of a large southern university I call Big State Alumni (BSA). The last two ethnographies were taken in the New England region of the United States between 2014 and 2017: an all-white, all-women, New England–based chapter of a patriotic lineage society I call the Daughters of Patriots (DOP) and an all-white, mixed-gender (predominately male), New England–based chapter of a civic association I call the Loyal Order of Benevolent Americans (LOBA) (see table 3).

I engaged in data triangulation of ethnographic fieldwork inclusive of meetings and informal activities; semistructured in-depth interviews (N = 204) with members of each group (NEA n = 24; WRJ n = 21; MAYEP n = 35; BSA n = 42; DOP n = 38; LOBA n = 44); content analysis of textual information such as paper and e-correspondence, archives, media advertisements, official documents, and office memos; and comparative vignettes. To secure Institutional Review Board approval, all potentially identifying information is either unreported or replaced with pseudonyms. I gained access after attending informational and recruiting meetings held by the organizations, by meeting influential members of the groups, and through word of mouth. My relationship with each group was that of a known researcher. I selected these six groups by their relative proximity to one another (NEA and WRJ, MAYEP and BSA, and DOP and LOBA), their status as chapters of larger, national associations, and as either purposeful or de facto all-white groups. The data analyzed come from a larger investigation of the relationships between white racial identity formation, organizational racial homophily and homogeneity, and white racial stratification beliefs about major social structures.

### FINDINGS

Findings are organized by education, employment, housing, and police-community relations. In each I present the content analysis of the Kerner report and then outline the patterns culled from the six ethnographic locations. I show a striking correspondence and relative stability in racial logics across time (from 1968 to 2018) and space (the six ethnographic locales), which in turn reveal several core assumptions about race in the United States.

### Education

The Kerner report created a three-tiered ranking of grievances among "Negro communities" in which "inadequate education" was a "second

**Table 3.** Ethnographic Descriptives

|  | NEA | WRJ | MAYEP | BSA | DOP | LOBA | Totals |
|---|---|---|---|---|---|---|---|
| **Organizational demographics** | | | | | | | |
| Participants active (n) | 24 | 21 | 35 | 42 | 38 | 44 | 204 |
| Mean years active (median, SD) | 3.29 (5, 2.77) | 4.38 (5, 2.08) | 3.83 (3, 3.18) | 6 (4, 7.87) | 10 (6.5, 9.51) | 14.73 (15, 10.15) | |
| Mean age in years (median, SD) | 37.18 (37, 8.19) | 36.76 (35, 10.88) | 26.29 (25, 4.72) | 31.45 (28, 10.93) | 45.95 (44, 12.83) | 56.84 (56.5, 11.79) | |
| Age range in years | 33 (25–58) | 40 (22–62) | 15 (20–35) | 41 (21–62) | 52 (25–77) | 51 (33–84) | |
| Gender ratio male/female | 23/1 | 19/2 | 15/20 | 24/18 | 0/38 | 35/9 | |
| | 95.8%/4.2% | 90.4%/9.6% | 42.86%/57.14% | 57.14%/42.86% | (0%/100%) | (79.55%/20.45%) | |
| **Religion** | | | | | | | |
| Catholic | 3 (12.5%) | 2 (9.5%) | 3 (8.57%) | 5 (11.90%) | 10 (26.32%) | 18 (40.9%) | 41 (21.08%) |
| Protestant | 16 (66.6) | 12 (57.1) | 25 (71.43) | 26 (61.90) | 7 (18.42) | 12 (27.27) | 98 (48.04) |
| Jewish | 0 (0) | 0 (0) | 0 (0) | 4 (9.52) | 0 (0) | 5 (11.36) | 9 (4.41) |
| Atheist | 1 (4.2) | 1 (4.8) | 2 (5.71) | 1 (2.38) | 7 (18.42) | 0 (0) | 12 (5.88) |
| Agnostic | 2 (8.3) | 2 (9.5) | 3 (8.57) | 4 (9.52) | 9 (23.68) | 0 (0) | 12 (5.88) |
| Spiritual/other | 2 (8.3) | 4 (19) | 2 (5.71) | 2 (4.76) | 5 (13.16) | 9 (20.45) | 12 (5.88) |
| **Region raised** | | | | | | | |
| Midwest | 6 (25%) | 2 (9.5%) | 2 (5.71%) | 3 (7.14%) | 3 (7.89%) | 4 (9.09%) | 20 (9.8%) |
| North | 3 (12.5) | 3 (14.3) | 3 (8.57) | 5 (11.90) | 30 (78.95) | 25 (56.82) | 69 (33.82) |
| South | 14 (58.3) | 16 (76.2) | 27 (77.14) | 28 (66.67) | 4 (10.53) | 9 (20.45) | 98 (48.04) |
| West | 1 (4.2) | 0 (0) | 3 (8.57) | 6 (14.29) | 1 (2.63) | 6 (13.64) | 17 (8.33) |
| **Political orientation** | | | | | | | |
| Democrat | 2 (8.3%) | 5 (23.8%) | 5 (14.29%) | 7 (16.67%) | 25 (65.79%) | 0 (0%) | 44 (21.57%) |
| Green | 0 (0) | 0 (0) | 2 (5.7) | 4 (9.52) | 2 (7.14) | 0 (0) | 8 (3.9) |
| Independent | 5 (20.8) | 12 (57.1) | 6 (17.14) | 6 (14.29) | 6 (15.79) | 8 (18.18) | 43 (21.08) |
| Libertarian | 0 (0) | 0 (0) | 3 (8.57) | 2 (4.76) | 0 (0) | 7 (15.91) | 12 (5.88) |
| Republican | 9 (37.5) | 1 (4.8) | 13 (37.14) | 19 (45.24) | 3 (7.89) | 23 (52.27) | 68 (33.33) |
| None/no answer | 8 (33.3) | 3 (14.3) | 6 (17.14) | 4 (9.52) | 2 (7.14) | 6 (13.64) | 29 (14.22) |

| | | | | | | |
|---|---|---|---|---|---|---|
| **Educational attainment** | | | | | | |
| No college | 0 (0%) | 0 (0%) | 0 (0%) | 0 (0%) | 0 (0%) | 9 (4.41%) |
| Some college | 5 (20.8) | 4 (19) | 5 (14.29) | 0 (0) | 0 (0) | 20 (9.8) |
| College degree or equivalent | 14 (58.3) | 7 (33.3) | 23 (65.71) | 33 (78.57) | 29 (76.32) | 131 (64.22) |
| Some graduate classes | 0 (0) | 3 (14.3) | 2 (5.71) | 4 (9.52) | 2 (5.26) | 11 (5.39) |
| Graduate degree | 5 (20.8) | 7 (33.3) | 5 (14.29) | 5 (11.90) | 7 (18.42) | 33 (16.18) |
| **Socioeconomic status (self-reported)** | | | | | | |
| Working class | 1 (4.2%) | 2 (5.71%) | 5 (11.90%) | 0 (0%) | 6 (13.64%) | 15 (7.36%) |
| Lower middle class | 2 (8.3) | 11 (831.43) | 5 (11.90) | 0 (0) | 8 (18.18) | 29 (14.22) |
| Middle class | 12 (50) | 21 (60.0) | 27 (64.29) | 8 (21.05) | 30 (68.18) | 106 (51.96) |
| Upper middle class | 9 (37.5) | 0 (0) | 5 (11.90) | 23 (60.53) | 0 (0) | 43 (21.08) |
| Upper class | 0 (0) | 0 (0) | 0 (0) | 7 (18.42) | 0 (0) | 10 (4.9) |
| **Yearly income** | | | | | | |
| Less than 25,000 | 2 (8.3%) | 2 (5.71%) | 3 (7.14%) | 0 (0%) | 0 (0%) | 8 (3.9%) |
| 25,000–49,999 | 9 (37.5) | 28 (80.0) | 20 (47.62) | 0 (0) | 3 (6.82) | 69 (33.82) |
| 50,000–74,999 | 11 (45.8) | 5 (14.29) | 14 (33.33) | 0 (0) | 7 (15.91) | 46 (22.5) |
| 75,000–99,999 | 2 (8.3) | 0 (0) | 5 (11.90) | 9 (23.68) | 12 (27.27) | 28 (13.73) |
| 100,000 or more | 0 (0) | 0 (0) | 0 (0) | 29 (76.32) | 22 (50.00) | 53 (25.98) |
| **Housing** | | | | | | |
| Own home | 13 (54.2%) | 3 (8.57%) | 16 (38.09%) | 33 (86.84%) | 39 (88.64%) | 114 (55.88%) |
| Rent | 11 (45.8) | 32 (91.43) | 26 (61.90) | 5 (13.15) | 5 (11.36) | 90 (44.12) |

*Source:* Author's compilation based on multisite ethnographies.

level of intensity." Most of the discussion on education centered on either racial disparities or the educational characteristics of rioters, but the place of whiteness in education was both implicitly and explicitly addressed.

*White Normativity in Education*
First, in the report, whites were the norm to which African Americans were most commonly compared. For instance,

> The bleak record of public education for ghetto children is growing worse. In the critical skills—verbal and reading ability—Negro students are falling further behind whites with each year of school completed.... If existing disadvantages are not to be perpetuated, we must drastically improve the quality of ghetto education. Equality of results with all-white schools must be the goal. (1968, 12)

Attention to the achievement gap was paramount in the report. On the heels of *Brown v. Board*,[3] the report assumes deprivational harm to the black psyche but submerges questions about white structural advantages (Carter 1990).[4] For the commission, educational inequality meant an embodied inferiority in black students. As a result, the black student was more scrutinized than the underlying pathology of white supremacist control of resources. Whiteness was the invisible norm by which disparities were measured and the presumed pathology-free student par exemplar to which students of color should aspire.

Contemporary racial logics of educational white normativity are exemplified in a statement by a white nationalist I call Tim (counselor, age thirty-three, four years in NEA). Tim explained that educational integration was "unnatural" and would hurt white children:

> Nonwhite children, people in general, need to be with their own.... integration is unnatural.... children are impressionable and could soak up, well, they could learn habits and customs that are not up to our white standard,... they need to learn our culture, that's the norm, white culture is the norm here.... nonwhites have a lower IQ and you want to put children with the smartest, not the dumbest, people in the room.

Such a white nationalist stance is to be expected. However, white antiracists often expressed similar rationales, such as one member named Sherrill (consultant, age thirty-five, eight years in WRJ):

> I'm not saying integration is bad.... it's the goal ... but everyone has a different culture.... for better or worse, white schools have more of a Eurocentric style and that's society's norm.... I'm afraid that white children sometimes suffer because, it's.... look, African American children are raised differently, there's a different culture, and their schools can be more Afrocentric and ... I believe in integration, but I don't see how it's pragmatic yet, like right now, ... I just don't think we need to fight these battles by using our children as the ammunition.

In groups not organized on the basis of white racial activism, such as the New England–based DOP, a member I call Emma (medical assistant, age forty-five, fifteen years in DOP) said,

> Schools have curricula and standards.... those are based on European history and knowledge, and culture ... white students learn more easily when around their own and are comfortable ... Of course, not all white students get it, some people fail [Author: "White students?"] Yeah, some just don't live up to their potential ... but the schools are set-up for white students, I think, in particular, to succeed. [long pause] I'm not so sure about black students.

---

3. *Brown v. Board of Education of Tokepa*, 347 U.S. 483 (1954).

4. Gregg Lee Carter reanalyzes data from the Kerner report's fifteen cities study and finds that despite a weak correlation between black grievances and deprivation, such a relationship did not link to riot activity, which leaves the report's claims of a psychological sense of desperation and frustration without evidence (1990).

Here we see a racial logic that evokes both an intra- and interracial boundary, which demarcates a white racial ideal—the right type of white student succeeds in school, by virtue of their racial-cultural orientation and fit in the educational system, opposed to both deficient white students and students of color.

Appeals to white children's intellectual development, white children's pedagogical comfort, and white safety were frequent both in the report and among the white participants of these six organizations. For instance, in referring to school desegregation efforts, Lara told me that her children would not be "used as guinea pigs in some social experiment, even if I agree that's how things should be" (human resources manager, age forty-four, twelve years in BSA).

### The Innocence of Everyday White People: White Violence Toward Desegregation

The Kerner report occasionally addresses violence toward desegregation efforts. For example, the following passage appears twice: "A climate that tends toward approval and encouragement of violence as a form of protest has been created by *white terrorism* [emphasis added] directed against nonviolent protest; by the open defiance of law and Federal Authority by state and local officials resisting desegregation" (1968, 5, 92).

Under this logic, some white people are singled out as, literally, terrorists who defy both the law and federal Authority. By framing white violence as the domain of a radical few, more commonplace and banal violent white activities by police and citizens were often marginalized. Even though the Kerner report finds that "Some 40 percent of the prior incidents [in Detroit over 1966 and 1967] involved allegedly abusive or discriminatory police actions" (1968, 69) and that "about 17 percent of the prior incidents [in Detroit over the same period] involved activities by whites intended to discredit or intimidate Negroes or violence by whites against Negroes" (70), this data did not sway the commission to posit white supremacy as a cause of the riots. Rather, the report stated that such episodes were "prior incidents" leading up to the violence and that none of the events occurring before the riots (labeled final incidents) "were classifiable as racist activity" (70).

Members of these six organizations often used similar racial logics. For instance, violence was framed as a possible, even natural, repercussion of "forced integration." Barney (plumber, age thirty-one, ten years in MAYEP) said,

> You can't tell people what to do. . . . if you force people, especially about their kids, then you're going to have resistance. . . . I wouldn't rule out violence, but when you're talking about people's kids, they are going to do whatever they have to do to protect them. . . . I don't care what kind of high-minded goal you got, but you know, if you go and, if you go and you start telling me what my children can and can't do and how they've got to learn, and I think it's bad, well just show me a parent that wouldn't do what they had to do.

Appeals to violence to "protect" white children from "unnatural" or "political" influences associated with school integration were common. Derrick (firefighter, age forty, seventeen years in LOBA) remarked,

> OK, let me be clear. I think integration could be fine and, well, . . . but you have to admit, there are some natural differences between the races, and there's nothing wrong with learning among your own. . . . the desegregation agenda is too political, and I'd fight some politician, or cop, or whoever it is, I'm talking tooth and nail, if they tried to force my son into being some pawn in their political agenda. It's unnatural.

And similarly, Fiona (homemaker, age thirty-one, one year in DOP) explained,

> I get that people want everyone to get along, but that's unnatural. . . . Listen, I'm not a violent person, but if someone tries to take my child and send them to some bad school that's full of, just, little criminals and delinquents . . . I, [a] real parent will stand up to

protect their child" [Author: "I'm sorry, who are the criminals and delinquents?"]. The kids, I mean, they are going to be soon. [Author: "The white kids in the integrated school?"] No, it's, you know what I mean, it's, listen, there are statistics that show that black, uh, African American students are more likely to commit crimes, . . . I don't want my children around that, and I'd fight anyone, I mean, if I had to hit, punch, kick, scream, or like chain myself to the schoolhouse door, if I had to, I would to, to protect my children.

White violence in defense of segregation qua children was used to construct the ideal white parent; a steadfast opponent of both "unnatural" integration and a protector from the "criminal and delinquent" characteristics believed natural to adolescent blackness.

*White Ignorance and Messianic Import*

The assumption that whites had a lack of racial understandings runs throughout the Kerner report. For example, "What white Americans have never fully understood—but what the Negro can never forget—is that white society is deeply implicated in the ghetto. White institutions created it. white institutions maintain it, and white society condones it" (1968, 1). In an often quoted line, the report places both blame and salvation of ghetto conditions in white knowledge. Following this logic, the report concludes that intercessions into ghetto conditions could be addressed via better communication with whites:

> In addition to establishing a foundation for needed legislative measures, these hearings would constitute a visible demonstration of governmental concern for the problems of ghetto residents. They would also provide a most useful means of bridging the communications gap, contributing to an improved understanding in the white community about the conditions of ghetto life. (1968, 152)

Although it is conceivable that some whites are unaware of their involvement in the creation and maintenance of inner-city social problems that hold disproportionate negative impacts on African Americans, the report's mention of white condonance (the acceptance, approval, or sanction of these conditions) betrays such a conclusion. This contradiction is apparent in the Kerner report's focus on white racial beliefs as "one of the major causes" for white migration away from inner cities (known as white flight). For instance,

> As the whites were absorbed by the larger society, many left their predominantly ethnic neighborhoods and moved to outlying areas to obtain newer housing and better schools. . . . Yet most Negro families have remained within predominantly Negro neighborhoods, primarly [sic] because they have been effectively excluded from white residential areas. . . . Another form of discrimination just as significant is white withdrawal from, or refusal to enter, neighborhoods where large numbers of Negroes are moving or already residing. . . . Once this happens, the remaining whites seek to leave, thus confirming the existing belief among whites that complete transformation of a neighborhood is inevitable once Negroes begin to enter. Since the belief itself is one of the major causes of the transformation, it becomes a self-fulfilling prophecy which inhibits the development of racially integrated neighborhoods. (1968, 119)

The report does not resolve this contradiction—a kind of "Schrödinger's whiteness" (Hughey 2018b)—that is simultaneously mindful of and oblivious to white involvement in black ghetto conditions and segregation. On the one hand, whites are simultaneously unaware of condoning ghetto conditions (and thus need better communication about them and their role in their creation, maintenance, and condonance), but on the other are all too aware of these conditions and explicitly leave them (thus both condoning African Americans to exclusively live in them while having "effectively excluded [African Americans] from white residential areas" [1968, 119]).

Temporarily ignoring white racial consciousness, the Kerner report places the cause of this supposed white ignorance at the feet of mass media:

They [the media] have not communicated to the majority of their audience;—which is white—a sense of the degradation, misery, and hopelessness of living in the ghetto. They have not communicated to whites a feeling for the difficulties and frustrations of being a Negro in the United States. They have not shown understanding or appreciation of— and thus have not communicated—a sense of Negro culture, thought, or history. (1968, 10, 210)

The report concludes that the media has crafted white ignorance in the collective consumption of newspapers and television:

> If what the white American reads in the newspapers or sees on television conditions his expectation of what is ordinary and normal in the larger society, he will neither understand nor accept the black American. By failing to portray the Negro as a matter of routine and in the context of the total society, the news media have, we believe, contributed to the black-white schism in this country. (1968, 211)

Media representations and narratives have been a part of whites' lack of "understanding or appreciation" in racial matters. However, it seems spurious to both insinuate, first, whites were not aware of the "negative" conditions they were fleeing to put their children in "better schools" free of African American children suffering from "disparities" (as well as excluding blacks from white suburban schools) and second, that a sudden realization of negative "ghetto conditions" would lead to a sea-change in white support for educational integration and equality.

The Kerner report is adamant that racial inequality and segregation is largely due to whites' ignorance and inaccuracy of them, but ethnographic data reveals that whites in fact seem to be hyperaware of these issues. As Michael (banker, age thirty-six, 4.5 years in WRJ) said, "I believe in integration, but I don't want to send my child to a black school because they're underfunded and troubled.... That's what segregation has done to black schools.... Integration is important, but I'm not going to sacrifice the well-being of my child." As Bianca (landscape architect, age thirty-eight, ten years in DOP) told me,

> I grew up close to Bridgeport [CT].... it was dangerous, with a police presence and surveillance, the poverty, the broken-down and underfunded schools. I knew it was because they were black. My school wasn't like that... that's "white privilege" [makes air quotes]. It's all because of race. And I think that's why most whites don't want to move there or send their kids there.... I'm not going to either.... in the end, what kind of parent would I be if my child doesn't get the best education?

Without difficulty, members of these six groups told me plainly about educational disparities across the color line and that those inequities were a (if not the) reason they would not send their children to "those" (black or Latinx) schools. Many did not seem ignorant as to the causes, extent, and mechanisms by which such educational segregation and inequality were reproduced, and none were unclear as to their consequences. Rather, discussions about schools always came down to the quality of the school that was measured with the proxy of race. From these interviews and witnessed discussions, it was clear that the ideal white parent would protect their child from the "dangerous" black schools, thereby delivering that child safety, innocence, and education.

Both the report and contemporary whites use a similar logic whereby white consciousness and benefaction will remedy educational inequality: "today's problems can be solved *only* [emphasis added] if white Americans comprehend the rigid social, economic and educational barriers that have prevented Negroes from participating in the mainstream of American life" (Kerner Report 1968, 95). The logic is that a cadre of kindly, white benefactors who, newly and acutely aware of educational segregation and inequality, will suddenly work to undo the system that continues to prop up their educational advantages. Such an assertion—and reliance on an idealized white savior figure—would be laughable if it were not the very real racial reasoning used in both the report and among varied whites today.

**Employment**
Rates, trends, and descriptions of a rioter's profile were the most common reference points for employment. Nevertheless, the Kerner report is replete with both implied and overt references to the intersection of whiteness and employment. Contemporary whites also hold these logics.

*The Blackness of the Culture of Poverty*
Describing black residents of the ghetto, the report states, "This pattern reinforces itself from one generation to the next, creating a 'culture of poverty' and an ingrained cynicism about society and its institutions." On the same page, the report continues, "The culture of poverty that results from unemployment and family disorganization generates a system of ruthless, exploitative relationships within the ghetto ... an environmental jungle characterized by personal insecurity and tension" (1968, 130).

Such a logic fails in distinguishing the differences between the "cultures" of white and black that supposedly keep the latter in a "pattern [that] reinforces itself from one generation to the next" (1968, 130). However, one passage compares current black realities with past white immigrant experiences, and critiques white historical romanticism:

> Finally, nostalgia makes it easy to exaggerate the ease of escape of the white immigrants from the ghettos. When the immigrants were immersed in poverty, they, too, lived in slums, and these neighborhoods exhibited fearfully high rates of alcoholism, desertion, illegitimacy and the other pathologies associated with poverty. Just as some Negro men desert their families when they are unemployed and their wives can get jobs, so did the men of other ethnic groups, even though time and affluence has clouded white memories of the past. (1968, 145)

The Kerner report acknowledges a strikingly similar form of pathologies across black and white communities, but addresses neither the nature of the affluence gained by white immigrants nor how affluence is achieved. White structural assistance is unmentioned while the report alludes to white immigrants simply giving up their pathologies and miraculously landing in economic affluence.[5] The report's pages drip with an implicit conflation of whiteness with a dysfunction-free culture, whereas African American culture fails to value work because, *circulus in probando*, African American people are underemployed.

Like the Kerner report, the evocation of black and Latinx pathologies and dysfunctions were frequent across these six organizations. For instance, Franklin (sales associate, age thirty-seven, five years in NEA) told me that

> Biological differences explain much of today's racial conflict.... Genetics makes clear that there is a connection between race and intelligence where the more melanin you have the less intelligent you are, you know, the less mental capacity you possess.... DNA and genetics are proving what we knew all along really. Blacks, Hispanics, darker-skinned people are more aggressive and dangerous.... It's not racist, it's a fact.

Franklin's interpretation is lockstep with NEA propaganda. However, this logic is not reducible to the political orientations of white nationalism and was shared by members of other white organizations.

Kenny (professor, age fifty-seven, thirteen years in BSA) explained his perspective: "The inner cities were destroyed after the Great Migration.... it's all vice there now.... Harlem looks like a war zone.... what kind of white people would live in a place like that?" Kenny admitted that he never has set foot in Harlem, but his self-assuredness was shared by many others, inclusive of the New England born-and-bred Haley (lawyer, age sixty-one, thirty-one years in DOP) who told me this:

5. Throughout much of the 1900s, whites had exclusive racialized access to bank loans, land grants, unemployment compensation, the minimum wage, labor unions, and the G.I. Bill during a segregated military.

I don't know if it's biology or just the way that blacks are socialized, or what it is really.... all I know is, and people don't want to admit this, but crime rates, drug use rates, mental illness, domestic violence, you name it, really, all of those, those ... you sociologists call them "social problems," all those things are overrepresented in black, uh, African American communities and families.... some white people have it, too, though. I guess we'd call them "white trash" ... the white people that don't, don't have their life together and have adopted some values from black people or from their native countries that don't fit here.

Both Kenny and Haley demonstrate a logic that relies on inter- and intraracial boundaries toward the pursuit of an ideal whiteness. First, spaces of color (for example, Harlem, African American communities and families) are framed as a "war zone" and as rife with "crime," "drug use," and "mental illness" alongside unnamed "white space" free of these dangers (Jackson 1999; Moore 2008; Anderson 2015). Second, whites who venture into these areas are somehow racially deficient (for example, "what kind of white people would live in a place like that" or "white trash" that "don't have their life together") and do not reflect the pursuit or attainment of the white hegemonic ideal.

It might be tempting to dismiss such remarks as the product of political leanings or generational cohorts, but many younger white self-reported Democrats and Independents voiced similar opinions in the company of their all-white organizations. Patrick (writer, age twenty-eight, two years in WRJ) said, "Blacks and Latinos, I don't know ... they just, let's be honest, they can't seem to get their stuff together.... you just want to say, 'Stop smoking crack, get a job, and, you know, stay in school!' ... yes, there is racism, but that's often an excuse." As Talia (retail sales, age twenty-two, one year in MAYEP) told me,

> Black-on-black crime is what's really holding black people back.... they blame white people for not getting along with them? Come on! ... if they got an education and a job, and stayed with it, then in a generation or two, there would be equality.... Most white people can do it, except for like rednecks and other losers who don't have an excuse [Author: "What do you mean, 'don't have an excuse'?"] Oh, well, because they're white [said matter-of-factly].

Both the inter- and intraracial divisions are quite clear in Talia's logic: whites have no excuse for unemployment because of the supposedly inherent value they place on work, whereas if people of color became more like whites, then they would have similar outcomes.

*White Control of Resources*

The Kerner report often mentions the lopsided white control of resources, acknowledging the role that segregated white communities and organizations played in excluding African Americans from economic opportunities. For example,

> Segregation played a role here too. The immigrants and their descendants, who felt threatened by the arrival of the Negro, prevented a Negro-immigrant coalition that might have saved the old political machines. Reform groups, nominally more liberal on the race issue, were often dominated by businessmen and middle-class city residents who usually opposed coalition with any low-income group, white or black. (1968, 144)

The report singles out racial segregation rather than culture of poverty as the causal variable for low occupational attainment, but often it intertwines the two. Hence, when it does address how white discrimination in employment and the economy are likely to drive the low socioeconomic status of blacks, the report often pivots toward renderings of white discrimination not as an objective reality (but rather a conclusion drawn from frustrated and dysfunctional black perceptions):

> Significant grievances concerning unfair commercial practices affecting Negro consumers were found in 11 of the 20 cities studied by the Commission. The fact that most of

the merchants who operate stores in Negro areas are white undoubtedly contributes to the conclusion among Negroes that they are exploited by white society. (1968, 139)

In this light, the riots of the 1960s were not a product of white repression, but of black perceptions of white repression. The report states that

> Much of the violence in recent civil disorders has been directed at stores and other commercial establishments in disadvantaged Negro areas. In some cases, rioters focused on stores operated by white merchants who, *they apparently believed* [emphasis added], had been charging exorbitant prices or selling inferior goods. Not all the violence against these stores can be attributed to "revenge" for such practices. Yet it is clear that many residents of disadvantaged Negro neighborhoods believe they suffer constant abuses by local merchants. (1968, 139)

Paradoxically, consensus shifted among the members of these six white groups regarding white control of economic resources. Despite agreement that whites hold more resources on average than people of color, members drew from a shared racial logic, attributing such dominance rarely to exploitation or unearned privileges but instead to hard work, cultural values, and natural ability. Yet, at other moments, members shared the reasoning that resources were being unfairly stripped from whites because of a "politically correct" system marked by "reverse racist" preferences for people of color. For instance, I once entered the meeting place of LOBA to find Aaron (contractor, age fifty-seven, nineteen years in LOBA), Eddie (mechanic, age fifty-nine, fifteen years in LOBA), and Rob (maintenance, age thirty-eight, one year in LOBA) in conversation:

AARON: "Obama's new tax plan is going to have a racial re-dis-trib-u-tive [said with punctuated emphasis] component, where they tax whites more than blacks and Mexicans and Asians.... they are going to fund affirmative action and welfare that way."

EDDIE: "How are they going to even measure, or uh, track that, I mean it's ...?"
ROB: [interrupting] "The census, man! Why do you think they started taking down people's race? They want to track the money to fund the handout programs."
AARON: "I heard they might merge the IRS and the census anyhow."
EDDIE: "Oh, that's that new box on the 1040 and 1099 I heard they are going to use, where they can garnish your income directly into jobs specifically for black people."
[AUTHOR: "How do you feel about all this?"]
AARON: "It's not fair. It just ain't right.... I worked hard, my daddy worked hard.... my money shouldn't go to some lazy nigger. [Aaron locked eyes with me] Look, I'm sorry, but that's who they are... I got a job, worked hard... I was taught the right values.... this is how you start a revolution, I tell you. Taxation without representation."

This conversation, and what ensued, was rife with discussions of whites' superior work ethic, worldview and values, and natural ability relative to people of color.

The same rationalizations were shared across the six white organizations. I would commonly ask members of these groups: "What makes white people different from other races?" Giving perhaps the most direct and brusque answer, Kylee (small business owner, age forty-three, three years in DOP) stated,

> We work harder, faster, and better. It's biological. It's cultural. It's taught. Just everything. It's ... look, I'll be honest with you, I read these studies by sociologists like you who document inequality.... I don't doubt the measurements.... White people come out on top in most areas. But the issue I have is with your explanations. You go out of your way to not say the obvious: White people are superior.... I don't like to advertise that opinion, because people will say I'm a racist.... here's a common-sense reason why I don't hire black people: ... white people work harder.

Kylee's worldview is overt, but was shared in more polite and nuanced forms by others. For instance, as Lance (postal worker, age twenty-eight, four years in BSA) told me,

> I graduated from [Big State] and couldn't find a job for a while. I didn't apply for welfare. I'm not some bum. . . . But I couldn't get a job in my field [marketing] because they were only hiring black people because of affirmative action. . . . it's everywhere, especially in federal jobs . . . . I finally found a job here with the local post office. [Author: "How did you a get federal job with all the affirmative action you mention?"] Well, I just kept trying. Hard work pays off. I didn't give up or wait for some hand out, like I told you.

### Housing

As it does for employment and education, the report concentrates on descriptive demographic variables such as fertility and mortality rates and migration patterns to emphasize white flight and black urbanization in the ghetto. Yet, racialized logics were often couched in between quantitative reports of trends and disparities.

*Black Underprivilege Without White Overprivilege*
Both the report and white group members engaged in one-sided appraisals of race relations whereby black disadvantage somehow existed without white advantage. For example, the report states that

> Social and economic conditions in the riot cities constituted a clear pattern of severe disadvantage for Negroes compared with whites, whether the Negroes lived in the area where the riot took place or outside it. . . . Although housing cost Negroes relatively more, they had worse housing—three times as likely to be overcrowded and substandard. When compared to white suburbs, the relative disadvantage was even more pronounced. (1968, 4)

When white upward social mobility in housing was mentioned, the specificity of assistance programs and structural disadvantage was unnamed. Consider the following Kerner report passage:

> But the later phases of Negro settlement and expansion in metropolitan areas diverge sharply from those typical of white immigrants. As the whites were absorbed by the larger society, many left their predominantly ethnic neighborhoods and moved to outlying areas to obtain newer housing and better schools. Some scattered randomly over the suburban area. Others established new ethnic clusters in the suburbs, but even these rarely contained solely members of a single ethnic group. As a result, most middle-class neighborhoods—both in the suburbs and within central cities—have no distinctive ethnic character, except that they are white. (1968, 119)

Here, white upward mobility occurred through assimilation via absorption even as the existence of white ethnic enclaves are dismissed and the racial advantages of whiteness go unnamed.

The respondents in the six all-white organizations rarely mentioned housing issues on their own. I often introduced the topic to gauge their understanding. Once presented, additional prompts were unnecessary. For instance, in asking Harry (lawyer, age thirty-eight, six years in NEA) about his choice of where he bought his home, he responded,

> "Location, location, location," that's what they say right? . . . quality of schools and the resale value were primary considerations. [Author: "What about race?"] Well, yeah! That goes without saying. I live in a nearly all-white neighborhood and I wasn't going to even think about living in an integrated neighborhood. . . . I wanted to leave my doors unlocked and windows open sometimes. . . . you need a crime-free, white neighborhood to do that. . . . whites won't, I mean, they just won't . . . I mean, almost never break into your home.

Harry, a white nationalist, repeats a commonly held belief about crime and neighborhood racial composition and frames whites as essentially innocent and nearly incapable of housing break-in. Others employed varied racialized logics to rationalize their choice to live in all-white neighborhoods. A member of a white antiracist organization, Philip (store owner, age fifty-three, five years in WRJ) told me,

> I know how it works and I'm not going to throw away my money.... if there's any "white flight" in the neighborhood then my property value is going to drop.... I'm not going to move into an integrated neighborhood where that's likely to happen or is already happening.... I believe in integration, but I can't go broke.

Most of the white members of these six organizations evoked similar overt racially or economically motivated rationales as Harry and Philip. Quick to point out the supposed disadvantages of living close to people of color, they were unable to address the advantages that both lead to and result from all-white segregated housing, instead dismissing such dynamics as either fictitious or inconsequential. For instance, at a BSA meeting, members admitted that "housing integration" might "artificially deflate" the value of homes, making even whites who favor neighborhood integration to be motivated by economic disincentives, as Alda (receptionist, age twenty-one, one year in BSA) remarked,

> I'm starting out having just graduated [from Big State] last year, and all I can afford are homes in integrated neighborhoods ... but I'm going to wait to save to buy in a white neighborhood because I can't risk pouring money into a home that's going to lose money over time. I see a home as a place to live *and* [said with elongated emphasis] a financial investment, like a 401K.

I shortly thereafter remarked, "If the entrance of people of color into neighborhoods artificially deflates the value of homes, would not the entrance of white people into neighborhoods artificially inflate the value of homes, so that any resale profit is generated from racial exclusion and discrimination?" My comment was summarily dismissed:

BRANDI (retail sales, age twenty-one, one year in BSA): "I don't think I quite get it, I mean, so, home values are just home values. Integration brings them down from where they should be normally, based on the market, so, I mean, I don't think I see what you're saying."

JOEL (insurance sales, age thirty-five, twelve years in BSA): "That's not right.... In actuarial science there's no measure of white inflation of home values, so, I think, I mean, I'm sorry, but that just sounds like something that someone made up."

JOY (medical assistant, age thirty-four, seven years in BSA): "That's what I was thinking, 'cause there's no way white people just simply moving in makes the housing values magically jump up a few thousand dollars.... the market value is based on the worth of the home, not the worth of the people living in it."

AUTHOR: "So, how do the values of homes fall when black people move into them?"

JOEL: "That's different, I mean, yeah, that's because of discrimination, but that's what we're saying, it brings the value down from where it naturally is.... There's no white housing value inflation or whatever you want to call it."

*The Causality of White Racist Attitudes*
The Kerner report uses the logic that individual, racist whites (in their attitudes that drive their actions) are the culprit for housing segregation and black disadvantage. For instance, "Within the cities, Negroes have been excluded from white residential areas through discriminatory practices. Just as significant is the withdrawal of white families from, or their refusal to enter, neighborhoods where Negroes are moving or already residing" (1968, 6). Furthermore, the report reads,

> Their exclusion has been accomplished through various discriminatory practices, some obvious and overt, others subtle and

hidden. Deliberate efforts are sometimes made to discourage Negro families from purchasing or renting homes in all-white neighborhoods. Intimidation and threats of violence have ranged from throwing garbage on lawns and making threatening phone calls to burning crosses in yards and even dynamiting property. More often, real estate agents simply refuse to show homes to Negro buyers. (1968, 119)

In summarizing the relationship of race to housing, the report asserts that

> the concentration of Negroes in central cities results from a combination of forces. Some of these forces, such as migration and initial settlement patterns in older neighborhoods, are similar to those which affected previous ethnic minorities. Others—particularly discrimination in employment and segregation in housing and schools—are a result of white attitudes based on race and color. (1968, 120)

However, the "subtle and hidden" practices and exact operation of "white attitudes" are not specified. And when factors are mentioned, such as exclusionary zoning, the cause of those practices stems from white cognitive racial prejudice or ignorance rather than systemic practices, laws, customs, and habits. In these passages, the report renders invisible the mechanisms that promote white advantage and posits these dynamics as a normative (read nonracial) process. The specific factors that created and maintained the "ghetto"—such as southern farming industrialization that increased the pace of the black Great Migration to northern urban centers, banking-mortgage denials to blacks, sundown towns, restrictive covenants in white suburbs, and redlining—were all but ignored, or only cursorily mentioned.

With a logic dismissive of white overprivilege in housing segregation, members of all-white groups did acknowledge the maintenance of all-white neighborhoods, and cite white racist attitudes as causal. However, such nods to attitudes were decoupled from actual discriminatory practices. For instance, while attending a DOP meeting, I raised the topic of white-only Federal Housing Act (FHA) loans, redlining, steering, and other housing discrimination mechanisms and was told the following:

BIANCA (landscape architect, age thirty-eight, ten years in DOP): "Okay, I mean, sure that happened, but, still, that was the past, and how much of a legacy, or an effect, I mean, that's not making segregation today. That was then, this is now."

WENDY (public relations manager, age forty-three, three years in DOP): "That's right. That was back when Jim Crow was the law of the land. Housing discrimination doesn't happen anymore. . . . the laws have changed, even if attitudes haven't."

CHARLOTTE (tax accountant, age forty-four, eight years in DOP): "Yeah, that's sad but uh, that doesn't happen anymore, and besides, I, I, well, it's just, that you, you have to just work hard in the face of adversity, so, so, when people are committed enough, they can, can overcome. . . . I always remember this quotation from Frederick Douglass that uh, it goes something like, uh "The limits of tyrants are controlled by the endurance of the oppressed"[6] which, uh, means, uh, to me it means that you can't be oppressed any more than you let yourself. . . . if people want to really want to buy a house they can with a persistent attitude."

For many members, white racial attitudes (as a causal factor in the creation of segregated neighborhoods) could only exist in their most overt form. For instance, Mark (corporate sales, age thirty-three, seven years in WRJ) told me, "Sure, there are some crazy Nazis out there that oppose integration." Such logic was employed by Ian (firefighter, age thirty-nine, one year in LOBA): "If you're a white supremacist Klan member who is using racial slurs every day, sure, that kind of racist attitude is surely going

---

6. The actual quotation is "The limits of tyrants are prescribed by the endurance of those whom they oppress" (Douglass 1857).

to stop you from wanting a black person in your neighborhood... or would cause you to move if one moved in."

Akin to the Kerner report, members of these six organizations also told me that housing segregation, and the creation of all-white and majority nonwhite enclaves, was the result not only of bad intentions, but also of either nonracial factors or ignorance. For example, Faith (counselor, age thirty-three, five years in MAYEP) said this:

> I can admit that segregation occurs, but sometimes that's just normal.... Aren't there bound to be segregated neighborhoods from place to place, on average?... and just because some people are prejudiced, that doesn't mean that they going to act on it.... Let's be fair, segregation occurs because of a variety of nonracial factors... when there's what you call white flight then can't that happen out of ignorance rather than because of prejudice?... maybe whites leave neighborhoods that blacks are moving into because they don't know any better, rather than any kind of bad intention.

### Police-Community Relations

Police, and their relationship with communities of color, are mentioned frequently in the Kerner report and among the white ethnographic settings. Various racial logics are used to rationalize and legitimate an ideal form of white identity and behavior.

*Condemning Attitudes and Excusing Behavior*
The report places great emphasis on the racist attitudes of white law enforcement. Toward the beginning, the report addresses a then commonly held assertion: the police were merely a spark that lit the already assembled kindling of riot-ready urban spaces:

> The police are not merely a "spark" factor. To some Negroes police have come to symbolize white power, white racism, and white repression. And the fact is that many police do reflect and express these white attitudes. The atmosphere of hostility and cynicism is reinforced by a widespread belief among Negroes in the existence of police brutality and in a "double standard" of justice and protection—one for Negroes and one for whites. (1968, 5)

Such police attitudes were on par with how the Kerner report views white attitudes generally: "the most fundamental [cause] is the racial attitude of white Americans toward black Americans. Race prejudice has shaped our history decisively in the past; it now threatens to do so again. White racism is essentially responsible for the explosive mixture which has been accumulating in our cities since the end of World War II" (1968, 203).

However, the report does not blame police–African American tension on white racist attitudes among the police, or white racist attitudes more generally, but instead all of society: "The abrasive relationship between the police and minority communities has been a major—and explosive—source of grievance, tension, and disorder. The blame must be shared by the total society" (1968, 8). The report suggests resolution to this tension not through legislation but rather by administrative policy changes within police departments. This is a curious solution, given that the report's prior evocation of racism among "the total society" is to be somehow remedied by additional administrative changes amid already white-dominated police leadership.

Furthermore, the report often explains away or excuses white racist behaviors on the part of the police. Although white racist attitudes are the cause of discrimination for whites in general, the report suddenly provides another explanation for police: discrimination by police becomes the result of limited knowledge or a lack of adequate personnel. First, the supposed limited knowledge of police officers:

> In a number of cities, the Commission heard complaints of abuse from Negro adults of all social and economic classes. Particular resentment is aroused by harassing Negro men in the company of white women—often their light-skinned Negro wives. "Harassment" or discourtesy may not be the result of malicious or discriminatory intent of police offi-

cers. Many officers simply fail to understand the effects of their actions because of their limited knowledge of the Negro community. (1968, 159)

Here, "harassment" is destabilized with scare quotes and is assumed not "the result of malicious or discriminatory intent" but rather the "limited knowledge of the Negro community." The report is vague on what knowledge is needed to avoid an intersecting patriarchal-colorism-racial harassment. Second, the report addresses the supposed inadequacies of personnel to respond to African American complaints in a timely way:

> The strength of ghetto feelings about hostile police conduct may even be exceeded by the conviction that ghetto neighborhoods are not given adequate police protection. This belief is founded on two basic types of complaint. The first is that the police maintain a much less rigorous standard of law enforcement in the ghetto, tolerating there illegal activities like drug addiction, prostitution, and street violence that they would not tolerate elsewhere. The second is that police treat complaints and calls for help from Negro areas much less urgently than from white areas. . . . Recent studies have documented the inadequacies of police response in some ghetto areas. . . . In a United States Commission on Civil Rights study, a review of police communications records in Cleveland disclosed that police took almost four times as long to respond to calls concerning robbery from the Negro district as for the district where response was next slowest. The response time for some other crimes was at least twice as long. (1968, 161–62)

Even with this evidence that the Kerner report itself supplied, the report continues that

> Because a basic problem in furnishing protection to the ghetto is the shortage of manpower, police departments should review existing deployment of field personnel to ensure the most efficient use of manpower. The Police Task Force of the Crime Commission stressed the need "to distribute patrol officers in accordance with the actual need for their presence." Communities may have to pay for more and better policing for the entire community as well as for the ghetto. (1968, 162)

This response lays bare the logic of excusing the police from racism, and is clear that no shortage of manpower exists for districts that are not "Negro." Rather, the key is not whether police manpower is adequate, but how that manpower is unequally distributed across racialized communities. Once equally distributed, one could then accurately ascertain whether a manpower problem exists.

Across these six all-white organizations, members regularly asserted that the police hold attitudes that are unhelpful in their interactions with the public, and most expressed the belief that the attitudes of law enforcement toward people of color are worse than those toward whites. As Lisa (secretary, age thirty-six, two years in NEA) told me,

> Sure, the police are racist. I think they attract all kind of prejudiced people within their ranks. It's like saying, "Hey, want a badge, stick, and a gun with a license to go bully people without consequence? Here's your chance!" . . . only psychos are attracted to that offer. . . . but that's what the police do, I mean, I guess every cop is a little bit prejudiced, some more or less, but all together more than you'd find on average.

Akin to the Kerner report, along with the admission of the prejudicial attitudes of the police, many simultaneously remarked that racially biased law enforcement behavior toward people of color—particularly African Americans—is the product of underfunded precincts, inadequate numbers of officers employed in nonwhite areas, and low or inadequate standards for police training, rather than a systematic program predicated on racialized surveillance. For instance, in addressing the New York Police Department (NYPD) stop-and-frisk program (most active between 2003 and 2013), most members of these organizations were of one accord. Kam (waitress, age twenty-five, two years in BSA) stated, "Black people commit more crime than whites, that's just a fact.... some might think profiling isn't nice, but it works." Even the white antiracist member Duncan (corporate sales, age thirty, 2.5 years in WRJ) said,

> Yes, yes, yes, the police are racist. We know this.... at the same time, I think that it's fair to say that while there are racist cops, there are also criminals.... I think it's true that black people consume more drugs and commit more violent crimes than whites, so it's not a zero-sum game.... lots of police are racist and lots of black people engage in crime.

In the midst of the NYPD stop-and-frisk program, most research concluded that "Whites were stopped on suspicion of possessing a weapon at a rate lower than their weapon-possession arrest rate [while] Blacks were stopped on suspicion of possessing a weapon at a rate greater than their weapon-possession arrest rate" (Ridgeway 2007). Stop-and-frisk "generated a high volume of unproductive police stops that had little crime reduction benefit" (MacDonald, Fagan, and Geller 2016). The logic of white innocence and black guilt appeared to consistently trump facts about racism and policing.

This framing was rationalized via the logic that if people of color acted in more calm, disciplined, and obedient manner, then such prejudiced officers would not act on those prejudices. Joseph (lawyer, age fifty-two, twenty-eight years in BSA) explained it this way: "underneath those statistics are a lot of variables that are not measured, like one's attitude and disposition, you know?.... if black people didn't walk and talk like they do, I think there would be less of a problem." This stance was often bookended by a converse logic. In this second rationale, the racially prejudiced attitudes and behaviors of the police should be excused because they are simply ignorant of the norms, customs, and culture of communities of color. Hailey (lawyer, age sixty-one, thirty-one years in DOP) was adamant that

African Americans should be more patient with the police.... they need to work harder to educate them as to the differences in their culture.... maybe what a white cop thinks is threatening is to them [African Americans] a kind of posture or stance that means something else completely.... I don't see why they don't just sit down and talk about how their culture is with the police.... the police are so unfairly demonized and not appreciated for what they do.... I'm sure they would want to do some kind of training where they learn the different black norms so that they can better avoid the constant claims that they have done something "racist."

Similarly, Martin (grant writer, age forty-four, one year in LOBA) matter-of-factly remarked

> the police have different customs and so do black people.... if black people want to stop being harassed, and, I know, I agree it's not all fair or deserved, then, why don't their leaders tell the police about their different cultural differences." [Author: "How do you think this works with police of color? With black police officers?"]. I guess that [long pause], I think the cops just have a different culture, and most cops are white and so, you probably wouldn't have to teach black cops about the things they already know.

In both cases, the prejudicial attitudes and behaviors of the police are excused because of the implicit whiteness of the law. In the former, whiteness is not shown deference. People of color's actions are interpreted as strangely foreign and threatening; they must alter their behavior to bring them into a different focus under white eyes. In the latter, whiteness should be shown patience to learn how to clearly view racial Others through the opaque filter of nonwhite culture.

*Deracializing Internal Police White Supremacy*
The Kerner report finds disproportionate white administrative control within the police precincts where rioting had occurred. After identifying a systemic racial bias within policing, the report then reads, "In a number of cities,

particularly larger ones, police officials are not only willing but anxious to appoint Negro officers. There are obstacles other than discrimination. While these obstacles cannot readily be measured, they can be identified" (1968, 166). Here is an instance in which the report a priori assumes phenomena to be obstacles, but without evidence. That is, it is untenable to assume a phenomenon an obstacle to a goal without, first, measuring the concept and, second, gauging if the phenomenon functions as an obstacle. The report did neither. Nevertheless, the report continued to identify several nonracial "obstacles" to hiring black police officers:

> One is the relatively high standards for police employment. Another is pay; better qualified Negroes are often more attracted by other, better paying positions. Another obstacle is the bad image of police in the Negro community. There also are obstacles to promotion apart from discrimination, such as the more limited educational background of some Negro officers. (1968, 166)

Even if we assume the report's criteria (1 = high standards in policing; 2 = low pay in policing; 3 = bad images of the police, and 4 = limited educational backgrounds of African Americans) are in fact real obstacles to hiring black police officers, never does the Kerner report explain first, how or why the high standards function in a racialized pattern to exclude blacks but include whites. This first point is even more puzzling when considering the report's own discovery of particularly low standards of performance and behavior among white police officers. Second, the report is silent on how or why low pay attracts whites rather than blacks to policing. Third, the report does not address how or why the bad images function as an exclusionary mechanism. Fourth, the report fails to examine why or whether limited educational backgrounds limit black police participation, especially in lieu of low educational levels among already employed white police officers. Moreover, even if these supposed obstacles were overcome, the report never addresses how the hiring of black officers would result in their promotion and rise in the ranks to become leaders and administrators within policing. Overall, the double standards identified by "the Negro community" find reproduction in the Kerner report's discussion of those same double standards. In the end, systemic white supremacy in police hierarchies is left both unexamined and unchallenged.

Rarely was the internal racial dynamics of police mentioned across the six all-white groups. However, four police officers were members in three of the organizations. Paige (age thirty-four, five years in MAYEP), Micah (age twenty-five, four years in BSA), Robert (age thirty-four, five years in NEA) and Paul (age forty-nine, five years in NEA). They spoke bluntly when I interviewed them. Paige informed me, "I've never had a supervisor who wasn't white." When I asked her why, she responded, "I think because law enforcement gets such a bad rap, that a black or Latino captain would be biased toward other white officers . . . they would try to overcorrect." Micah, who majored in criminology and dreamed of being a police officer, remarked,

> We have a hard time recruiting people of color to be police . . . and it's not for everyone. . . . there's a lot of racist jokes in policing culture. . . . I don't think black or Latino supervisors happen often for that reason [Author: "What reason?"] Comfort. Fit. I guess there's some bias, but, I mean, [laughing] where isn't there?

The two white nationalist police officers (Robert and Paul) were the most adamant. After multiple conversations about confidentiality and a couple no-so-veiled threats that they, as police officers, could "make my life difficult," they told me the following as we sat in the corner of a bar in a Washington, D.C., suburb:

PAUL: "There are plenty of us [white nationalists] in law enforcement . . . local, state, federal. We've always been there. I'm not going to let some Afro American into my department if I can do anything about it . . . sure as hell are not going to get promoted."
ROBERT: "I feel the same. Look, we're being honest and you want to know so, . . . white people are genetically, the most civilized and intelligent. . . . white civilization has to

be defended and so many white people, like you, sorry, but you asked, are diluting and selling out our people. . . . other races need to be kept in check and stopped from corrupting white culture. . . we invented a culture of law and order."

PAUL: "Well put."

For these police officers, the law defends civilization and civilization is white. Although Paige and Micah would have shunned the white nationalist label, they evoked a similar logic.

## DISCUSSION: HOW FAR HAVE WE COME?

In addition to the Kerner report discourse and ethnographic case studies, the online appendix to this article[7] outlines the larger trends of racial logics related to employment, education, and housing.[8] Drawn from the General Social Survey, such generalizable data—held in companion with the explanatory data from the content and ethnographic analyses—indicates the resiliency of white comfort with both the racial logics we might deem racist or white supremacist as well as deeply unequal and segregated conditions (Smith et al. 2017; compare Homans 1974). For example, although housing segregation across all racial groups in major U.S. metropoles has declined over the past century, levels of black-white housing segregation remain significantly high (on the overall decline, Massey and Tannen 2015; on high black-white rates, Lichter, Parisi, and Taquino 2015). Recent white retreats into ever more racially homogenous suburbs exacerbates such segregation (Logan and Zhang 2011). Answering the question of "How far have we come?" requires that we both temper optimism and abandon untenable teleological assumptions about the supposed decline of racial consequence and instead engage with the "homeostatic principle of the entire system of racial domination" (Patterson 1989, 480).

## What Worked and What Did Not Work?

Since 1968, rollback and attack on the most progressive policies, laws, and practices the Kerner report suggests have been considerable. For instance, the report proposed six million new and existing housing units between 1968 and 1973 for low- and moderate-income families (targeting African American families). These were never realized. The report also suggested a "comprehensive and enforceable federal open housing law to cover the sale or rental of all housing" (1968, 13), partially realized two months later in the FHA (part of Title VIII of the Civil Rights Act of 1968). However, even with the 1989 amendments to the act,[9] the FHA provides few tools to compel compliance and relies on aggrieved home-seekers to file complaints with the U.S. Department of Housing and Urban Development (HUD) and then sue if HUD fails to obtain "voluntary compliance."[10] The orientation of such laws, like the FHA, places the recognition of discrimination, burden of evidence, and related costs on the racial underclass.

Among the dominant racial class, such laws assume an increasing desire for, and willingness to pursue, integration and equality. The white worldviews culled from the ethnographic data (and in the online appendix) indicate such assumptions are unfounded. Since 1990, an average of 25 percent of white U.S. residents op-

---

7. Available at: https://www.rsfjournal.org/doi/suppl/10.7758/RSF.2018.4.6.04.

8. Eduardo Bonilla-Silva writes, "Traditional survey research is rooted in methodological individualism and assumes that racial beliefs are pathological (that is, that 'racists' are ignorant or crazy people). . . . In contrast, the racial ideology paradigm is rooted in the notion that the races constitute different social groups with distinct interests, and interprets the ideas, views, and affects of actors on racial matters as their social representations of how the world is and how it ought to be" (2003, 78). I see the General Social Survey research as representative of white groupness and white racial interests rather than an aggregate of individual attitudes.

9. Amendments extended the time to file housing discrimination complaints, covered attorney's fees and court costs for prevailing plaintiffs, and empowered judges to award greater compensation.

10. The Fair Housing Act mirrored the language of the Kerner report's suggestions that parties engage in desegregation via "voluntary community action" (1968, 263).

pose living in a neighborhood where half of the neighbors are black (see table 3B in the online appendix). Additionally, in 1968, the homeownership rate for African Americans was approximately 42 percent. Fifty years later, in January 2018, it remains at 42 percent, thirty points behind the white homeownership rate of 73 percent (which saw modest gains over the same period).[11] Here we see a reproductive feedback loop; white worldviews are both product and producer of hypersegregated white spaces. Many of the Kerner report's proposals were doomed because they relied on white efforts to voluntarily desegregate but took few actions to break apart the segregated white spaces that incubate white worldviews.[12]

## What Are the Implications for the Twenty-First Century?

The Kerner report's discussion of whiteness and the ethnographic case studies together reveal how racialized logics supportive of inequality and segregation in employment, education, housing, and policing continue to resonate with whites over the past half-century. What might first appear as arbitrary lines in a government report or atomistic attitudes from various actors are, when aggregated and analyzed, illustrative of deep-seated and "commonsensed" white racial logics. The preceding analysis gestures toward a sobering conclusion: we will not have effective policies or practices to address racial inequality and segregation in so long as these logics remain dominant. Together, these nine themes reveal several core presuppositions that must be dislodged to address racial inequality and segregation in the twenty-first century.

First, the two themes of "the blackness of the culture of poverty" and "deracializing internal police white supremacy" reveal the inference of antiblackness via beliefs in dysfunctional, abnormal, and criminal values and behavior. Consider the Kerner report's descriptive section titled "The Jungle" or the preceding passage that reads "many ghetto children spend the bulk of their time on the streets.... The image of success in this world is not that of the 'solid citizen,'... but rather that of the 'hustler' who promotes his own interests by exploiting others" (1968, 129).[13] Such condescending language, coupled with the strategic omission of white behaviors that pursue "interests by exploiting others," is also witnessed in contemporary white worldviews. Judgmental condescension and paternalism—what the sociologist W. E. B. Du Bois aptly described as being measured "by the tape of a world that looks on in amused contempt and pity" (1903, 7)—leaves public policy and legal recommendations to address racial inequality and segregation bereft: as long the state treats people of color as less than solid citizens, good faith policies, laws, and practices are not possible.

The themes of "white normativity in education," "the innocence of everyday white people," "causality of white racist attitudes," and "condemning attitudes and excusing behavior" together indicate the second presupposition of white normativity—the taken-for-granted ideas and practices that make whiteness appear natural, logical, and moral. If the "primary goal must be a single society, in which every citizen will be free to live and work according to his capabilities and desires, not his color," then assimilation is the report's recommended method to achieve that goal (1968, 11). As long as policies and laws rely on black engagement with assimilation to prove their worth via the acquisition of the prerequisite skills, education, and cultural mores somehow deemed appropriate, the United States moves not toward equality, but masks an iron first of domination within a velvet glove of paternalism.

---

11. In March 2018, HUD Secretary Ben Carson moved to strike the word *inclusive* and the phrase *free from discrimination* from HUD's mission statement, indicating further rollbacks of HUD Fair Housing Act enforcement.

12. Recall Senator Walter Mondale's 1967 comments, a month after the Kerner Commission was established, that exhibited faith in white people to engage in fair housing: "I think that there is a crucial debate under way in American ghettos, and that debate involves a dispute about the basic decency of white America" (U.S. Congress 1967, 2).

13. The sociologist Steven Steinberg contends that the Kerner report is "a white document, written by white writers, and aimed at a white audience—*about* [emphasis in original] black people" (2007, 93).

In this vein, the Kerner report presents "three choices open to the Nation" (1968, 10). The first is the "present policies choice" in which the United States would stay the course and endure a continuation of riots and inequality. Second, the "enrichment choice" (or the "gilding the ghetto" option) calls for federally backed manpower training and expanded War on Poverty programs to develop black capitalism and abandon racial integration. Third is the "integration choice" in which residential and educational segregation were identified as key limitations toward black employment opportunities and central variables increasing the likelihood of rioting. Favoring the third option, the report dismisses the second option: "This premise has been vigorously advocated by Black Power proponents. . . . This argument is understandable, but there is a great deal of evidence that it is unrealistic" (1968, 223). Hence, the report calls for "policies which will encourage Negro movement out of central city areas" (1968, 10), ostensibly to assist in black integration into white-dominated neighborhoods, schools, jobs, and police forces. However, in 2018, just as in 1968, such assimilation is resisted, implemented half-heartedly or not at all, and ill equipped to offer equal access to resources.

The third presupposition is white entitlement. Revealed in both the content analysis and ethnographic data, whites are rarely expected to change their behaviors. The themes of "white ignorance and messianic import," "white control of resources," and "black underprivilege without white overprivilege" show a concerted effort to label some whites as racist bad apples or alternatively to issue a vague condemnation of white society. Rarely are white practices, or institutions (that benefit whites to the exclusion of people of color), specifically identified for either divestment or demolition. Refusal to both name and remove white domination in corporations, universities, courts, political bodies, cultural life, and other social collectives warrants their continuation. Neither equality nor integration are possible so long as policy and law refrains from asking "whither whiteness?"

What could be done differently? The United States cannot effectively redress discrimination, segregation, and inequality until recognition of the interrelated impact of antiblackness, white normativity, and white entitlement. Without confronting these central presuppositions, discrimination appears irrational and atypical rather than systematically methodical and banal. To confront these primary traditions systematically, antidiscrimination laws would be proactive rather than remedial, attuned to conditions rather than individually focused, and counterhegemonic. That is, rather than waiting for individuals to recognize and report overt discrimination, laws would actively search for violations, immediately dismantle the hypersegregated white spaces that rationalize and legitimate discrimination, and have broader reach in combating hate-speech and antiblack propaganda. I am skeptical of such an orientation without a new constitutional convention; the United States will fail to either systematically sanction or change discrimination and segregation because such proposals may run afoul of the First Amendment. Without such a radical departure, the United States will have more riots, more reports, and fewer results.

## CONCLUSION

The article has addressed, first, how the Kerner report described the intersection of whites with education, employment, housing, and police-community relations, and, second, how whites today across geographic areas, political persuasions, and socioeconomic divides make meaning of their intersection with these four areas. It has demonstrated the existence of specific racial logics in both the Kerner report and the ethnographic data. Such racialized reasoning legitimates white advantage and appears stable and robust over both space (varied all-white locales) and time (between 1968 and 2018).

In light of this analysis, future research on both state reports and modern white-dominated organizations would be well served to focus on variations in racialized logics, their common denominators, and the contexts of racial homogeneity and homophily that may constrain or enable the rationalization and legitimation of those logics. We know little about the precise reproductive mechanisms within the feedback loop between logics and conditions. Without more attention to how intersubjectively shared racial logics create path dependencies of action and order (particularly toward the promotion of specific white racial interests), and how unequal and segregated white spaces promote the creation, maintenance, and defense of racial logics, social science runs the risk of missing the key apparatus and social processes by which larger inequities reproduce. With more knowledge of social reproduction in the commonplace ways of speaking and interacting, we can better understand (and possibly dismantle) the logics and spaces that function as co-constitutive barriers to practices, policies, and laws to address inequality and segregation.

## REFERENCES

Altheide, David L., and Christopher J. Schneider. 2013. *Qualitative Media Analysis*. Thousand Oaks, Calif.: Sage Publications.

Anderson, Elijah. 2015. "The White Space." *Sociology of Race and Ethnicity* 1(1): 10–21.

Blumer, Herbert. 1954. "What Is Wrong with Social Theory?" *American Sociological Review* 19(1): 3–10.

Boger, John Charles. 1992. "Race and the American City: The Kerner Commission in Retrospective—An Introduction." *North Carolina Law Review* 71: 1290–350.

Bonilla-Silva, Eduardo. 2003. "Racial Attitudes or Racial Ideology? An Alternative Paradigm for Examining Actors' Racial Views." *Journal of Political Ideologies* 8(1): 63–82.

Calmore, John O. 1992. "Spatial Equality and the *Kerner Commission Report*: A Back-to-the-Future Essay." *North Carolina Law Review* 71: 1487–518.

Carter, Gregg Lee. 1990. "Black Attitudes and the 1960s Black Riots: An Aggregate-Level Analysis of the Kerner Commission's '15 Cities' Data." *Sociological Quarterly* 31(2): 269–86.

Douglass, Frederick. 1857. "West India Emancipation." Speech delivered August 3, 1857, Canandaigua, New York. Accessed April 24, 2018. http://rbscp.lib.rochester.edu/4398.

Du Bois, W. E. B. 1903. *The Souls of Black Folk*. Chicago: A.C. McClurg & Co.

Fogelson, Robert M., Gordon S. Black, and Michael Lipsky. 1969. "Review Symposium Report of the National Advisory Commission on Civil Disorders." *American Political Science Review* 63(4): 1269–81.

Homans, George. 1974. *The Nature of Social Science*. New York: Harcourt, Brace and World, Inc.

Hughey, Matthew W. 2018a. "Of Riots and Racism: Fifty Years since the Best Laid Schemes of the Kerner Commission (1968–2018)." *Sociological Forum* 39(3). DOI: 10.1111/socf.12436.

———. 2018b. "Schrödinger's Whiteness." *Contexts* 17(2): 17–19.

Jackson, Ronald L., II. 1999. "White Space, White Privilege: Mapping Discursive Inquiry into the Self." *Quarterly Journal of Speech* 85(1): 38–54.

Johnson, James H., and Walter C. Farrell Jr. 1992. "The Fire This Time: The Genesis of the Los Angeles Rebellion of 1992." *North Carolina Law Review* 71: 1403–20.

Kerner Commission. 1968. *Report of the National Advisory Commission on Civil Disorders*. Washington: Government Printing Office.

Lichter, Daniel T., Domenico Parisi, and Michael C. Taquino. 2015. "Toward a New Macro-Segregation? Decomposing Segregation Within and Between Metropolitan Cities and Suburbs." *American Sociological Review* 80(4): 843–73.

Lipsky, Michael. 1971. "Social Scientists and the Riot Commission." *Annals of the American Academy of Political and Social Science* 394(1): 72–78.

Lipsky, Michael, and David J. Olson. 1977. *Commission Politics: The Processing of Racial Crisis in America*. New Brunswick, N.J.: Transaction Books.

Loessberg, Rick. 2017. "Two Societies: The Writing of the Summary of the Report of the National Advisory Commission on Civil Disorders." *Journal of Urban History* DOI: 10.1177/0096144216689087. Accessed April 24, 2018. http://journals.sagepub.com/doi/abs/10.1177/0096144216689087.

Logan, John, and Wenquan Zhang. 2011. "Global Neighborhoods: New Evidence from Census 2010." New York: Russell Sage Foundation and American Communities Project of Brown University.

MacDonald, John, Jeffrey Fagan, and Amanda Geller. 2016. "The Effects of Local Police Surges on Crime and Arrests in New York City." *PLoS ONE* 11(6): e0157223. DOI: 10.1371/journal.pone.0157223.

Marx, Gary. 1970. "Two Cheers for the National Riot (Kerner) Commission Report." In *Black Ameri-*

cans: A Second Look,* edited by J. F. Szwed. New York: Basic Books.

Massey, Douglas S., and Jonathan Tannen. 2015. "A Research Note on Trends in Black Hypersegregation." *Demography* 52(3): 1025–34.

Moore, Wendy Leo. 2008. *Reproducing Racism: White Space, Elite Law Schools, and Racial Inequality.* Lanham, Md.: Rowman & Littlefield.

Patterson, Orlando. 1989. "Toward a Study of Black America." *Dissent Magazine* Fall 1989: 476–86.

Reed, Adolph, Jr. 2017. "The Kerner Commission and the Irony of Antiracist Politics." *Labor: Studies in Working-Class History of the Americas* 14(4): 3–38.

Ridgeway, Greg. 2007. *Analysis of Racial Disparities in the New York Police Department's Stop, Question, and Frisk Practices.* Santa Monica, Calif.: RAND Corporation.

Rosenbaum, James, Nancy Fishman, Alison Brett, and Patricia Meaden. 1992. "Can the Kerner Commission's Housing Strategy Improve Employment, Education, and Social Integration for Low-Income Blacks." *North Carolina Law Review* 71: 1519–56.

Smith, Tom W., Peter V. Marsden, Jeremy Freese, and Michael Hout. 2017. *General Social Survey, 1972–2016.* [Machine-readable data file]. Principal Investigator, Tom W. Smith; Co-Principal Investigator, Peter V. Marsden; Co-Principal Investigator, Michael Hout; Sponsored by National Science Foundation, Chicago: National Opinion Research Center at the University of Chicago [producer and distributor].

*Social Service Review.* 1968. "The Kerner Commission Report." 42(2): 261–63.

Steinberg, Steven. 2007. *Race Relations: A Critique.* Stanford, Calif.: Stanford University Press.

Stoesz, David. 1992. "Poor Policy: The Legacy of the Kerner Commission for Social Welfare." *North Carolina Law Review* 71: 1675–91.

U.S. Congress. Senate Committee on Banking and Currency. 1967. *Fair Housing Act of 1967: Hearings Before the Subcommittee on Housing and Urban Affairs.* 90th Cong., 1st sess., August 21–23, 1967.

# Measuring the Distance: The Legacy of the Kerner Report

RICK LOESSBERG AND JOHN KOSKINEN

On its release in 1968, the Kerner report, with its "two societies" warning, was the subject of intense public attention. However, within a year, concerns arose that the report's influence was limited and that its recommendations were not being implemented. This perception has not changed noticeably since then. Fifty years later, it is important to accurately assess the report's legacy and whether the nation has avoided becoming two societies. It has become clear, however, that the report has been implemented more than previously thought and that it has been and continues to be influential. It has also been determined that despite progress toward eliminating the disparity between blacks and whites, it has unfortunately not yet been as extensive as is needed.

**Keywords:** urban policy, racial discrimination, public policy, civil rights, African American socioeconomic status, riots

> We know more than we understand. We understand more than we can explain.
>
> —Claude Bernard

It has now been fifty years since the Kerner report (the 1968 account of the National Advisory Commission on Civil Disorders, see Kerner Commission) sought to provide a traumatized nation with answers as to why the rioting of 1967 occurred. Its unequivocal conclusion, that discrimination—not radicals, riffraff, or a conspiracy—had been responsible for the rioting and its pointed warning that America was moving toward "two societies, one white, one black—separate and unequal" instantly focused the nation's attention on race and the conditions of the inner city as no other governmental report had ever done. Newspapers led with headlines of "White Racism Blamed in Riots," network television devoted special coverage to the report, and the public rushed to purchase copies of it (Lipsky and Olson 1977). By the end of its first month, more people had bought copies of it than the Warren Commission report on the assassination of President Kennedy during that report's first month (Raymont 1968). Within three months, 1.6 million copies of the Kerner report had been sold (Lipsky and Olson 1977).

Yet, even on the report's first anniversary,

**Rick Loessberg** is director of planning and development for Dallas County, Texas. **John Koskinen** was commissioner of the Internal Revenue Service.

© 2018 Russell Sage Foundation. Loessberg, Rick, and John Koskinen. 2018. "Measuring the Distance: The Legacy of the Kerner Report." *RSF: The Russell Sage Foundation Journal of the Social Sciences* 4(6): 99–119. DOI: 10.7758/RSF.2018.4.6.05. Please direct correspondence to: Rick Loessberg at rloessberg@dallascounty.org, 411 Elm St., 3rd Floor, Dallas, TX 75202.

Open Access Policy: *RSF: The Russell Sage Foundation Journal of the Social Sciences* is an open access journal. This article is published under a Creative Commons Attribution-NonCommercial-NoDerivs 3.0 Unported License.

**Table 1.** Kerner Commission Interviewees

| Individual | Position | Year(s) Interviewed |
|---|---|---|
| Fred Harris | Commission member | 2015 |
| Victor Palmieri | Deputy executive director | 2015, 2017 |
| David Chambers | Special assistant to executive director | 2015, 2017 |
| John Koskinen | Special assistant to deputy executive director | 2015, 2017 |
| Robert Shellow | Assistant deputy director–research | 2016 |
| Dick Nathan | Associate director for program research | 2015, 2017 |
| Gary Marx | Consultant–research staff | 2016, 2017 |
| Jay Kriegel | Assistant to commission vice chairman | 2015, 2017 |
| Peter Goldmark | Assistant to commission vice chairman | 2015, 2017 |
| Herbert Gans | Consultant | 2017 |
| Jack Rosenthal | Special consultant | 2015 |

*Source:* Author's compilation.

many of its supporters were already concerned that the report's influence was limited and that its many recommendations were being ignored (Herbers 1969). Successive years and accounts have not changed this perception noticeably (Lipsky and Olson 1977; Lupo 2011; Zelizer 2016). Many excellent efforts have been undertaken to determine whether the country has been successful in avoiding becoming two societies (Bernstein 1995; Shapiro, Meschede, and Osoro 2013; Goodman, Zhu, and Pendall 2017). However, because of the complexity of this task, these efforts are frequently only able to concentrate on a particular aspect or characteristic, such as wealth inequality (De La Cruz et al. 2018), rather than provide an overall assessment. This matter is further complicated when some areas (such as the incidence of poverty) show noticeable improvement and others (such as the ratio of black unemployment to white unemployment) virtually no change.

Fifty years is a point at which we often assess the significance of a career, a movie, or a marriage. What then is the legacy of the Kerner report? To what extent has it been influential or implemented? To what extent have we made progress since 1968? And what do the people who were responsible for writing the report believe?

For a report that sought to explain the origins of a horrendous wave of destruction and to understand the nature of race in this country (a country that has become even more racially diverse since 1968), these questions deserve to be answered. Given that three-fourths of the nation's present population was not yet born when the Kerner report was written and so may not understand how troubling 1967 was (NBC said in a documentary at the time that the nation was "in the worst crisis we have known since the Civil War") or appreciate how things may or may not have changed, this determination is even more critical.

This article seeks to address these issues. To do so, the authors have taken their direct personal knowledge and combined it with recent interviews with other Kerner Commission participants (see table 1). They have also extensively reviewed the status of many of the report's recommendations, researched what happened to other presidential reports from the same era, and examined the many ways a government report can be influential. Because statistics do not and cannot tell the entire story—we sometimes forget that data represent actual people—they have supplemented this research with interviews of African Americans from across the country to see how they view America and how that view compares with what they (or their parents) may have held fifty years ago.[1]

---

1. Twenty African Americans were interviewed for this article with the assurance that their identities would remain confidential. They were all friends of the authors or friends of friends. Most the authors have known well for at least ten years, and most are bankers, lawyers, accountants, engineers, and administrators. They have lived

What emerges from this effort is a view that may surprise some—a report that is more influential that what has been commonly thought—and an increased understanding of what has transpired for black Americans over the past five decades.

## THE KERNER COMMISSION'S DECISION-MAKING PROCESS

Public opinion polls presently disclose that the nation is now as politically divided as it has been at any time since 1968, and therefore it is especially important to look into how a report dealing with a matter as sensitive as race could be unanimous and so bold. It is even more significant given that at the time little indicated that this would occur. According to Tom Wicker, the eleven-member Kerner Commission had "seemed an unpromising group" when first appointed, and the conclusions of previous riot panel reports had generally been considered underwhelming (Kerner Report 1968; Platt 1971; Lupo 2011). The complexity of the task before the commission also did not lead one to believe that the outcome of this group would be any different, John Kenneth Galbraith remarking that, instead of appointing a commission on rioting and calling for a national day of prayer as President Lyndon Johnson had done, "it might have been more constructive to establish a commission on prayer and declare a national day of rioting" (Rosenthal 1969). Yet, through a combination of urgency, commitment, respect, and skillful management, the commission overcame these obstacles and produced a surprisingly forceful and comprehensive report.

One of the most important decisions that led to the development of such a report was the early decision by David Ginsburg, the commissioner's executive director, that the commission be given every paragraph of every draft section, that these would be read aloud, and that the commission would not move onto the next section until agreement was reached or the section had been sent back for revisions. This brilliant brick-by-brick strategy allowed the commission to focus on the matter at hand, enabled the report to become the commission's rather than the staff's, and eliminated the need to have a final vote on the entire report (Loessberg 2017).

Previous accounts of the commission's work and recent interviews with commission participants indicate that the major disagreements that arose among commission members were not over what was the cause of the rioting, but on semantics and what should be done to prevent future rioting. Commission members Fred Harris, John Lindsay, Roy Wilkins, and Otto Kerner were usually supportive of more ambitious proposals; fellow members I. W. Abel, William McCulloch, Katharine Peden, and Charles Thornton were typically more concerned about their costs or political realities. The commission's remaining members—Herbert Jenkins, James Corman, and Edward Brooke—moved between the two primary groups depending on the issue. With many key matters decided on six-to-five votes, the respect that commission members showed one another allowed them to proceed under what was a very short schedule and to subsequently adopt a unanimous final report (Loessberg 2017).[2]

---

in or are from states as far west as Nevada and Arizona; as far south as Louisiana, Mississippi, and Florida; as far east as Washington, D.C.; and as far north as New York and Ohio. Although this population obviously does not constitute a randomly drawn sample, the authors believe their views on discrimination and whether there has been progress since 1968 are nonetheless significant. All of the interviewees are professional in both occupation and appearance. Yet, they can all cite recent instances of encountering some type of discrimination or social slight. Most are also the first members of their family to have a college education or to firmly become part of the black middle class. Because many of their siblings and childhood friends have not experienced the same success, they understand that their success is still unique and was not preordained.

2. Under the instructions issued by President Johnson on the creation of the commission, it was to make an interim report in seven months by March 1, 1968, and a final report five months later. Given the complexity and the enormity of the assignment, delivering a final report in twelve months was already going to require significant effort. However, in December 1967, factors beyond the commission's control led to a decision to eliminate the interim report and to shorten the schedule for the final report even further to March 1, 1968. Some speculated

However, for all of this skill, hard work, and courtesy, it was not until the very end that it became clear that the report would be unanimous. As commission member Fred Harris noted, despite elements in the report that some members may not have liked (such as its call for new taxes), not to have had a unanimous report when the nation seemed to be in crisis would have been "a catastrophe."[3] Such an attitude is in marked contrast to today, when one needs not just to win, but to win only on one's terms.

## The Status of "Two Societies"

The Kerner report's warning that the nation was moving toward two societies is perhaps one of the most vivid and best-remembered phrases of any governmental report. Even without any other description or supporting data, the phrase instantly produces a stark picture of what the commission found.

The origination of this phrase can be credited to Jack Rosenthal, who wrote much of the report's narrative. In a chapter titled "The Future of the Cities," Rosenthal used similar wording ("the nation is rapidly moving toward two increasingly separate Americas") to describe the suburbanization of employment opportunities and the white population under way at the time. He used it to emphasize the increasing geographic and economic separation of blacks and whites, but other Kerner staff, principally Jay Kriegel and Peter Goldmark, recognized the powerful potential of the phrase, polished it, and incorporated into the report's widely read summary (Loessberg 2017).

In using this phrase, the commission was not implying that the nation had once been "a single society" and was now in danger of losing this distinction—the report's chapter on the history of racism in America, which was based on information provided by African American historian John Hope Franklin, makes this quite clear. Rather, it was using the phrase to express its findings and its concerns.

The report did not just rely on the evocative phrase to make its case about the status of blacks; it invoked numerous statistics across a variety of subject areas—housing, life expectancy, income, educational attainment, and so on—to demonstrate that black America was substantially different from white America. Re-

---

at the time and since then that this was an effort to cut short the individual city investigations or to rush through a final report without consideration of alternative drafts. The reality is much more straightforward. In early December, the commission's executive director (David Ginsburg), his deputy executive director (Victor Palmieri), and the special assistant to the deputy executive director (John Koskinen) were called to the White House to meet with Bureau of the Budget (now the Office of Management and Budget) Director Charles Shultz. Shultz explained that the commission had been funded to that point out of the $1 million emergency fund of the president. Those funds were nearing depletion, and the planned supplemental budget request to Congress, which normally occurred in December, would not be made. Shultz did not explain in detail why, but President Johnson at the time was struggling to fund both "guns and butter." In this case, he was anxious to continue to fund domestic social programs at the same time funding was provided for the Vietnam War and anticipated that a supplemental appropriation request would trigger a public debate about the strains on the budget. In any event, the message from Shultz was that the commission would get no more direct funding and that the staff would have to work with other agencies—such as the departments of Defense; Commerce; and Health, Education, and Welfare—to fund specific commission projects. Clearly, this meant that the work that had begun on an interim report would now be focused on a single, final report that would have to be completed in the next few weeks. Palmieri and Koskinen soon held a meeting with the Kerner Commission staff, which by that time included more than two hundred people, in mid-December to advise them that most of them would not be employed after the end of the year. Although the decision not to seek a supplemental appropriation created significant stress for the commission and its staff, the final result of a single report that was focused on the nature of the problem no doubt had a much more significant impact than two reports separated by five or six months would have had. And, although no one knew it at the time, the riots that erupted after Martin Luther King's assassination in April 1968 further sharpened focus on the commission report and its finding that the country was moving toward two societies, separate and unequal.

3. Fred Harris, interview with Rick Loessberg, May 26, 2015.

**Table 2.** Educational Attainment and Economic Characteristics

|  | 1968 | 2015 |
|---|---|---|
| Blacks with high school diploma or GED | 30.1 | 84.8 |
| Whites with high school diploma or GED | 55.0 | 88.8 |
| Blacks with college degree | 4.3 | 20.3 |
| Whites with college degree | 11.1 | 31.8 |
| Black families in poverty | 32.4 | 21.6 |
| White families in poverty | 8.4 | 8.3 |
| Ratio of black unemployment to white unemployment | 2.15 | 2.29 |
| Ratio of black household med income to white household med income | 0.61 | 0.62 |

*Source:* Author's compilation based on 1968 Current Population Reports, 1969 Current Population Reports, 1974 Current Population Reports, 2011–2015 American Community Survey, 2015 Bureau of Labor Statistics, 2015 American Community Survey.
*Note:* All numbers in percentages except ratios.

visiting these same statistics fifty years later, as well as several other indices, some improvements are especially noticeable. Life expectancy, for instance, has increased dramatically for blacks, from 64.1 years in 1969 to 75.5 in 2013 and is now only 4.6 years less than that for whites (in 1969, the difference was almost eight years).

Significant progress has also been made in closing the educational attainment gap between blacks and whites. As shown in table 2, blacks now complete high school at almost the same rate as whites, and whereas whites once had a college education rate that was three times greater than that of blacks, the difference is now only about one-third.

With this increase in education has come a noticeable decline in the poverty rate for black families. More important, the black middle class has expanded and is now almost proportionate to the black population's relationship to the nation (Pew Research Center 2015).[4] Paul Jargowsky, who has studied housing patterns and the concentration of poverty, notes that we now "have a very robust black middle class" and that you "don't have to look at the data . . . it is there to see."[5] Similarly, Robert Shellow, who oversaw the commission's field data analysis, points to a "huge surge of blacks in the middle class."[6] Accompanying this growth in the black middle class has been an increase in the percentage of blacks holding white-collar jobs. In 1972, for instance, only 34.8 percent of blacks were employed in such positions. By 2006, however, this figure had risen to 49.5 percent (Ware and Davis 2012).

Unfortunately, as shown in table 3, not all of the benefits associated with improved education have readily translated to other economic advancement. Black median income is still only about 60 percent of whites', and the black unemployment rate continues to remain twice that of whites. The homeownership rate for blacks is basically unchanged, and the relative median value of their home has changed only marginally.

One area, though, where positive change has begun to occur is in the residential patterns of urban America. At the time of Kerner, neighborhoods were highly segregated. In 1970, it was estimated that 79 percent of either the black or white population in most cities would have to move for the proportion of blacks and whites in a city's census tracts to be representative (Logan and Stults 2011); when blacks began moving into white neighborhoods, whites often ha-

---

4. In this instance, middle class is defined as those households whose incomes fall into the middle of three tiers and is equal to at least two-thirds of the nation's median household income and no greater than twice this amount.

5. Paul Jargowsky, interview with Rick Loessberg. June 29, 2017.

6. Robert Shellow, interview with Rick Loessberg. March 23, 2016.

**Table 3.** Housing Characteristics

|  | 1970 | 2015 |
|---|---|---|
| Black households owning | 41.6% | 42.2 % |
| White households owning | 62.9 | 67.0 |
|  | 1968 | 2015 |
| Ratio of black median home value to white median home value | 0.62 | 0.69 |

*Source:* Author's compilation based on 1970 Census of Housing, 1973 Annual Housing Survey, 2000 Census, 2011–2015 American Community Survey, 2015 American Housing Survey, Collins and Margo 2001.

rassed their new neighbors or seemingly moved out en masse (Rothstein 2017).

However, according to research from a variety of sources, although segregation continues, "most neighborhoods are becoming more diverse" (Farrell and Lee 2011). For example, although in 1960 nearly 50 percent of the black population lived in neighborhoods where they made up at least 80 percent of the residents, in 2010, only 20 percent did (Glaeser and Vigdor 2012). Not surprisingly, the percentage of the black or white population in 2010 that would have to move to achieve a proportional distribution had fallen to 59 percent (Logan and Stults 2011).

Such an improvement holds several important long-term consequences. First, it appears that much of the integration has involved African Americans leaving older, more segregated, cities for the suburbs and for relatively newer Sunbelt cities (Glaeser and Vigdor 2012; Lee, Iceland, and Sharp 2012). Given that suburbs and the Sunbelt often have more employment opportunities and better school systems, such integration should help reduce the continuing black-white economic disparity. This change also apparently reflects a significant cultural and attitudinal shift, in that 64 percent of white Americans said in 1972 that homeowners should be allowed to racially discriminate when selling their homes (Bobo et al. 2012).

Another area showing important progress is the rise of black elected officials. Although the Kerner Commission was clearly concerned about the sense of powerlessness it detected during its many site visits, it did not anticipate the effect that the 1965 Voting Rights Act and the relatively recent one-man-one-vote principle of *Baker v. Carr* would have on the political landscape.[7] As a result, the report includes little discussion about increased black political representation and only then in the context of when a city became majority-minority. However, since 1965, the number of African American elected officials has increased from less than a thousand to more than ten thousand, and the percentage of blacks in the 2015 House of Representatives approached the proportion of the black U.S. voting age population (Brown-Dean et al. 2015). Black mayors have been elected in cities that were not predominantly minority (such as Dallas and Los Angeles) and black senators in states that were primarily white (Massachusetts, New Jersey, South Carolina, and Illinois), and an African American was, of course, elected president in 2008 and reelected in 2012.

Unfortunately, whenever a Douglas Wilder has been elected governor of a primarily white state, this has generally turned out to be a gratifying, but isolated, event: the number of black U.S. senators, governors, city councilpersons, and state legislators is still much lower than the percentage of the nation that is black (Brown-Dean et al. 2015). Perhaps, much as was initially the case when integration began in white neighborhoods, it was not that a black moving into the neighborhood was the issue; it was the number of blacks. The same may be true for the electoral process—whites are pres-

7. *Baker v. Carr*, 369 U.S. 186 (1962).

ently comfortable with having a few black elected officials, but no more than that.

## ASSESSING CHANGES IN WHITE ATTITUDES AND OPINIONS

Because the Kerner report concludes that white discrimination and prejudice had been responsible for the disparate living conditions of most blacks, no meaningful change in the socioeconomic status of African Americans can ever realistically occur without a simultaneous significant change in white attitudes. A review of various public opinion polls, existing research, and interviews with African Americans conducted for this article yields various indications that some important changes have occurred.

As noted earlier, neighborhood integration has become established in many cities. Also, it is generally thought that the most overt and blatant forms of racism and discrimination have disappeared and that other social customs have changed noticeably (Pager and Shepherd 2008; King and Jones 2016). As one interviewee for this article simply and bluntly remarked, he can now inadvertently make eye contact with a white woman and not feel as if he is going to be lynched. A comprehensive review of General Social Survey results from 1972 to 2008 similarly concludes that the data "documents a sweeping and fundamental change in norms regarding race" and "strongly points to a large and growing orbit of social and political acceptance for African Americans" (Bobo et al. 2012, 73–74).

Illustrating this change is a daily scene in the food court of a major downtown Dallas office building. When one of the authors began frequenting this food court in the mid-1980s, almost all the people eating their lunches were white. Today, not only is the clientele racially diverse, but so are the people sitting around individual tables. Such a situation not only reflects more integrated social groupings and a more integrated work force, but as Elijah Anderson explains, it also presents an opportunity to influence others (2012).

However, for all of this improvement, discrimination continues to occur, albeit perhaps on a more subtle basis. According to a 2013 study for the Department of Housing and Urban Development, black homebuyers are typically shown or told about fewer homes than comparable white homebuyers (Turner et al. 2013). Similarly, a 2004 study that examined employment discrimination found that job applicants with "Anglo-sounding" names, such as Brad and Emily, were offered interviews at a rate about 50 percent higher than comparable applicants with "African American–sounding" names, such as Jamal and Lakisha (Bertrand and Mullainathan 2004).

A 2016 Pew Research Center study disclosed that 18 percent of surveyed blacks felt that police had unfairly stopped them within the previous year. Such findings are similar to the responses given by blacks interviewed for this article; these individuals cite examples of being stopped because a bicycle in the neighborhood had been stolen, their car headlights were not working properly, they had out-of-state license plates, or the front bumper of their car extended past the line at an intersection. Because of the unfortunate outcome that can arise if such encounters are not handled properly, the blacks interviewed explain that, early on, they have to have "the talk" with their children, especially their sons. However, whereas for whites the talk usually deals with "the birds and the bees," for blacks it deals with how to interact with the police.

Besides the continuation of such discrimination, another factor that complicates America's ability to make progress is the discrepancy between blacks and whites as to whether discrimination continues to exist. For example, whereas in 2016, 52 percent of whites felt that minorities had the same employment opportunities as whites, only 20 percent of blacks agreed. Eighty percent of whites also thought that blacks were treated the same in local stores; only 47 percent of blacks felt the same (Gallup 2016).

Such a discrepancy may indicate that perhaps whites still do not fully understand the many forms that discrimination and prejudice can take above and beyond being a member of the Klan. Gary Marx, who was on the commission's research staff, has long maintained that the commission should have explained what it meant when it wrote, "white society is deeply implicated in the ghetto. White institutions created it, white institutions maintain it, and white society condones it" (Kerner Report 1968, 1; Marx 1970, 2016). He believes that the report would have been far more influential had it differentiated institutional racism from idiosyncratic racism, racist attitudes from racist behavior, and self-conscious and intended racism from subconscious, nonreflective, and unintentional behavior, and attitudes that may have racist consequences.

Discrimination often being so subtle, such an explanation could have helped those whites who finally understood that requiring blacks to use separate bathroom facilities was inappropriate, but who did not realize how some of their other long-standing preferences, practices, or comments still constituted discrimination (Martin 2016; Banaji and Greenwald 2016). Matthew Hughey's recent study of white attitudes shows that even whites that belong to organizations that were created to support racial equality express personal opinions that are seemingly contradictory to the purpose of these organizations (2017).

The African Americans interviewed for this article also repeatedly gave examples of subtle forms of discrimination that they encounter: being followed in stores "unless they are wearing a coat and tie," encountering sales people who chat with white customers but say almost nothing to them, and having people not hold doors open for them. Another interviewee told of being a waitress while working her way through college and being by asked by the white wait staff to handle tables with black customers because "they don't tip much, or they don't buy much." Such instances cause John Wiley Price, the first African American to be elected as a county commissioner in Texas, to say that blacks are required to have a second I.Q.—an "insult quota"—and whether these actions are intended to be discriminatory and prejudicial or deliberate, subconscious, rationalized, or completely accidental, they still have the effect of continuing an America with two societies.[8]

## WHAT DOES IT ALL MEAN?

According to the vast majority of the commission staff, "enormous change" has occurred since 1968. However, as Gary Marx notes, what progress you see depends upon where you stand.[9] One of the authors, who was on the Kerner Commission's staff, similarly compares the situation to the scene that one views through a kaleidoscope. Twisting the end of this kaleidoscope can give someone else a very different image.

Given how traditional the members of the Kerner Commission itself were, they would likely be pleased with the increase in black educational attainment and the size of the black middle class that has been achieved. However, they would also likely be dismayed by the corresponding lack of relative change in median income and unemployment.

Peter Goldmark, who was one of Commission Vice Chairman John Lindsay's assistants, believes that Lindsay would be "very distressed" by the events of the past few years (efforts to restrict and complicate minority voting, continued police shootings, and so on), but that "he would still see that there had been progress."[10] David Chambers, who was David Ginsburg's special assistant, is a little less sanguine about how the commission would view today's world.[11] Although Chambers says that he does "not doubt for a minute that we've made progress," he is concerned that more has still not been achieved, and he believes that the commission would feel the same, suggesting that, if the progress of the last fifty years had occurred within a decade, then the commission would have been "stunned" by what had happened. However, on discovering that it had actually taken fifty years to get to this point, they would be very disappointed.

Richard Nathan, the commission's associate director for program research, and commission

---

8. John Wiley Price, interview with Rick Loessberg, June 19, 2017.

9. Gary Marx, interview with Rick Loessberg, June 15. 2017.

10. Peter Goldmark, interview with Rick Loessberg, June 24, 2017.

11. David Chambers, interview with Rick Loessberg, May 5, 2017.

member Fred Harris have similar views as to the progress that has been made. Both believe that progress was made on "virtually every aspect of race and poverty" for a period of time (National Public Radio 2017).[12] However, globalization and the automation and export of the U.S. manufacturing base—and one can also add double-digit inflation, the AIDS crisis, Watergate, and the emergence of homelessness—greatly complicated this progress. So despite an expanded black middle class today and many blacks now having more opportunities than ever, a large group has been left behind in the inner city. For example, in 1966, more than about one-half of America's blacks lived in the central city; by 2016, about one-third did.

The change in our manufacturing base also helps explain why, despite increased educational attainment, relative median income, relative black-white unemployment, black homeownership, and black wealth have changed little. Traditionally, manufacturing provided many unskilled workers with entry-level jobs, relatively higher wages, and a chance to acquire skills and be promoted. However, as manufacturing employment began to decline rapidly in the 1970s and 1980s, this opportunity also declined significantly, as did the corresponding ability to earn a higher income, become a homeowner, and accumulate wealth.

These Kerner Commission participant views are quite similar to those of the African Americans interviewed for this article. However, the interviewees tend to see the glass being more half-full than the Kerner participants. The black interviewees believe that things "have changed significantly," one explaining, "I know what it is like to drink from a colored fountain . . . we have made great progress." Yet, this same individual, along with others, also specifically acknowledges that parts of cities still do not look much different than they did before the report. "We are unquestionably better off," said another, "but we still have more to go."

Both groups attribute the lack of even more significant progress to the lingering effects of past practices and the institutional barriers that remain. As an example, many people find out about job openings and career possibilities from friends. However, until the 1964 Civil Rights Act (which made discrimination in employment illegal), many occupations were realistically not available to African Americans. As a result, blacks generally have only recently had the opportunity to develop contacts and networks in a variety of fields previously closed to them. This, when combined with the noted reduction in manufacturing, has made black economic advancement even more difficult.

In addition, some discussion among both groups has focused on whether fifty years is realistically enough time to eliminate the vast disparity between blacks and whites, given the other issues that have competed for the nation's attention and the difficulty of race in the United States. As one African American interviewee remarked, "fifty years seems like a long time until you turn fifty." Considering that it took one hundred years after slavery ended for blacks to just be able to sit next to a white person in a restaurant, the progress of the last fifty years may begin to look different—though still not where it should be.

The Kerner staff and the black interviewees again have identical views on whether the recent trend of cell phone–recorded police incidents indicates an increased level of racism among police. Both groups view this as the product of increased technology, not proof that police racism is increasing. One interviewee suggested that the recording and the repeated disclosure of such incidents could help reduce these police incidents and help whites realize that racism still exists: "sometimes whites need to see things to believe them." Peter Goldmark also believes that these incidents do not represent a step backward (interview, see note 10). "Despite what we see today . . . we are not going back."

## HOW COMMISSION REPORTS CAN BE INFLUENTIAL

The influence of the Kerner report is often assessed on the basis of whether its many recommendations were actually adopted (Lupo 2011). This is understandable given the number of recommendations (about one-fifth of the nearly seven hundred pages were devoted to this) and

12. Richard Nathan, interview with Rick Loessberg, June 12, 2017.

the significance that the report attached to having them implemented—"There can be no higher priority for national action and no higher claim on the nation's conscience."

However, a document like the Kerner report can be influential several other ways. It can educate, which, says David Flitner, who has extensively studied presidential commissions, "is no small thing in a democracy," and it can inform and persuade (Rosenbaum 2005, 3). It can inspire, provide a platform, or provide justification and credibility. It can provide new data and a new way of thinking; it can guide decisions about policy; and it can offer a course of action. A review of the Kerner report over the past fifty years, shows, perhaps surprisingly so, how active it has been in all of these roles.

## EDUCATING AND INFORMING AMERICA

From its beginning, the commission realized that, regardless of how dire the conditions that it saw were, unless it could convincingly convey that information to white America, what was recommended did not matter. A September 21, 1967, memo from the commission's deputy executive director to its executive director emphasized that one of the objectives of the report was "to focus the attention of the American people—particularly the suburban white population—on the critical issues presented by the riots" (Lipsky and Olson 1977). A memo from commission member James Corman to the commission's executive director a month later made a similar point: "Testimony before the Commission has repeatedly referred to an appalling ignorance among white Americans concerning current conditions in urban ghettos. It is essential that the Commission be brutally honest in this regard" (1967).

With the understanding that it would first have to educate, the commission set out to present a report that would forcefully describe the many ways in which black America differed from white America. *Newsweek* singled out the report for "its unsparing detail," and its ability to "sketch . . . the pattern of economic exclusion, unresponsiveness by local government, abrasive police tactics and 'pervasive discrimination' that has left the Negro uniquely isolated and embittered" (1968, 19). Jack Rosenthal was especially proud of how the report served as "a pistol shot in the ear of the nation."[13] Richard Rothstein, who has studied housing patterns and the federal government's role in creating residential segregation, says the report was "very influential in terms of informing people's awareness that the ghetto was not created by accident and not created by the choice of its residents."[14] Even conservative Congressman Dan Kuykendall, who criticized the report for blaming "everyone and everything" for the riots "except the two principal culprits—the lawless, who seize any excuse to pillage and destroy, and the politicians, who for political advantage, overpromise the disadvantaged," recognized that "there is no doubt the problems outlined in the report do exist."[15]

The report's efforts to educate were further enhanced by the standing of the commission that produced it and the attention that the report received. These aspects helped give it credibility and a platform from which to reach the public. As mentioned, the response the report received was intense; for several weeks, it monopolized the nation's attention, no small feat given that the Tet Offensive had just turned the Vietnam War upside down, and America had begun what would become one of the most dramatic presidential campaigns in its history.

That the report, which presented such a deplorable picture of black urban America, was unanimously adopted by a commission that included not ivory tower professors, fiery radicals, or black nationalists, but a senator from Oklahoma (Fred Harris), a police chief from the South (Herbert Jenkins), a radio station operator from Kentucky (Katherine Peden), and a small-town Republican congressman (William McCulloch), gave it a sense of respectability

---

13. Jack Rosenthal, interview with Rick Loessberg, March 3, 2015.

14. Richard Rothstein, interview with Rick Loessberg, June 6, 2017.

15. 114 Cong. Rec. 5280 (1968).

that was critical.[16] Peter Goldmark says that this was one of the first times that so many political leaders of different backgrounds came together to talk about race in this manner (interview, see note 10). Former Attorney General Nicholas Katzenbach also said at the time that the attention and the prestige that the report carried greatly mattered to African Americans. "Statements by the Kerner Commission like 'white racism' are extremely important. They help restore the confidence of the black community in the integrity of government and public institutions" (Rosenthal 1969, 60).

Besides educating white America about the living conditions of many urban blacks, the report also helped begin to dispel the strongly held sentiment that the rioting had been caused by some combination of outside agitators, a conspiracy, and local riffraff. A variety of polls taken in 1967 showed that as many as 71 percent of whites thought the rioting was organized and that 45 percent thought that the organizing was done by outside parties (Woods 2016). Other polls showed that about one-third of whites thought that the "main cause" of the 1967 rioting had been "looters and other undesirables" (Campbell and Schuman 1968, 47).

However, using intelligence reports from the Federal Bureau of Investigation, testimony from J. Edgar Hoover, and interviews with more than 1,200 people who witnessed the rioting, the commission found no evidence of a conspiracy or the involvement of outside agitators; and when this information was combined with a special analysis of the arrest reports of 13,102 rioters in twenty-two cities, it found that the typical rioter was no more representative of the criminal element than other members of his neighborhood (Fogelson and Hill 1968) and was

> in many ways very different from the stereotypes. He was not a migrant. He was born in the state and was a life-long resident of the city in which the riot took place. Economically his position was about the same as his Negro neighbors who did not actively participate in the riot [and] . . . although he had not, usually, graduated from high school, he was somewhat better educated than the average inner-city Negro. (Kerner Report 1968, 128)

According to the sociologist Seymour Spilerman, this was one of the first times that the "riffraff" theory could be empirically refuted.[17] With white America having already begun blaming conspiracies and extremists for the rioting and the rise of law and order being one of the major campaign issues of 1968 (White 1969), this determination was invaluable as the country sought to move forward after the events of 1967.

Polling data shows how white beliefs about the causes of the rioting changed before and after the report was released. In a Harris poll taken immediately after the Newark and Detroit riots, whites were asked to identify "the two or three main reasons" for the riots (*Newsweek* 1967). Forty-five percent said outside agitation, the most-cited explanation. Only 16 percent identified prejudice. However, in a Harris poll conducted about a month after the report was released, 37 percent of whites now said that the riots were "brought on mainly by white racism" (Harris 1968, A5). Although this change in opinion still did not represent the view of a majority of white opinion, it did represent a doubling of what was previously thought, and it helped diminish the then-prevailing sentiment and prevented it from dangerously expanding further.

The analysis of who rioted, the detailed descriptions of how riots unfolded (which were called "the best-documented record of civil disorders, certain to become a prime reference work," *Business Week* 1968, 31), and the extensive surveying that was conducted in fifteen cities have subsequently provided the foundation for much of the research on riots and collective behavior that has been conducted since. The

---

16. The commission's other seven members were also establishment types: I.W. Abel was a labor union president; Charles Thornton was a defense contractor; Edward Brooke was a senator from Massachusetts; John Lindsay was mayor of New York; Roy Wilkins was the head of the NAACP; James Corman was a congressman from California; and Otto Kerner was the governor of Illinois.

17. Seymour Spilerman, interview with Rick Loessberg. July 7, 2017.

surveying of racial attitudes done on behalf of the commission has been called "groundbreaking for understanding race relations in the United States" (Michalos 2014, 782). Spilerman, whose work from 1970 to 1976 is regarded as being "the definitive word on the 1960s riots" (Myers 1997, 94), relied on the report for both background and data (interview, see note 18). Others, such as Nathan Caplan and Jeffrey Paige (1968), Clark McPhail (1994), and Daniel Myers (1997) similarly used the report in their work on riots, Myers saying later that the report was "absolutely central to the riot literature that emerged" after 1968.[18]

The report also helped educate a generation of college graduates, leaders, business people, policemen, and public administrators. The report's analysis of what had happened and why found its way into numerous sociology, government, and urban studies textbooks during the 1970s, many of these books quoting the report extensively (Dye 1969, 1972; Fickers and Graves 1971; Berger 1978; Cousins and Nagpaul 1979). Copies of the report also continued to be sold during the early 1970s at a rate of about 2,500 per year for use by the public and in corporations, schools, police departments, and community organizations (Lipsky and Olson 1977).

## IMPLEMENTATION OF RECOMMENDATIONS

The Kerner Commission first sought to educate a nation, but it ultimately wanted the nation to take action and to adopt the recommendations it was prescribing. As a result, although "a legislative box score" is not, and should not, be the sole measure of whether a commission report has been influential (Rosenbaum 2005), the analysis should be made, especially for a report whose recommendations were premised on preventing future rioting. However, trying to assess whether the Kerner report's recommendations have been implemented is difficult given the sheer number of them and the various forms they took. Some, such as calling for the passage of a federal fair housing law, are specific, so determining whether they have been implemented is very straightforward. Others, though, such as improving program coordination, are far more difficult to determine, given their vagueness.

Recognizing this, the authors have sought to assess the implementation status of the thirty-one recommendations for national action identified in the report's summary as well as the recommendations that the report made that pertain to law enforcement and the media. These are not only the report's most significant recommendations, but they also generally lend themselves to some type of implementation assessment.

As shown in table 4, some form of action was taken on many of the report's recommendations, much of it within the first five years of publication—a position also shared by the commission's executive director David Ginsburg (1988). Some action was on a very significant scale; the 1968 Housing Act, for instance, created new housing programs and national assisted-housing goals and was called by Senate House Banking Committee Chairman John Sparkman as "the most comprehensive housing and urban development bill . . . ever presented to the Senate."[19] Funding for Model Cities and Urban Renewal doubled in a very short time. The Fair Housing Act was approved. The Equal Employment Opportunity Commission was substantially strengthened. The House passed a bill in 1970 that would have revolutionized welfare. The Comprehensive Employment and Training Act consolidated ten employment and training programs into one. Funding for education doubled in many areas. Such accomplishments would run counter to the statement that "while the Johnson Administration reacted harshly to the recommendations and refused to implement them, the Nixon Administration [which took office a year after the report was produced] did so to an even greater degree, making it nearly impossible for any of the recommendations to become policy" (Lupo 2011, 149).

Granted, some of the action taken was often piecemeal and of a much lesser scale than envisioned. Funding for the JOBS training pro-

---

18. Daniel Myers, interview with Rick Loessberg, August 2, 2017.

19. 114 Cong. Rec. 14943 (1968).

gram and for school desegregation never amounted to much, the percentage of the eligible population that participates in Head Start today is about the same as it was in 1968, and only about one-third of the report's five-year housing goal was met. It is these results that lead others to conclude that the report's implementation has not been "consistent with the scope and urgency" of its recommendations (Lipsky and Olson 1977, 141), a finding much closer to the reality than those who say that no or little action was ever taken (Lupo 2011, 149–51).

Given that so much of the discussion about the influence of the Kerner report usually centers on whether its national action recommendations were adopted, it is understandable that the report's law enforcement and media recommendations often get overlooked. However, given the intense level of resentment that the police generated in many black neighborhoods, that almost all of the major riots that occurred in 1967 began with a fairly routine police encounter, and that poor police responses sometimes caused these encounters to explode into major confrontations, the report's law enforcement recommendations were, in many respects, actually more important than those that dealt with housing or education. In fact, these recommendations were so important that the commission immediately began releasing some of them rather than waiting six months to include them in the final report.

On August 10, 1967, only two weeks after it had been appointed, the commission recommended that the number of blacks in the National Guard be substantially increased and that its riot training be expanded and improved as rapidly as possible. Eight weeks later, on October 7, 1967, the commission recommended that the Justice Department begin providing training to local police departments on improving community relations, crowd control techniques, crisis situation decision making, and joint operations. The commission's final report, which was released on March 1, 1968, then contained more detailed recommendations regarding the need to diversify local police departments, develop strong citizen complaint processes, improve police tactics, increase crowd control training, develop new codes of conduct, and review existing field procedures.

Although it is difficult to determine the extent to which some of these recommendations, such as reviewing field procedures, have been implemented nationally, for others it is possible to do so. As an example, during the winter of 1967–1968, the Justice Department conducted four, one-week, conference sessions on the topics suggested by the commission for four hundred mayors, city managers, and police officials from the 136 largest cities in the country (Urban America and The Urban Coalition 1969). National Guard training was also quickly expanded (GAO 1972; Urban America and The Urban Coalition 1969). Many other cities began revising their training programs and operational practices, some cities (such as Atlanta and Boston) also requiring their police officers to read the Kerner report (Jenkins 1969; Bratton 2016).

It is thought that, collectively, these Justice Department conferences, local efforts, and new National Guard training explained the lesser property damage and lower loss of life during the April 1968 riots that followed Martin Luther King's death than what had occurred in 1967. According to the executive director of the International Association of Chiefs of Police: "There is no question that the lessons learned from the report by the police and National Guard made it possible to handle the riots which sprang up. I believe considerable credit for the collection and dissemination of meaningful lessons belongs to the Commission and the work it stimulated" (Gillon 2017, 326).

The International City Managers Association reached a similar conclusion: "Police departments have become more adept at handling potential riot situations. While riot potential was greater in 1968 than in 1967, the triggering events were rapidly controlled and large-scale disorders thus were avoided" (Urban America and The Urban Coalition 1969, 69–70).

More contemporary accounts have also continued to attribute the relatively few civil disturbances that have occurred since 1968 to the training and strategy that have become common-place since the report was issued (Herbers 1988; Barnhart 2008). In fact, Jay Kriegel, another of John Lindsay's assistants, says

**Table 4.** Implementation of Report's Recommendations for National Action

| Report Recommendation | Implementation Status |
| --- | --- |
| 1. Consolidate existing manpower programs to avoid fragmentation and duplication | Ten employment and training programs consolidated into one program (CETA) in 1973 |
| 2. Create one million public-sector jobs and one million private-sector jobs within three years for hardcore unemployed | PEP created 185,000 public employment jobs in 1972; CETA created 755,000 in 1978; targeted Jobs Tax Credit created about 700,000 private-sector jobs in mid-1980s |
| 3. Reimburse private employers for on-the-job training of hardcore unemployed | Federal funding for JOBS program increased from $90 million in FY68 to $169 million in FY71 |
| 4. Provide tax incentives for investment in rural and urban poverty areas | Such incentives provided in 1993 with establishment of Empowerment Zones |
| 5. Prevent unemployment discrimination by strengthening the EEOC | EEOC given new authority in 1972; funding increased from $6.8 million in FY68 to $63 million in FY75 |
| 6. Provide substantial federal aid to desegregated school districts | Emergency School Aid Act approved in 1972; Funding ranged from $228 million in FY73 to $274.7 million in FY77 |
| 7. Eliminate racial discrimination in northern and southern schools | Difficult to assess |
| 8. Extend early childhood education to every disadvantaged child | Funding increased from $333.9 million in FY69 to $403.9 million in FY75, but no change in percentage of eligible population participating |
| 9. Improve education for disadvantaged children through provision of year-round schooling | Funding increased from $1.1 billion in FY69 to $1.9 billion in FY76, but year-round schooling did not occur |
| 10. Provide greater funding for adult basic education | Funding increased from $255 million in FY69 to $932 million in FY77 |
| 11. Increase opportunities for parent and community participation in public schools | Difficult to assess |
| 12. Reorient vocational education toward work experience training | Funding increased from $260 million in FY69 to $844 million in FY77 |
| 13. Increase federal assistance to disadvantaged for higher education | Funding increased from $418 million in FY69 to $908 million in FY72 |
| 14. Revise state aid formulas for poor schools | Difficult to assess |
| 15. Establish uniform national welfare payments | Attempt passed House in 1970; unsuccessful in Senate; significant state disparities still exist |
| 16. Establish AFDC-UP nationally | Attempt passed House in 1970, but unsuccessful in Senate; approved in 1988 |
| 17. Federal payment of at least 90 percent of state welfare costs | No significant change; states continue to provide about as much assistance as federal government |
| 18. Provide more social services, including family planning, through neighborhood centers | Difficult to assess |
| 19. Increase incentives for those on welfare to seek training and employment | WIN program funded beginning in FY69 with $33 million; funding reached $370 million in FY77 |
| 20. Repeal 1967 AFDC freeze | AFDC freeze repealed in 1969 |

**Table 4.** (continued)

| Report Recommendation | Implementation Status |
|---|---|
| 21. Eliminate welfare residency requirements | Residency requirements declared unconstitutional in 1969 |
| 22. Enact federal fair housing law | Adopted in 1968 |
| 23. Reorient federal housing programs to place more assisted units outside of ghetto areas. | Repeated location of assisted housing in minority areas declared unconstitutional in 1969 |
| 24. Build six million low-moderate income housing units within five years | 1968 Housing Act authorized construction of six million within ten years; about 1,800,000 actually constructed within five years |
| 25. Expand rent supplement program | No meaningful change in funding until establishment of Section 8 program in 1974 |
| 26. Modify below-market interest rate program for nonprofit housing sponsors | Provided for by 1968 Housing Act |
| 27. Create low-income homeownership program | Provided for by 1968 Housing Act |
| 28. Provide interest rate subsidy for privately developed moderate-income housing | Provided for by 1968 Housing Act |
| 29. Expansion of public housing | Amount of new public housing built each year increased from eighty thousand in FY69 to one hundred thousand in FY71 |
| 30. Expansion of Model Cities | Federal funding almost doubled from $400 million in FY68 to $750 million in FY70 |
| 31. Expansion and reorientation of urban renewal | Funding increased from $589 million in FY69 to $1.2 billion in FY72; program required to provide low/moderate income housing |

*Source:* Author's compilation.

that the report's "greatest lasting impact" is the influence that it has had on the handling of disorders,[20] a conclusion shared by Patrick Gillham and Gary Marx (2018).

Improved training and tactics were not the only law enforcement recommendations from the report to have been implemented. Just as the Kerner Commission had hoped, minority representation on local police forces has increased. In 1967, a survey of twenty-eight cities conducted by the commission found that only about 6 percent of the police forces were black. However, in 2013, 27.3 percent were minority (Maciag 2015). In addition, several of the police chiefs of some of the nation's major cities (Denver, Dallas, Fort Worth, San Francisco, Philadelphia, and Charlotte) are now African American, some of the chiefs leading departments in cities (such as Dallas and Fort Worth) where not only is the city not predominantly black but also African Americans are not even its largest minority.

The report's emphasis on improving community relations and patrol strategies is also credited with helping establish the community policing strategy that later emerged (Page 2014). The report also led the Ford Foundation to create the Police Foundation, the nation's largest private agency dedicated exclusively to police work (Police Foundation n.d.).

Because of the role of the media in U.S. society, the report's media recommendations were also important. Jack Rosenthal in particular thinks that the report's media recommendations were among its most noteworthy.[21] Two of the more significant media recommenda-

20. Jay Kriegel, interview with Rick Loessberg, June 27, 2017.

21. Jack Rosenthal, interview with Rick Loessberg, May 8, 2015.

tions dealt with increasing both the number and the visibility of blacks in journalism and the media. For a population that has since become accustomed to regularly seeing African Americans as news anchors, major characters in television programs, and as individuals in commercials promoting everything from credit unions to cereal, it may be difficult to understand how all-white television and journalism once were and why these recommendations were made. In the 1960s, persons of color were seen on television only if they were a singer or a comedian on a variety show. The report itself states that fewer than 5 percent of U.S. journalists at the time were black, and it is thought that most of them worked for the black press.

For many African Americans, the report was instrumental in changing this almost-all-white world. Les Payne, who helped found the National Association of Black Journalists, says "the Kerner Report . . . was our affirmative action program. Before the Report came out, there were very few blacks in the media industry. So once that Report came out, major newspaper editors, for example, began to hire black journalists" (Mondale 2016).

Charlene Hunter-Gault similarly credits the report for opening doors and changing the rules. "I'm finding it difficult to remember a time," she said in 1988, "before there was a Kerner Commission so profoundly it has affected a generation of journalists and journalism." For many, she said, the report found its place in the libraries of black journalists, right alongside the copies of *The Elements of Style* and *Webster's Unabridged Dictionary* that many journalists kept back then. She said that she also owed her "very existence to the Kerner Commission Report" as she got her first job in television in 1968 immediately following a conference of editors and journalists that had been held to discuss how to implement the Kerner report's media recommendations (C-SPAN 1988).

As of 2014, 22.4 percent of television journalists were minority. For radio and newspaper journalists, the figures were at 13 percent each (White 2015). Although these figures are still not representative of the nation's total minority population and though the figures for minority producers and directors are even smaller, these changes are nonetheless significant: they now allow for a constant and frequent minority presence on our screens and in our newspapers.

## INFLUENCING FAIR HOUSING–HOUSING DESEGREGATION POLICY

The Kerner report's involvement in the evolution of fair housing and the desegregation of assisted housing is a prime example of how a presidential commission report can influence public policy. Before the report, no federal fair housing law was on the books, and earlier efforts to secure one had been unsuccessful. In both 1966 and 1967, congressional attempts had failed, and prospects did not appear much better in 1968 when three motions to end a filibuster on a proposed bill were also defeated. Then, on March 4, 1968, in the first cloture vote since the report's release three days earlier, enough support was finally secured to end the debate when three senators changed their previous positions. All said that the report had influenced their decision.[22] With the filibuster having been ended, the Senate soon passed what became the last of the great civil rights laws of the 1960s.

Senator Allen Ellender, who had opposed the measure, accused the commission of deliberately releasing its report when it did to coincide with the fair housing debate.[23] Senator Howard Cannon, who was one of the three who changed his vote on the motion to end the filibuster, explained his reason for doing so:

> At no point has institutional discrimination . . . been more clearly dramatized [than] by the report of the Presidential Commission on Civil Disorders, filed only a few days ago. Against a backdrop of the prospects of more rioting in American streets this summer, we have the challenge of improving the quality of life. Money and programs, in my view, are secondary to the far more urgent need to demonstrate in open and clear fashion that

22. 114 Cong. Rec. 4954–56 (1968).

23. Ibid., 4960.

Americans have the will to meet these problems. The vote today offers an alternative to the present course of our national turmoil, and it is fitting that this course should be charted and set in the U.S. Senate.[24]

One year later, the report contributed to the nation's first successful public housing desegregation lawsuit (*Gautreaux v. Chicago Housing Authority*), which found that the Chicago Housing Authority's repeated and consistent placing of assisted housing in predominantly minority neighborhoods was in violation of federal law. In announcing this decision, the court, in its key summary judgment, ended with the following Kerner report citation and an echoing of the report's two societies warning: "On the basis of present trends of Negro residential concentration and of Negro migration into and White migration out of the central city, the President's Commission on Civil Disorders estimates that Chicago will become 50% Negro by 1984. By 1984 it may be too late to heal racial divisions."[25]

This landmark ruling, which, over the next twenty to thirty years, subsequently provided the legal basis for a series of other challenges across the country (see, for instance, *Jaimes v. Lucas Metropolitan Housing Authority, Walker v. Dallas Housing Authority, Ortero v. New York City Housing Authority, Mahaley v. Cuyahoga Metropolitan Housing Authority, Thompson v. HUD*), led to the end of high-rise public housing and the emergence of scatter-site housing.

The Kerner report continued to influence public housing policy in the 1990s when the Clinton administration sought to deal with the nation's supply of severely distressed public housing. Edward Blakely, who participated in this effort, said the report's discussion of segregation and its warning of two societies helped guide this work and culminated with the creation of the HOPE VI program, which demolished more than ninety-eight thousand severely distressed public housing units, many located in minority areas, and replaced them with about ninety-seven thousand mixed-income units in more dispersed locations (U.S. Department of Housing and Urban Development n.d.).[26]

In 2015, a major Supreme Court decision, *Texas Department of Housing and Community Affairs v. The Inclusive Communities Project*, demonstrated the report's continuing influence in housing discrimination and desegregation.[27] The Court not only ruled that the method that the state of Texas used to select low-income housing tax credit projects perpetuated segregation, but also established for the first time that, under the Fair Housing Act, intent does not need to be first proved to determine whether a specific action is discriminatory.

In its majority opinion, the Court cited the Kerner Commission's findings that "residential segregation and unequal housing and economic conditions in the inner cities" created the "significant, underlying causes of the social unrest" that the nation experienced in the 1960s, and that "both open and covert racial discrimination prevented black families from obtaining better housing and moving to integrated communities." It concluded with "the Fair Housing Act must play an important part in avoiding the Kerner Commission's grim prophecy that '[o]ur Nation is moving toward two societies, one black, one white—separate and unequal.'"[28] Mike Daniel, one of the attorneys representing the party that challenged the state's method, says that the legal team carefully assembled the material that was submitted to the Supreme Court and that it emphasized the Kerner report because it was "one of the two seminal works" on race in this country (the other being Gunnar Myrdal's *American Dilemma*) and because it so forcefully pointed out the consequences of continued housing segregation. He further notes that the report's influence was even more significant because it was

---

24. 114 Cong. Rec. 4960 (1968).

25. *Gautreaux v. Chicago Housing Authority*, 296 F. Supp. 907 (7th Cir. 1999).

26. Edward Blakely, email message to Rick Loessberg, July 20, 2017.

27. 576 U.S. ___ (2015), No. 13-1371.

28. Ibid.

"a government report" from "our government" that unhesitatingly described the conditions that existed for blacks.[29]

## THE REPORT AS SOCIOECONOMIC-RACIAL SHORTHAND

Of the many ways in which the report has been influential—as a platform, as a call to action, as a provider of information—the one which continues to endure (and which was totally unanticipated in 1968) is how it, and in particular, its two societies warning, have become such a part of our public consciousness and political vocabulary. Both are cited when studies chronicle the existence of residential segregation (Jargowsky 1997) or the economic disparity between whites and blacks (Goldsmith and Blakely 2010). They are also quickly invoked whenever there is a tragic police incident, whether it be Miami in 1980 (*Time* 1980), Los Angeles in 1992 (Steel 1992), Ferguson in 2014 (Cobb 2014), or Baltimore in 2015 (Western 2015). Peter Goldmark has remarked that he can go to an event almost anywhere and find people who recognize the two societies phrase (interview, see note 10).

In so doing, the report has, in short, become a reference point. It has the power to convert a statistic or a finding from a study into a distinct image. It has the power when a questionable police shooting occurs to quickly remind us that not as much progress has been made as thought (or hoped). It has, as John Wiley Price says, provided the country with a measuring stick that allows it to assess the distance it has covered, both statistically and rhetorically (interview, see note 8).

That the report continues to be frequently invoked after fifty years is remarkable. That it is often quoted verbatim is also extraordinary, especially given that it is not readily possible to remember any wording whatsoever from other historically significant commission reports, such as the Warren report or the 9/11 report.

A review of the *New York Times* illustrates how frequently the Kerner report has been cited. From 1968 to 2017, the commission and its report were cited a total of 349 times. In comparison, three other urban commissions (Katzernbach, Kaiser, and Douglas) from the same period were collectively mentioned only eighty-nine times. Moreover, the frequency with which the report has been cited is not just because of the intense attention it received on publication. Two-thirds (235) of the references to the report that the *Times* has made occurred in 1970 or later. The other three commissions and their reports have been cited only a total of twenty-three times over the same period, suggesting that the Kerner report, unlike the others, has developed and sustained a significant presence over several generations.

## CONCLUSION

The Kerner report dramatically called America's attention to the grave disparity between blacks and whites and provided a comprehensive agenda for eliminating this disparity. Although the report did not lead to another Great Society or to "unprecedented levels of funding" as the commission had hoped, a surprising number of the recommendations were implemented; the report also provided the foundation for much of the diversity in today's media, many law enforcement principles, and many housing policy decisions. In so doing, America has become more inclusive, additional violence has been prevented, and new opportunities for where people can live, go to school, and work have been created. Although this influence has not been enough to eliminate the two societies that the report warned about, there has nonetheless been, by many accounts, important progress over the last fifty years.

The report's greatest legacy, though, may now be how it has endured and how it continues to influence and educate. Several generations have come of age since the report was written; yet, it is still quoted and remembered while other reports from the same era have been forgotten. As Gary Marx notes, "what the Kerner Report really did is . . . to document the gap between the values we hold and the realities" that exist and to demonstrate "that we are not living up to the American ideal" (interview, see note 9). This ability to remind America and to constantly measure the current situation,

---

29. Mike Daniel, interview with Rick Loessberg, November 30, 2017.

whatever it may be, after fifty years is critical, for as America's past has shown, the journey to equality is a long one.

**REFERENCES**

Anderson, Elijah. 2012. *The Cosmopolitan Canopy: Race and Civility in Everyday Life.* New York: W. W. Norton.

Banaji, Mahzaron, and Anthony Greenwald. 2016, *Blind Spot: Hidden Biases of Good People.* New York: Bantam Books.

Barnhart, Bill. 2008. "Kerner Report: The Lessons." *Chicago Tribune.* March 2. Accessed May 1, 2018. http://articles.chicagotribune.com/2008-03-02/news/0802291088_1_kerner-report-national-advisory-commission-final-report/.

Berger, Alan S. 1978. *The City: Urban Communities and Their Problems.* Dubuque, Iowa: William C. Brown Company.

Bernstein, Jared. 1995. "Where's the Pay-Off?" Washington, D.C.: Economic Policy Institute. Accessed April 25, 2018. http://www.epi.org/files/page/-/old/studies/wheres_the_payoff-FULL.pdf.

Bertrand, Marianne, and Sendhil Mullainathan. 2004. "Are Emily and Greg More Employable than Lakisha and Jamal? A Field Experiment on Labor Market Discrimination." *American Economic Review* 94(4): 991–1013.

Bobo, Lawrence D., Camile Z. Charles, Maria Krysan, and Alicia D. Simmons. 2012. "The Real Record on Racial Attitudes." In *Social Trends in American Life*, edited by Peter V. Marsden. Princeton, N.J.: Princeton University Press.

Bratton, William J. 2016. "The Practice of Policing; Evolution in the Police Profession." *Cityland.* February 2. Accessed April 25, 2018. http://www.citylandnyc.org/copmmissioner-bratton-policing-evolution.

Brown-Dean, Khaliah, Zoltan Hajnal, Christina Rivers, and Ismail White. 2015. "50 Years of the Voting Rights Act: The State of Race in Politics." Washington, D.C.: Joint Center for Political and Economic Studies.

*Business Week.* 1968. "Congress Is Cool on Riot Study." March 9, 31–32.

Campbell, Angus, and Howard Schuman. 1968. "Racial Attitudes." In *Supplemental Studies for the National Advisory Commission on Civil Disorders.* Washington: Government Printing Office.

Caplan, Nathan, and Jeffrey M. Paige. 1968. "A Study of Ghetto Rioters." *Scientific American* 219(2): 15–21.

Cobb, Jelani. 2014. "Crimes and Commissions." *The New Yorker.* December 8. Accessed April 25, 2018. http://www.newyorker.com/magazine/2014/12/08/crimes-commissions.

Collins, William J., and Robert A. Margo. 2001. "Race and The Value of Owner-Occupied Housing, 1940–1990." Working paper no. 00-W25R. Nashville, Tenn.: Vanderbilt University.

Corman, James. 1967. Memo to David Ginsburg, October 17. National Advisory Commission on Civil Disorders Collection, "Letters to Governor Kerner," series 47, box 1, LBJ Library.

Cousins, Albert N., and Hans Nagpaul. 1979. *The Sociology of Cities and Urban Society.* New York: John Wiley & Sons.

C-SPAN. 1988. "Two Decades After the Kerner Commission Report." Videorecording of Annual Convention of American Society of Newspaper Editors. April 13, 1988.

De La Cruz-Viesca, Melany, Paul M. Ong, Andre Comandon, William A. Darity Jr., and Darrick Hamilton. 2018. "Fifty Years After the Kerner Commission Report: Place, Housing, and Racial Wealth Inequality in Los Angeles." *RSF: The Russell Sage Foundation Journal of the Social Sciences* 4(6): 160–84. DOI: 10.7758/RSF.2018.4.6.08.

Dye, Thomas R. 1969. *Politics in States and Communities.* Englewood Cliffs, N.J.: Prentice-Hall.

———. 1972. *Understanding Public Policy.* Englewood Cliffs, N.J.: Prentice-Hall.

Farrell, Chad R., and Barrett A. Lee. 2011. "Racial Diversity and Change in Metropolitan Neighborhoods." *Social Science Research* 40(4): 1108–23.

Fickers, Victor B., and Herbert Graves, eds. 1971. *Social Sciences and Urban Crisis: Introductory Readings.* New York: MacMillan.

Fogelson, Robert M., and Robert H. Hill. 1968. "Who Riots? A Study of Participation in the 1967 Riots." In *Supplemental Studies for the National Advisory Commission on Civil Disorders.* Washington: Government Printing Office.

Gallup, Inc. 2016. "Race Relations." Accessed April 24, 2018. http://news.gallup.com/poll/1687/race-relations.aspx.

Gillham, Patrick F., and Gary T. Marx. 2018. "Changes in the Policing of Civil Disorders Since the Kerner Report: The Police Response to Ferguson, August 2014, and Some Implications for the Twenty-First Century." *RSF: The Russell Sage*

Foundation Journal of the Social Sciences 4(6): 122–43. DOI: 10.7758/RSF.2018.4.6.06. Gillon, Steven M. 2017. *Separate and Unequal: The Kerner Commission and the Unraveling of American Liberalism*. New York: Basic Books.

Ginsburg, David. 1988. Interview by Michael Gillette, November 11. LBJ Oral Histories, LBJ Presidential Library.

Glaeser, Edward, and Jacob Vigdor. 2012. "The End of the Segregated Century: Racial Separation in America's Neighborhoods, 1890–2010." Civic Report no. 66. New York: Manhattan Institute. Accessed April 25, 2018. https://www.manhattan-institute.org/pdf/cr_66.pdf.

Goldsmith, William W., and Edward J. Blakely. 2010. *Separate Societies: Poverty and Inequality in U.S. Cities*. Philadelphia, Pa.: Temple University Press.

Goodman, Laurie, Jun Zhu, and Rolf Pendall. 2017. "Are Gains in Black Homeownership History?" *Urban Wire*, February 14. Accessed May 1, 2018. https://www.urban.org/urban-wire/are-gains-black-homeownership-history.

Harris, Louis. 1968. "Differences in Races' Opinions." *Los Angeles Times*, April 16.

Herbers, John. 1969. "U.S. A Year Closer to Two Societies, New Study Finds." *New York Times*, February 23.

———. 1988. "The Kerner Report: A Journalist's View." In *Quiet Riots*, edited by Fred R. Harris and Roger Wilkins. New York: Pantheon.

Hughey, Matthew W. 2018. "Whither Whiteness? The Racial Logics of the Kerner Report and Modern White Space." *RSF: The Russell Sage Foundation Journal of the Social Sciences* 4(6): 73–98. DOI: 10.7758/RSF.2018.4.6.04.

Jargowsky, Paul A. 1997. *Poverty and Place: Ghettos, Barrios, and the American City*. New York: Russell Sage Foundation.

Jenkins, Herbert. 1969. Interview by T. H. Baker, May 14. LBJ Library Oral Histories. LBJ Presidential Library.

Kerner Commission. 1968. *Report of the National Advisory Commission on Civil Disorders*. Washington: Government Printing Office.

King, Eden, and Kristen Jones. 2016. "Why Subtle Bias Is So Often Worse than Blatant Discrimination." *Harvard Business Review*, July 13. Accessed May 1, 2018. http://hbr.org/2016/07/why-subtle-bias-is-so-often-worse-than-blatant-discrimination.

Lee, Barrett A., John Iceland, and Gregory Sharp. 2012. "Racial and Ethnic Diversity Goes Local: Charting Change in American Communities over Three Decades." US2010 Census Project. Providence, R.I.: Brown University. Accessed April 25, 2018. https://s4.ad.brown.edu/Projects/Diversity/Data/Report/report08292012.pdf.

Lipsky, Michael, and David J. Olson. 1977. *Commission Politics: The Processing of Racial Crisis in America*. New Brunswick, N.J.: Transaction Books.

Loessberg, Rick. 2017. "Two Societies: The Writing of the Summary of the Report of the National Advisory Commission on Civil Disorders." *Journal of Urban History*, January 30. DOI: 10.1177/0096144216689087.

Logan, John R., and Brian J. Stults. 2011. "The Persistence of Segregation in the Metropolis: New Findings from the 2010 Census." US2010 Census Project. Providence, R.I.: Brown University. Accessed April 25, 2018. https://s4.ad.brown.edu/Projects/Diversity/Data/Report/report2.pdf.

Lupo, Lindsey. 2011. *Flak-Catchers*. Lanham, Md.: Lexington Books.

Maciag, Mike. 2015. "Where Police Don't Mirror Communities and Why It Matters." *Governing*, August 28. Accessed April 25, 2018. http://www.governing.com/topics/public-justice-safety/gov-police-department-diversity.html.

Martin, Brian. 2016. "Subtle Prejudice." *Brian's Comments* (blog), July 1. Accessed April 25, 2018. http://comments.bmartin.cc/2016/07/01/subtle-prejudice/.

Marx, Gary T. 1970. "Two Cheers for the National Riot (Kerner) Commission Report." In *Black Americans: A Second Look*, edited by J. F. Szwed. New York: Basic Books.

———. 2016. "Inside the Tent: Some Reflections on Working for the 1967 Kerner Commission." In *The Harvest of Racism*, ed. Robert Shellow. Ann Arbor: University of Michigan Press.

McPhail, Clark. 1994. "The Dark Side of Purpose: Individual and Collective Violence in Riots." *Sociological Quarterly* 35(1): 1–32.

Michalos, Alex C. 2014. "Angus Campbell: A Pioneer in Social Indicators and Social Reporting." *Applied Research Quality Life* 9(3): 781–82.

Mondale, Arthur. 2016. "National Association of Black Journalists: Kerner Report Key to African-American Breakthrough in Media Industry." *Pentagram*, February 18. Accessed April 25, 2018. http://www.army.mil/article/162632.

Myers, Daniel. 1997. "Racial Rioting in the 1960s: An Event History Analysis of Local Conditions." *American Sociological Review* 62 (February): 94–112.

National Public Radio. 2017. "50 Years On, Sen. Fred Harris Remembers Great Hostility During 1967 Race Riots." *All Things Considered*, July 20. Accessed April 25, 2018. https://www.npr.org/2017/07/20/538370689/50-years-on-sen-fred-harris-remembers-great-hostility-during-1967-race-riots.

NBC Broadcasting. 1967. "Summer 1967: What We Have Learned." Television documentary, directed by Fred Freed. Broadcast, September 15.

*Newsweek*. 1967. "The Basic Causes of the Negro Rioting." August 21.

———. 1968. "Roots of Riot—Call to Battle." March 11, 39–42.

Page, Clarence. 2014. "Forgotten Lessons of '60s Urban Riots." *Chicago Tribune*, August 22. Accessed April 25, 2018. http://www.chicagotribune.com/news/opinion/page/ct-oped-page-lessons-urban-riots-1960s-0824-20140822-column.html.

Pager, Devah, and Hana Shepherd. 2008. "The Sociology of Discrimination: Racial Discrimination in Employment, Housing Credit, and Consumer Markets." *Annual Review of Sociology* 34(1): 181–209.

Pew Research Center. 2015. "The American Middle Class Is Losing Ground." Washington, D.C.: Pew Research Center. Accessed April 25, 2018. http://www.pewsocialtrends.org/2015/12/09/the-american-middle-class-is-losing-ground/.

———. 2016. "On Views of Race and Inequality, Blacks and Whites Are Worlds Apart." Washington, D.C.: Pew Research Center. Accessed April 25, 2018. http://www.pewsocialtrends.org/2016/06/27/on-views-of-race-and-inequality-blacks-and-whites-are-worlds-apart.

Platt, Anthony M., ed. 1971. *The Politics of Riot Commissions*. New York: Collier.

Police Foundation. n.d. "History." Accessed August 10, 2017. https://www.policefoundation.org/about/history/.

Raymont, Henry. 1968. "Riot Book Big Best Seller." *New York Times*, March 14, 49.

Rosenbaum, David E. 2005. "Commissions Are Fine, But Rarely What Changes The Light Bulb." *New York Times*, October 30. Accessed April 25, 2018. http://www.nytimes.com/2005/10/30/weekinreview/commissions-are-fine-but-rarely-what-changes-the-light-bulb.html.

Rosenthal, Jack. 1969. "Study Panels Flourish in Capital." *New York Times*, December 15.

Rothstein, Richard. 2017. *The Color of Law*. New York: Liversight Publishing.

Shapiro, Thomas, Tatjana Meschede, and Sam Osoro. 2013. "The Roots of the Widening Racial Wealth Gap." *Research and Policy Brief*. February 2013. Institute on Assets and Social Policy. Accessed May 1, 2018. https://iasp.brandeis.edu/pdfs/Author/shapiro-thomas-m/racialwealthgapbrief.pdf.

Steel, Ronald. 1992. "Broken Promises, Empty Dreams." *New York Times*, May 7, A27.

*Time*. 1980. "Fire and Fury." June 2, 18.

Turner, Margery Austin, Rob Santos, Diane Levy, Doug Wissoker, Claudia Aranda, and Rob Pitingolo. 2013. *Housing Discrimination Against Racial and Ethnic Minorities 2012*. Washington: Urban Institute and the U.S. Department of Housing and Urban Development.

U.S. Department of Housing and Urban Development. n.d. "Hope VI Data Compilation and Analysis." Accessed April 25, 2018. https://www.huduser.gov/portal/pdredge/pdr-edge-research-032017.html#.wy0v0zX15t0.email.

U.S. General Accounting Office (GAO). 1972. "Training and Equipping the Army National Guard for Maintaining Order During Civil Disturbances." Washington: Government Printing Office. Accessed April 25, 2018. https://www.gao.gov/assets/210/203694.pdf.

Urban America and The Urban Coalition. 1969. *One Year Later*. New York: Praeger.

Ware, Leland, and Theodore J. Davis. 2012. "Ordinary People in an Extraordinary Time: The Black Middle Class in the Age of Obama: III. Occupational Advances." *Howard Law Journal* 55(2): 533–74.

Western, Bruce. 2015. "The Man Who Foresaw Baltimore." *Politico*, April 30. Accessed April 25, 2018. http://www.politico.com/magazine/story/2015/04/baltimore-riots-kerner-commission-117515_full.html.

White, Gillian B. 2015. "Where Are All the Minority Journalists?" *The Atlantic*, July 24. Accessed April 25, 2018. http://www.theatlantic.com/business/archive/2015/07/minorities-in-journalism/399461.

White, Theodore. 1969. *The Making of the President 1968*. New York: Atheneum.

Woods, Randall B. 2016. *Prisoners of Hope*. New York: Basic Books.

Zelizer, Julian E. 2016. "Introduction to the 2016 Edition." *The Kerner Report*. Princeton, N.J.: Princeton University Press.

# PART II
# Policing, Law, and Communities

# Changes in the Policing of Civil Disorders Since the Kerner Report: The Police Response to Ferguson, August 2014, and Some Implications for the Twenty-First Century

PATRICK F. GILLHAM AND GARY T. MARX

*The Kerner Commission identified factors contributing to police ineffectiveness during the 1960s civil disorders. Since release of the Kerner report, the frequency and intensity of civil disorders has declined and the policing of disorders has changed. Using the report recommendations as a framework, we analyze changes in police disorder management during the 2014 events in Ferguson as these involve operational planning and equipment. Data for the Ferguson case are constructed from media reports, police and activist accounts, after action reports, and field observations. We link changes seen in Ferguson to larger institutional changes in law enforcement over the last fifty years. We conclude with discussions on what did and did not work in the policing of Ferguson and highlight implications for policing of protest and disorder in the twenty-first century.*

**Keywords:** Kerner Commission, National Advisory Commission on Civil Disorders, democratic policing, protest, riots, Ferguson

> Police departments have become more adept at handling potential riot situations. While riot potentials were greater in 1968 than in 1967, the triggering events were rapidly controlled and large-scale disorders thus were avoided.
>
> —Urban America 1969

> It is our hope that the lessons learned in Ferguson will provide guidance to . . . police departments around the country and will prepare these agencies to respond *effectively* and *constitutionally* to the challenges of mass demonstrations in the 21st century. [emphasis added]
>
> —Institute for Intergovernmental Research 2015

**Patrick F. Gillham** is assistant professor of sociology at Western Washington University. **Gary T. Marx** is professor emeritus at MIT.

© 2018 Russell Sage Foundation. Gillham, Patrick F., and Gary T. Marx. 2018. "Changes in the Policing of Civil Disorders Since the Kerner Report: The Police Response to Ferguson, August 2014, and Some Implications for the Twenty-First Century." *RSF: The Russell Sage Foundation Journal of the Social Sciences* 4(6): 122–43. DOI: 10.7758/RSF.2018.4.6.06. The authors thank Blake Gardner and Hugh Jones for field assistance in Ferguson. In addition, they thank participants in the RSF Conference on the Fiftieth Anniversary of the Kerner Commission Report and anonymous reviewers at RSF for their insightful comments on this manuscript. Direct correspondence to: Patrick F. Gillham at pat.gillham@wwu.edu, Department of Sociology, 516 High St., MS-9081, Bellingham, WA 98225; and Gary T. Marx at gtmarx@mit.edu, http://www.garymarx.net.

Open Access Policy: *RSF: The Russell Sage Foundation Journal of the Social Sciences* is an open access journal. This article is published under a Creative Commons Attribution-NonCommercial-NoDerivs 3.0 Unported License.

Police were a central factor in the 1967 disorders studied by the National Advisory Commission on Civil Disorders (the Kerner Commission, thus the Kerner report [1968]). The commission's "Supplement on Control of Disorder" considered problems related to operational planning, logistical needs, training, control equipment, coordination, and legal needs. We use some of their 1968 recommendations as the framework to contrast police behavior then and now. For the contemporary period, we consider the policing of protests that emerged with a case study of Ferguson, Missouri, following the police killing of Michael Brown.

The Ferguson protests and disorder and the overwhelming police response to this social unrest provide a reminder that, more than any other institution, police symbolize the American racial order. Despite improvement in some areas, the combustible mix that led to the 1960s disorders is still here. Police remain the fulcrum for accumulated grievances.

In the 1960s, incidents (and sometimes rumors) of police violence were most often what drew protesters, rioting protesters, and opportunistic rioters to the streets. Once on the street, police responses were a central factor in whether violence escalated. In 1967 police action could often be described as too much too soon or too little too late. Sometimes there were two riots—the police and those they sought to control. Other factors include instances of firecrackers being heard as gunshots, of police mistakenly firing at each other, of police covering their badges; and of leadership, equipment, strategic, and logistical failures that limited effectiveness and increased anger on all sides (Marx 1971a). This article explores how the policing of civil disorders in a context of protest has changed since the 1960s.

We begin with a consideration of factors relevant to the relative absence of the large-scale disorders since the 1960s. Paralleling changes in the forms of disorder, we note a shift by researchers to study the policing of disorders as a factor more broadly tied to efforts to control social movements and protest. Then, we review several problems with the policing of disorders identified by the Kerner Commission and the commission's recommendations to mitigate them. We use the case of Ferguson in 2014 to illustrate significant changes in the policing of protests since Kerner. We consider three central questions: What changes in the policing of protest and civil disorder are most noticeable since Kerner? What police practices "worked" in Ferguson and what practices did not? What are implications for the twenty-first century?

## THE ABEYANCE OF LARGE-SCALE CIVIL DISORDERS

We have in general not seen a repeat of the massive state violence in response to crowd situations that was responsible for hundreds of deaths in the 1960s (Tilly 2003). Even the assassination of Martin Luther King Jr. did not lead to extended and continued rioting beyond the initial outbursts, nor was it as heavy handed a police response as in previous times.[1] The decline in the frequency of civil disorders has been documented (Olzak and Shanahan 1996; Olzak, Shanahan, and McEneaney 1996; Gooden and Myers 2018; Bentley-Edwards et al. 2018), but little research has been undertaken on reasons for the decline and on changes in policing of disorders. Since the 1970s, scholars have shifted their focus away from disorders as such and toward the policing of social movements and protest events (see, for example, Marx 1970a, 1988; della Porta and Reiter 1998; Earl, Soule, and McCarthy 2003; Vitale 2005; della Porta, Peterson, and Reiter 2006; Waddington 2007; Soule and Davenport 2009; Earl 2011; Starr, Fernandez, and Scholl 2011; Gillham, Edwards, and Noakes 2013; Wood 2014). This shift

---

1. The Kerner report with its call for improved police responses appeared shortly before King's death. Yet independent of the Kerner report awareness had increased within law enforcement of the need to avoid the kinds of failures seen in Detroit, Newark, and Watts. This statement is of course relative to American history, internationally and since the 1960s. Examples of post-1960s failures in policing of civil disorders include the 1979 Greensboro massacre, the 1980 Miami race–McDuffie riots, and the six-day Rodney King riots in Los Angeles in 1992 (Moore 2012; Webster and William 1992).

away from studying civil disorders is no doubt related to their relative absence. Relevant factors in the decline likely include improved ways for filing grievances against police, the spread of civilian review boards, greater court receptiveness to police liability cases, and establishment of protest permitting systems (McCarthy and McPhail 1998; McPhail, Schweingruber, and McCarthy 1998; Schneider 2014).[2] Yet, as many of the articles in this issue suggest, the racial injustices seen by the commission persist and in some ways have been worsened by the devastating impacts of the war on drugs (Alexander 2011; Oliver 2008).

## VARYING POLICE RESPONSES TO PROTEST AND DISORDERS

Given the contemporary saliency of protests and the fact that disorders often ignite from protest events (such as Ferguson, Baltimore, Standing Rock, and Charlottesville), for this article we draw on scholarship from the policing of social movements and protest events to theorize the changes in policing of civil disorders. By civil disorders, we mean larger scale, disruptive, public events directed at a dominant social order that can include acts of civil disobedience and direct action, confrontations with law enforcement and counter protesters, and behavior such as looting, arson, and physical violence (Body-Gendrot 2017). Collective and individual acts that occur during civil disorders involve violence rituals, coordinated destruction, and opportunism whether directed at commodities, competing groups, or both (Tilly 2003; Waddington 2007). Our definition recognizes that such actions may represent political acts seen as being of last resort (Hobsbawm 1964; Piven and Cloward 1979). Whether police view crowd behavior as protest or crime has important implications for where responses fall on a continuum moving from communication to coercion (Earl and Soule 2006; Wood 2007).

Contemporary research on the U.S. policing of protest and disorderly events has focused primarily on national special security events (such as G20 meetings), disruptive protest events extensively covered by the media (such as Occupy Wall Street), and on policing in large metro areas like New York City and Washington, D.C., where protests are routine (Gillham and Marx 2000; Vitale 2005, 2007; Fernandez 2008; Starr, Fernandez, and Scholl 2011; Gillham, Edwards, and Noakes 2013; Wood 2014; King 2017). This research finds that the policing of protest and disorder has changed dramatically since the 1960s, although scholars debate whether the changes are driven more by innovations in police behavior or by changes in protest tactics (Earl 2011).

Police actions can facilitate, channel, or repress protests (Marx 1988; Earl 2003). During the 1950s and 1960s cycles of protest, police applied escalating levels of force to prevent or constrain protests and disorders (McCarthy and McPhail 1998). Such actions could result in on-the-job troubles such as injuries, deaths, and property damage, and in-the-job troubles such as public criticism, commissions, and pressure from political elites (Walker 1968; Waddington 1994).

In the aftermath of the Kerner Commission and others (such as the Violence Commission) researchers noted the development of a less confrontational approach by leading law enforcement agencies that emphasized negotiating with protesters the time, manner, and place of demonstrations. Adopted first in Washington, D.C., in the early 1980s, the *negotiated management* style of protest policing developed around an *event permitting process*, which in turn led to increased communication and co-

---

2. Just how independent, transparent, and effective current methods are is a different question, but the presence of these mechanisms, however imperfect, matters. In addition, when disorders occur they are likely to receive more balanced attention in the mass media and from the Justice Department than fifty years ago. Other possible factors for the abeyance of disorders include the appearance of stronger neighborhood, local community and professionalized national and other nongovernmental organizations (Noakes and Gillham 2006), and moves toward community policing, or at least greater receptiveness to community concerns. Finally, just as the war on drugs has devastated many minority communities by moving many black males younger than thirty into prison or placing them under some type of judicial supervision, this "war" has also removed potential participants from the pool of people who could participate in social movements and other forms of political activity (Oliver 2008).

operation between police and protesters and an extended period of calm (McPhail, Scheingruber, and McCarthy 1998; McCarthy, McPhail, and Crist 1999). Yet, since the disruptive World Trade Organization protests in Seattle in 1999 police-protester relations have been frequently more adversarial. Trust, cooperation, and communication have declined on both sides as police sought to incapacitate protest and activists resisted such efforts (Noakes, Klocke, and Gillham 2005; Vitale 2005, 2007; Gillham and Noakes 2007; Gillham 2011; King 2017).

These changes are noticeable relative to the 1960s. Drawing on media reports, police and activist accounts, official after-action reports, and our direct field observations from August 16 through August 18, we analyze policing of the 2014 Ferguson Missouri protests and disorder that developed. The Ferguson case is important because it provides an opportunity to study an infrequent occurrence of civil disorder and law enforcement's response, and illustrates some broader national changes seen in many law enforcement agencies since the release of the Kerner report.

## KERNER FINDINGS

Among problems identified by the Kerner Commission were those involving operational planning and police control equipment (see table 1). The first set of *operational planning* problems involved weaknesses in the dispatch-oriented command and control structure for policing disorders (Kerner Report 1968, 268). In the 1960s, departments used a dispatch-driven command and control system according to which orders were delivered from a central location via car radio to line officers on patrol. Officers responding to the scene of a crowd incident radioed back to dispatch for help to disperse the crowd. Yet, when supporting officers arrived at the scene, their presence and actions could increase tensions among those already angry and distrustful of police. Because radios were anchored to the patrol vehicle, officers at the scene were unable to easily communicate with commanders at headquarters. By the time commanders realized they and additional officers were needed on-site, it was often too late as disorder rapidly spread and escalated, as was the case in Detroit, Milwaukee, and Newark (Kerner Report 1968).

After a large-scale disorder was under way, police often had difficulty communicating with each other because they did not have radios on their person and no special radio frequencies had been established to handle the additional radio traffic associated with the disorder response. Many departments did not have adequate organizational and technical means to communicate either with police in neighboring jurisdictions or with state police and sheriff departments. When other law enforcement agencies were present, their radio frequencies were frequently incompatible, making it difficult to respond quickly in an organized way (Kerner Report 1968, 269).

To mitigate these command and control troubles, the commission recommended that, first, a model operational plan providing guidelines for responding to incidents and civil disorders developed by the commission be distributed to all police departments;[3] second, the federal government fund the development of miniaturized and portable radios for law enforcement; and, third, the Federal Communications Commission make enough frequencies available to police and other first responders (Kerner Report 1968, 269–70).

The second set of operational planning problems involved the lack of information or intelligence available to police about the planning of protests and disorder events, and about disorder events once they started (Kerner Report 1968, 172–73, 269). The commission noted that many departments had little understanding about the causes of unrest within primarily black urban areas, had poor relations with people living in these segregated neighborhoods, and generally lacked reliable means for gathering information about looming civil unrest. The lack of broad understanding, poor relations, and relevant pre-disorder information pre-

---

3. The plan was integrated into a larger *Guidelines for Civil Disorder and Mobilization Planning* prepared by the Research, Development and Planning Division of the International Association of Chiefs of Police (Smith and Kobetz 1968). It was released six months after the Kerner report.

**Table 1.** Kerner Findings: Mismanagement Factors, Problems, and Recommendations Related to Operational Planning and Police Equipment

| Mismanagement Factor | Problems | Recommendation |
|---|---|---|
| Operational planning | Dispatch driven command and control system provides insufficient structure for responding to incidents and civil disorders | Police need operational plans that provide guidelines for responding to incidents and civil disorders |
| | Line officer radios located in patrol vehicle. Thus, cannot communicate with dispatch unless in vehicle | Federal government should initiate and fund portable radio development programs |
| | No special radio frequency available to use for public order emergencies; limited means to communicate with neighboring law enforcement agencies; neighboring agencies used incompatible radio frequencies | FCC should make enough frequencies available to police and related public safety services to meet needs for public order emergencies |
| | Limited information gathered before and during civil disorder. Thus, unable to make reliable assessment and decisions in the field and unable to counter rumors | Develop intelligence units to gather, evaluate, analyze, and disseminate information about potential and actual civil disorders |
| Police equipment | Minimal self-protection equipment available for frontline officers resulting in officer injury | Provide proper equipment and clothing to protect against threat to bodily harm |
| | Batons and hand guns, the primary control tools available for local law enforcement, are insufficient for responding to civil disorders | Federal government should initiate program to test and evaluate nonlethal weapons for use by police, provide support to develop national standards to stimulate the private sector to produce these weapons, and direct funds to develop these weapons for local and state law enforcement agencies |

*Source:* Authors' tabulations.

vented police from preparing adequately. Moreover, once civil disorders erupted, police had limited skills and methods for gathering information. This made responding to rumors difficult. Furthermore, few formal ways to disseminate accurate information about an incident or disorder were in place, leaving rumors and media to shape the public's view of events. The commission recommended that police develop intelligence units to gather, evaluate, analyze, and disseminate information about potential civil disorders and during civil disorders (269).

Another set of problems identified involved police protective and control equipment. Most police departments did not provide officers adequate self-protection equipment against rocks, bottles, and other projectiles. Wooden batons and service revolvers were the primary methods of control (Kerner Report 1968, 176). The commission questioned the justification for using deadly force during civil disorders, noting the risk of killing or wounding innocent people, that the property crimes committed during disorder events did not warrant the use of lethal force, and that excessive force (including the inappropriate display of weapons) could provoke further disorder. The commission saw a need for control tools in the "middle range of physical force" that could be used "more humanely" and effectively for regular policing and during times of unrest (176).

The commission recommended that the federal government undertake a program to test and evaluate "nonlethal" weapons for use by police, provide support "to establish criteria and standards specifications to stimulate [private industry to produce] such items," and direct funds "to be used to develop appropriate tools . . . for local and state law enforcement agencies (Kerner Report 1968, 272). The commission further warned against militarizing local police because doing so risked "destroy[ing] the concept of civilian police as a public service agency dependent for effective operations on community cooperation and support" (272).

We next compare the commission's recommendations with what we saw in Ferguson to illustrate changes in the policing of disorder. The contrast between policing of the 1960s and today is clear, just as are commonalities. Although many factors are involved, the changes in law enforcement seen in the illustrative case study that follows are consistent with the basic thrust of the Kerner recommendations and certainly had an important impact.

## TRANSFORMATION IN THE POLICING OF DISORDER

We next consider key events in Ferguson over the sixteen days between the killing of Michael Brown and his funeral. We then use the Ferguson case to highlight changes in police operational planning and equipment since Kerner and note some institutional forces contributing to these changes.

### The Ferguson Case (August 9–August 25, 2014)

On August 9, shortly after noon, a Ferguson police officer shot and killed eighteen-year-old Michael Brown, an unarmed African American man. Backup officers from the Ferguson Police Department (PD) and the St. Louis County Police Department (SLCPD) rushed to the scene and pushed back an agitated crowd that had gathered. Officers reported an increasingly chaotic scene, with some crowd members making death threats to police and shots being fired nearby. In response, the SLCPD deployed their Tactical Operations Unit, then initiated the county's Code 1000 Plan, which mobilized aid from neighboring police departments and activated the Riot A Channel for exclusive communication between responding law enforcement agencies (IIR 2015, 5–9). More than fifty officers from multiple agencies quickly arrived and staged at two nearby locations. Crowds continued to grow at the homicide scene and formed at the police staging areas and outside the Ferguson PD headquarters. Protests continued at these locations until early morning August 10 (10–11).

Mid-morning of August 10, crowds reassembled around the city. In response, SLCPD and Ferguson police chiefs established an "informal joint command" within the Ferguson PD headquarters and used the Code 1000 plan to request more officers from surrounding jurisdictions. After an evening candle-light vigil at the site of the shooting, angry protesters surged into streets chanting "no justice, no peace." They were met by police in riot gear holding rifles and shields (*New York Times* 2014). After this confrontation, the first civil disorder began when several protesters vandalized police vehicles, damaged property, and looted businesses along West Florissant Avenue (Barker 2014). Police deployed armored vehicles and canine units to protect officers from thrown projectiles and more reported gun fire.

The SLCPD chief took charge as incident commander and extended the Code 1000 Plan by initiating a formal Incident Command System (ICS) framework. The ICS, an organizational framework first developed by FEMA and adopted nationally by first responders, is "a standardized personnel management tool" that establishes an integrated organizational command and control framework which designates an incident commander to manage all personnel and make critical decisions (Bigley and Roberts 2001; St. Louis County 2013, 6). As part of the ICS police established an official command post in a mall on West Florissant Avenue. After allegedly giving dispersal orders, tactical teams fired smoke canisters and tear gas, pushing protesters and looters north into the town of Dellwood. That night, police made thirty-two arrests (Barker 2014; Giegerich, Bogan, and Bell 2014; Institute for Intergovernmental Research 2015, 11–15).

Over the next several days, a similar cycle persisted of peaceful protests during the daytime and a mix of peaceful, unruly, and illegal actions during the night. According to police reports, at night some citizens looted and burned businesses, threw Molotov cocktails and other projectiles at police lines, fired guns, and destroyed civilian and police vehicles. Police forcefully responded by driving armored vehicles into the streets, deploying tear gas and other less-lethal weapons, and making arrests (IIR 2015, 15–17, 58).

As news of the unrest spread through conventional media and social media outlets, police intelligence reports indicated that people from across the region and country had begun arriving in Ferguson, some to protest and others with intent to exploit opportunities for personal gain (IIR 2015, 18, 58). Local, county, and state political leaders, frustrated by the increased disorder and negative media attention wanted the incident commander replaced. On August 14, Governor Nixon responded by declaring a state of emergency and making Missouri State Highway Patrol Captain Johnson, an African American, incident commander. Protester and police interactions were calmer that night, perhaps because of the governor's action (20).

The calm, though, was short lived. On August 15, the Ferguson Police Department identified Darren Wilson as the officer who had killed Michael Brown and released a surveillance video showing that Brown had allegedly stolen a package of cigars from a convenience store shortly before he was stopped by Wilson. A later unedited version of the video indicated that Brown may not have stolen the cigars (Smith 2017). Hundreds of people assembled outside the Ferguson Police Department headquarters to condemn release of the video, seen by many in the community as a ploy to demonize Brown and justify the shooting. Like previous nights, people again engaged in rioting and looting while peaceful protesters looked on. This time, police stood by choosing not to act out of concern they would only make things worse (IIR 2015, 21–23).

August 16, Governor Nixon declared a state of emergency and imposed a midnight to 5:00 a.m. curfew. In the streets, officers with helmets, face protectors, gas masks, riot batons, shields, and Kevlar vests formed lines separating people on the streets and sidewalks from local businesses. Tactical teams in full battle gear moved small groups of people around the streets and sidewalks and stood guard at roadblocks. That night police again used armored vehicles, lines of officers, less-lethal weapons, and arrests to disperse crowds (IIR 2015, 24–25).

On the evening of August 17, police reported that a large crowd attempted to overtake the command post. It is unclear whether this was the intent of those in the crowd or they had assembled simply to protest police actions or the curfew order. Police dispatched a helicopter to provide overhead surveillance and a line of officers led by SWAT units used smoke bombs, tear gas, and other less-lethal weapons to move the crowd back north on West Florissant Avenue. Several businesses were looted and a brawl between 150 people broke out. As the chaos increased, all police teams were pulled back in hope to diffuse the anger of people in the streets. But the disorder raged on as the most violent night of unrest yet. The next day, Governor Nixon lifted the curfew and ordered the National Guard to protect the command post, freeing up police officers to help with disorder control (IIR 2015, 26–28).

August 19 was a turning point. Hostile interactions continued between protesters and police, but less rioting, property damage, and shots fired were reported. Over the next several days "a calm began to emerge"—as fewer people protested and less anger was exhibited (IIR 2015, 28). On August 21, the governor ordered the Missouri National Guard to withdraw from Ferguson. By August 24, police report that protest had continued to decrease in size and "a sense of normalcy was returning." On August 25, Michael Brown was laid to rest. At his father's request, no protests occurred during the funeral (IIR 2015, 28–29).

**Fifty Years After Kerner**
We use the Ferguson case to consider our first major question: What has changed in the policing of protest and civil disorder since the

**Table 2.** Police Command and Control System, Intelligence Practices, and Protective and Control Equipment During Disorders in the 1960s and in Ferguson in 2014

| | 1960s | Ferguson |
|---|---|---|
| Command and control system | Dispatch driven | Code 1000 Plan and ICS |
| | No special radio frequency for emergencies | RIOT A radio frequencies |
| | Radios located in patrol vehicles incompatible with radios used by neighboring jurisdictions | Vehicle and portable radios, cell phones, and text messaging across command chain |
| Intelligence practices | No formal intelligence units in most PDs | Joint intelligence unit formed from SLCPD, SLMPD, SL Fusion Center; assistance from MO Info Analysis Center |
| | Limited information gathered before civil disorder | No information gathered before civil disorder |
| | Limited information gathered during civil disorder | Event data collected by intel unit in static and real time via undercover officers, officers in streets, permits, aircraft, police video-streaming, social media monitoring |
| | | Information about outside protest groups collected by intel unit; relied on cross-national diverse intelligence information systems including fusion centers |
| Self-protection equipment | Minimal self-protection available | Helmets, gas masks, Kevlar vests, and shields (line officers and tactical units) |
| | | Military grade body armor, battle dress, and armored vehicles (tactical units) |
| Control equipment | Baton and guns | Less-lethal weapons to disperse and incapacitate, such as impact, acoustic, and chemical irritants (line officers and tactical units) |
| | | Armored vehicles and displayed military firepower to deter and intimidate (tactical units) |

*Source:* Authors' tabulations.

Kerner report? We limit our analysis to changes in police operational planning related to command and control and the gathering and analysis of intelligence, and police equipment used (see table 2). After highlighting some of these changes, we identify institutional forces that have contributed to the changes.

*Command and Control in Ferguson*
Commanders' abilities to quickly receive assistance from other agencies and to communicate effectively across the chain of command has improved significantly since Kerner. For many years, St. Louis County has had a Code 1000 Plan that aides nearby agencies in planning and control for civil disorders and disasters (St. Louis County 2013). When activated on August 9, the nearest twenty-five police cars from various jurisdictions were immediately dispatched to the homicide scene along with a crowd-control mobile response team. Other officers self-deployed when they heard the Code 1000

request (Belmar and Kleinknecht 2016; IIR 2015). Besides providing a mechanism to promptly mobilize mutual aid, the Code 1000 Plan also provided a framework for managing personnel during the early hours of the crises. For example, for each five officers that responded to the Code 1000 request, a commanding officer was deployed. The commanding officer then made decisions in the field and communicated with the SLCPD chief who had initiated the Code 1000 (IIR 2015).

Once it became clear that the civil disorder would not quickly dissipate, law enforcement officials initiated an ICS framework, which formally designated the incident commander and required establishment of an operations command post and lines of communication across the ICS chain of command, designated an operations officer to coordinate tactical operations and a public information officer to communicate to the media and community, established law enforcement staging areas, and assigned support staff (St. Louis County 2013, 6; Bigley and Roberts 2001; FEMA 2013). Reliance on such extensive and versatile operational guidelines as provided by the Code 1000 Plan and ICS framework indicates an organizational shift in law enforcement's command and control structure far beyond what the Kerner Commission envisioned.

Relatedly, communication technologies have of course changed dramatically since Kerner. Police agencies now have access to portable radios on the same frequencies as vehicle radios and as radios in other jurisdictions. In Ferguson, the county dispatcher could contact agencies needed to respond to the initial call for assistance and special RIOT channels were available. Most radios synced well, despite interoperability issues still common elsewhere (IIR 2015; Weiser 2007). When there were failures, a communications officer activated the IP Interoperability and Collaboration System and bridged communication networks across all agencies (Kanowitz 2016). Interoperability was also provided through officers' smart phones which received bulk message texts via a private messaging service (IIR 2015, 106) and likely allowed the sharing of maps, photos, and videos among officers in the streets and command center.

*Intelligence in Ferguson*

Intelligence practices have also radically changed. Today, police departments rely on in-house intelligence units, new surveillance technologies, and cooperation among law enforcement across a national network of fusion centers (IIR 2015; Gillham 2011; Narr et al. 2006). Ferguson police did not have an active intelligence unit when the uprising began. However, once the ICS protocol was initiated, a joint intelligence unit was established to monitor the civil disorder and related issues. The unit drew officers and other resources from the separate intelligence units of the SLCPD and St. Louis Metropolitan Police Department, the St. Louis Fusion Center, and the Missouri State Fusion Center (IIR 2015, 82).

The quickly assembled intelligence unit was able to gather event data as the protests mobilized and the disorders spread (IIR 2015, 129). The intelligence unit relied on various local resources including local agency helicopters equipped with the latest forward-looking infrared (FLIR) night vision and moving map technologies, undercover intelligence officers circulating among the crowds, and officers tracking social media (St. Louis County Police Department 2014, 19; IIR 2015, 82, 101). Much of this locally based intelligence gathering was conducted using "new surveillance technologies" (Marx 2002, 2016), such as Geofeedia, a surveillance platform that links social media posts with the location of the posting. Geofeedia showed the intelligence unit the exact locations of the worst disorder from pictures and video posted by protesters (Ozer 2016).

The joint intelligence unit also relied on outside assistance. FBI aerial surveillance pinpointed the location of fires and where people were gathered (Tucker 2015). National law enforcement and private sector analysts provided the intelligence unit "information through diverse intelligence information systems" (IIR 2015, 83), including the hub-and-spoke network of seventy-eight fusion centers distributed nationwide (82).

Although secrecy surrounding a sensitive topic inhibits a full understanding of where information came from and how it was used internally, the public information officer used some information to counter rumors and protester narratives of events, and to portray police in a positive light (IIR 2015). The use of public information officers in these ways is a common national practice (Gillham, Edwards, and Noakes 2013; Narr et al. 2006). The surveillance and information acquisition and sharing capacity has expanded significantly since the 1960s.

*Self-protection Equipment in Ferguson*
Police involved in management of the Ferguson disorder were well equipped in protective gear relative to the 1960s (see table 2). Line officers in Ferguson wore their regular duty uniforms and Kevlar vests and were issued protective equipment depending on the officer assignment. Agents policing the most disorderly locations (such as the SLCPD and Missouri State Highway Patrol) had helmets, handheld shields, face shields, and gas masks (IIR 2015, 57). More visually and technically striking was the protective gear worn by tactical officers: "battle dress uniforms," some in camouflage, military boots, utility belts and web guns, Kevlar helmets with night vision equipment, goggles, gasmasks, "level-three heavy vests," and some body armor. They also had available armored vehicles for safe transit and to extract officers and injured citizens from volatile settings (IIR 2015; Pickler 2015; Belmar and Kleinknecht 2016).

*Control Equipment in Ferguson*
The range of mid-level weapons that augmented officers' batons and service revolvers contrasted markedly with the 1960s. Line officers and tactical units had electronic control weapons such as Tasers and an arsenal of various projectiles, which had varying levels of impact on their human targets. Less painful and less likely to cause serious injury were hand-thrown Stingerball devices that released rubber balls and pyrotechnic fire and sounds. More painful and likely to injure people were bean bag rounds fired from shotguns, and Pepper-Ball rounds and wooden batons both fired from handheld launchers. Smoke canisters were fired to disorient people in the streets, break up groups, and assess wind direction before deploying tear gas (IIR 2015, 46–49).

Police had more than mid-level weapons available, however. Tactical units relied heavily on military-grade equipment and techniques. They carried automatic rifles, had strapped to their vests high-capacity magazines containing one to two hundred rounds of ammunition for their weapons, and used armored vehicles to disperse crowds (IIR 2015). The Lenco Bearcat, a close cousin to the U.S. military mine-resistant, ambush-protected vehicle, was the most prominent type of armored vehicle deployed. The SLCPD's Bearcat was twenty feet long and ten feet wide, weighed eighteen thousand pounds, and had an elevated platform that would allow access to the third floor of a building (Lenco 2014; Belmar and Kleinknecht 2016, 36). Tactical officers used the platform to post lookouts and snipers who pointed their rifles at people in the crowd while using their high-powered sights to search for people with weapons (IIR 2015). Attached to the Bearcat was a military long-range acoustical device or "sound cannon," which would transmit verbal announcements or warnings across long distances or high-pitched, ear-damaging tones to disperse crowds.

**Institutional Forces of Change**
Several institutional forces contributed to these organizational and technological response changes. Closely connected to the Kerner Commission recommendations was creation of the National Institute of Justice (NIJ) to research and standardize police equipment and technologies. Another important set of institutional forces link to the U.S. Department of Homeland Security (DHS). These include requirements that law enforcement agencies receiving federal grants must adopt the ICS framework, creation of the fusion center network, and the establishment of antiterrorism grant programs.[4]

*National Institute of Justice and Development of Police Technologies*
The various mid-level weapons and communication and surveillance technologies available

---

4. Space limitations prevent us from elaborating on other similar institutional forces including the rise of paramilitary police units and the Department of Defense 1033 Program that leases military equipment to local law enforcement agencies (see Kraska and Cubellis 1997; Kraska and Kappeler 1997; Balko 2013; Wood 2014).

to law enforcement in Ferguson and nationally were developed with assistance from the NIJ, the research branch of the U.S. Department of Justice. The NIJ was formed in 1969 following recommendations made by President Johnson's 1966 Commission on Law Enforcement and Administration of Justice and the Kerner Commission report. A central purpose of the NIJ was to promote the innovation and adoption of police technologies used to manage protest and disorder (National Institute of Justice 1994, 10, 44.).

The NIJ promoted this innovation and adoption through four mechanisms. First, in the early 1970s, the Institute developed the Police Weapons System Program to assess "policies and practices in the acquisition and use of offensive and defensive weapons by law enforcement" and evaluated existing police weapons systems not yet widely adopted (1994, 45). Second, simultaneously it launched the Law Enforcement Standards Laboratory with the dual purpose of establishing "scientifically based, voluntary commercial manufacturing standards" and certifying a nationwide network of "laboratories where equipment items could be evaluated according to those standards" (45). By 1975, the laboratory had developed performance standards for technologies recommended by the Kerner report including portable radios and defensive gear such as riot helmets, light weight body armor, and ballistic shields. Over the years, the NIJ has continued to update these standards, including for new surveillance technologies (National Institute of Justice 1994; Nunn 2001).

Third, the NIJ provided research grants to improve existing weapons and develop new ones. These grants were distributed through projects such as the Less-Lethal Technologies Program started in 1986, and Joint Non-Lethal Weapons Program started in 1996 (Wood 2014). Through these grants, less-lethal products such as pepper spray and adjustable-velocity projectile launchers were developed (National Institute of Justice 1994, 52). Fourth, the NIJ joined with universities and the private sector to disseminate knowledge about these technologies through commercial trade journals, trade shows that coincided with police conventions, and guides for less-lethal weapons (Weapons and Protective Systems Technologies Center 2010; Wood 2014).

By the time of the Ferguson protests, a market had been created whereby law enforcement agencies across the country could find powerful and affordable middle-range weapons and other technologies (Wood 2014; Balko 2013).

*Department of Homeland Security and Change*
The DHS, created in the aftermath of the terrorist attacks of September 11, 2001, has been responsible for three other institutional forces that have shaped law enforcement's adoption of the ICS framework and new technologies used in response to protest and civil disorder. The first is the requirement that state and local agencies who receive federal grants must adopt FEMA ICS protocols.

The ICS structure was initially developed by the U.S. Forest Service and supporting state and local agencies in reaction to several organizational problems encountered by first responders during catastrophic wildfires in California in 1970 (Chase 1980).[5] After the Forest Service and other fire agencies adopted the ICS framework, FEMA adopted ICS as a best practice and recommended that other first responder agencies, including law enforcement, do the same (Cardwell and Cooney 2000). However, most law enforcement agencies were slow to adopt ICS (Cardwell and Cooney 2000; Buck, Trainor, and Aguirre 2006).

After establishing the DHS, President George W. Bush directed state and local agencies that receive federal grant funds, including law enforcement agencies, to adopt FEMA's ICS approach for managing emergencies.[6] Today, as a consequence of this directive, most law enforcement departments have adopted a

---

5. These problems (similar to the organizational planning problems identified in the Kerner report) included "overloaded spans of control..., lack of reliable information, inadequate and incompatible communication,... and unclear lines of authority" (Lutz and Lindell 2008, 123).

6. HSPD-5, Directive on Management of Domestic Incidents, February 28, 2003 (accessed May 4, 2018, https://www.dhs.gov/sites/default/files/publications/Homeland%20Security%20Presidential%20Directive%205.pdf).

FEMA modeled ICS for responding in emergency situations, including situations like the civil disorder that broke out in Ferguson (IIR 2015).

Another DHS-related institutional force was the establishment of a national fusion center network. Fusion centers, paid for with post-9/11 federal grants, are charged with receiving, analyzing, gathering, and sharing threat-related information across federal, state, local, tribal, territorial, and private-sector partners (DHS 2017). Analysts in local or state fusion centers send information to other centers and to the central DHS watch center (DHS 2017). As noted in our case, this network provided vital information to the Ferguson intelligence unit as they have to local police agencies responding to other recent protests and disorders (Gillham, Edwards, and Noakes 2013; Police Executive Research Forum 2015; Meyer 2017).

A final institutional force is DHS grants provided to law enforcement agencies for national security. Since 2003, Urban Areas Security Initiative (UASI) grants have provided more than $500 million annually to the largest metropolitan areas in the United States, enabling police to acquire military equipment and less-lethal weapons (Balko 2013; DHS 2014; IIR 2015, 58). These funds are intended to "address the unique planning, organization, equipment, training, and exercise needs of high-threat, high-density urban areas, and assists them in building an enhanced and sustainable capacity to prevent, protect against, respond to, and recover from acts of terrorism" (FEMA 2010, 2). But these funds pay for equipment used for more than anti-terrorism measures. The SLCPD used UASI grants to purchase their Bearcat, protective gear, and less-lethal weapons used during the Ferguson unrest (Belmar and Kleinknecht 2016; IIR 2015).

In sum, the provision of federal resources and funding requirements helped standardize practices, improved communication across agencies, and provided support for new practices and technologies unlikely to be locally funded. Clearly, in important ways the policing of protest has dramatically changed since Kerner. Next, we consider what worked and what did not work as a consequence of the described changes.

## HOW MANY CHEERS? SOME IMPACTS IN FERGUSON AND BEYOND

Besides organizational and technical changes, we note changes in police culture, specifically, better empirical understanding of crowd behavior and the rights of citizens. In many cases this has resulted in a softening of, and greater differentiation in, police responses, even as this brings risks of under-reaction. Yet simultaneously some law and order responses to crowds have hardened, bringing risks of over-reaction (for example, blurring the lines between local police and the military with respect to available tools, tactics, and cooperation).

Given the vast time period and significant variation across places and types of events any conclusions about consequences of "what worked and what has not worked since Kerner?" must be tentative. Furthermore, any consideration of what works in the context of a semi-secret institution with unique powers of coercion charged with maintaining an unequal status quo must be qualified more than for other less adversarial institutions. Yet, some broader conclusions can be drawn from the Ferguson case with respect to current police command and control systems, intelligence practices, and equipment (see table 3).

The organizational and equipment changes seen in Ferguson were not accompanied by civilian or police fatalities. As noted in table 3, policing practices employed during Ferguson worked in some ways to deal with issues raised by the Kerner Commission (such as rapid mobilization, clearer chain of command, improved communication within and between agencies and officers, dispelling of rumors through public information officers, better intelligence during events, safety equipment, use of less-lethal weapons).

Yet, paradoxically, these practices can be accompanied by ironic or unforeseen consequences. Consider the ways local police have become more militarized—a factor the Kerner report clearly warned against. Although increasing militarization provides protective equipment for police and superior force to potentially deter violent assaults against police or others, it can also reinforce feelings of fear and anger and the view that police are an occupying army rather a public force that protects and

**Table 3.** Police Command and Control System, Intelligence Practices, and Protective and Control Equipment Used in Ferguson in 2014

| | Worked | Did Not Work |
|---|---|---|
| **Command and control system** | | |
| 1000 Plan/ICS Plan | Provided efficient mechanism to rapidly mobilize officers from multiple agencies<br>Established clear chain of command for decision-making, communicating orders, and communicating with public to dispel rumors | Drew self-deploying officers undertrained in disorder control and without direct supervision<br>Incident commander communicated orders inconsistently resulting in contradictory and under-enforcement that escalated disorder<br>Misinformation provided in cigar video inflamed community members and escalated disorder |
| RIOT radio frequency, portable radios, cell phones, and text messaging | Facilitated efficient and closed communication between officers<br>Prevented communication system overload | Closed communications minimized public transparency about police actions |
| **Intelligence practices** | | |
| Local intelligence unit with extensive in-house surveillance and analytic tools available | Used extensive in-house surveillance and analytic tools to gather and analyze multiple sources and large amounts of static and real-time information; able to quickly assess risk and respond, and to collect evidence for prosecution | Revealed extent of national surveillance system with capacity to violate privacy rights; created distrust and chilled protest |
| National fusion center network | Used extensive national surveillance and analytic tools to gather and analyze multiple sources and large amounts of static and real-time information; able to inform Ferguson intelligence unit about events there and potential outsider threats | Revealed extent of national surveillance system with capacity to violate privacy rights; created distrust and chilled protest |
| **Control equipment and techniques** | | |
| Self-protection equipment | Minimized individual injury to officers in the field | Distanced officers from community members, chilled protest |
| Deployment of military grade equipment | Display of firepower may have deterred some disorder; armored vehicles provided way to extract officers and injured protesters from volatile settings | Frightened and angered community members, delegitimized police in local communities and nationally, may have escalated disorder, risk of mass fatalities |
| Use of less-lethal weapons | Prevented deaths and reduced incident of serious injuries | Frightened and angered community members, delegitimized police in local communities and nationally, more people affected by police use of force, may have escalated disorder |

*Source*: Authors' tabulations.

serves its community. First Amendment activities may be chilled, already damaged relations may be worsened, and police further delegitimized. If disorder persists, a militarized force can attract more people into the streets out of curiosity, excitement, or anger (Gillham and Marx 2000). Another risk is that officers armed with automatic weapons might inadvertently kill many citizens or other officers.

Less-lethal weapons also raise questions. In Ferguson, the police use of less-lethal weapons might have prevented fatalities. Yet the methods were controversial. Police claimed they used tear gas to disperse crowds. But complaints were lodged that police used it to punish protesters, gave either no or inadequate warnings to disperse before using, and gas seeped into adjacent homes (IIR 2015, 49–51). As is true of military-grade equipment, the use of less-lethal weapons worked in some ways, even as it created problems. The question of what worked and what did not is in many ways a question of the trade-offs, paradoxes, and ironies inherent in any intervention in complex social environments.

## Implications for the Twenty-First Century

We conclude with two sets of issues—one empirical and one evaluative to address a final question: What are the implications of changes in policing of disorder for a democratic American society in the twenty-first century?

*Empirical Issues*

Social scientists generally have a terrible reputation for predicting the future. Thus, a note of caution is needed regarding sweeping conclusions and predictions about the trends we identified. It is too easy to assume that the patterns from the past will be present in the future, or, if they are, that they will be found in the same ratios and be accounted for by the same causal factors as previously. In the research presented here, any conclusions must be tempered by the fact that there is an always evolving, dynamic, and fluid conflictual dance between police and those involved in protest and disorder (Gillham and Marx 2000). But, holding apart questions about trying to predict the future, we build off Marx's (1998) earlier reflections on the developing ethos of U.S. policing since the late 1960s to draw some empirical conclusions relevant for today (see table 4).

In the decades since Kerner, rather than taking an explicitly adversarial and intentionally violent approach specifically against protests, police have often sought a more velvet-gloved, neutral, measured stance, even as the nearby, out of sight, iron fist of the National Guard, military, and hardware with varying degrees of lethality could be quickly mobilized. The policing of protest has thus become more accepted and better understood as a routine part of local policing. Although the police hardly welcome them, mass demonstrations today in general no longer arouse the hostility or fear they previously did. Yet large-scale disorders that spill out of protests like that in Ferguson still create conditions where police may react in ways that violate civil liberties, have a chilling effect on nonviolent protest, and escalate disorders, just as they did in the 1960s and historically, whether the issue was race or unions.

But today law enforcement is less quick to automatically categorize all those in the streets as riffraff, criminals, rebellious adolescents, manipulated students, or agents of a foreign power. Rather, they are often seen as citizens with rights, though they are expected to keep their disorder within bounds. More than in the 1960s, police view their job to be managing rather than repressing protest, protecting the right to demonstrate and guaranteeing due process of law and to use a minimum amount of force to restore order (even to those whose views they may find intolerable). The presence of video, cell phone cameras, and body cameras, with their potential for accountability can support this.

Exceptions to this trend are numerous (see note 1). The pattern of police pacification itself involves a series of interrelated developments and may not continue in the face of wrenching social changes or widespread social unrest. Nor is it unilateral across dimensions, groups, or contexts—as any venture into marginalized, ethnically diverse, lower-income areas or discussions with those who have had their rights violated and their bodies assaulted can attest (Wood 2007). But viewed in comparative and historical terms in which the

**Table 4.** The Evolving Ethos of the Policing of Protests and Civil Disorders in the United States Since 1967

1. Police are servants of the law rather than the private army of whoever happens to be in power.
2. Law and policy are extended to tactics that had once been ignored and unregulated.
3. The law must be viewed flexibly, and a broad pragmatic view of the likely consequences of police action needs to be taken.
4. The primary goal of police in conventional crowd situations is to manage them to see that they do not get out of hand.
5. Emphasis is on prevention rather than responding after the fact.
6. A *coproduction of order* should involve a decentralized and delegated reliance on citizens to enforce the law and to control themselves.
7. Emphasis is placed on science and technology involving, first, efforts to engineer physical and social environments while minimizing to the extent possible the militarization of local police or using a technical method simply because it is available, and, second, relatively dispassionate intelligence gathering and analysis. Information technology is central to police managing information about police themselves, events, and protesters.
8. *Efforts are made to learn from past events to be better prepared the next time, yet with flexibility, avoiding being rigidly captured by current en vogue doctrines.*
9. *The federal leadership role is stronger from the start. This involves an effort to develop uniform approaches across soft as well as hard police methods; to increase communication, integration, and cooperation to create more uniform, standardized operations and procedures across local, state, and federal authorities; and to create national standards and best practices.*
10. *Police are more militarized, particularly with regards to equipment. Logistical, organizational, and communication borders between local, regional, and state control agencies, and between them and the military, are weaker.*

*Source:* Authors' tabulations (adapted from Marx 1998).
*Note:* Italicized text are additions.

standard police response was, and in many countries still is, to prohibit demonstrations or to fire or charge into crowds, the trends matter. The ethos of demonstration policing Marx saw thirty years after Kerner, holds, if with some changes in 2018 (Marx 1998; see table 4 and appendix).

*Moral and Political Issues*
Apart from what can be seen or empirically demonstrated are questions of interpretation involving moral and political judgments. With respect to the latter, what can be said about the impact of more controlled (and what are seen conventionally to be effective) police responses? We need to ask effective for whom and by what standards?

How should we judge developments in the management of disorders? Is law enforcement's ability to avoid killing protesters in the streets or to intervene preventively a sign of progress? Is this a cause for some modest celebration, or at least appreciation? Certainly, the avoidance of provocation, injury or loss of life, cities on fire, and escalation, as well as decreasing hatred and alienation are positive. Full-scale riots leave deep reservoirs of bitterness on all sides and are conducive to backlash and draconian policies. We saw that clearly with the backlash and weakening of the civil rights movement related to Nixon's presidency. It is hard to see who really profited from the prolonged 1960s disorders. It is much easier to see short-run costs (Shellow et al. 2018).[7]

The development of a more pacific, demo-

---

7. Rob Shellow and his colleagues note how outcomes varied in the short run aftermath by city characteristics and type of event.

cratic policing ethos is not without contradictions, challenges, risks and trade-offs relative to other models (Marx 1988; Gillham and Marx 2000). As noted earlier, we need to ask what does it mean to say that a police response works? With health care or schools, we seek maximum effectiveness. But for police in a democratic society we need optimal (rather than maximal) effectiveness. Practices must be continually reexamined given changing conditions, tactics, and actors. In the case of efforts to create more professional police and to regulate discretion in crowd situations, the challenge is in finding the right mix such that honoring discretion does not put police beyond the law and responsible political control, and that regulating discretion does not introduce undue rigidity. Order needs to be maintained and the law (with its vagaries and conflicts) followed, but not at great cost to citizens' rights, the elimination of protest as a tool for social change, or the permanent institutionalization of strong control responses temporarily created and justified by a major crisis (such as 9/11). In such cases, strong oversight and renewal procedures are necessary to keep responses measured and proportionate.

There is no guarantee that the enhancements of police powers relative to crowds will be used to protect, rather than to undermine democracy. A democratic society must continually ask the question, "how efficient do we want police to be?" Democratic societies have traditionally been willing to sacrifice a degree of order for increased liberty, but not in times of crisis. At such times the danger of a creeping (or galloping) downhill spiral is ever present. When liberty is reduced on behalf of order, transparency is particularly important, as is avoiding the risk of artificially created or exaggerated crises to justify that sacrifice.

We can ask that a bandage or pain reliever do its job and certainly not make an injury worse, even as it is not a cure. President Johnson's charge to the commission was muddied regarding the link between his three often-cited questions ("what happened, why did it happen and what can be done to prevent it happening again"). The *it* was taken to mean riot stoppage. But what was really needed was a fourth question separating it as riot control from it as racial injustice (Marx 1970b, 2018). What it takes to prevent or stop a civil disorder is distinct (other than the issue of police abuse that can precipitate and contribute to disorder) from changes in economic and political opportunity, education, housing, health, and the many other factors related to inequality that propel disorders.

Improved and more effective police responses can often stop disorders from escalating. But to the extent that they are unfairly repressive and deter legitimate protest, they may deepen racial injustice and the anger and despair that help fuel disorders.

Democratic societies experience a continual tension between the desire for order and the desire for liberty. Although, as the case of the police state suggests, one can have the former without the latter, it is not possible to have a society with liberty that does not also have a minimum degree of order. The balance between these will vary depending on the context and time period. Policing in a democracy seeks to avoid the extremes of either anarchy or repression.

In an open democratic society that respects the dignity of the individual and values voluntary and consensual behavior and the nonviolent resolution of conflicts, police—with their power, secrecy, and use of violence and deception—are an anomaly. They are charged with using undemocratic means to help create democratic ends. Police offer an ethical and moral paradox that should forever make democratic citizens vigilant.

This paradox is evident in the fact that a democratic society needs protection both by police and from police. Restrictions on police power are not an adequate guarantee of freedom. Taken too far, they may even guarantee its opposite, as private interests reign unchecked or citizens take the law into their own hands in the face of increased disorder, or both. Yet a police force with too much power is also a danger. President Abraham Lincoln posed the dilemma well when he asked, "must a government, of necessity, be too strong for the liberties of its' own people, or too weak to maintain its' existence?" This paradox remains one of the major challenges of democratic governance.

## APPENDIX: WORKING FOR THE KERNER COMMISSION AND RELATED REFLECTIONS

Gary T. Marx had the good fortune to work for the commission as part of a research group led by Rob Shellow and studied police behavior and types of disorder. When the Kerner Commission studied questions of the police and civil disorders, very little social science research had been undertaken to inform the analysis; the dominant control ethos was a hardline, law and order approach in a context of a decentralized federal law enforcement system.

Marx describes the experience of working for the commission and on a suppressed report *The Harvest of Racism* (2018; Shellow et al. 2018), published on the fiftieth anniversary of its writing. For Marx, the focus on these issues helped define over five decades of scholarly work. The chance to work on these questions at the beginning of a career with the abundant resources, legitimation, and access of a national commission was most fortuitous and sustaining. That experience provided data, research questions, and scholarly connections that lasted a lifetime on topics such as police behavior in riots and intelligence gathering, types of riot, counter-rioters and community police patrols, the implications of the minority or majority group identity of activists and researchers, and, more broadly the study of social movements and mass behavior and of the requisites for social order (Marx 1970a, 1970b, 1971a, 1971b, 1974, 1988, 1998, 2002, 2016; Marx and Archer 1971; Marx and Useem 1971; Marx and McAdam 1994; Gillham and Marx 2000, 2003).

Working for the Kerner Commission sensitized Marx to the importance and neglect of the softer ethos as applied to crowds. The importance of this was heightened in a candid conversation with a high-ranking member of the Chicago Police Department shortly after the police violence during the 1968 Democratic Convention. The commander indicated how unprofessional his department had behaved. He said that as a commander in a protest situation he is willing to listen, to negotiate, to tolerate minor infractions, and to keep a low profile. He felt strongly that saving lives should be more important than protecting property or symbols. He believed that demonstrations could actively help create, rather than undermine, political stability (at least relative to not permitting or responding violently to them). The extensive media coverage of Chicago police attacking protesters was a public relations disaster and such behavior made the police job much more difficult. At the time, his views were heretical and he left the police soon after, but in the decades since they have become more widely shared among major police leaders in the United States. The management of disorders continues to evolve.

How control agents frame events bears directly on control responses. If they are defined as (or only as) violations of law and order and the criminal code, then hard repression is the more likely response. If, in contrast, they are also seen as connected to understandable protests because grievances are present (apart from whether police are in sympathy with these) or because citizen's have the right to express their concerns, then a soft communications approach, particularly at the outset, is more likely (Tilly 2000; Gillham and Noakes 2007). Adopting either approach to the exclusion of the other brings risks of unwanted under- or overreaction.

Apart from the institutional and cultural factors discussed in the article, the greater prominence of softer approaches is likely tied to a shift from the late 1960s to the present in the ratio of non- or less focused crowd-protest events to ones where a protest theme is more directly in evidence. A conflict is also possible in the communications offered the public by police and political leaders, versus that coming from protest groups. For the former, the tilt is toward a definition of disorder and criminal behavior; for the latter, it is toward a protest definition. Within these groups are conflicts as well, control groups divided over soft and hard approaches and protest groups divided between orderly disorder (to coin a phrase) and random destruction and assaults (favored by fringe groups).

The social and psychological characteristics and location of control agents are related to such definitions, but more objective characteristics also are likely to be. Thus the presence of a widely shared belief among those in the streets that direct action is needed to call attention to a problem, within a context of an ongoing political dispute and a planned event whose organizers go through a permitting process are likely to be differentiated from spontaneous, less organized, or unorganized gatherings that have no clear leader or group to communicate with, nor a specific precipitating event (Gillham and Noakes 2007). Marx considers these and other factors in seeking objective measures for how events are likely to be labeled as either protest or disorder (1970a). However, because events often show much internal variation (by types of participant, activities, places, and times within the event) rarely will an event approach the ideal type at either end of the continuum.

The views expressed by the officer mentioned contrast markedly with those found in totalitarian regimes, which blur or erase the line between politics and crime. Any oppositional politics is defined as crime. But they also contrast with the creation of the first modern police department in Paris at the end of the seventeenth century in which the protection of public order was also equated with the protection of the political order. Indeed, for many observers the connection has been reversed. That is, protecting the right to protest against the political order is defined as the best way of protecting it—at least if the political order is broadly defined to involve a set of democratic principles, rather than the particular persons or groups in power. The conditions under which democracies can accept nonelectoral political challenges and yet remain democracies is an issue of enduring importance. As James Madison observed, "you must first enable the government to control the governed; and in the next place, oblige it to control itself."

## REFERENCES

Alexander, Michelle. 2011. *The New Jim Crow: Mass Incarceration in the Age of Colorblindness*. New York: The New Press.

Balko, Radley. 2013. *Rise of the Warrior Cop: The Militarization of America's Police Forces*. New York: Public Affairs.

Barker, Tim. 2014. "Ferguson-Area Businesses Cope with Aftermath of Weekend Riot." *St. Louis Post-Dispatch*, August 12.

Belmar, Jon M., and Gil Kleinknecht. 2016. "Tactical Operations (SWAT)." St. Louis County, Missouri Police Department, February 14.

Bentley-Edwards, Keisha L., Malik Chaka Edwards, Cynthia Neal Spence, William A. Darity Jr., Darrick Hamilton, and Jasson Perez. 2018. "How Does It Feel to Be a Problem? The Missing Kerner Commission Report." *RSF: The Russell Sage Foundation Journal of the Social Sciences* 4(6): 20–40. DOI: 10.7758/RSF.2018.4.6.02.

Bigley, Gregory A., and Karlene H. Roberts. 2001. "The Incident Command System: High-Reliability Organizing for Complex and Volatile Task Environments." *Academy of Management Journal* 44(6): 1281–99.

Body-Gendrot, Sophie. 2017. *Public Disorder and Globalization*. New York: Routledge.

Buck, Dick A., Joseph E. Trainor, and Benigno E. Aguirre. 2006. "A Critical Evaluation of the Incident Command System and NIMS." *Journal of Homeland Security and Emergency Management* 3(3): 1–27.

Cardwell, Michael D., and Patrick T. Cooney. 2000. "Nationwide Application of the Incident Command System: Standardization Is the Key." *FBI Law Enforcement Bulletin* 69(10): 10–15.

Chase, Richard A. 1980. "FIRESCOPE: A New Concept in Multiagency Fire Suppression Coordination." General Technical Report PSW-40. Berkeley, Calif.: Pacific Southwest Forest and Range Experiment Station.

della Porta, Donatella, Abby Peterson, and Herbert Reiter, eds. 2006. *The Policing of Transnational Protest*. Burlington, Vt.: Ashgate.

della Porta, Donatella, and Herbert Reiter, eds. 1998. *Policing of Protest: The Control of Mass Demonstrations in Western Democracies*. Minneapolis: University of Minnesota Press.

Earl, Jennifer. 2003. "Tanks, Tear Gas, and Taxes: Toward a Theory of Movement Repression." *Sociological Theory* 21(1): 44–68.

———. 2011. "Political Repression: Iron Fists, Velvet Gloves, and Diffuse Control." *Annual Review of Sociology* 37(1): 261–84.

Earl, Jennifer, and Sarah A. Soule. 2006. "Seeing Blue: A Police-Centered Explanation of Protest Policing." *Mobilization* 11(2): 145–64.

Earl, Jennifer, Sarah A. Soule, and John D. McCarthy. 2003. "Protest Under Fire? Explaining the Policing of Protest." *American Sociological Review* 68(4): 581–606.

FEMA. 2010. *Fiscal Year 2010 Homeland Security Grant Program: Guidance and Application Kit, December 2009.* Washington: U.S. Department of Homeland Security. Accessed December 27, 2017. https://www.fema.gov/pdf/government/grant/2010/fy10_hsgp_kit.pdf.

——. 2013. "IS-0100.B: Introduction to the Incident Command System (ICS) Instructors Guide." Accessed June 5, 2017. https://training.fema.gov/is/courseoverview.aspx?code=IS-100.b.

Fernandez, Luis. 2008. *Policing Dissent: Social Control and the Anti-Globalization Movement.* New Brunswick, N.J.: Rutgers University Press.

Giegerich, Steve, Jesse Bogan, and Kim Bell. 2014. "Ferguson Day Two Wrap-up: Day of Protests, Night of Frenzy." *St. Louis Post-Dispatch*, August 11. Accessed December 20, 2017. http://www.stltoday.com/news/local/crime-and-courts/ferguson-day-two-wrapup-day-of-protests-night-of-frenzy/article_f9d627dc-e3c8-5bde-b2ab-7f0a3d36a083.html.

Gillham, Patrick F. 2011. "Securitizing America: Strategic Incapacitation and the Policing of Protest Since the 11 September 2001 Terrorist Attacks." *Sociology Compass* 5(7): 636–52.

Gillham, Patrick, F., Bob Edwards, and John A. Noakes. 2013. "Strategic Incapacitation and the Policing of Occupy Wall Street in New York City, 2011." *Policing and Society* 23(1): 82–103.

Gillham, Patrick F., and Gary T. Marx. 2000. "Complexity and Irony in Policing and Protesting: The World Trade Organization in Seattle." *Social Justice* 27(2): 212–36.

——. 2003. "Ironies in Protest and Policing: The World Trade Organization in Seattle." In *Representing Resistance: Media, Civil Disobedience, and the Global Justice Movement*, edited by Andy Opel and Donnalyn Pomper. Westport, Conn.: Greenwood.

Gillham, Patrick F., and John A. Noakes. 2007. "More Than a March in a Circle: Transgressive Protests and the Limits of Negotiated Management." *Mobilization* 12(4): 341–57.

Gooden, Susan T., and Samuel L. Myers Jr. 2018. "The Kerner Commission Report Fifty Years Later: Revisiting the American Dream." *RSF: The Russell Sage Foundation Journal of the Social Sciences* 4(6): 1–17. DOI: 10.7758/RSF.2018.4.6.01.

Hobsbawm, Eric. 1964. *Primitive Rebels.* Glencoe, Ill.: Free Press.

Institute for Intergovernmental Research (IIR). 2015. *After-Action Assessment of the Police Response to the August 2014 Demonstrations in Ferguson, Missouri.* COPS Office Critical Response Initiative. Washington: U.S. Department of Justice, Office of Community Oriented Policing Services.

Kanowitz, Stephanie. 2016. "How Missouri Police Deliver On-Scene Interoperable Communications." *GCN*, March 21. Accessed December 17, 2017. https://gcn.com/articles/2016/03/21/missouri-emergency-comm.aspx?admgarea=TC_STATELOCAL.

Kerner Commission. 1968. *Report of the National Advisory Commission on Civil Disorders.* Washington: Government Printing Office.

King, Mike. 2017. *When Riot Cops Are Not Enough: The Policing and Repression of Occupy Oakland.* New Brunswick, N.J.: Rutgers University Press.

Kraska, Peter B., and Louis J. Cubellis. 1997. "Militarizing Mayberry and Beyond: Making Sense of American Paramilitary Policing." *Justice Quarterly* 14(4): 607–29.

Kraska, Peter B., and Victor E. Kappeler. 1997. "Militarizing American Police: The Rise and Normalization of Paramilitary Units." *Social Problems* 44(1): 1–18.

Lenco. 2014. "The Reason for Armored Vehicles? To Keep Police Safe While They Do Their Jobs." *Lenco News*, August 30. Accessed May 2, 2018. http://www.lencoarmor.com/the-reason-for-armored-vehicles-to-keep-police-safe-while-they-do-their-jobs/.

Lutz, Leslie D., and Michael K. Lindell. 2008. "Incident Command System as a Response Model Within Emergency Operation Centers during Hurricane Rita." *Journal of Contingencies and Crisis Management* 16(3): 122–34.

Marx, Gary T. 1970a. "Issueless Riots." *Annals of the American Academy of Political and Social Science* (September): 21–33.

——. 1970b. "Two Cheers for the National Riot (Kerner) Commission Report." In *Black Americans: A Second Look,* edited by John F. Szwed. New York: Basic Books.

——. 1971a. "Civil Disorder and the Agents of Social Control." *Journal of Social Issues* (Winter): 19–57.

——. 1971b. *Racial Conflict Tension and Change in American Society.* Boston, Mass.: Little Brown.

——. 1974. "Thoughts on a Neglected Category of Social Movement Participant: The Agent Provocateur and the Informant." *American Journal of Sociology* 80(2): 402–42.

———. 1988. "External Efforts to Damage or Facilitate Social Movements: Some Patterns, Explanations, Outcomes, and Complications." In *Dynamics of Social Movements: Resource Mobilization, Social Control, and Tactics*, edited by Mayer N. Zald and John D. McCarthy. Lanham, Md.: University Press of America.

———. 1998. "Some Reflections on the Democratic Policing of Demonstrations." In *Policing of Protest: The Control of Mass Demonstrations in Western Democracies*, edited by Donatella della Porta and Herbert Reiter. Minneapolis: University of Minnesota Press.

———. 2002. "What's New about the 'New Surveillance'? Classifying for Change and Continuity." *Surveillance and Society* 1(1): 9–29.

———. 2016. *Windows into the Soul: Surveillance and Society in an Age of High Technology.* Chicago: University of Chicago Press.

———. 2018. "Inside the Tent: Some Reflections on Working for the 1967 Kerner Commission." In *The Harvest of Racism*, edited by Robert Shellow, David Boesel, Gary T. Marx, and David Sears. Ann Arbor: University of Michigan Press.

Marx, Gary T., and Dane Archer. 1971. "Citizen Involvement in the Law Enforcement Process: The Case of Community Police Patrols." *American Behavioral Scientist* 15(1): 52–72.

Marx, Gary T., and Doug McAdam. 1994. *Social Movements and Collective Behavior.* Englewood Cliffs, N.J.: Prentice Hall.

Marx, Gary T., and Michael Useem. 1971. "Majority Involvement in Minority Movements: Civil Rights, Abolition, Untouchability." *Journal of Social Issues* 27(1): 81–104.

McCarthy, John D., and Clark McPhail. 1998. "The Institutionalization of Protest in the United States." In *The Movement Society: Contentious Politics for a New Century*, edited by David S. Meyer and Sidney Tarrow. Boulder, Colo.: Rowman and Littlefield.

McCarthy, John D., Clark McPhail, and John Crist. 1999. "The Diffusion and Adoption of Public Order Management Systems." In *Social Movements in a Globalizing World*, edited by Donatella della Porta, Hanspeter Kriesi, and Dieter Rucht. London: Palgrave.

McPhail, Clark, David Schweingruber, and John D. McCarthy. 1998. "Policing Protest in the United States: 1960–1994." In *Policing of Protest: The Control of Mass Demonstrations in Western Democracies*, edited by Donatella della Porta and Herbert Reiter. Minneapolis: University of Minnesota Press.

Meyer, Josh. 2017. "Virginia Received DHS Warning Before Charlottesville Rally." *Politico*, August 29. Accessed February 23, 2018. https://www.politico.com/story/2017/08/29/charlottesville-violence-homeland-security-242140.

Moore, Maloy. 2012. "Los Angeles Riots: Remember the 63 People Who Died." *Los Angeles Times*, April 26. Accessed November 17, 2017. http://latimesblogs.latimes.com/lanow/2012/04/los-angeles-riots-remember-the-63-people-who-died-.html.

Narr, Tony, Jessica Toliver, Jerry Murphy, Malcolm McFarland, and Joshua Ederheimer, eds. 2006. *Police Management of Mass Demonstrations; Identifying Issues and Successful Approaches.* Washington, D.C.: Police Executive Research Forum.

National Institute of Justice. 1994. "Twenty-Five Years of Criminal Justice Research." Washington: U.S. Department of Justice, Office of Justice Programs. Accessed May 2, 2018. https://www.ncjrs.gov/pdffiles1/nij/151287.pdf.

*New York Times*. 2014. "Michael Brown's Shooting and Its Immediate Aftermath in Ferguson." Timeline of Events. Last updated August 25, 2014. Accessed May 2, 2018. https://www.nytimes.com/interactive/2014/08/12/us/13police-shooting-of-black-teenager-michael-brown.html#/#time348_10366.

Noakes, John A., and Patrick F. Gillham. 2006. "Aspects of the 'New Penology' in the Police Response to Major Protests in the United States, 1999–2000." In *The Policing of Transnational Protest*, edited by Donatella della Porta, Abby Peterson, and Herbert Reiter. Burlington, Vt.: Ashgate.

Noakes, John A., Brian Klocke, and Patrick F. Gillham. 2005. "Whose Streets? Police and Protester Struggles over Space in Washington, D.C., September 29–30, 2001." *Policing and Society* 15(3): 235–54.

Nunn, Samuel. 2001. "Police Technology in Cities: Changes and Challenges." *Technology in Society* 23(1): 11–27.

Oliver, Pamela. 2008. "Repression and Crime Control: Social Movement Scholars Should Pay More Attention to Mass Mobilization as a Form of Repression." *Mobilization* 13(1): 1–24.

Olzak, Susan, and Suzanne Shanahan. 1996. "Deprivation and Race Riots: An Extension of Spilerman's Analysis." *Social Forces* 74(3): 931–61.

Olzak, Susan, Suzanne Shanahan, and Elizabeth H. McEneaney. 1996. "Poverty, Segregation, and Race Riots: 1960–1993." *American Sociological Review* 61(4): 590–613.

Ozer, Nicole. 2016. "Police Use of Social Media Surveillance Software Is Escalating, and Activists Are in the Digital Crosshairs." *ACLU*, September 22. Accessed December 27, 2017. https://www.aclu.org/blog/privacy-technology/surveillance-technologies/police-use-social-media-surveillance-software.

Pickler, Nedra. 2015. "The Obama Administration Just Took Huge Step Toward Demilitarizing U.S. Police Forces." *Associated Press*, May 18. Accessed December 27, 2017. http://www.businessinsider.com/obama-announces-new-rules-to-reverse-militarization-of-local-police-2015-5.

Piven, Francis Fox, and Richard A. Cloward. 1979. *Poor People's Movements: Why They Succeed, How They Fail*. New York: Vintage Books.

Police Executive Research Forum. 2015. *Lessons Learned from the 2015 Civil Unrest in Baltimore*. Washington, D.C.: Police Executive Research Forum.

Schneider, Cathy Lisa. 2014. *Police Power and Race Riots*. Philadelphia: University of Pennsylvania Press.

Shellow, Robert, David Boesel, Gary T. Marx, and David Sears. 2018. *The Harvest of Racism*. Ann Arbor: University of Michigan Press.

Smith, Dean R., and Richard W. Kobetz. 1968. *Guidelines for Civil Disorder and Mobilization Planning*. Washington, D.C.: International Association of Chiefs of Police.

Smith, Mitch. 2017. "New Ferguson Video Adds Wrinkle to Michael Brown Case." *New York Times*, March 11. Accessed March 3, 2018. https://www.nytimes.com/2017/03/11/us/michael-brown-ferguson-police-shooting-video.html.

Soule, Sarah A., and Christian Davenport. 2009. "Velvet Glove, Iron Fist, or Even Hand? Protest Policing in the United States, 1960–1990." *Mobilization* 14(1): 1–22.

St. Louis County Police Department. 2014. "St. Louis County Police Department Annual Report." Clayton, Missouri. Accessed May 4, 2018. https://www.stlouisco.com/Portals/8/docs/document%20library/police/reports/14Annual.pdf.

St. Louis County. 2013. "The Code 1000 Plan for St. Louis County and Municipal Law Enforcement Agencies." Clayton, Missouri. Accessed May 4, 2018. https://stlouisco.com/LawandPublicSafety/EmergencyManagement/Code1000.

Starr, Amory, Luis Fernandez, and Christina Scholl. 2011. *Shutting Down the Streets: Political Violence and Social Control in the Global Era*. New York: New York University Press.

Tilly, Charles. 2000. "Spaces of Contention." *Mobilization* 5(2): 135–59.

———. 2003. *The Politics of Collective Violence*. New York: Cambridge University Press.

Tucker, Eric. 2015. "Comey: FBI Used Aerial Surveillance Above Ferguson." *Associated Press*, October 22.

Urban America Inc., and the Urban Coalition. 1969. *One Year Later*. New York: Praeger.

U.S. Department of Homeland Security (DHS). 2014. "DHS Announces Grant Allocations for Fiscal Year (FY) 2014 Preparedness Grants." Washington: U.S. Department of Homeland Security, July 25. Accessed May 2, 2018. https://www.dhs.gov/news/2014/07/25/dhs-announces-grant-allocations-fiscal-year-fy-2014-preparedness-grants.

———. 2017. "State and Major Urban Area Fusion Centers." Washington: U.S. Department of Homeland Security. Accessed July 25, 2017. https://www.dhs.gov/state-and-major-urban-area-fusion-centers.

Vitale, Alex S. 2005. "From Negotiated Management to Command and Control: How the New York Police Department Polices Protests." *Policing and Society* 15(3): 283–304.

———. 2007. "The Command and Control and Miami Models at the 2004 Republican National Convention: New Forms of Policing Protests." *Mobilization* 12(4): 403–15.

Waddington, David P. 2007. *Policing Public Disorder: Theory and Practice*. Portland, Ore.: Willan Publishing.

Waddington, Peter A. J. 1994. *Liberty and Order: Public Order Policing in a Capital City*. London: U.C.L. Press.

Walker, Daniel. 1968. *Rights in Conflict: Chicago's 78 Brutal Days: Report on the Chicago Study Team of the National Commission on the Causes and Prevention of Violence*. New York: Grosset and Dunlap.

Weapons and Protective Systems Technologies Center. 2010. *A Guidebook for Less-Lethal Devices: Planning for, Selecting, and Implementing Technology Solutions.* University Park: Pennsylvania State University Applied Research Laboratory. Accessed May 2, 2018. https://www.nccpsafety.org/assets/files/library/Guidebook_for_Less-lethal_Devices.pdf.

Webster, William H., and Hubert William. 1992. *The City in Crisis. A Report by the Special Advisor to the Board of Police Commissioners on the Civil Disorder in Los Angeles, October 21, 1992.* Los Angeles, Calif.: Office of the Special Advisor.

Weiser, Philip J. 2007. "Communicating During Emergencies: Toward Interoperability and Effective Information Management." *Federal Communications Law Journal* 59(3): 547–74.

Wood, Lesley J. 2007. "Breaking the Wave: Repression, Identity, and the Seattle Tactics." *Mobilization* 12(4): 377–88.

———. 2014. *Crisis and Control: The Militarization of Protest Policing.* London: Pluto Press.

# The Effects of the Neighborhood Legal Services Program on Riots and the Wealth of African Americans

JAMEIN P. CUNNINGHAM AND ROB GILLEZEAU

This article uses newly collected data on communities receiving Neighborhood Legal Services Programs (NLSP) grants between 1965 and 1975 to evaluate the impact of NLSPs on civil disorders and resulting changes in property values in African American communities. We employ several empirical strategies, all of which confirm the NLSP's effectiveness in combatting civil disorders and indicate a robust, positive relationship between NLSPs and property values. We find that NLSP funding increased property values by 2 percent. These results are consistent with a substantial reduction in riot propensities due to target government funding, and further support claims by the Kerner Commission report that the NLSP mitigated the damage resulting from the civil disorders.

**Keywords:** legal services, War on Poverty, Kerner Commission, property values, riots

Starting in 1964, a series of civil demonstrations escalated into widespread uprisings across the United States. One of the many policy responses was to include the Neighborhood Legal Service Program (NLSP) in the War on Poverty. The NLSP was introduced to equip the poor with alternative paths to remediate grievances, particularly those concerning local police misconduct.[1] Under the program, lawyers redressed grievances by bringing civil cases against local police departments and other government agencies. The early success of the NLSP was highlighted by the Kerner Commission report (1968), which called for its expansion to reduce the likelihood of future civil disorders. This qualitative assessment has since

**Jamein P. Cunningham** is assistant professor of economics in the Fogelman College of Business and Economics at the University of Memphis. **Rob Gillezeau** is assistant professor of economics at the University of Victoria.

© 2018 Russell Sage Foundation. Cunningham, Jamein P., and Rob Gillezeau. 2018. "The Effects of the Neighborhood Legal Services Program on Riots and the Wealth of African Americans." *RSF: The Russell Sage Foundation Journal of the Social Sciences* 4(6): 144–57. DOI: 10.7758/RSF.2018.4.6.07. This project was generously supported by an NICHD center grant to the Population Studies Center at the University of Michigan (R24 HD041028). The authors would like to thank William Collins and Robert Margo for sharing their data. Direct correspondence to: Jamein P. Cunningham at jamein.p.cunningham@memphis.edu, University of Memphis, Fogelman College of Business and Economics, 3675 Central Ave., Memphis, TN 38152; and Rob Gillezeau at gillezr@uvic.ca, University of Victoria, Department of Economics, 3800 Finnerty Rd., Victoria, British Columbia V8P 5C2.

Open Access Policy: *RSF: The Russell Sage Foundation Journal of the Social Sciences* is an open access journal. This article is published under a Creative Commons Attribution-NonCommercial-NoDerivs 3.0 Unported License.

1. This approach is consistent with the broader redirection of War on Poverty organizing resources in the Community Action Program towards hearing and addressing grievances from the African American community. The success of this approach is documented (Gillezeau 2015).

been verified, the NLSP found to reduce the number of riots by 3.6 percent and the severity by as much as 56 percent (Cunningham 2018). However, although the NLSP was deemed successful in reducing uprisings, the impact of the program on individuals' economic well-being has not been assessed.

The primary mechanisms through which the 1960s riots undermined the economic well-being of many in the African American community have been a permanent depression in the value of African American properties and worsened labor market outcomes for African Americans (Collins and Margo 2007; Collins et al. 2004).[2] Given the substantial reduction in riot propensities found in Cunningham (2018), it is plausible that the NLSP mitigated the damages from civil disorders and violent protests. To examine the possibility, we exploit the variation in timing and location of the establishment of NLSP projects to estimate the causal impact of the NLSP on racial disparities in wealth by focusing on property values.

Our analysis uses recently collected data on the communities receiving legal services grants between 1965 and 1975. We rely on the differential timing of NLSP's implementation in cities across the United States as well as variation in the location and intensity of treatment to imply a causal relationship. In addition, we use the age of local law schools to isolate the relationship between funding and riot propensities, exploiting the fact that neighborhood law firms were frequently affiliated with nearby law schools.

Our results show that legal services reduced both the number of riots and their severity, the effect being substantially larger on severity. Over the long run, the results further show that the NLSP has a robust positive relationship with property values. Using our most conservative estimates, we find that federally funded legal services increased black-owned property values by 2 percent. These findings are consistent with the narrative that the NLSP created access to social justice by providing additional channels for blacks in urban communities to settle disputes. This is consistent with the Kerner Commission report call for the expansion of legal services. Given renewed attention on police-community relations, this analysis contributes to the literature by deepening our understanding of policy initiatives that deal with unresolved community grievances that at times lead to violent rebellions.[3]

## A BRIEF HISTORY OF THE LEGAL SERVICE PROGRAM

In March of 1876, the first legal aid society opened its doors in New York City (Hollingsworth 1977; Johnson 2014). The German Legal Aid Society, financed through membership dues, provided legal assistance to German immigrants unable to acquire legal counsel. In 1890, the organization opened its doors to all ethnic groups, changing its name to the Legal Aid Society. To meet the needs of the poor, the organization expanded and opened additional branches, one for seamen and another for women. The women's branch dealt with legal needs, largely pertaining to divorce and domestic relations. In response to underwhelming demand by women, the mission of that branch shifted and the office serviced the legal needs of all, but the majority of the clientele were men.

The need for legal aid by women led to the first legal aid office in Chicago. In 1886, the Protective Agency for Women and Children provided legal assistance to young women in areas related to unpaid wages, debt schemes, and licentious employment practices (Katz 1982). In 1888, the Bureau of Justice joined the Protective Agency for Women and Children providing legal aid for Chicago's poor regardless of ethnicity and gender. At the turn into

---

2. Beyond that, evidence suggests that the 1960s civil disorders may have hastened the white flight phenomenon from America's urban core and decreased voter participation (Boustan 2010; Wasow 2015).

3. We do not provide an in-depth review of the civil disorder literature. It is robust, largely originating from sociology, regarding the causes of the racialized civil disorders of the 1960s (Spilerman 1970; Downes 1968; Olzak, Shanahan, and McEneaney 1996; Myers 1997) and corrective policy measures (Carter 1987; Wasow 2015; Ariel, Farrar, and Sutherland 2015) as well as economic outcomes (DiPasquale and Glaeser 1998; King 2003; Collins and Smith 2004; Collins and Margo 2007).

the twentieth century, legal societies began springing up across the country from Jersey City to Denver. Harvard opened its first legal clinic for the poor in 1913. This massive expansion in legal aid provision led to the first national convention for legal aid societies in 1914 in Chicago and the formation of the National Alliance of Legal Aid Societies, which would later become the National Legal Aid and Defender Association.

By the 1960s, more than two hundred legal aid societies were servicing the legal needs of the poor (Hollingsworth 1977).[4] Although legal assistance was free, many services were not provided due to a lack of funds, excess demand, and individual beliefs on the type of services the poor should receive. However, a reliance on charitable donations to fund legal aid threatened lawyers' ability to take on controversial cases, and lawyers turned away cases that would bring negative attention and influence charitable donations (Johnson 1974). Lawyers also refrained from cases involving bankruptcy and divorce, shunned challenging large corporations, and refused to challenge government agencies (Wright 1967; Stumpf 1975; Katz 1982). Furthermore, the lack of funds restricted lawyers' ability to appeal cases. As a result, the tendency was to focus on simple cases or to just provide advice to clients rather than pursue justice. The limitations were not restricted to the kinds of service provision. The location and hours of operation of legal aid offices often prevented the poor from seeking justice (Levitan 1969). Many of these offices were located in the city center, away from the poor. Regular business hours made it difficult for the typical worker to make the commute to the legal aid office and not miss work.

### Legal Services and the War On Poverty

The legal aid movement of the 1950s and the early 1960s coincided with social movements that sought the inclusion of marginalized groups into the greater democracy of America. The Kennedy administration and the Ford Foundation, through demonstration projects, financed antipoverty programs to deal with issues resulting from wartime migration into urban areas (Boustan 2010; Hinton 2016). Demonstration programs in New York City, New Haven, Connecticut, and Washington, D.C., included legal agencies to deal with civil and criminal matters the poor often encountered (Johnson 1974). These demonstration programs provided the blueprint for the community-oriented social service programs introduced in President Lyndon Johnson's War on Poverty.

The incorporation of the "civilian perspective" into the War on Poverty was motivated by Jean and Edgar Cahn in the *Yale Law Review*.[5] The Cahns proposed that university-affiliated, neighborhood law firms be established to serve as intermediaries between the community and antipoverty bureaucracies (Cahn and Cahn 1964). Law firms would provide free legal representation in areas related to divorce, eviction, welfare fraud, coerced confessions, arrest, police brutality, and installment buying. The article details their experience and advocates for the development of a nationwide program. A draft of the manuscript was first circulated among colleagues for comment and eventually landed in the hands of Associate Justice Arthur Goldberg. Justice Goldberg was persuaded to send letters to President Johnson advocating for the inclusion of a nationwide legal services program under the War on Poverty (Johnson 1974). As a result, Sargent Shriver brought the Cahns into the Office of Economic Opportunity (OEO) to spearhead the development and implementation of the program. The support of the American Bar Association (ABA) was vital to the rollout of the legal services program. National support from the ABA helped insulate

---

4. Most of the growth in legal aid societies occurred in the 1950s. American lawyers and bar associations were energized by Great Britain's federally funded legal aid society. Acting in opposition to a centralized authority in the law profession, bar associations across the country established charitable legal aid offices to meet the needs of the poor. An estimated forty-nine legal aid societies were operating in 1949. By 1961, the number rose to 236 (Johnson 1974).

5. The Cahns operated one of the three neighborhood law firms financed by the Ford Foundation in the early 1960s.

the program from the attacks of local bar associations when controversial cases were undertaken against powerful entities. On February 8, 1965, the ABA fully endorsed the NLSP.

Following the Cahns' proposal, the Neighborhood Legal Services Program was launched as part of the War on Poverty in 1965. Neighborhood law firms were financed by grants from the OEO and operated under the Community Action Program (CAP). The OEO was responsible for the antipoverty programs, and CAP projects were one of its largest initiatives. The community-based approach created wide variation in how federally funded grants were not only used but received. The OEO grants avoided local and state roadblocks and went directly to community organizations, allowing federal funds to be spent rapidly with wide variation for intended purposes (Johnson 1974; Gillette 1996).

The first year of the legal services program under the OEO resulted in the issuance of more than 155 grants backed by a total budget of more than $20 million. By 1967, the legal services program doubled in size, issuing more than three hundred grants with an annual budget of more than $40 million. By the end of 1967, the federal legal service program was funding 250 projects and providing legal assistance in forty-eight states (Levitan 1969). The rapid expansion of the program was the result of existing legal aid societies' willingness to adopt the neighborhood approach of the NLSP. This included opening legal services offices in poor neighborhoods with nontraditional hours of operation. NLSP agencies were able to provide services in areas that existing legal aid societies were reluctant to handle. This included divorce, bankruptcy, as well as challenging laws, government agencies, and large corporations. Nearly 40 percent of the initial grantees were existing legal aid societies (Levitan 1969). Law schools were just as vital to the roll-out of the program. As stated earlier, the program was designed to take advantage of cheap labor and expertise provided by a local law school. Law schools provided newly trained lawyers to staff legal services offices, designed new curriculum in poverty law, and opened and operated legal services offices in nearby communities.[6]

## Legal Services and Civil Disorder

The neighborhood law firms established by the NLSP were inundated with new clients. In 1968, legal services offices handled 282,000 cases. The typical NLSP lawyer had fifty to one hundred new cases a month, including ten to twenty related to criminal matters and juvenile delinquency (Levitan 1969). Although NLSP attorneys could not represent clients in felony criminal procedures, many criminal issues were related to perceived illegal police activity, thus allowing legal services to serve as a community advocate for the poor and disenfranchised in these circumstances. According to Legal Services Agency Survey of 1970, NLSP lawyers spent approximately 30 percent of their time in community advocacy and educational activities, playing a role in the enforcement of new laws related to police conduct and judicial procedure (Champagne 1974). In addition, approximately 7 percent of NLSP cases were devoted to law reform. These cases challenged local, state, and federal law in areas primarily related to welfare rights (Levitan 1969). Test cases were often brought against police departments, challenging police procedures and practices that negatively impacted the poor (Cunningham 2016).

Legal services lawyers brought lawsuits on behalf of the black community against police departments in Los Angeles, Cleveland, Washington, D.C., and Camden, New Jersey (*Los Angeles Sentinel* 1971). Advocates of the program claimed that NLSP lawyers were influential not only in reducing police brutality, but also in reducing the likelihood and severity of riots. Legal services lawyers often showed up at demonstrations to ease frustrations and prevent violence. For example, at a Senate subcommittee hearing, NLSP lawyers were lauded for averting violence after a police shooting of residents in Cleveland (U.S. Congress 1969). NLSPs often served as clearinghouses for local com-

---

6. Clinical legal education gained attention and the requisite funding through the expansion of legal aid in the 1960s and 1970s through the legal services program. Before the program, only a select few law schools provided legal aid to the poor through legal clinics (Johnson 2014).

plaints of police brutality. The purpose was to reduce the impulse to partake in violent demonstrations and to help build cases against illegal police behavior. Even in instances when violent protests occurred, NLSP lawyers served the community through city panels and organizations to help local and police officials redress the community's grievances.

NLSP lawyers often represented individuals at the heart of conflicts between police and the black community, such as the taxi cab driver whose physical confrontation with police sparked the 1967 Newark riot (Finman 1971). This led to a federal lawsuit accusing Newark's police department of violating the constitutional rights of black residents and requested a complete overhaul of the Newark Police Department. The success of the program was highlighted by the Kerner Commission report, which called for the expansion of the program as an antiriot initiative (Kerner Report 1968).

## Expected Effects of the Legal Service Program

Neighborhood law firms provided representation, consultation, and referrals for the poor at a cost substantially lower than private law firms would. NLSP lawyers were also involved in community organizing and community advocacy. In particular, NLSP lawyers were willing to articulate grievances against state institutions, which was a dramatic shift from previous behavior. The NLSP may have influenced the decision to riot and subsequent outcomes related to civil disorders through several mechanisms. More precisely, legal services should have both direct effects, increases in the number of police complaints (Cunningham 2016; Pedroza 2017), and indirect effects, changes in riot behavior (Cunningham 2018). The direct effect is a result of the indigent using lawyers to access public services, in this case, adequate and nondiscriminatory policing. The indirect effect, however, could improve the relationship between the police and the community (reduce riot propensities) or escalate tension (increase riot propensities).

An improvement in police-community relations may occur if the police become less likely to use excessive force or if citizens are more likely to use the judicial system to resolve conflicts. A statement from the Office of Economic Opportunity at a Senate Subcommittee Hearing in 1969 provides anecdotal evidence to this effect: "Legal services lawyers have won the confidence of angry young men and women and have channeled their grievances into democratic procedures. This capability and achievement mark a major victory for those concerned with maintaining law and order" (U.S. Congress 1969, 102). Conversely, free legal aid and information may embolden citizens into more militant actions. For instance, a police officer accused NLSP lawyers of organizing the protest that escalated into the Newark Uprising of 1967. He criticized NLSP lawyers for emboldening criminals and interfering with the police ability to control the crowd stating, "You can carry a machete through the streets of Newark and not get locked up" due to the presence of NLSP lawyers (Herbers 1967, 24). Police retaliation against the community for filing lawsuits or citizens exaggerating claims of police use of force to NLSP lawyers are also possible. The indirect effects on riot propensities and severities are ambiguous. These claims have been tested, providing evidence that NLSPs reduce riot propensities and severities, but the indirect mechanisms are unclear (Gillezeau 2015; Cunningham 2018).

Given that rioting caused a dramatic decrease in the property values of African American homes and reduced the labor market opportunities for blacks, we could expect the NLSP to have noticeable impacts on these outcomes (Collins and Margo 2007; Collins et al. 2004). Because most individuals accumulate wealth through homeownership, the 1960s uprisings contributed significantly to generational wealth disparities (Toney 2016). The NLSP, either directly (through legal consultation) or indirectly (by reducing riot propensities and severities), should have a positive impact on wealth accumulation through property appreciation.

## EMPIRICAL STRATEGY

To test the impact of the NLSP on wealth accumulation of African Americans, we first must establish a link between NLSPs and riots. After establishing that linkage, we then analyze the impact of the NLSP on property values. We follow the general approach used by Jamein Cunningham to identify the relationship between NLSPs and riot propensities (2018). However, the dependent variable in our analysis is the cumulative funding of an NLSP, not funding in a given year. In our case, the impact of funding does not depreciate after one year, allowing a NLSP to build on existing efforts.

The empirical strategy used to determine the effectiveness of the NLSP as an antiriot policy is a continuous difference-in-difference analysis. The treatment variable of interest is cumulative NLSP funding in millions of dollars.[7] For cities in the control group, this variable is always zero (never receive a grant). For those in the treated group, it is initially zero (before treatment) and increases as a city receives federal grants over time. Our analysis accounts for key cross-sectional differences between funded and unfunded cities by controlling for observable demographic characteristics as well as including fixed effects to capture unobserved heterogeneity that is time invariant.[8] The dependent variable of interest is the number of riots in a city in a given year or the severity of those riots. The riot severity measure is the total number of arrests, arsons, injuries, and people killed due to rioting in a city relative to the total share of arrests, arsons, injuries, and people killed due to rioting between 1964 and 1971 (see Collins and Margo 2007).

To identify a causal effect, NLSP funding must be unrelated to existing trends in riot propensities. Urban civil disorders, regarding violence and destruction of property within the black community in response to perceived injustices, were relatively rare before 1964. Riots or mobs resulting in interracial conflict occurred before the 1960s. However, civil disorders similar to those that occurred in the 1960s did occur in Detroit and Harlem in the 1940s as well as in Harlem in 1935. Despite riots being relatively rare events prior to the 1960s (Lieberson and Silverman 1965), the NLSP was promoted as an antiriot program and more than likely implemented in communities more likely to explode. If so, this will attenuate the impact of the program on riot propensities.

As a robustness check, we use the age of the oldest nearby law school as an instrument to deal with endogeneity related to the timing, location, and intensity of treatment.[9] Law schools were directly related to the implementation and rollout of the program as well as unrelated to existing trends in riot behavior due to their age and the fact that legal clinics mostly came about through NLSP funding (Cunningham 2018; Johnson 2014). Law schools are an ideal instrument because the program was designed to be affiliated with law schools. The exclusion restriction is satisfied by the fact that urban riots occur well after the implementation of legal education through universities in the United States.

We link the NLSP to wealth accumulation by using property values as a measurement of wealth. For robustness, we use two techniques to examine the relationship between NLSPs and wealth. The first approach is a difference-in-difference regression model. The dependent variable is the log of the median residential property value for black homeowners.[10] The

---

7. This variable captures cumulative legal services funding and is lagged by one year. So in census year 1970, this will include NLSP funding through 1969. And for 1980, this will account for NLSP funding through 1979.

8. Demographic characteristics are from the 1960, 1970, and 1980 censuses as covariates. The covariates are the proportion of the nonwhite population, the percentage of the population with more than twelve years of education, population per square mile, median age, and family median income. We include city fixed effects to capture unobserved heterogeneity that varies across cities but is time invariant. We also include region-by-year fixed effects to deal with riot contagion that varies by region and year. The literature on riots highlights the importance of the geographical region of a city.

9. For this variable, zeroes refer to cities without a law school.

10. Property value serves as a measurement of wealth. We use the median property value of black-owned homes for the city due to the fact that riots will have direct impact on the values of homes in rioting communities as well as indirect impact on nearby areas including other black communities in the city. For instance, white flight hastened by the riots would influence the median property value of all homes in a city (Boustan 2010). Second,

treatment variable is cumulative NLSP funding in a city prior to census year 1960, 1970, or 1980. In addition, an indicator variable identifies cities that experienced a high-severity riot and another indicator variable identifies cities that experienced a medium-severity riot. The zero and low-severity group are the reference group.

The second approach follows the specification outlined by William Collins and Robert Margo (2007). Now the dependent variable is the change in the log median residential property value for all black homeowners. Similar to the previous specification, the treatment variable is cumulative funding of the NLSP. We include the riot severity indicator variables. We also estimate a specification that includes a riot severity measure where a city with zero riots or low-severity riots is coded as 0, medium-severity riots as 1, and high-severity riots as 2. The key difference in this specification is the inclusion of regional fixed effects instead of city fixed effects and conducting a cross-sectional analysis. Also the covariates vary by the specification but include total population, the percentage of the population black, the proportion of workers in manufacturing, the change in property value between 1950 and 1960, the crime rate in 1962, and a measure of residential segregation. These covariates are used to replicate and compare our results to those of Collins and Margo (2007).[11]

## DATA

Data on the recipients of federal legal services grants were compiled from National Archives Community Action Program (NACAP) files. NACAP provides information on the city, county, and state for which funds were received. These data also include the date the grant was issued, the amount of the grant, the name and address of the grantee, and a brief description of the intended purpose of the grant. Data on property values and other city characteristics are taken from 1960, 1970, and 1980 census city and county data books. The city-level demographic information was constructed by linearly interpolating between 1960, 1970, and 1980 data. Data on civil disorders has been provided courtesy of Collins and Margo (2007) and originally collected by Greg Carter (1986). The Carter data include the location and duration of race riots between 1964 and 1971 as well as the number of people killed, injured, or arrested, and the number of arsons reported or discovered by police during a race riot. Because the riot data contain civil disorders only between 1964 and 1971, we focus on legal service spending and provision before 1972.

The riot data provided by Collins and Margo differ from other sources of race riots (2007). For comparison purposes, Susan Olzak provides detailed accounts of ethnic protests in standard metropolitan statistical areas (SMSAs) during our sample period, 1964 to 1971 (2015).[12] Figure 1 highlights the differences in the frequency of protests by events and data source. Carter race riots are represented by the line without a marker (1986), and Olzak by the line with a circle marker.[13] The two main differences from these series are the definition of a riot and the source information. According to Carter, a race riot is defined as a demonstration involving at least thirty participants, some of whom must be black, that results in some property damage or violence (1986). In addition, the event has to occur outside of a school setting or an organized civil rights demonstration. Olzak defines a riot as a demonstration involving at least fifty participants, involving some form or act of violence, and lasting longer than two hours (2015). Additionally, Olzak identifies ethnic conflicts using the *New York Times* and Carter collects information on riots from the *New York Times*, the *Washington Post*, Lemberg

---

Collins and Margo show that riots influence the median property value of all homes and black-owned homes in a city (2007).

11. In addition, we use rainfall in April of 1968. Collins and Margo show that rainfall is an important predictor of riot severity (2007). To compare our estimates with theirs, we instrument for riot severity group using the rainfall variable they provide.

12. Olzak documents ethnic conflicts from 1954 to 1992.

13. Olzak race riots are black initiated riots according to the event type and initiating ethnic group (2015).

**Figure 1.** Frequency of Riots by Data Source

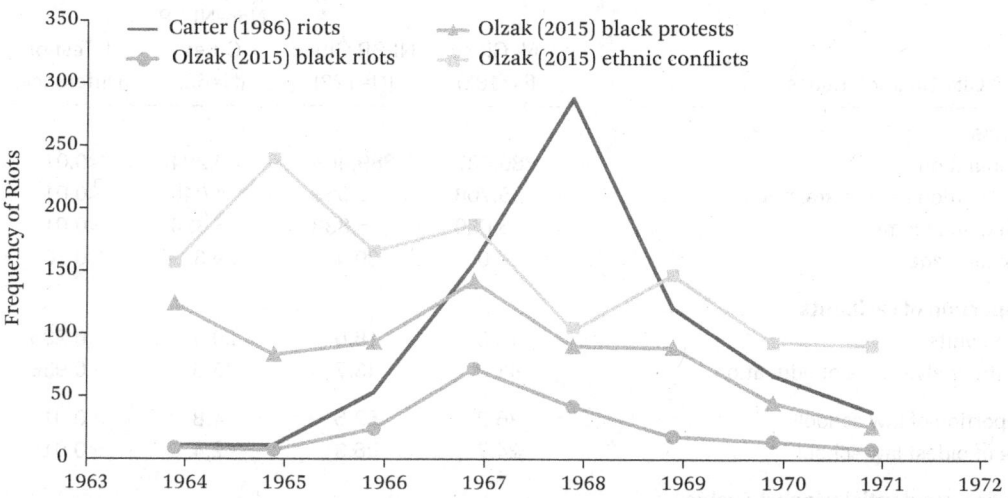

*Source:* Authors' calculation based on tabulations from Collins and Margo 2007 and Olzak 2015.
*Notes:* Carter (1986) original source of race riots between 1964 and 1971, which are identified by the line without a marker. Race riots are identified by the line with a circle marker. Black protests (including riots) are identified with a triangle marker. All ethnic conflicts recorded by Olzak (2015) are identified by the line with a square marker. The sample is restricted to capture events between 1964 and 1971.

Center for the Study of Violence, *Congressional Quarterly Almanac*, and congressional reports.[14]

Despite the differences in the data collection efforts, we use the Carter data to take advantage of city level variation in the outcome variables of interest (rioting and property values) and the treatment variable (legal services). A SMSA will include multiple cities of interest such as Dallas–Fort Worth. Our estimating strategy takes advantage of the fact that Dallas received an NLSP grant before Fort Worth. This allows Fort Worth to serve as a comparison for Dallas before Fort Worth is treated. Another example is Raleigh-Durham. Durham received an NLSP grant, but Raleigh was not treated. Considering the similarities of these two cities, we use Raleigh as a comparison for Durham. We also use Carter to compare our results with the literature (1986).

The final sample consists of city-level observations of federal legal service funding, riots, property values, and census demographic information for 185 cities. The selection of cities is based on the availability of median black-owned property values in published census tables for 1960, 1970, and 1980. The final sample contains 122 cities that received NLSP grants, the treatment group, and sixty-three nongrant cities, the comparison group. As shown in table 1, treated cities are typically larger, denser, and more affluent. Within these cities, median property values of black homeowners are less than all homeowners. Black-owned property values are higher in treated cities, but these cities experience more rioting and more severe rioting when compared to nongrant cities.

### RESULTS

Our results show that NLSP funding is inversely related to the number of riots. Table 2 reports estimates for the effects of NLSP funding on the number of riots and riot severity. Columns 1 and 4 report estimates from the full sample; columns 2 and 5 restrict the analysis to cities that received NLSP grants. Columns 3 and 6 limit the sample to cities included in the Collins and Margo analysis (2007). Last, columns 4 through 6 report estimates using the age of

---

14. It is quite possible that Carter overstates the number of riots in the 1960s and Olzak understates them (Carter 1986; Olzak 2015). Both sources identify major severe riots during this period.

**Table 1.** Summary Statistics

| 1960 City Characteristics | All Cities (N=185) | NLSP Cities (N=122) | Non-NLSP Cities (N=63) | T-Test of Difference |
|---|---|---|---|---|
| **Means** | | | | |
| Population | 280,437 | 389,469 | 69,294 | <0.01 |
| Population per square mile | 5,708 | 6,569 | 4,040 | <0.01 |
| Median income | 5,680 | 5,833 | 5,384 | <0.01 |
| Median age | 30.0 | 30.4 | 29.3 | 0.10 |
| **Proportion of residents** | | | | |
| Nonwhite | 18.8 | 18.0 | 20.3 | 0.235 |
| With twelve years of education | 43.6 | 43.7 | 43.5 | 0.936 |
| Proportion of law schools | 36.2 | 52.5 | 4.8 | <0.01 |
| Age of oldest law school | 24.7 | 36.3 | 2.4 | <0.01 |
| **Median residential property value** | | | | |
| Black home owners | 8,719 | 9,185 | 7,817 | <0.01 |
| All home owners | 12,264 | 12,411 | 11,978 | 0.389 |
| **Means between 1964 and 1971** | | | | |
| Number of riots | 2.29 | 3.09 | 0.75 | <0.01 |
| Severity of riots | 1.91 | 2.73 | 0.31 | <0.01 |

*Source:* Authors' calculations based on Collins and Margo 2007 and U.S. Census Bureau 1960.
*Notes:* Riot data (Collins and Margo 2007); means (U.S. Census Bureau 1960).

the oldest law school as an instrumental variable. Column 4 reports estimates from our preferred specification.

According to our preferred specification (column 4), a $1,000,000 increase in NLSP funding reduced the number of riots by 3 percent. The typical size of an NLSP grant was $200,000, implying a treatment effect of 0.6 percent decrease in rioting due to NLSP.[15] Although we exploit the variation in timing and location, columns 2 and 5 provide suggestive evidence that the results are not driven by cities that never received an NLSP grant. Point estimates are typically larger in the NLSP-only sample relative to the full sample, but the results are not statistically different. Estimates using age of the oldest law school as an instrument in panel A are smaller than ordinary least squares (OLS) results but remain statistically significant in columns 4 and 5.

Although the treatment effects in the first panel are small, most of the direct antiriot efforts of poverty lawyers operating NLSPs involved efforts to reduce the severity of riots. Advocates of the NLSP and the Kerner Commission Report viewed poverty lawyers as vital to resolving grievances that lead to civil disorders. Similar to the first, the second panel shows that NLSP funding is inversely related to riot severity. According to column 4, a $1,000,000 increase in NLSP funding reduced riot severity by 48 percent. This implies that the typical NLSP grant reduced the severity of riots by approximately 10 percent, which is a substantial treatment effect. The results are statistically significant in columns 1, 4, and 5. Moreover, results in columns 4 through 6 are at least 50 percent larger than OLS estimates. These results suggest that public officials were more likely to fund a NLSP in more volatile

15. Both Jamein Cunningham (2018) and Rob Gillezeau (2015) find much larger effects of NLSP on the number of riots. However, both analyses rely on different sample periods and sample selection criteria.

**Table 2.** Estimates of Cumulative NLSP Funding on Riot Propensities

|  | 1 | 2 | 3 | 4 2SLS | 5 2SLS | 6 2SLS |
|---|---|---|---|---|---|---|
| **Number of riots** | | | | | | |
| Legal service grant (in millions) | −0.106** | −0.109** | −0.0904* | −0.0673* | −0.0718* | −0.0609 |
|  | [0.0446] | [0.0520] | [0.0461] | [0.0376] | [0.0397] | [0.0391] |
| $R^2$ | 0.741 | 0.772 | 0.785 | 0.807 | 0.828 | 0.838 |
| **Riot severity** | | | | | | |
| Legal service grant (in millions) | −0.585* | −0.611 | −0.504 | −0.914* | −0.926* | −0.808 |
|  | [0.351] | [0.378] | [0.313] | [0.490] | [0.480] | [0.498] |
| $R^2$ | 0.620 | 0.637 | 0.666 | 0.664 | 0.678 | 0.704 |
| Covariates (X) | X | X | X | X | X | X |
| Treated sample only |  | X |  |  | X |  |
| Collins and Margo sample |  |  | X |  |  | X |
| Observations | 1,480 | 976 | 808 | 1,480 | 976 | 808 |
| Number of cities | 185 | 122 | 101 | 185 | 122 | 101 |

*Source:* Authors' calculations.
*Notes:* Table displays weighted-least-squares estimates. All columns include city and state-by-year effects and covariates from 1960, 1970, and 1980 censuses linearly interpolated in columns. All columns use 1960 population as weights.
***$p < .01$; **$p < .05$; *$p < .10$

communities. If so, OLS underestimates the true effect of the NLSP on riot severity.

### Legal Services and Property Values

Table 3 displays the results for the impact of NLSP on wealth accumulation. Columns 1 through 3 refer to the difference-in-difference approach where the dependent variable is the log of the median residential property value for black homeowners. Columns 4 through 7 refer to the cross-section OLS approach where the dependent variable is the change in the log of the median property value of black homeowners. Column 1 excludes NLSP funding to compare results using a difference-in-difference approach with Collins and Margo cross-section analysis. Column 2 includes NLSP funding and column 3 limits the sample to the cities used in Collins and Margo (2007). For comparability, columns 4 and 5 replicate results from table 3B in Collins and Margo (2007), which highlights the impact of riots on black-owned property value not accounting for the endogeneity of riots. Columns 6 and 7 replicate the results from table 6 in Collins and Margo (2007), which uses rainfall in April of 1968 as an instrument for the severity of riots.

Using the difference-in-difference approach, the results in columns 1 through 3 identify an inverse relationship between property values and riots. The results are statistically significant only for black-owned homes in a community that experienced severe riots. Including NLSP funding reduces the negative impact of high-severity riots on black-owned property values.[16] According to column 2, high-severity riots reduce property value by 14 log points (12.9 percent). Restricting the sample to the cities in

---

16. Legal Services as an antirioting program should reduce the duration and severity of riots and as a result have a positive effect on property values relative to places that are not funded or receive very little funding. Moreover, NLSP should reduce the likelihood of additional riots, which will also have a positive effect on property values. Because legal services are correlated with rioting, the specification that does not include legal services will capture that positive relationship, making the point estimates smaller. Therefore, accounting for legal services should increase (in absolute terms) the coefficient on riot severity, though this is not the case in each specification.

**Table 3.** Estimates of NLSP and Riots on Log of Median Black-Owned Property Value, 1960–1980

|  | Log | | | Change in Log | | | |
| --- | --- | --- | --- | --- | --- | --- | --- |
|  | 1 | 2 | 3 | 4 | 5 | 6 | 7 |
| NLSP funding |  | 0.0180* | 0.0232** |  | 0.0224** |  | 0.0441** |
|  |  | [0.00978] | [0.00962] |  | [0.0101] |  | [0.0199] |
| High-severity group (0/1) | −0.153*** | −0.138*** | −0.0997** | −0.139** | −0.193*** |  |  |
|  | [0.0411] | [0.0452] | [0.0477] | [0.0593] | [0.0558] |  |  |
| Medium-severity group (0/1) | −0.0282 | 0.00706 | 0.0491 | −0.0845** | −0.0939** |  |  |
|  | [0.0367] | [0.0413] | [0.0465] | [0.0391] | [0.0389] |  |  |
| Severity group (0–2) |  |  |  |  |  | −0.220* | −0.355* |
|  |  |  |  |  |  | [0.129] | [0.190] |
| Collins and Margo sample |  |  | X |  |  |  |  |
| Observations | 555 | 555 | 303 | 101 | 98 | 104 | 101 |
| $R^2$ | 0.402 | 0.437 | 0.391 | 0.599 | 0.625 | 0.445 | 0.327 |
| Number of cities | 185 | 185 | 101 | 101 | 98 | 104 | 101 |

*Source:* Authors' calculations.
*Notes:* Table displays least-squares estimates. The dependent variable is the log of the median property values for black-owned homes provided in the published tables from the 1960, 1970, and 1980 censuses. Covariates are from the 1962, 1972, and 1983 city and county data books. Each regression in column 1 through 3 is weighted by 1960 population. Heteroskedasticity-robust standard errors are presented beneath each estimate in brackets.
***$p < .01$; **$p < .05$; *$p < .10$

Collins and Margo reduces the impact of high-severity riots even further than estimates in columns 1 and 2 (2007). The marginal effect in column 3 implies high-severity riots reduce black-owned property values by 10 log points (9.5 percent). The impact of NLSP funding is statistically significant or marginally statistically significant and positive. According to results in column 2, a $1,000,000 increase in NLSP funding would have increased black-owned property values by 1.8 percent. Limiting the sample implies a 2.3 percent increase in property values.

Similarly, columns 4 and 5 highlight the inverse relationship between riots and black-owned property values. Column 4 reproduces estimates from Collins and Margo (2007). Column 5 augments their analysis by including NLSP funding. Using the cross-sectional approach, high-severity riots and medium-severity riots are found to have a negative and statistically significant effect. Also, legal services appear to be an important omitted variable in this analysis, which is evident from table 2 as well as column 5 in table 3. Including NLSP funding increases the estimate of high-severity riots by 39 percent. As shown in column 5, high-severity riots reduce property values by 19 log points (17.6 percent), medium-severity riots reduce them by 9 log points (8.9 percent), and NLSP funding increases them by 2 log points (2.2 percent).

Columns 6 and 7 report estimates using rainfall in April of 1968 as an instrument. Column 6 reproduce estimates from Collins and Margo (2007), and column 7 adds NLSP funding to the analysis. As in columns 4 and 5, including NLSP funding dramatically increases the marginal effects of riot severity on black-owned property values, by 52 percent. Also, using rainfall as an instrument increases the size of the treatment effect. According to column 7, a $1,000,000 increase in NLSP is associated with a 4.4 percent increase in black-owned property values.[17]

We estimate the overall effect of the NLSP

---

17. NLSP funding is likely correlated with unobserved factors correlated with property values. In regard to property values, law schools no longer serve as a valid instrument due to possible violation of exclusion restrictions.

on black-owned property values by using the estimated effects in column 2 of table 3, to predict the counterfactual log of median property values in 1980 for each city. These predicted values are calculated by subtracting the estimated value added due to NLSP funding in treated cities. Using the number of owner-occupied housing units in each city as weights, the weighted average of property values in 1980 across cities is calculated to construct an average counterfactual value of black-owned homes. The weighted average of property values in the non-NLSP counterfactual in 1980 is $10,486. The weighted average of the actual property in 1980 is $12,136. The difference between the actual and counterfactual property values implies an additional $2,139 increase in property value due to NLSP funding. The average number of black owner-occupied housing units in 1980 across cities is 6,394. Using this number, the NLSP is associated with a $10.5 million increase in property values by 1980.

## CONCLUSION

In closing, we reflect on these results in light of the broader questions framing this volume. These questions reflect on the historical success of the government's legal services program in discouraging civil disorders, the kind of progress we have made today, and the lessons that we should take from this work into the future.

### What Worked and What Did Not Work?

Together, the results present a compelling story for the importance of the NLSP. The program may have only had a modest impact in reducing the number of riots that occurred in the United States, but spending on the NLSP substantially reduced the severity of the rioting that occurred. This is a particularly important finding given that riot severity has important impacts on urban development and African American outcomes over the long-run. A one-time investment of $1,000,000 in NLSP may have increased black-owned property values by as much as 2 to 4 percent over the long term. This is a substantial and persistent impact that shows just how cost-effective antiriot programs can be. The finding is particularly salient given that riot prevention was not even the primary goal of the program. The findings of long-run mitigating impacts on the accepted economic costs of riots are a further verification that the NLSP was truly an effective program in lessening riot severity.

More broadly, these results suggest that the War on Poverty and many of its component programs may provide a template for future efforts to discourage or mitigate civil disorders. Despite limited evidence that direct income transfers were successful in discouraging riots, this work is part of a growing literature suggesting that programs designed to empower individuals and address grievances were effective in discouraging civil disorder.

### How Far Have We Come?

The NLSP is one of several War on Poverty programs that, in some form, survived the dismantling of the Office of Economic Opportunity by the Nixon administration in the form of the independent Legal Services Corporation (LSC) and its depoliticized mandate. However, even in this new form funding has been rocky throughout the decades. In the 1980s, the LSC budget was cut severely, although Democrats successfully blocked efforts to discontinue the LSC. The following decades marked a period of stability for LSC, although the Trump administration sought to eliminate the LSC in the president's 2017 proposed budget. Despite the current political climate, there appeared to be some degree of consensus that the LSC serves an important role even if funding is limited.

More broadly, however, there is still a long way to go. Unaddressed grievances and unequal treatment helped drive the riots of the 1960s, but it is clear that unfair treatment by state institutions, including the police and the judiciary, are driving factors behind the riots that have occurred since 1970. Although publicly funded legal services programs could potentially help address these injustices, other sys-

---

When using age of law school as an instrument for NLSP, the coefficient on NLSP funding and severity group are dramatically larger in magnitude (four times larger for NLSP funding and two times for severity group) but statistically insignificant.

tematic changes in policing and the legal treatment of officers involved in shootings of unarmed African Americans may have more substantial impacts.

## What Are the Implications for the Twenty-First Century?

The results are of particular relevance to the ongoing Black Lives Matter movement. Because grievances are so explicitly grounded in accusations of police abuses, reasons are strong to believe that legal supports designed to challenge local and state institutions could prove an effective mechanism to calm tensions. Given how often existing legal institutions are perceived to favor police officers engaged in shootings of unarmed African American civilians, the case to be made that a more activist form of legal services as envisioned in the 1960s could have a strong impact in lessening the associated protests is a strong one.

### REFERENCES

Ariel, Barak, William A. Farrar, and Alex Sutherland. 2015. "The Effect of Police Body-Worn Cameras on Use of Force and Citizens' Complaints Against the Police: A Randomized Controlled Trial." *Journal of Quant Criminology* 31(3): 509–35.

Boustan, Leah Platt. 2010. "Was Postwar Suburbanization 'White Flight'? Evidence from the Black Migration." *Quarterly Journal of Economics* 125(1): 417–43.

Cahn, Edgar, and Jean Cahn. 1964. "The War on Poverty: A Civilian Perspective." *Yale Law Journal* 73(8): 1317–52.

Carter, Gregg Lee. 1986. "The 1960s Black Riots Revisited: City Level Explanations of Their Severity." *Sociological Inquiry* 56(2): 210–28.

———. 1987. "Local Police Force Size and the Severity of the 1960s Black Rioting." *Journal of Conflict Resolution* 31(4): 601–14.

Champagne, Anthony. 1974. "An Evaluation of the Effectiveness of the OEO Legal Service Program." *Urban Affairs Review* 9(4): 466–89.

Collins, William J., and Robert Margo. 2007. "The Economic Aftermath of the 1960s Riots in American Cities: Evidence from Property Values." *Journal of Economic History* 67(4): 849–83.

Collins, William J., Robert Margo, Jacob Vigdor, and Daniel Myers. 2004. "The Labor Market Effects of the 1960s Riots." *Brookings-Wharton Papers on Urban Affairs* 2004: 1–46. Accessed April 29, 2018. https://muse.jhu.edu/article/170965/pdf.

Collins, William J., and Fred H. Smith. 2004. "A Neighborhood-Level View of Riots, Property Values, and Population Loss: Cleveland 1950–1980." *Explorations in Economic History* 44(3): 365–85.

Cunningham, Jamein P. 2016. "An Evaluation of the Federal Legal Services Program: Evidence from Crime Rates and Property Values." *Journal of Urban Economics* 92 (March): 76–90.

———. 2018. "The Language of the Unheard: Legal Services and the 1960s Race Riots." Working Paper. Memphis: University of Memphis.

DiPasquale, Denise, and Edward L. Glaeser. 1998. "The Los Angeles Riot and the Economics of Urban Unrest." *Journal of Urban Economics* 43(1): 52–78.

Downes, Bryan T. 1968. "Social and Political Characteristics of Riot Cities: A Comparative Study." *Social Science Quarterly* 49(3): 504–20.

Finman, Ted. 1971. "OEO Legal Service Programs and the Pursuit of Social Change." *Wisconsin Law Review* 1971(1): 1001–1084.

Gillette, Michael L. 1996. *Launching the War on Poverty: An Oral History*. New York: Twayne Publishers.

Gillezeau, Rob. 2015. "Did the War on Poverty Stop the 1960s Race Riots?" Working Paper. Ann Arbor: University of Michigan.

Herbers, John. 1967. "Newark Jailer Says Poverty Aides Stirred Riots." *New York Times*, August 8.

Hinton, Elizabeth. 2016. *From the War on Poverty to the War on Crime: The Making of Mass Incarceration in America*. Cambridge, Mass.: Harvard University Press.

Hollingsworth, Ellen J. 1977. "Ten Years of Legal Services for the Poor." In *A Decade of Federal Antipoverty Programs*, edited by Robert H. Haveman. New York: Academic Press.

Johnson, Earl, Jr. 1974. *Justice and Reform*. New York: Russell Sage Foundation.

———. 2014. *To Establish Justice for All*. Santa Barbara, Calif.: Praeger.

Katz, Jack. 1982. *Poor People's Lawyers in Transition*. New Brunswick, N.J.: Rutgers University Press.

Kerner Commission. 1968. *Report of the National Advisory Commission on Civil Disorders*. Washington: Government Printing Office.

King, Mary C. 2003. "Race Riots and Black Economic Progress." *Review of Black Political Economy* 30(4): 51–66.

Levitan, Sar. 1969. *The Great Society's Poor Law.* Baltimore, Md.: Johns Hopkins University Press.

Lieberson, Stanley, and Arnold Silverman. 1965. "The Precipitants and Underlying Conditions of Race Riots." *American Sociological Review* 30(6): 887–98.

*Los Angeles Sentinel.* 1971. "Legal Services: Challenging the Power." May 27, A8.

Myers, Daniel J. 1997. "Racial Rioting in the 1960s: An Event History Analysis of Local Conditions." *American Sociological Review* 62(1): 94–112.

Olzak, Susan. 2015. *Ethnic Collective Action in Contemporary Urban United States — Data on Conflicts and Protests, 1954–1992.* ICPSR34 341-v1. Ann Arbor, MI: Inter-university Consortium for Political and Social Research [distributor], 2015-03-04. DOI: 10.3886/ICPSR34341.v1.

Olzak, Susan, Suzanne Shanahan, and Elizabeth H. McEneaney. 1996. "Poverty, Segregation, and Race Riots: 1960 to 1993." *American Sociological Review* 61(4): 590–613.

Pedroza, Juan M. 2017. "Making Noncitizens' Rights Real: The Safety Net, Legal Aid Services, and Immigration Legal Services Fraud." Working Paper. Stanford, Calif.: Stanford University.

Spilerman, Seymour. 1970. "The Causes of Racial Disturbances: A Comparison of Alternative Explanations." *American Sociological Review* 35(4): 627–49.

Stumpf, Harry. 1975. *Community Politics and Legal Services.* Beverly Hills, Calif.: Sage Publications.

Toney, Jermaine. 2016. "Is There Racialized Legacy in Wealth Across Generations? Evidence from Panel Study, 1984–2013." Working Paper. New York: The New School.

U.S. Census Bureau. 1960. *1960 Census of Population and Housing.* Washington: Government Printing Office. Accessed April 29, 2018. https://www.census.gov/prod/www/decennial.html.

U.S. Congress. Senate. Subcommittee on Employment, Manpower and Poverty of the Committee on Labor and Public Welfare. 1969. *Legal Services Program of the Office of Economic Opportunity*, Hearing, November 14. Washington: Government Printing Office.

Wasow, Omar. 2015. "Nonviolence, Violence, and Voting: Effects of the 1960s Black Protests on White Attitudes and Voting Behavior." *Working Paper.* Princeton University, Princeton.

Wright, Eric W. 1967. "Competition in Legal Services Under the War on Poverty." *Stanford Law Review* 19(3): 579–92.

# PART III

# Urban Cities in Focus

# Fifty Years After the Kerner Commission Report: Place, Housing, and Racial Wealth Inequality in Los Angeles

MELANY DE LA CRUZ-VIESCA, PAUL M. ONG,
ANDRE COMANDON, WILLIAM A. DARITY JR.,
AND DARRICK HAMILTON

*Fifty years after the national Kerner Commission report on urban unrest and fifty-three years after California's McCone Commission report on the 1965 Watts riots, substantial racial disparity in education, housing, employment, and wealth is still pervasive in Los Angeles. Neither report mentions wealth inequality as a cause for concern, however. This article examines one key dimension of racial wealth inequality through the lens of home ownership, particularly in South Los Angeles, where the 1965 Watts riots took place. It also analyzes the state's role in housing development in codifying and expanding practices of racial and class segregation that has led to the production and reproduction of racial inequality in South Los Angeles compared with Los Angeles County.*

**Keywords:** urban policy, racial wealth inequality, housing, immigration, Los Angeles

**Melany De La Cruz-Viesca** is assistant director of the UCLA Asian American Studies Center and managing editor of *Asian American Pacific Islander (AAPI) Nexus Journal*. **Paul M. Ong** is research professor at UCLA's Luskin School of Public Affairs and director of the UCLA Center for Neighborhood Knowledge. **Andre Comandon** is a PhD student in the Department of Urban Planning at the Luskin School of Public Affairs. **William A. Darity Jr.** is Samuel DuBois Cook Professor of Public Policy, African and African American Studies, and Economics and director of the Samuel DuBois Cook Center on Social Equity at Duke University. **Darrick Hamilton** is director of the doctoral program in public and urban policy at the New School in New York, jointly appointed professor of economics and urban policy at the Milano School of International Affairs, Management, and Urban Policy and the Department of Economics at the New School, and co-associate director of the Cook Center for Social Equity at Duke University.

© 2018 Russell Sage Foundation. De La Cruz-Viesca, Melany, Paul M. Ong, Andre Comandon, William A. Darity Jr., and Darrick Hamilton. 2018. "Fifty Years After the Kerner Commission Report: Place, Housing, and Racial Wealth Inequality in Los Angeles." *RSF: The Russell Sage Foundation Journal of the Social Sciences* 4(6): 160–84. DOI: 10.7758/RSF.2018.4.6.08. This research is made possible by the generous support of the Ford Foundation's Building Economic Security Over a Lifetime initiative. We especially acknowledge our Ford Foundation Program Officers—Kilolo Kijakazi, Amy Brown, Leah Mayor, and John Irons. Funding was also provided by the UCLA Institute for American Cultures, UCLA Asian American Studies Center, UCLA Luskin Center for History and Policy, and the Haynes Foundation. This research is also part of the UCLA Center for Neighborhood Knowledge's (CNK) Kerner Revisited project. We are grateful to CNK staff, Chhandara Pech and Alycia Cheng, for their research and technical assistance. Direct correspondence to: Melany De La Cruz-Viesca at melanyd@ucla.edu, UCLA Asian American Studies Center, 3230 Campbell Hall, Los Angeles, CA 90095.

Open Access Policy: *RSF: The Russell Sage Foundation Journal of the Social Sciences* is an open access journal. This article is published under a Creative Commons Attribution-NonCommercial-NoDerivs 3.0 Unported License.

In its now well-known report, the National Advisory Commission on Civil Disorders (the Kerner Commission, thus the Kerner report) cited the 1965 Watts riots in Los Angeles as an omen of violence before the summer of 1967 (Kerner Report 1968; Farley 2008). The commission noted, "The Los Angeles riot, the worst in the United States since the Detroit riot of 1943, shocked all who had been confident that race relations were improving in the North" (Kerner Report 1968, 38). Fifty years after the Kerner Commission's report and fifty-three years after California's McCone Commission's report on Watts, we examine the extent to which a key component of racial inequality has or has not been addressed and the limitations of the solutions the two commissions put forth.[1]

The reports' findings are not surprising, and they mirror the findings of similar postmortems into other large-scale urban racial riots, massacres, and uprisings before and after the 1960s, including the 1871 Chinese Massacre, 1943 Zoot Suit riots, and the 1992 civil unrest in Los Angeles.[2] Both the Kerner and McCone reports recommend addressing racial disparities through emergency literacy and preschool programs, improved police-community ties, increased affordable housing, more job training projects, upgraded health-care services, more efficient public transportation, among many suggestions. However, none of the original proposals mention wealth inequality as a cause for concern.

This article examines one key dimension of racial wealth inequality through the lens of home ownership, particularly in South Los Angeles, where the 1965 Watts riots took place. Homeownership is the largest component of wealth for many Americans, particularly those in the middle class. Homeownership also has neighborhood benefits in terms of added stability. Yet, for many communities of color, homeownership is out of reach. Countless people of color are unable to move from "bad" neighborhoods or purchase a home in their community. This issue has reached crisis levels in Los Angeles, which ranks near the top in homelessness and near the bottom in homeownership (Lansner 2017).

## THE MCCONE REPORT, KERNER REPORT, AND THE 1965 WATTS RIOTS

On Wednesday evening of August 11, 1965, an African American motorist was arrested for speeding. A minor roadside argument broke out, and then escalated into a fight. The community reacted in outrage to allegations of police brutality that soon spread, and six days of looting and arson followed. Los Angeles police needed the support of nearly four thousand members of the California Army National Guard to quell the riots, which resulted in thirty-four deaths and more than $40 million in property damage (Kerner Report 1968; Hinton 2016).[3] The riots were blamed principally on police racism and brutality. It was the city's worst civil unrest until the 1992 acquittal of the policemen who assaulted Rodney King.

The uprisings of 1967 in hundreds of cities across the nation involved blacks fighting against local symbols of white privilege in black neighborhoods, rather than against white individuals. It was only after the Watts riots and the many black uprisings that took place across America in the late 1960s that major municipal or federal commissions were appointed to investigate the depth of social and material inequality in urban centers, revealing a pervasive lack of awareness of the scale of the issues within government institutions and society.

---

1. A commission under California Governor Pat Brown, headed by former CIA director John A. McCone and thus known as the McCone Commission, investigated the Watts–Los Angeles riots. On December 2, 1965, it released a 101-page report titled *Violence in the City—An End or a Beginning?* (McCone and Christopher 1965).

2. The attack on Chinese was the single largest racially motivated mass lynching in the United States (Johnson 2011). The Zoot Suit riots, a series of racial attacks on primarily Mexican youth by American military servicemen, occurred during World War II, when many migrants arrived for the defense effort and newly assigned servicemen engulfed the city.

3. The race of the thirty-four individuals killed is not identified in either the McCone or the Kerner report.

The reports document how social and economic conditions in the riot cities represented a systematic pattern of severe disadvantage for blacks relative to whites. Although racially biased police practices were the precipitating factors largely responsible for igniting the 1965 Watts civil unrest, both the Kerner and McCone Commissions point to inadequate housing conditions as one of the most severe root causes.[4]

The McCone Commission provided a more detailed account of the conditions in Los Angeles, uncovering how residents of the Watts area lived in conditions inferior to the citywide average and strikingly inferior to newer sections of the city. The commission also noted that conditions were not nearly as bleak as the highly visible deterioration of northern slums. Assessing the issues required peeling away at the structural differences in housing. Overcrowding stood out as one of the greatest sources of housing disparity. An average of 4.3 persons lived in each Watts household, versus an overall county average of 2.94 per household (Los Angeles County and City Human Relations Commissions 1985). Furthermore, 88.6 percent of the total black population lived in areas considered segregated and concentrated within South-Central Los Angeles (McCone and Christopher 1965).

The McCone Commission, despite its assessment that the area was neither "gem nor slum," does express a major concern that a "serious deterioration of the area was in progress." Homes in the area were old and required constant maintenance to remain inhabitable, and more than two-thirds were owned by absentee landlords (McCone and Christopher 1965). The barriers to homeownership residents faced exacerbated this situation creating a general deficit in housing investments. The McCone report states, "Compounding the problem is the fact that both private financial intuitions and the Federal Housing Authority consider the residential multiple unit in the curfew area an unattractive market because of difficult collection problems, high maintenance costs, and a generally depreciating area resulting from the age of surrounding structures" (1965, 79).

The recommendations of the McCone and Kerner reports focus on the preservation of and increased presence of affordable rental units, in large part by subsidizing private and nonprofit investors and developers. Hypothetically, this strategy could address the challenge of improving the lack of decent and affordable housing, assuming that developers would significantly expand the supply, use government support to lower rents, and continue to maintain the housing stock.

There were three flaws with this approach. First, it was unlikely that funding would be adequate, thus overall impact would be minimal relative to the size of the housing problem. Second, the reports do not offer any detailed mechanisms to ensure the desired outcome from private developers; consequently the commissions implicitly relied on a simplistic assumption that market forces would be sufficient, that more competition would keep rents low and force absentee owners to pass along savings from the subsidies. However, it was just as likely that the housing market was operating to give the balance of economic power to landlords. Under these conditions, governmental support would end up in the developers' pocket.

Third, the recommendations do little to address the lack of local ownership of land and housing, which meant that inequalities in asset and wealth holding would remain, or become worse. Indeed, it would have been better had the commissions recommended or given more priority to increasing access to financial resources to residents, ending discriminatory practices in mortgage lending, and encourag-

---

4. Although specific grievances varied from city to city, at least twelve deeply held grievances were identified and ranked into three levels of relative intensity. The first level of intensity consisted of police practices, unemployment and underemployment, and inadequate housing. The second level of intensity comprised inadequate education, poor recreation facilities and programs, ineffectiveness of the political structure and grievance mechanisms. The third level included disrespectful white attitudes, discriminatory administration of justice, inadequacy of federal programs, inadequacy of municipal services, discriminatory consumer and credit practices, and inadequate welfare programs.

ing and providing incentives for home ownership at manageable fees. Not only would this have increased local households' wealth; it also could have generated the positive externalities and community stability that come with the presence of more homeowners.

Unfortunately, many of the recommendations were either not implemented or only partially implemented, and South Los Angeles remained a marginalized community. Nineteen years after the 1965 McCone report, the Los Angeles County and City Human Relations Commission found that housing remained one of the most critical problems in South Central Los Angeles.[5] The persistent socioeconomic problems and frustration felt by local residents eventually led to another sociopolitical explosion, the 1992 civil uprising.

## THE MULTIETHNIC RIOTS OF 1992

The 1985 Los Angeles County and City Human Relations Commissions report recommends that the mayor and city council request the City Planning Commission to develop a plan, including legislation if necessary, to address the critical housing problems of South-Central Los Angeles. The report concludes, "We cannot emphasize too strongly the critical nature of the problems described in this report and the implications of continued inaction. We should not have to wait for a second Los Angeles riot to erupt to bring these problems to serious public attention" (Los Angeles County and City Human Relations Commissions 1985, 16). Seven years later, Los Angeles would witness a massive second uprising—riots precipitated by the failure of a jury empaneled in Simi Valley to convict policemen who had engaged in a taped beating of Rodney King.[6]

The growing economic disparity in Los Angeles caused by corporate restructuring and government deregulation produced a widespread feeling of frustration and powerlessness among communities of color. The King beating verdicts, like the police force abuse of 1965, acted as the spark that set off the cumulative resentment in a violent expression of collective public protest (Davis 1992b). One main difference between the 1992 King riots and the 1965 Watts civil unrest was the multiethnic involvement of Koreans and Latinos, demonstrating that tensions were not limited to segregated black neighborhoods (Pastor 1995). This shift reflected a new racial paradigm that was taking shape not only in Los Angeles, but throughout America. This required a parallel shift in the analysis of issues such as segregation and access to decent housing from focusing solely on disparities between black and white people to one that is cross-cutting and multidimensional. The history of civil unrest in Los Angeles from the Chinese Massacre of 1871 to the 1965 Watts civil unrest, the 1968 Chicano Blowouts, and the 1992 Los Angeles uprising becomes part of a continuum of systematic oppression of communities of color that should spur renewed critical conversations about race, economics, and justice in America.[7]

---

5. The McCone Commission urged the immediate creation of a city human relations commission to develop comprehensive educational programs designed to enlist the cooperation of all groups, both public and private, in eliminating prejudice and discrimination in employment housing, education, and public accommodations.

6. On April 29, a trial jury acquitted four white officers of the Los Angeles Police Department of the use of excessive force in the videotaped arrest and beating of an African American, Rodney King. In response, South-Central Los Angeles was once again a site of protest, where protestors blocked freeway traffic and beat motorists, wrecked and looted numerous downtown stores and buildings, and set more than one hundred fires. The three days of rioting killed more than sixty people, injured almost two thousand, led to seven thousand arrests, and caused nearly $1 billion in property damage, including the burnings of more than three thousand buildings (Crogin 2002; Thomas 2016).

7. The East Los Angeles Walkouts, or Chicano Blowouts, were a series of 1968 protests by Chicano students against unequal conditions in the Los Angeles Unified School District high schools. The first protest took place on March 1, 1968. The students who organized and carried out the protests were primarily concerned with the quality of their education. This movement involved thousands of students in the Los Angeles area and was one of the first mass mobilizations by Mexican Americans in Southern California (*Los Angeles Times* 1968; Torgerson 1992).

## THE ROLE OF PLACE AND RACE IN CREATING HOMEOWNERSHIP DISPARITIES

Unlike New York or San Francisco, Los Angeles is decentralized in its structure. Its major commercial, financial, and cultural institutions are geographically dispersed rather than concentrated in a single central urban core. This spatial structure led to urban sprawl, which arguably intensified the creation of racially segregated neighborhoods (Le Goix 2005). However, the structure of segregation in Los Angeles was created through racial discrimination, restrictions, and systematic displacement long before the metropolis sprawled to its contemporary limits.

In one of the more blatant uses of state power to displace people of color, the City of Los Angeles used eminent domain with funds from the Federal Housing Act of 1949 to acquire land largely owned by Mexican Americans in Los Angeles' Chavez Ravine (Normark 1999). The city used California's redevelopment law to justify massive "poor removal," uprooting more than one thousand Mexican Americans (Davis 1992b; Becerra 2012). The land then was used to construct Dodger Stadium.

Federal subsidies for urban sprawl led to disinvestment in the central city and increased development of suburban areas, which, concomitant with the displacement of poorer residents and people of color, gave rise to contemporary patterns of segregation. This pattern was reinforced through two mechanisms. Although legalized housing discrimination and practices by the Fair Housing Authority (FHA) ended with the Fair Housing Act of 1968, the outcomes it gave rise to persist. For example, the systematic exclusion from the broader appreciating housing market and exploitive housing market-based strategies that have specifically targeted people of color (Kain and Quigley 1972; Sharp and Hall 2014, Massey 2005; Steil et al. 2017). The exodus of many of the wealthier and white households to the suburbs further contributed to marginalization as employment and commercial growth would follow, creating problems of spatial mismatch for poor residents of central cities (Davis 1992a; De Graaf and Taylor 2001; Pastor 2001b).

A growing post–World War II economy coupled with a severe labor shortage forced the federal government to finally abolish the national origins formula that had been in place since the 1924 Immigration Act and replace it with the 1965 Hart-Cellar Immigration Act (Chan 1991).[8] This more open immigration policy coupled with the international episodes of war and large-scale violence in which the United States was involved opened the door both to more targeted programs, such as the Indochina Migration and Refugee Act of 1975, which provided refugees who fled from Cambodia and Vietnam with assistance in domestic resettlement (Takaki 1989; Chan 1991; Ong, Bonacich, and Cheng 1994), and to a greater influx from Latin America following the political upheaval of the 1970s and 1980s, in particular in the Central American nations of El Salvador, Guatemala, Honduras, and Nicaragua (Chinchilla and Hamilton 2004). Moreover, the ratification of the North American Free Trade Agreement in 1994 created favorable economic conditions and insourcing of immigrant labor from Mexico for U.S. firms until the late 2010s (Kelly and Massey 2007). Together, these events combined with Los Angeles' size and strategic location have contributed to the region's becoming home to some of the largest clusters of immigrant populations.[9]

---

8. The national origins formula was an American system of immigration quotas between 1921 and 1965 that restricted immigration on the basis of existing proportions of the population. It aimed to reduce the overall number of unskilled immigrants, to allow families to reunite, and to prevent immigration from changing the ethnic distribution of the population. The 1924 Immigration Act included the Asian Exclusion Act that barred specific origins from the Asia Pacific Triangle, which included Japan, China, the Philippines, Thailand, Laos, Vietnam, Cambodia, Singapore, Korea, Indonesia, Burma, India, Sri Lanka, and Malaysia (Office of the Historian 2016).

9. According to the 2015 American Community Survey five-year estimates, the Los Angeles metro area was home to the most Salvadorians, 447,788, followed by Houston, 169,935.

Los Angeles offers a wide range of opportunities to immigrants that continues to make it an attractive destination despite the high cost of life in the region (Ley 2007). Despite the deindustrialization of the late 1970s, Los Angeles was able to thrive because of federal spending on defense in the Reagan-Bush era. It became a key center of the military industrial complex, primarily creating low-skilled assembly and manufacturing firms alongside higher-tech firms linked to electronics and media (Pastor 2001a). However, despite a relatively strong economic recovery following the withdrawal of the defense industry (thanks in part to financial investments from the Asia Pacific region and labor from Mexico), this path to development promoted a strong economic bifurcation that reinforced the creation of lower- to middle-wage jobs (Ong, Bonacich, and Cheng 1994; Storper et al. 2015).

The preponderance of low-wage employment available to new migrants locked many in conditions that make acceding to homeownership or renting more difficult and promoted suboptimal housing conditions (Painter and Yu 2008). In general, differences in socioeconomic status are the main source of disparity in homeownership between white households and Asian and Latino households (Kuebler and Rugh 2013). However, Latinos in Los Angeles in particular have a large degree of heterogeneity in nativity, citizenship, and legal status. Eileen McConnell finds that undocumented migrants were substantially less likely to be homeowners and that authorized noncitizens were also less likely than naturalized Latinos to be homeowners (2015).

Although immigration status creates further barriers to homeownership, many of the same obstacles apply to all residents of segregated central cities. Casey Dawkins explains that for individuals working low-wage jobs, access to transit is a necessity which creates a locational tradeoff (2005). Greater transit connectivity is required to access jobs, but such locations tend to have higher rents that prevent acquiring a car and moving to a location with lower rent and better access to higher-paying jobs. This trade-off also significantly delays ownership, further impeding the accumulation of wealth through home equity (see also Hilber and Liu 2008).

The housing downturn that began in 2006 had distinctive geographic patterns. The Pew Research Center reports that more than two in five of the nation's Latino and Asian American households lived in Arizona, California, Florida, Michigan, and Nevada. These five states had the steepest declines in home prices in 2005. In contrast, about one in five of the nation's white or black households lived in these five states and were not affected as severely (Kochhar, Fry, and Taylor 2011).

Nationally, Rakesh Kochhar and his colleagues estimate that the crisis cut the median net worth of Asian American households in half, from $168,103 in 2005 to $78,066 in 2009. Hispanic households' net worth was only a third of what it was in 2009 ($18,359 to $6,325) while black households lost over half of their wealth ($12,124 to $5,677). Derek Hyra and Jacob Rugh find that black wealth was significantly reduced through systemic predatory lending practices by major lending institutions and mortgage brokers, who directed black borrowers into high-cost, high-risk loans that left them susceptible to default, foreclosure, and loss of home equity during the great recession (2016). In contrast, the white decline in median net worth was 16 percent, from $134,992 to $113,149 (Kochhar, Fry, and Taylor 2011).

In 1965, Martin Luther King Jr. had noticed the extreme levels of inequality unique to Los Angeles. Commenting on the proximity of Watts to affluent areas, he noted that the average black person in "Watts is closer to the affluence of our society and further away from it than any other American community." Indeed, fifty years later, for every dollar of wealth held by the average white household, black and Mexican households have 1 cent, Koreans 7 cents, other Latinos 12 cents, and Vietnamese 17 cents (De La Cruz-Viesca et al. 2016).

The foreclosure crisis exacerbated the vulnerable position of people of color in Los Angeles, but it also affected them differently. African Americans and Latinos were more exposed to foreclosure, joblessness, and home value declines than other groups (Bocian, Li, and Ernst 2010; U.S. Census Bureau 2011). Asian Americans experienced lower unemployment rates and home value declines than non-Hispanic whites, but shouldered increased housing cost burdens to avoid foreclosure (U.S. Census Bureau 2011).

## DATA AND METHODS

This study relies primarily on summaries of key indicators pertaining to housing outcomes in South Los Angeles between 1960 and 2015. Detailed statistical analysis of the data is beyond the scope of this article, but we ran simple logit regressions for homeownership to isolate the effect of residing in South Los Angeles above and beyond its socioeconomic composition.

All demographic and socioeconomic data come from the Integrated Public Use Microdata Sample for 1960 (Ruggles et al. 2017), the decennial U.S. Census Bureau public-use micro samples (PUMS) for 1990, and the five-year American Community Survey PUMS for 2015. Home equity data were derived from the 2011 and 2013 Department of Housing and Urban Development's American Housing Survey (AHS), and the National Asset Scorecard and Communities of Color Survey administered by the Samuel DuBois Cook Center on Social Equity at Duke University, that report information on race, and other key demographics such as income, education, and housing information.[10]

We use South Los Angeles as the focal area, which we contrast to Los Angeles County as a measure of broader patterns. There are many definitions of South Los Angeles and boundaries are fluid. We use the definition of the *Los Angeles Times* because it fully encompasses the historical curfew area which the McCone Commission relied on, allows for the gradual expansion of the relevant area over time, and closely matches the units within which data are available (for details, see the appendix).

Data availability and compatibility constrained the analysis to the years 1960, 1990, and 2015. Nonetheless, each year corresponds to meaningful historical junctures: 1960 captures Los Angeles on the eve of the Watts riots, but also the complete shift in socioeconomic structure. The year 1990, in addition to providing an overview of pre-1992 Los Angeles, shows the effect of major transformations due to the national recession of the early 1990s, global restructuring of the economy, and shifts in demographic patterns. Finally, 2015 represents contemporary Los Angeles.

### Demographic Changes

Between 1960 and 2015, Los Angeles County's white population as a share of the county total fell from 4,719,780 to 2,637,477 (from 80 percent to 27 percent). The black population remained relatively stable (at about 8 percent). The Asian population grew exponentially, from 2 percent to 14 percent. Hispanics outpaced all groups, from 11 percent in 1960 to 49 percent in 2015, becoming the largest group by 1990 (see figure 1 and figure A1 and table A1 in the appendix). Meanwhile, the resident population of the county as a whole increased from six to ten million.

The population of South Los Angeles grew more slowly, increasing by a third since 1960. Still, at more than seven hundred, it would be the fifth largest city in California were it a municipality. In 1960, South Los Angeles was 53 percent black with a substantial but far smaller white population (around a third of the area total) and a smaller Hispanic population, a stark comparison to Los Angeles County. At the time, South Los Angeles was geographically divided between the western half, where most whites resided, and the predominantly black eastern half, with little overlap (see figure 1).

By 1990, the growth of the Hispanic population in South Los Angeles (LA) and the relative stability of the black population translated to a near complete disappearance of whites from the area. Geographically, this marked the largest extent of the black community in South LA. Most Hispanics were spatially clustered in the northeast corner of the area, and the neighborhood boundary extended much further east and was moving

---

10. The NASCC survey was developed to supplement existing national data sets that collect data on household wealth in the United States but rarely collect data disaggregated in detail by race and ethnicity. The survey targets five metropolitan areas in order to collect data about the asset and debt positions of racial and ethnic groups at a detailed ancestral-origin level.

**Figure 1.** Residential Settlement by Race in South Los Angeles

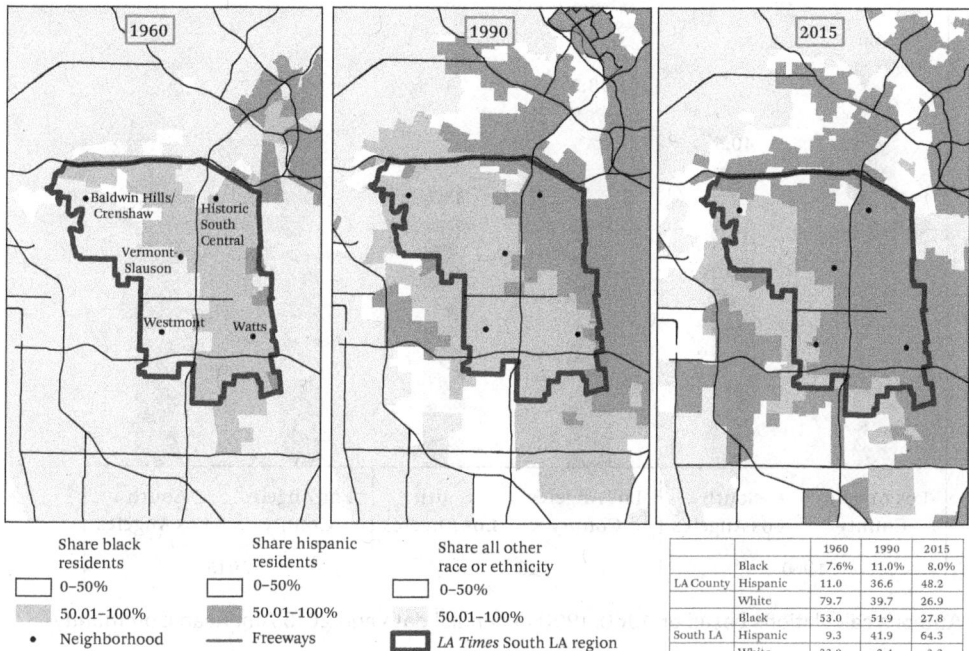

*Source:* Author's calculations based on 1960, 1990 decennial data and 2015 American Community Survey.

gradually west. The expansion westward of the Latino community made the area majority Hispanic (64 percent) by 2015. The black population, after a dramatic relative decline from 53 percent to 28 percent, was clustered at the western edge of South LA. This decline was not just relative: the number dropped by nearly one hundred thousand from 1960.

These patterns are not solely the results of demographic pressures. Both the Kerner and McCone reports explicitly state that the regulations of the Federal Housing Administration, such as redlining, were major factors in creating substandard housing conditions in South Los Angeles. Redlining practices emerged with the first wave of the Great Migration from the South to northern and western cities in the 1920s. They became institutionalized and systematically implemented in large cities through the initiative of a set of institutions of which the Home Owners' Loan Corporation (HOLC) was the central player. At its height, the HOLC recruited and trained mortgage lenders, developers, and real estate appraisers in nearly 250 cities to create maps that color-coded credit worthiness and risk on neighborhood and metropolitan levels (for map and details, see figure A2 in the appendix). Among other things, these practices had long-term effects through the erection of high barriers to either investing in one's neighborhood or moving out of neighborhoods deemed too risky (Dymski, Veitch, and White 1994). Redlining is no longer legal, but research shows that other nefarious practices have emerged, this time with the consequence of displacing many families (Pfeiffer et al. 2014; Berg 2017).[11]

### Homeownership 1960, 1990, and 2015

Homeownership is a primary asset for most Americans with positive net worth. The federal tax code also provides incentives for homeownership by providing tax savings associated with mortgage interest deductions. Moreover, own-

---

11. Neighborhood upscaling is the combination of a decrease in low-income households and an increase in high-income households due to luxury housing and transit orientated development.

**Figure 2.** Homeownership Rates for Los Angeles County and South Los Angeles

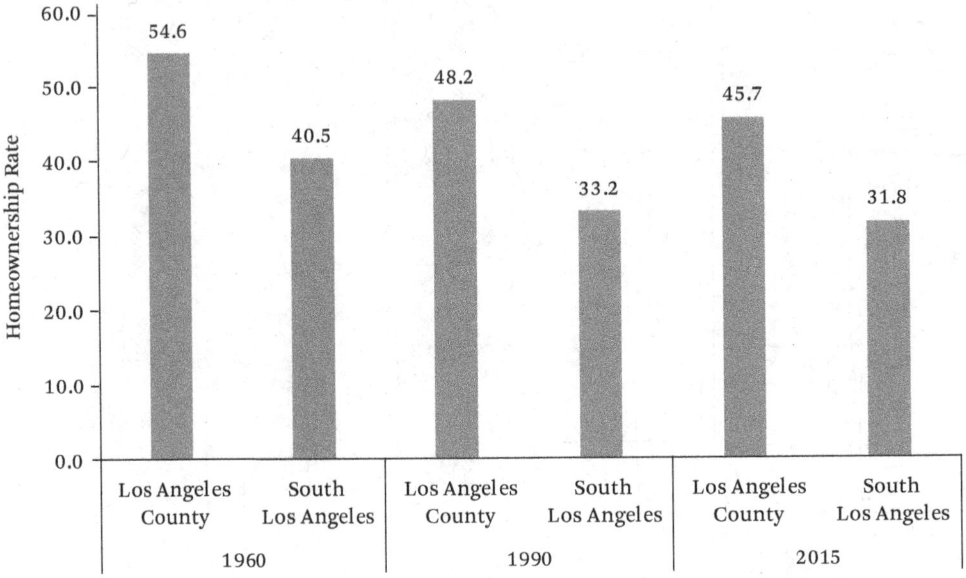

*Source:* Author's calculations based on 1960, 1990 decennial data and 2015 American Community Survey.

ing a home offers other benefits, such as access to a good public school district, convenient shops, and parks. Finally, fairly or unfairly, the purchase of a home and regular on-time mortgage payments leads to higher Fair, Isaac and Company (FICO) credit scores than families that regularly make on-time payments for rent.

As figure 2 shows, homeownership rates in Los Angeles County have fallen from 55 percent in 1960 to 48 percent in 1990 and again to 46 percent in 2015. The rate in South Los Angeles ran parallel to the declining trend in Los Angeles County from 1960 to 2015. However, rates in South Los Angeles continually lagged behind county rates on average by 15 percentage points and did not reach parity over fifty years.

In 1960, the black homeownership rate (36 percent) was the lowest of all racial groups in South Los Angeles (figure 3). By 1990, the percentage of blacks who owned homes improved slightly, to 37 percent, the corresponding percentage of Hispanic population fell 19 points to 22 percent. In 2015, blacks (33 percent), by a slight margin, continued to have a higher homeownership rate than Hispanics (30 percent) in South LA. Across all periods, whites have the highest homeownership rates, though low by the national standard, dipping below 40 percent by 2015.

During this period, growth of the foreign-born population in all major racial and ethnic groups was significant, but increases were much higher among Asians and Hispanics. By the 1960s, 35 percent of the Asian population and 19 percent of the Hispanic population in Los Angeles County were foreign born (Ong et al. 2016). By the 1980s, these figures nearly doubled, to 62 percent of Asians and 45 percent of Hispanics (Ong et al. 2016). The share of black and white immigrants also increased, but from much lower levels and peaking in 2014 at 18 percent for whites and 7 percent for blacks (Ong et al. 2016).

As seen in figure 4, the overall homeownership rates in South Los Angeles decreased over time, in particular the historic South-Central, Watts, and Westmont neighborhoods. In historic South-Central, a high percentage of tracts had homeownership rates between 26 percent and 50 percent in 1960. By 1990 and 2015, homeownership ranged between 0 percent and 25 percent in much of the area. In Watts, the majority of tracts had rates between 51 percent and 75 percent in 1960. By 1990, homeowner-

**Figure 3.** Homeownership Rates by Race in South Los Angeles

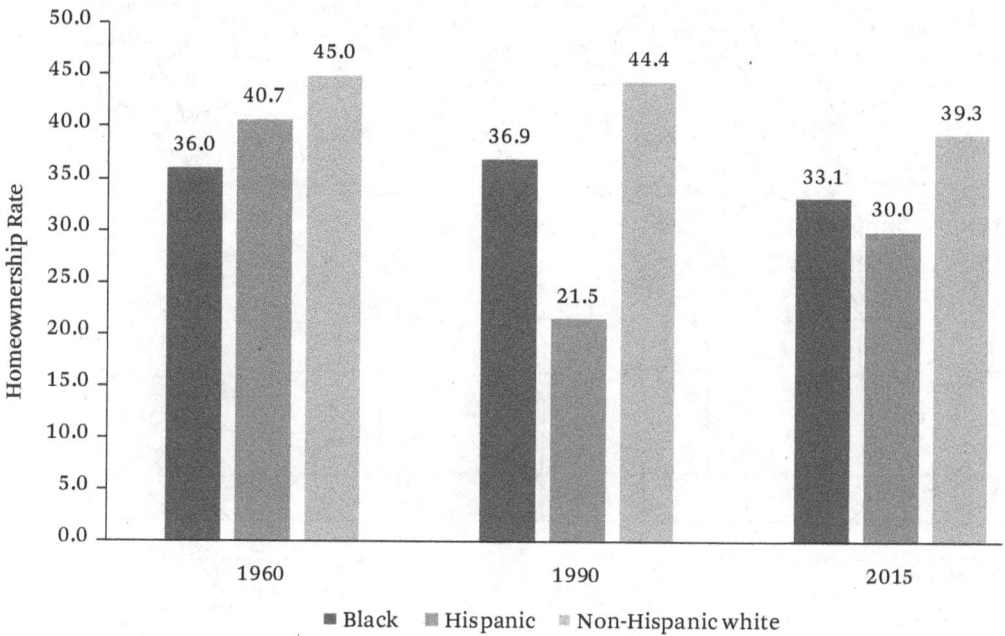

*Source:* Authors' calculations based on 1960, 1990 decennial data and 2015 American Community Survey.

ship decreased to between 26 percent and 50 percent and remains the same in 2015. In Westmont, the largest share of tracts had rates between 51 percent and 75 percent in 1960. The proportion declined to between 26 percent and 50 percent in 1990 and to between 0 percent and 25 percent in 2015.

The foreclosure crisis contributed significantly to the patterns of homeownership in South Los Angeles by creating pockets of concentrated vacancies or rental conversions in distressed communities. Subprime lending increased for all racial groups, but blacks and Hispanics were much more likely than whites to receive higher-cost mortgages. In 2005, more than half of all loans to blacks and Hispanics were subprime, versus only 16 percent for whites. Moreover, black and Hispanic homebuyers were approximately 40 percent to 75 percent more likely than their white counterparts to receive high-risk loans during the 2005–2007 boom period. Throughout the 2007 to 2012 recession period, Hispanics had the highest rate of foreclosure (13 percent), followed by blacks (12 percent)—three times higher than that of whites (Ong, Pech, and Pfeiffer 2014). These trends for the greater Los Angeles region provide insights as to why homeownership rates in South Los Angeles dipped in 2015.

To measure the impact of some of these hard-to-measure factors specific to South Los Angeles, we ran a model of homeownership to control for life cycle, ethnoracial, education, and income variables on the likelihood of owning a home. We report the odds ratio to summarize the output (see table A2). In this case, the odds ratio is the odds that a household will own their home given that they live in South Los Angeles rather than the county, after controlling for all other variables. In other words, an odds ratio of one indicates no difference in the odds of owning in South Los Angeles and the county. A number higher or lower than one signifies that the odds of owning is higher or lower.

The gap in homeownership between South Los Angeles and the county remained fairly constant, fluctuating between 14 and 15 percentage points from 1960 to 2015. Over this half century, household attributes—particularly

**Figure 4.** Homeownership Patterns in South Los Angeles

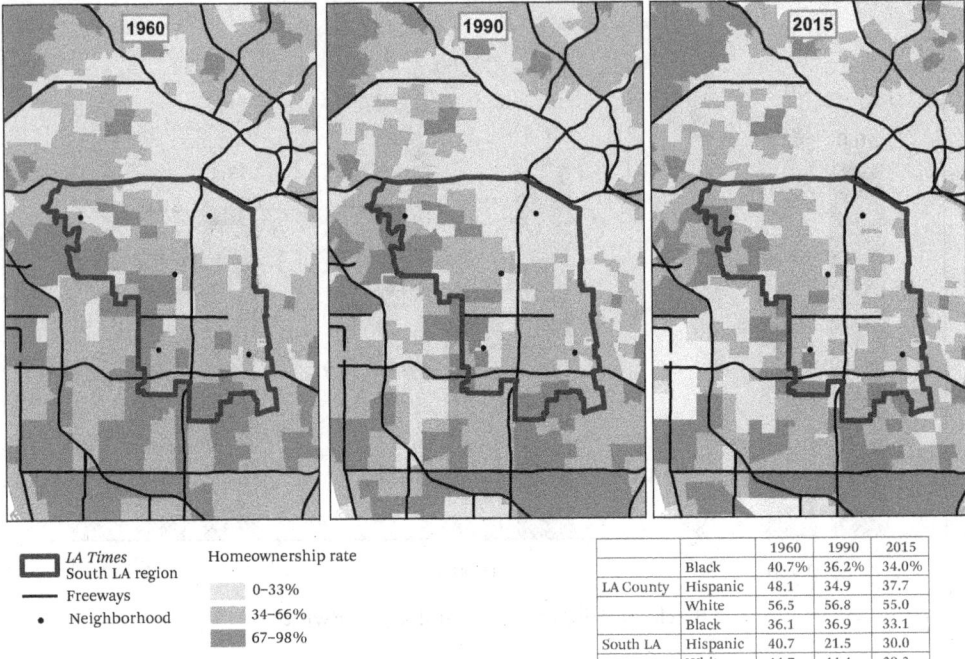

*Source:* Authors' calculations based on 1960, 1970 decennial data and 2015 American Community Survey.

race, nativity, and income—are the key drivers of disparities in homeownership. However, the odds of owning a home correlated with residing in South Los Angeles have had a large and significant effect. In 1960, the ratio was 0.68, qualitatively lower than the rest of the county, ceteris paribus. This same number decreased to 0.65 in 1990 but increased to 0.89 in 2016. The role of South Los Angeles as a place has therefore decreased over time in that more of the gap is explained by the composition of the resident population.

### Home Values, 1960, 1990, and 2015

The county's median home values adjusted to 2015 dollars have risen over time from $131,000 in 1960 to $383,000 in 1990 to $420,000 in 2015 (see figure 5).[12] In contrast to the consistently low homeownership rate in South Los Angeles, the property value gap relative to the county closed from 1990 to 2015. This is in part due to an increase in values between 1990 and 2015 that far outpaced the county's (South LA's values increased by 60 percent against 10 percent for the county). However, despite this relative convergence, over the entire period South Los Angeles trails the county. In 1960, the gap in median home value between South Los Angeles and the county was about $20,000. By 1990, the gap had widened considerably to more than $190,000, making home values in South Los Angeles approximately half that of the county. In 2015, thanks to the convergence in values, the gap shrank to approximately $150,000.

The Los Angeles housing market experi-

---

12. The data reported in this section suffers from a number of limitations due to differences in how property values were reported in 1960, 1990, and 2015. The main difference is that the 1960 and 1990 data are reported as ordinal data where each household belongs to a bin with a range of values. In contrast, the 2015 data is reported as a continuous variable. Thus, the values in 1960 and 1990 correspond to the midpoint of the bin within which the median household falls. See the appendix for a detailed discussion of the variable and the range of each bin (for a detailed discussion, see Collins and Margo 2003).

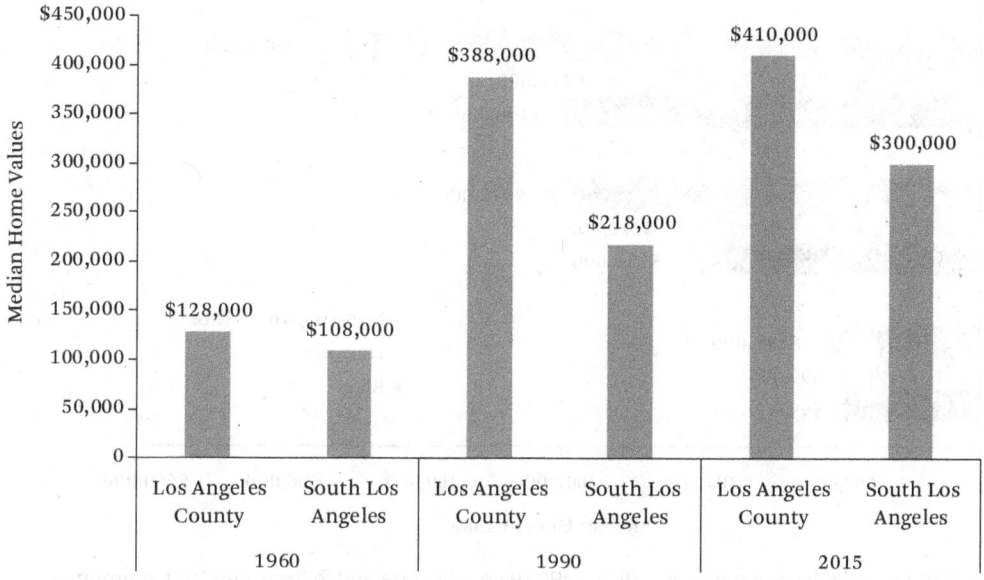

**Figure 5.** Median Home Values (2015 Dollars) in LA County and South LA

*Source:* Authors' calculations based on 1960, 1990 decennial data and 2015 American Community Survey.

enced a robust recovery following the 2006 foreclosure crisis, and the concurrent lag in new construction has created a growing housing shortage. In this context, it is to be expected that South Los Angeles home values would increase faster since it has a concentration of relatively affordable homes in proximity to major job centers (downtown and El Segundo). However, this also means that home owners are not benefiting equally from home equity.

Home equity value is the main measure of the financial gains homeownership confers. Equity is the value of the home minus what is owed on the property. Therefore, for homeowners who own their home outright, the entire value of the property is their equity, and equity will continue to grow as property values rise. On the other hand, equity can be negative if owners owe more than the property is worth, a situation that became widespread during the 2006 crisis, leading to many people losing their entire wealth. In the early 2010s, black homeowners' equity was only 54 percent of that of non-Hispanic white owners. Hispanic homeowners' equity was only 45 percent of non-Hispanic white owners'; the statistics for Asians is only 66 percent of non-Hispanic white owners.

The combination of high barriers to achieving homeownership with lower home values creates stark disparities between nonwhite racial and ethnic groups and whites. Figure 6 demonstrates how the median home values of black households do not appreciate as greatly as those of white households in South Los Angeles. Median home value for blacks and whites was similar in 1960: $91,000 and $111,000 respectively. However, that $20,000 gap increased to $96,000 in 1990 and $150,000 in 2015. In light of the lower equity levels found, these housing disparities between communities of color and whites in Los Angeles are even starker than they appear.

In terms of parity, the home value of blacks and Hispanics in South Los Angeles failed to catch up to whites in the county. For both groups, home values were about 80 percent of non-Hispanic whites' home values in 1960, but by 2015 that figure had worsened to 67 percent for blacks and 58 percent for Hispanics. In contrast, non-Hispanic whites in South Los Angeles did not experience a relative decline compared with non-Hispanic whites in the county.

Median income trends help explain why the homeownership rate is low in South LA. House-

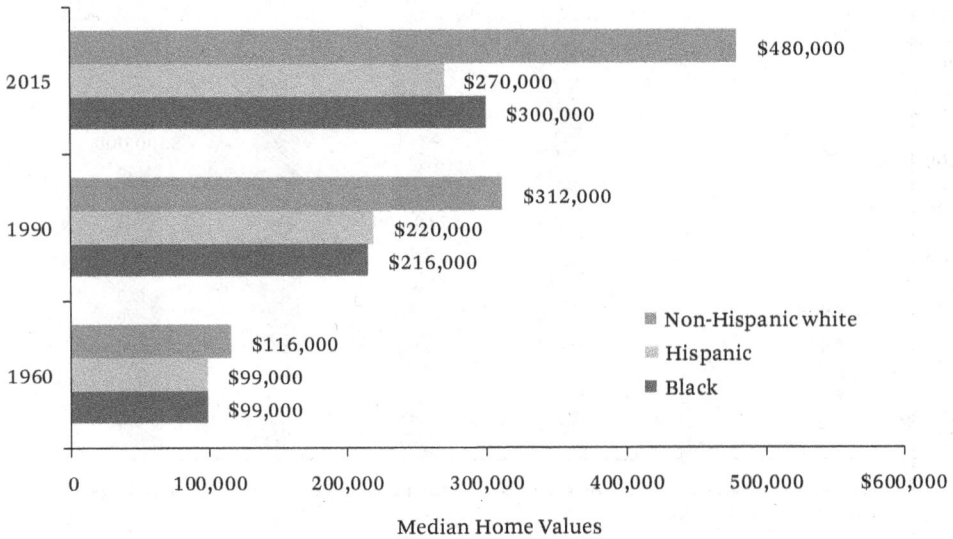

**Figure 6.** Median Home Values (2015 Dollars) by Race in South Los Angeles

*Source:* Authors' calculations based on 1960, 1990 decennial data and 2015 American Community Survey.

holds with limited income are unable to afford a mortgage, among many other high housing costs, and are more likely to be renters. Given the regional trends in housing, rents have also increased, putting an ever-growing number of households under severe housing burdens and locking them into not only renting but also renting in locations that may not be optimal for accessing jobs and educational opportunities. Figure 7 shows the median income adjusted to 2015 constant dollars for blacks in South Los Angeles and how it decreases over time. Given that housing costs have clearly outstripped inflation in Los Angeles, the median household income decrease of $7,000 understates the magnitude of the increasing demands housing puts on households. We see an even more pronounced trend among Hispanics whose median income decreases by $11,000 over the half century. This is not a common trend. Although the drop in median income for whites between 1960 and 1990 is consistent with the trend for the area, by 2015 whites' incomes recovered to levels $5,000 or higher than in 1960.

In addition, South Los Angeles became a hot spot of speculative real estate investments in the wake to the 2006 crisis. A disproportionate number of units have been bought up by corporate investors, such as Blackstone developers (see figure A3), adding to the pressure on home prices. Many of these units are being renovated and turned into luxury housing. Moreover, neighborhood upscaling spillover effects from the new University of Southern California village housing and commercial development, the new Los Angeles Stadium at Hollywood Park in Inglewood, and the renovation of Crenshaw Plaza with a new transit station are driving gentrification in South Los Angeles, making the prospects of a more accessible housing market all the fainter.

## WHAT WORKED AND WHAT DID NOT WORK

As we reflect on the findings from the Kerner Commission report, we focus on racial wealth inequality through the lens of homeownership and the role of place by studying South Los Angeles, where the 1965 Watts riots took place. Through our research, we fill the gap within the existing literature by examining how housing influences wealth building, a clear component missing in the recommendations from both the Kerner and McCone reports. The two commission reports failed to adequately ad-

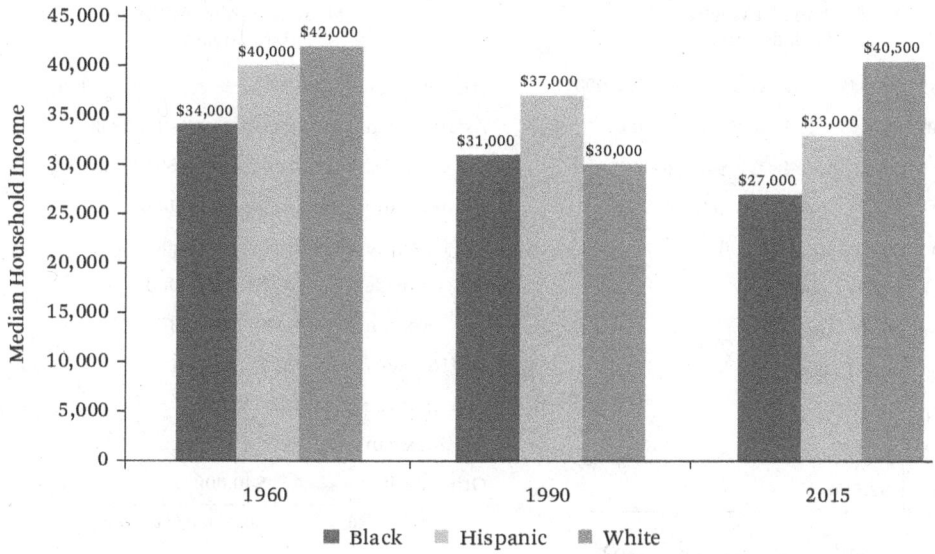

**Figure 7.** Median Household Income (2015 Dollars) by Race in South Los Angeles

*Source:* Authors' calculations based on 1960, 1990 decennial data and 2015 American Community Survey.

dress the paramount pathway toward economic security via wealth accumulation including homeownership. Mainly, the recommendations focused on increasing the supply of affordable rentals. This is a policy failure that perpetuates wealth inequality. Both reports document poor housing conditions and high housing burden as underlying causal factors, but both focused on the rental sector. The solutions were to increase good and affordable rental units, but by and large ignore homeownership. In a sense, this silence means implicitly perpetuating the lack of asset building through remedial policy, thus the reproduction of wealth inequality. The housing recommendations dealt with some symptoms but not the deeper roots of racial economic inequality.

Another issue largely missed by both the Kerner and McCone reports was the increasing racial complexity in Los Angeles that was so nascent at the time of the release of the Kerner and McCone reports. The 1968 Chicano Blowouts and the 1992 Rodney King riots are examples of shifting demographics that challenged the black and white relations binary. These changes are embedded in the demographic shift in South LA, again something that the two commissions did not foresee. Thus, the two reports lacked the ability to predict the evolving nature of racial inequality in Los Angeles.

However, the current state of South Los Angeles is a mixed picture. The median home value data suggest an uptick in the area. This is a positive development because it may increase a homeowner's equity and allow them to gain wealth over time, but only for a minority of the households, and, as this article demonstrates, home value appreciation rates are not equally shared across racial and ethnic groups both across and within neighborhoods. Nonetheless, overwhelmingly, renters are missing out on gains across the board. If this is the case, policymakers, advocates, and community leaders must develop new ideas on what can be done to increase homeownership opportunities and build wealth.

Overall, Los Angeles has failed to remedy the housing problem in South Los Angeles despite the recommendations and political promises. If the high cost of housing (for example, higher rents and home prices) and neighborhood upscaling continue to drive gentrification and displacement, Los Angeles may be headed into a new round of problems given growing

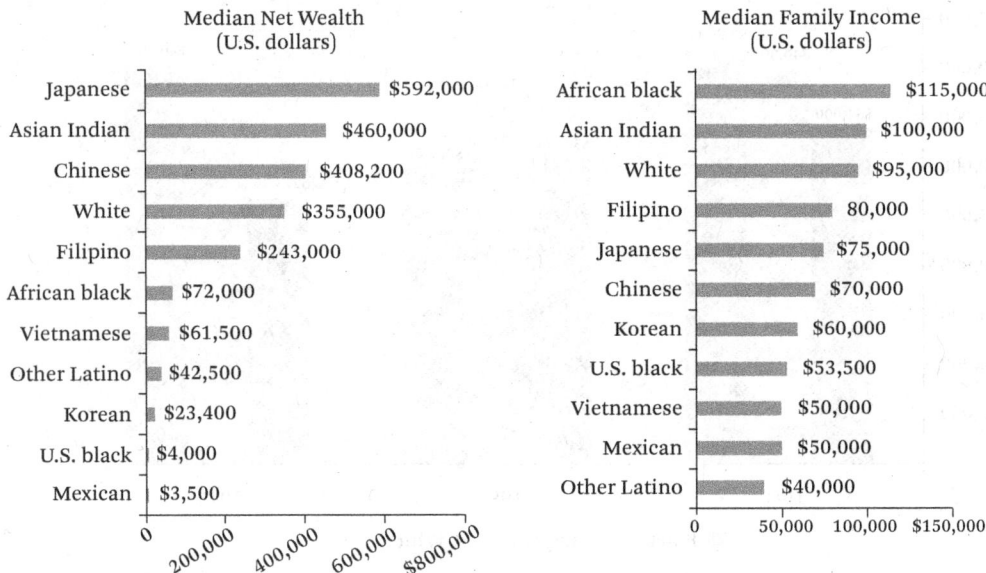

**Figure 8.** White and Nonwhite Household Wealth and Family Income in Los Angeles

*Source:* Authors' calculations based on 2014 National Asset Scorecard and Communities of Color Survey (De La Cruz-Viesca et al. 2016).

economic inequality and declining housing affordability. The demographics may have changed dramatically, but South Los Angeles remains at the margins of the economy, as well as society.

## WHAT ARE THE IMPLICATIONS FOR THE TWENTY-FIRST CENTURY

Wealth is derived from taking the total market value of all physical and intangible assets owned, then subtracting all debts. Although homeownership is a primary asset for the majority of Americans with positive net worth, it is not a driver of wealth. Data from the National Asset Scorecard and Communities of Color (NASCC) collected in 2014 found that one of the wealthiest ethnic groups in Los Angeles, Asian Indians, have a lower rate of homeownership than blacks—whose low level of wealth indicates a population overwhelmingly reliant upon income (De La Cruz-Viesca et al. 2016). As figure 8 shows, the median net worth for Asian Indians is $460,000 in contrast with $4,000 for non-immigrant blacks in Los Angeles and homeownership rates are 40 percent and 42 percent, respectively (De La Cruz-Viesca et al. 2016). The median net wealth of Asian Indians is most likely attributed to higher incomes, stock ownership, and savings. Thus, not all high wealth racial groups are homeowners. Wealth is also derived from assets such as intergenerational wealth transfers, savings, stocks, and retirement.

Moreover, when we examine differences by nativity, a more nuanced picture emerges. NASCC data revealed that for the Los Angeles metro area, the median wealth for African immigrants is $72,000. Figure 9 shows the median wealth for Mexican immigrants is $3000 compared with $58,000 for U.S.-born Mexicans (Biu et al. 2017). Even more noteworthy is the difference in homeownership rates between Mexican immigrants (35 percent) and U.S.-born Mexicans (63 percent) (Biu et al. 2017). The NASCC data sheds light on within-group differences by nativity and ethnicity and demonstrates the great diversity that exists within each racial group.

Also, the socioeconomic status of immigrants prior to entering the United States plays an important role in influencing the wealth position of particular groups. The majority of immigrants who arrived after the passage of the 1965 Immigration Act are highly educated, pos-

**Figure 9.** U.S.-Born and Immigrant Household Wealth and Homeownership in Los Angeles

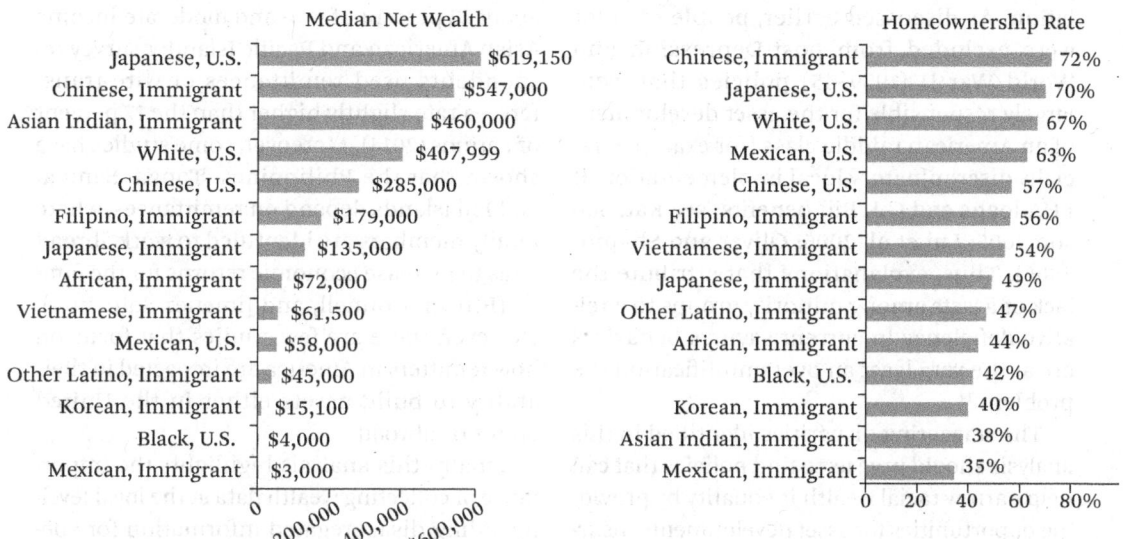

*Source:* Authors' calculations based on 2014 National Asset Scorecard and Communities of Color Survey (Biu et al. 2017).

sess higher levels of wealth than the average American, and are highly skilled professionals who are more likely to hold jobs with higher earnings levels (Lee and Zhou 2015). Thus, the selectivity status of immigrants to Los Angeles has vital implications for how they are able to accumulate assets over time, especially relative to primarily native-born populations. It is critical to understand how the nature of inequality has been transformed by immigration and the overall growth of income and wealth inequality.

Furthermore, one study has shown that income differences are only a small fraction in producing ethnoracial residential segregation and that segregation is largely driven by ethnic and racial differences (Ong et al. 2016). Though most social scientists point to individual prejudices and structural racism, others counter that segregation is a mere byproduct of systematic economic differences. For example, some minority groups are poorer and thus disproportionately concentrated in low-income neighborhoods. The Ong report indicates that although black-white segregation has been decreasing steadily in Los Angeles, segregation levels remain high while increasing between Hispanics and non-Hispanic whites (2016).[13] Nonetheless, we observe evidence that even in the same neighborhoods, black and Hispanic homeownership rates, home values, and appreciation rates are lower than among their white neighbors.

The findings provide us with a better understanding of what might influence racial wealth disparities. A review of the economic literature demonstrates that inheritances, bequests, and intrafamily transfers also account for more of the racial wealth divide than any other demographic and socioeconomic indicators, including education, income, and household structure (Hamilton and Chiteji 2013; see also, for example, Blau and Graham 1990; Menchik and Jianakoplos 1997; Conley 1999; Charles and Hurst 2003; Gittleman and Wolff 2007). Thus, it is important to understand the racial differences in resource transfers across generations.

It is beyond the scope of this article to identify the causal mechanisms influencing racial wealth disparity in Los Angeles, but the find-

---

13. This is in part due to the white population share falling and in part to the Hispanic population rising.

ings outlined in this paper do help us identify potential factors influencing wealth accumulation. As discussed earlier, people of color were excluded from post-Depression and World War II (1939–45) policies that were largely responsible for the asset development of an American middle class (for example, racially discriminatory local implementation of FHA loans and G.I. Bill benefits; see Katznelson 2005; Lui et al. 2005; Oliver and Shapiro 2006). Thus, explanations that attribute the lack of assets among minority groups to a relative deficiency in current savings behaviors are at the very least an oversimplification the problem.[14]

The staggering disparities identified in this analysis should urge us to find policies that can help narrow racial wealth inequality by providing opportunities for asset development; ensuring fair access to housing, credit, and financial services; ensuring equal opportunity to well-paying jobs regardless of race or ethnicity; strengthening retirement incomes; promoting access to education without overburdening individuals with debt; and providing access to health care while helping minimize medical debt.[15] All policies aimed at bridging the wealth gap also should consider the wide diversity among nonwhite populations and be targeted or adapted accordingly. Policy solutions are complex and need to use a multifaceted approach that includes input from practitioners who are familiar with the unique needs and challenges that different communities of color face.

We also need to broaden the analysis of how transnational capital has affected household assets. For example, the importance of remittances for many immigrants inhibits their ability to save or accumulate assets in the United States or abroad. The Alliance for Stabilizing Our Communities found that about 22 percent of low- and moderate-income Asian American and Pacific Islander survey respondents used remittances or wire transfers—a rate slightly higher than the 17 percent of Latinos (2014). Moreover, some studies have shown that the Philippines, Tonga, Samoa, and Fiji islands depend on remittances, where family members are identified to work abroad so as to increase economic returns for the family (Brown, Connell, and Jimenez-Soto 2014). However, there are few studies that focus on how remitters in America are impacted in their ability to build assets either in the United States or abroad.

Finally, this analysis highlights the importance of collecting wealth data at the local level, including disaggregated information for specific national origin groups. Having access to this type of data is an important step to help shape policymakers', practitioners', and foundations' responses to the enormous challenges communities of color experience across the country. Wealth is perhaps more important than income in better understanding economic inequality, and wealth is critical in ensuring financial security and opportunity for future American families.

More needs to be done to ensure that the diverse voices of nonwhite groups are included in public debates and to understand the reasons behind the enormous differences uncovered in this analysis. More than ever, it is important to include data and analysis of indigenous and communities of color that are often overlooked in traditional studies in the development of a more inclusive, fair, and comprehensive narrative about racial inequality and financial justice in America.

---

14. Economists ranging from Milton Friedman (1957) to Marjorie Galenson (1972), to Marcus Alexis (1971), have found that, after accounting for household income, blacks have a slightly higher savings rate than whites. More recently, Maury Gittleman and Edward Wolff (2007) using the Panel Study on Income Dynamics (PSID) have found that, after controlling for household income, if anything blacks had a mild savings advantage compared to whites (Hamilton and Chiteji 2013).

15. Two of the authors of this report have previously proposed universal gradationally endowed based familial wealth position at birth child trust accounts, "baby bonds." The accounts would be used as seed money to purchase an asset like a home or a new business that might appreciate over a lifetime (Hamilton and Darity 2010; Aja et al. 2014).

## APPENDIX

In this section, we define key terms and technical documentation about the data used in this article. The variables are analyzed at the individual level for the entire sample.

*Race and ethnicity.* The questions asked about race and ethnicity changed across the decades we examine (1960, 1990, and 2015) leading to some discrepancies in definition. In 1960, the question that comes closest to the later definition of Hispanic relates to whether the respondents have a Spanish surname. In later decades, the question about self-identified Hispanic origin is used. Asian respondents in 1960 are identified by the categories Japanese, Chinese, and Filipino. Later decades are both more comprehensive and consistent in their definition. In 1960, the share of respondents that were not black, white, or Asian was extremely small and is included with the white population.

*Household variable.* For household variables, data for all respondents belonging to the same unit are aggregated. This is of particular relevance in 1960 when no household income variable existed. In that case, the incomes of individuals belonging to the same household were added up to obtain the household value. In summarizing household data by race and ethnicity, no information regarding who owns the home is available. Therefore, following Collins and Margo (2003), we assume that the home belongs to the head of household and his or her race and ethnicity to subset the data.

*Property values.* The data reported in this section suffer a number of limitations due to differences in how property values were reported in 1960, 1990, and 2015. The main difference is that the 1960 and 1990 data are reported as ordinal data where each household belongs to a bin with a range of values. In contrast, the 2015 data are reported as a continuous variable. As such, the values in 1960 and 1990 correspond to the midpoint of the bin within which the median household falls.

Home values are reported differently in 1960, 1990, and 2015. In all three surveys, the values were self-reported. This is a common issue about which evidence is contradictory as to the potential bias, but not much can be done to mitigate it. The main difference comes from the format of the data. In 1960, home values were coded into ten bins with ranges of $2,500 (about $20,000 in 2015 dollars) between $5,000 and $20,000. Then, $20,000 to $24,900, $25,000 to $34,900, and more than $35,000. In 1990, there were twenty-five bins starting with less than $10,000 as its lowest value. The values increase in $5,000 (a little less than $9,000 in 2015) increments up to $80,000. Then, $10,000 increments up to $100,000; $25,000 increments up to $200,000; $50,000 increments up to $300,000. The last two are $300,000 to $399,999 and $400,000 and more. In 2015, the data are continuous but granular in that values tend to be rounded and recur at relatively high frequency.

In handling the 1960 and 1990 data, we assign the midpoint of the bin within which the household falls to calculate the median values. For example, a household falling in the bin $100,000 to $124,999 in 1990 would be assigned the value $112,500. This method has limitations given that the ranges can be quite wide. However, no alternative data sources that would allow us to replicate this analysis with greater accuracy are available. As an alternative, we fitted the data to parametric functions and found that the results were close to those obtained with the simpler estimation based on midpoints.

However, in interpreting the values we provide, rather than the single value we provide for clarity and simplicity, median home values fall within the range of the bin containing that value. To use the same example, if the median home value in 1990 were $112,500, this value should be interpreted as the median falling between $100,000 and $125,000.

*Home equity.* The American Housing Survey (AHS) is funded by the U.S. Department of Housing and Urban Development and conducted by the U.S. Census Bureau. Collected every two years, the AHS is a national longitudinal survey that collects very detailed information on housing units and their occupants. The AHS is a reliable data source to examine housing assets because it includes questions on home ownership, total mortgage, home value, and basic demographic information such as age, race, and place of birth.

**Table A1.** Population Number by Race, Los Angeles County and South Los Angeles

|  | 1960 | | 1990 | | 2015 | |
| --- | --- | --- | --- | --- | --- | --- |
|  | LA County | South LA | LA County | South LA | LA County | South LA |
| Asian | 102,560 | 25,360 | 921,768 | 16,992 | 1,379,767 | 18,536 |
| Black | 448,020 | 285,680 | 955,542 | 337,085 | 773,488 | 197,356 |
| Hispanic | 651,140 | 50,080 | 3,175,651 | 272,221 | 4,795,770 | 459,724 |
| White | 4,719,780 | 177,740 | 3,446,863 | 15,463 | 2,637,477 | 18,130 |

*Source:* Authors' calculations based on 1960, 1990 decennial data and 2015 American Community Survey.

**Table A2.** Odds Ratio Based on Output of Logit Regression

|  | Odds Ratio 1960 | Odds Ratio 1990 | Odds Ratio 2015 |
| --- | --- | --- | --- |
| (Intercept) | 0.001 | 0.001 | 0.001 |
| Education in years | 1.027 | 1.046 | 1.052 |
| Age | 1.152 | 1.163 | 1.147 |
| Age squared | 0.999 | 0.999 | 0.999 |
| Married | 2.948 | 2.645 | 1.979 |
| Persons | 1.372 | 1.019 | 1.113 |
| Household income | 1.204 | 1.217 | 1.154 |
| Income squared | 0.996 | 0.993 | 0.999 |
| Black | 0.828 | 0.503 | 0.421 |
| Latino | 0.776 | 0.763 | 0.890 |
| Asian | 0.721 | 1.094 | 1.243 |
| Other |  | 0.776 | 0.694 |
| Female | 1.480 | 1.190 | 1.134 |
| Foreign born | 0.980 | 0.805 | 0.746 |
| English proficiency | 1.219 | 2.367 | 2.215 |
| Median PUMA |  |  |  |
| Home value | 1.028 | 0.736 | 0.823 |
| South LA | 0.681 | 0.647 | 0.894 |

*Source:* Authors' calculations.
*Note:* Dependent value is homeownership. All coefficients significant at the 5 percent level or higher.

**Figure A1.** Percent of the Total Population by Race

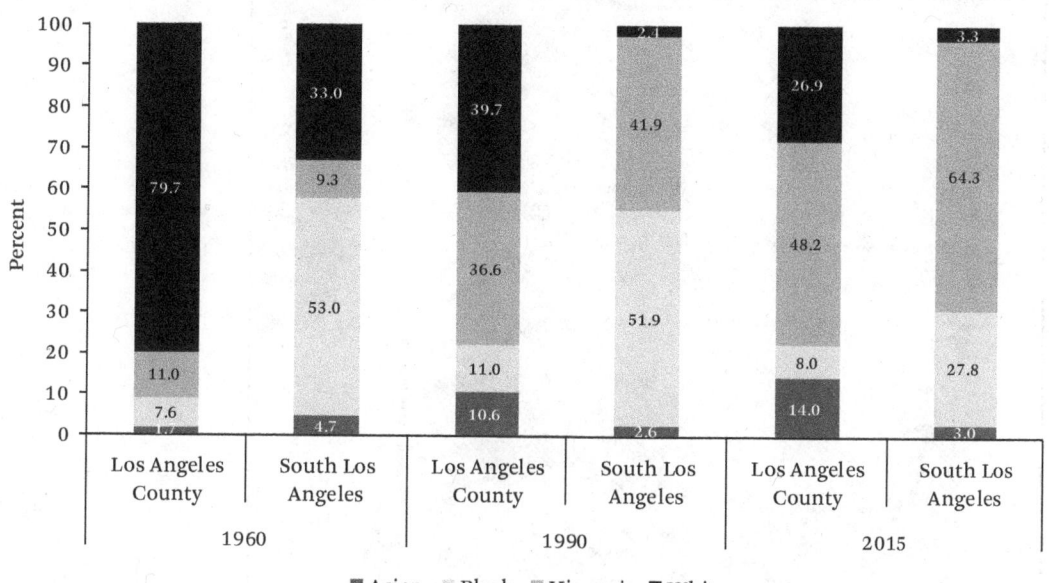

*Source:* Authors' calculations based on 1960, 1990 decennial data and 2015 American Community Survey.

**Figure A2.** Federal Housing Administration Redlining Map of South Los Angeles

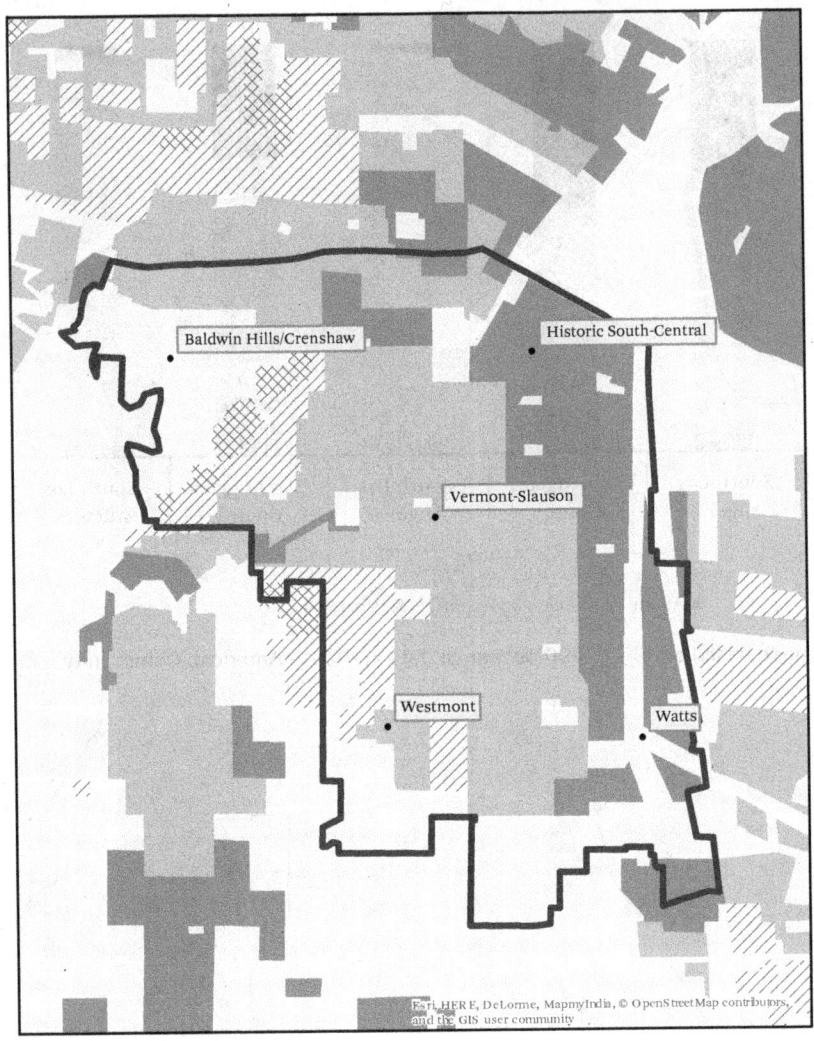

Redlining zones
- ▩▩▩ Area A = Best
- ▨▨▨ Area B = Still desirable
- ░░░ Area C = Definitely declining
- ▓▓▓ Area D = Hazardous
- ▢ *LA Times* South LA boundaries

*Source:* Home Owners Loan Corporation 1939.
*Note:* Testbed for the redlining archives of California's exclusionary spaces. Maps throughout this article were created using ArcGIS® software by Esri. ArcGIS® and ArcMap™ are the intellectual property of Esri and are used herein under license. Copyright © Esri. All rights reserved. For more information about Esri® software, please visit www.esri.com.

**Figure A3.** Corporate Investor Hot Spots in Los Angeles

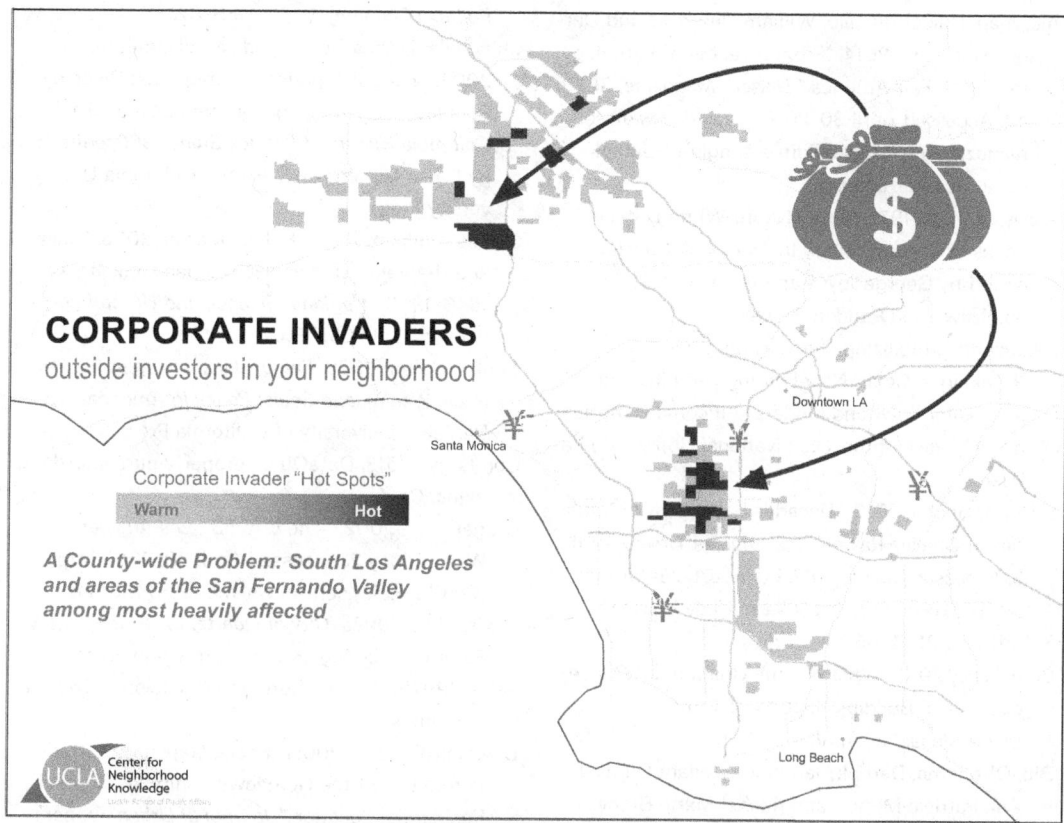

*Source:* Authors' calculations based on 2013 DataQuick property data (CoreLogic 2013).

## REFERENCES

Aja, Alan, Daniel Bustillo, William Darity Jr., and Darrick Hamilton. 2014. "From a Tangle of Pathology to a Race-Fair America." *Dissent Magazine*, 38–42. Accessed April 30, 2018. http://www.dissentmagazine.org/article/from-a-tangle-of-pathology-to-a-race-fair-america.

Alexis, Marcus. 1971. "Some Negro-White Differences in Consumption." In *The Black Consumer*, edited by George Joyce and Norman A. P. Govoni. New York: Random House.

Alliance for Stabilizing Our Communities. 2014. "Banking in Color: New Findings on Financial Access for Low- and Moderate-Income Communities." Washington, D.C.: National Council de La Raza.

Becerra, Hector. 2012. "Decades Later, Bitter Memories of Chavez Ravine" *Los Angeles Times,* April 5. Accessed May 4, 2017. http://articles.latimes.com/2012/apr/05/local/la-me-adv-chavez-ravine-20120405.

Berg, Nate. 2017. "What Are the Unintended Consequences of Building the City of Tomorrow?" *UCLA Magazine*, April.

Biu, Ofronama, Darrick Hamilton, William Darity Jr., Ana Patricia Muñoz, and Rachel Marie Brooks Atkins. 2017. "Place, Race, and Immigration: Assets, Debts, and Transfers Across Ethnic Groups." Paper presented at 32nd session of the OECD Working Party on Territorial Indicators, Paris (May 17).

Blau, Francine D., and John W. Graham. 1990. "Black-White Differences in Wealth and Asset Composition." *Quarterly Journal of Economics* 105(2): 321–39.

Bocian, Debbie Gruenstein, Wei Li, and Keith S. Ernst. 2010. "Foreclosures by Race and Ethnicity: The Demographics of a Crisis." Durham, N.C.: Center for Responsible Lending. Accessed April 30, 2018. http://www.responsiblelending.org/mortgage-lending/research-analysis/foreclosures-by-race-and-ethnicity.pdf.

Brown, Richard P. C., John Connell, and Eliana V. Jimenez-Soto. 2014. "Migrants' Remittances, Poverty and Social Protection in the South Pacific: Fiji and Tonga." *Population, Space and Place* 20(5): 434–54.

Chan, Sucheng. 1991. *Asian Americans: An Interpretive History*. Boston, Mass.: Twayne Publishers.

Charles, Kerwin, and Erik Hurst. 2003. "The Correlation of Wealth Across Generations." *Journal of Political Economy* 111(6): 1155–82.

Chinchilla, Norma Stoltz, and Nora Hamilton. 2004. "Central American Immigrants: Diverse Populations, Changing Communities." In *The Columbia History of Latinos Since 1960*, edited by David Gutierrez. New York: Columbia University Press

Collins, William. J., and Robert Margo. 2003. "Race and the Value of Owner-Occupied Housing, 1940–1990." *Regional Science and Urban Economics* 33(3): 255–86.

Conley, Dalton. 1999. *Being Black, Living in the Red: Race, Wealth, and Social Policy in America*. Berkeley: University of California Press.

CoreLogic. 2013. DataQuick property purchase data. Irvine, Calif.

Crogan, Jim. 2002. "The L.A. 53." *Los Angeles Weekly*, May 2. Accessed April 30, 2018. http://www.laweekly.com/news/the-la-53-2134716.

Davis, Mike. 1992a. *City of Quartz: Excavating the Future in Los Angeles*. London: Verso Press

———. 1992b. "In L.A., Burning All Illusions." *The Nation*, June 1.

Dawkins, Casey J. 2005. "Racial Gaps in the Transition to First-Time Homeownership: The Role of Residential Location." *Journal of Urban Economics* 58(3): 537–54.

De Graaf, Lawrence, and Quintard Taylor. 2001. "Introduction." In *Seeking El Dorado: African Americans in California*, edited by Lawrence De Graaf, Kevin Mulroy, and Quintard Taylor. Los Angeles: Autry Museum of Western Heritage; Seattle, Wash.: University of Seattle Press.

De La Cruz-Viesca, Melany, Zhenxiang Chen, Paul M. Ong, Darrick Hamilton, and William A. Darity Jr. 2016. "The Color of Wealth in Los Angeles." Durham, N.C. / New York / Los Angeles: Duke University / The New School / University of California, Los Angeles.

Dymski, Gary A., John M. Veitch, and Michelle White. 1994. "Taking It to the Bank: Race, Poverty, and Credit in Los Angeles." In *Residential Apartheid: The American Legacy*, edited by Robert D. Bullard, Charles Lee, and J. Eugene Grigsby III. Los Angeles: University of California, Center for Afro-American Studies, UCLA, 1994.

Farley, Reynolds. 2008. "The Kerner Commission Report Plus Four Decades: What Has Changed? What Has Not?" Population Studies Center Research Report no. 08–656. Ann Arbor: University of Michigan Institute for Social Research.

Friedman, Milton. 1957. *A Theory of the Consumption Function*. Princeton, N.J.: Princeton University Press.

Galenson, Marjorie. 1972. "Do Blacks Save More?" *American Economic Review* 42: 211–16.

Gittleman, Maury, and Edward N. Wolff. 2007. "Racial and Ethnic Differences in Wealth." In *Race and Economic Opportunity in the Twenty-First Century*, edited by Marlene Kim. London: Routledge.

Hamilton, Darrick, and Ngina Chiteji. 2013. "Wealth." In *International Encyclopedia of Race and Racism*, 2nd ed., edited by Patrick L. Mason. New York: Macmillan.

Hamilton, Darrick, and William Darity Jr. 2010. "Can 'Baby Bonds' Eliminate the Racial Wealth Gap in Putative Post-Racial America?" *Review of Black Political Economy* 37(3,4): 207–216.

Hilber, Christian A. L., and Yingchun Liu. 2008. "Explaining the Black–White Homeownership Gap: The Role of Own Wealth, Parental Externalities and Locational Preferences." *Journal of Housing Economics* 17(2): 152–74.

Hinton, Elizabeth. 2016. *From the War on Poverty to the War on Crime: The Making of Mass Incarceration in America*. Cambridge, Mass.: Harvard University Press.

Home Owners Loan Corporation. 1939. Redlining Map of South Los Angeles. Washington.

Hyra, Derek, and Jacob S. Rugh. 2016. "The U.S. Great Recession: Exploring Its Association with Black Neighborhood Rise, Decline and Recovery." *Urban Geography* 37(5): 700–26.

Johnson, John, Jr. 2011. "How Los Angeles Covered Up the Massacre of 17 Chinese." *Los Angeles Weekly*, March 10. Accessed September 6, 2017. http://www.laweekly.com/news/how-los-angeles-covered-upthe-massacre-of-17-chinese-2169478.

Kain, John F., and John M. Quigley. 1972. "Housing Market Discrimination, Home-Ownership, and Savings Behavior." *American Economic Review* 62(3): 263–77.

Katznelson, Ira. 2005. *When Affirmative Action Was White: An Untold History of Racial Inequality in Twentieth-Century America*. New York: W. W. Norton.

Kelly, Patricia Fernández, and Douglas S. Massey. 2007. "Borders for Whom? The Role of NAFTA in Mexico-U.S. Migration." *Annals of the American Academy of Political and Social Science* 610(1) (March): 98–118.

Kerner Commission. 1968. *Report of the National Advisory Commission on Civil Disorders*. Washington: Government Printing Office.

Kochhar, Rakesh, Richard Fry, and Paul Taylor. 2011. "Wealth Gaps Rise to Record Highs Between Whites, Blacks and Hispanics." Washington, D.C.: Pew Research Center.

Kuebler, Meghan, and Jacob Rugh. 2013. "New Evidence on Racial and Ethnic Disparities in Homeownership in the United States from 2001 to 2010." *Social Science Research* 42(5): 1357–74.

Lansner, Jonathan. 2017. "Half of Us Rent." *Orange County Register*, July 27. Accessed May 6, 2018. http://www.ocregister.com/2017/07/27/los-angeles-orange-county-homeownership-rate-2nd-lowest-in-u-s.

Le Goix, Renaud. 2005. "Gated Communities: Sprawl and Social Segregation in Southern California." *Housing Studies* 20(2): 323–43.

Lee, Jennifer, and Min Zhou. 2015. *The Asian American Achievement Paradox*. New York: Russell Sage Foundation.

Ley, David. 2007. "Countervailing Immigration and Domestic Migration in Gateway Cities: Australian and Canadian Variations on an American Theme." *Economic Geography* 83(3): 231–54.

Los Angeles County and City Human Relations Commissions. 1985. "McCone Revisited: A Focus on Solutions to Continuing Problems in South Central Los Angeles." Los Angeles: Los Angeles County and City Human Relations Commissions.

*Los Angeles Times*. 1968. "Student Disorders Erupt at 4 High Schools; Policeman Hurt." March 7.

Lui, Meizhu, Barbara Robles, Betsy Leondar-Wright, Rose Brewer, and Rebecca Adamson. 2005. *The Color of Wealth: The Story Behind the U.S. Racial Wealth Divide*. New York: The New Press.

Massey, Douglas. S. 2005. "Racial Discrimination in Housing: A Moving Target." *Social Problems* 52(2): 148–51.

McCone, John A., and W. M. Christopher. 1965. *Violence in the City—An End or a Beginning? A Report*. Los Angeles: California, Governor's Commission on the Los Angeles Riots.

McConnell, Eileen D. 2015. "Hurdles or Walls? Nativity, Citizenship, Legal Status and Latino Homeownership in Los Angeles." *Social Science Research* 53(1): 19–33.

Menchik, Paul L., and Nancy Ammon Jianakoplos.

1997. "Black-White Wealth Inequality: Is Inheritance the Reason?" *Economic Inquiry* 35(2): 428–42.

Normark, Don. 1999. *Chávez Ravine, 1949: A Los Angeles Story*. San Francisco: Chronicle Books.

Office of the Historian. 2016. "The Immigration Act of 1924." Washington: U.S. State Department. Accessed May 6, 2018. https://history.state.gov/milestones/1921-1936/immigration-act.

Oliver, Melvin, and Thomas Shapiro. 2006. *Black Wealth/White Wealth: A New Perspective on Racial Inequality*, 2nd ed. New York: Routledge.

Ong, Paul M., Edna Bonacich, and Lucie Cheng, eds. 1994. *The New Asian Immigration in Los Angeles and Global Restructuring*. Philadelphia, Pa.: Temple University Press.

Ong, Paul, Chhandara Pech, Jenny Chhea, and C. Aujean Lee. 2016. "Race, Ethnicity, and Income Segregation in Los Angeles." Los Angeles: University of California, Center for Neighborhood Knowledge. Accessed September 7, 2017. http://www.anderson.ucla.edu/Documents/areas/ctr/ziman/ZimanSegregation-LA-Ong.pdf.

Ong, Paul M., Chhandara Pech, and Deirdre Pfeiffer. 2014. "The Foreclosure Crisis in Los Angeles." In *California Policy Options*, edited by Daniel J. B. Mitchell. Los Angeles: University of California, Luskin School of Public Affairs. Accessed August 8, 2017. http://www.lewis.ucla.edu/wp-content/uploads/sites/2/2014/02/California-Policy-Options-forInstructor1.pdf.

Painter, Gary, and Zhou Yu. 2008. "Leaving Gateway Metropolitan Areas in the United States: Immigrants and the Housing Market." *Urban Studies* 45(5–6): 1163–91.

Pastor, Manuel, Jr. 1995. "Economic Inequality, Latino Poverty, and the Civil Unrest in Los Angeles." *Economic Development Quarterly* 9(3): 238–58.

——. 2001a. "Poverty, Race, and Immigration in Los Angeles County." In *Asian and Latino Immigrants in a Restructuring Economy: The Metamorphosis of Southern California*, edited by Marta López-Garza and David Diaz. Stanford, Calif.: Stanford University Press.

——. 2001b. "Looking for Regionalism in All the Wrong Places: Demography, Geography, and Community in Los Angeles County." *Urban Affairs Review* 36(6): 747–82.

Pfeiffer, Deirdre, Karna Wong, Paul Ong, and Melany De La Cruz-Viesca. 2014. "Pathways to Trouble: Homeowners and the Foreclosure Crisis in Los Angeles Ethnic Communities." Los Angeles: University of California, Asian American Studies Center.

Ruggles, Steven, Katie Genadek, Ronald Goeken, Josiah Grover, and Matthew Sobek. 2017. "Integrated Public Use Microdata Series: Version 7.0" [dataset]. Minneapolis: University of Minnesota.

Sharp, Gregory, and Matthew Hall. 2014. "Emerging Forms of Racial Inequality in Homeownership Exit, 1968–2009." *Social Problems* 61(3): 427–47.

Steil, Justin P., Len Albright, Jacob S. Rugh, and Douglas S. Massey. 2017. "The Social Structure of Mortgage Discrimination." *Housing Studies* published online November 3. DOI: 10.1080/02673037.2017.1390076.

Storper, Michael, Thomas Kemeny, Naji P. Makarem, and Taner Osman. 2015. *The Rise and Fall of Urban Economies: Lessons from San Francisco and Los Angeles*. Stanford, Calif.: Stanford Business Books.

Takaki, Ronald. 1989. *Strangers from a Different Shore: A History of Asian Americans*, rev. ed. Boston, Mass.: Little, Brown.

Thomas, Dexter. 2016. "Three Black Journalists Talk About the L.A. Riots, 24 Years Later." *Los Angeles Times*, April 29. Accessed August 2, 2017. https://medium.com/la-times/three-black-journalists-talk-aboutthe-l-a-riots-24-years-later-d8dc2d72899e.

Torgerson, Dial. 1992. "'Brown Power' Unity Seen Behind School Disorders." *Los Angeles Times*, July.

U.S. Census Bureau. 2011. "Facts for Features: Asian/Pacific American Heritage Month: May 2011." CB11-FF.06. Accessed May 6, 2018. http://www.census.gov/newsroom/releases/archives/facts_for_features_special_editions/cb11-ff06.html.

# The Evolution of Black Neighborhoods Since Kerner

MARCUS D. CASEY AND BRADLEY L. HARDY

*This article studies the evolution of African American neighborhoods since the publication of the groundbreaking Kerner Commission report in 1968. We first examine how black and riot-affected neighborhoods evolved in four representative cities—Detroit, Newark, Los Angeles, and Washington, D.C.—during this period. Among black neighborhoods in these cities, we find that black neighborhoods not directly affected by riots fare better but trend similar to those that were. Notably, a number of disparities the commission identified as policy priorities—such as relatively lower income, higher poverty, and higher unemployment—persist despite declines in racist attitudes, extreme segregation, and an increased suburbanization of blacks. Fifty years after its publication, these findings suggest that the concerns of the Kerner Commission report remain relevant.*

**Keywords:** neighborhoods, urban economic development, race, Kerner Commission, riots

The National Advisory Commission on Civil Disorders, colloquially known as the Kerner Commission, was tasked by Lyndon B. Johnson (LBJ) to examine the causes and propose solutions to the destructive urban rioting that marked the 1960s. The resulting report (1968) focused primarily on the abject living conditions in many African American communities as a principal cause of the rioting. Its narrative voiced the growing recognition that efforts culminating in the adoption of civil rights legislation and Great Society programs were not enough to quell rising discontent within many black communities. Rampant housing and labor market discrimination driven by white racism, the report argues, contributed to the formation and maintenance of black ghettos, places characterized by extreme segregation,

---

**Marcus D. Casey** is David M. Rubenstein Fellow in Economic Studies at the Brookings Institution and assistant professor in the Department of Economics at the University of Illinois at Chicago. **Bradley L. Hardy** is associate professor in the Department of Public Administration and Policy at American University.

© 2018 Russell Sage Foundation. Casey, Marcus D., and Bradley L. Hardy. 2018. "The Evolution of Black Neighborhoods Since Kerner." *RSF: The Russell Sage Foundation Journal of the Social Sciences* 4(6): 185–205. DOI: 10.7758/RSF.2018.4.6.09. We thank the editors and three anonymous reviewers for helpful comments that improved the paper. We also thank William Collins for allowing us access to a subset of the Collins and Margo tract-level data on riot locations for use in this study. Finally, we would like to acknowledge the seminar participants at the Russell Sage Foundation and the Institute on Research on Race and Public Policy, University of Illinois at Chicago. Direct correspondence to: Marcus D. Casey at mcasey@brookings.edu, 1775 Massachusetts Ave. N.W., Washington, D.C. 20036; and Bradley L. Hardy at hardy@american.edu, 4400 Massachusetts Ave. N.W., Washington, D.C. 20016.

Open Access Policy: *RSF: The Russell Sage Foundation Journal of the Social Sciences* is an open access journal. This article is published under a Creative Commons Attribution-NonCommercial-NoDerivs 3.0 Unported License.

concentrated poverty, poor public good provision, and limited access to mainstream jobs. The commission outlined a program for direct government investments in housing, education, and employment coupled with active antidiscrimination campaigns especially in suburban areas. Deemed radical by many then, as well as by many today, the commission's omnibus recommendations were largely ignored (Kerner Report 1968; Russell 2004).

The Kerner Commission understood that neighborhood living conditions are a large component of individual and family-level socioeconomic well-being and the report notes that prior to the 1960s, neighborhood conditions facing blacks in cities outside the South remained quite difficult. The "promised land" in the north—away from the southern Jim Crow regime—had provided little of the prosperity that many black migrants sought (Olzak, Shanahan, and McEneaney 1996). The roughly fifty years since the report's publication, however, have seen a dramatic change in the overall institutional environment. Blacks as a group have made substantive gains both socially and economically; overt efforts to exclude blacks or constrain where blacks can live have largely disappeared. In particular, as Reynolds Farley describes in this volume about Detroit, peripheral city neighborhoods and formerly all-white suburbs now boast large or majority-black populations (2018). Yet, despite these apparent advancements in other sectors of society, racial segregation continues to characterize cities; blacks face lower educational attainment levels and higher unemployment; disparities in income and wealth persist at levels near those that commission chairman Otto Kerner and his colleagues described five decades ago.

This article examines how the features of black neighborhoods that concerned the Kerner Commission have evolved. Ultimately, we seek to understand how, in light of the attention brought by the Kerner report and others focused on problems in urban neighborhoods, these black neighborhoods have evolved vis-à-vis their white and other nonblack counterpart neighborhoods. Despite reductions in racial animus and discrimination over time, as recognized by the authors of the Kerner report, blacks still remain largely in segregated neighborhoods. Hence, it is important to determine what relative progress in black neighborhood quality, if any, has occurred since the Kerner report issued its call for black neighborhood improvement fifty years ago.

To conduct our analysis, we combine U.S. census data harmonized across five decades in the Neighborhood Change Database with tract-level information on the location of riots in these cities (Collins and Margo 2004). We match these riot locations to tracts in our set of cities and compare these areas to those that did not directly experience rioting. We focus particularly on the re-sorting of residents: What were the characteristics of neighborhoods that retained high proportions of black residents? How did neighborhoods elsewhere change? We characterize population counts, racial composition, educational levels, income, poverty, and public assistance use across five decades spanning 1970 through 2010 for black and transitional neighborhoods, and then compare these outcomes across census tracts representative of America's urban core that have disproportionately higher shares of black and other minorities, census tracts outside this core, and urban core census tracts directly affected by rioting of the 1960s.

Our descriptive analysis yields several key stylized facts. Consistent with earlier research, we find that, on average, the population in tracts directly affected by riots fell dramatically between 1970 and 2010. We document that these areas initially became more nonwhite and poor in the intervening decades. By contrast, tracts in riot-affected cities that did not directly experience rioting violence had relatively stable populations. However, they have evolved to become much more diverse racially, ethnically, and socioeconomically in part as a consequence of Hispanic population growth. Moreover, we find that neighborhoods directly affected by riots in the cities we study remain among the most economically disadvantaged today. In particular, we find that black movement from the urban core to peripheral city neighborhoods and suburbs accelerated after 1970, that amenity declines consistent with neighborhood divestment coincided with urban riots and ultimately helped foster ongoing gentrification observed in many urban neighborhoods (for example, Hyra 2012), and that socioeconomic gaps persist between black neighborhoods—with and without any history of rioting—and neighborhoods without a large concentration of black residents.

We discuss several policies in the spirit of those advocated by the Kerner Commission that, adopted in recent decades, have been aimed at improving living conditions and life chances for residents of disadvantaged neighborhoods. These policies include those aimed at desegregation, those that have generally focused on promoting economic development and employment, and those geared toward improving the quality of educational choices in these neighborhoods. Echoing the existing literature that seeks to evaluate the success of these policies, it is apparent that desegregation initiatives have had only minimal effect. Likewise, those aimed at increasing economic development and employment in black neighborhoods have largely been ineffective or have engendered complaints of gentrification and displacement. By contrast, policies that have sought to improve educational quality and choice in these neighborhoods have had more, albeit mixed, success.

We expand the scope of our inquiry to provide a descriptive comparison of U.S. neighborhoods where blacks typically live as of 2010. Given that changes in attitudes and other features of American life had led to a racial resorting both within the urban areas affected by the rioting and across the nation, the types of neighborhoods where blacks typically reside in the twenty-first century have broadened. A simple comparison reveals that blacks still live in neighborhoods that lag on a number of key indicators. In concert with the comparisons presented from the riot cities analysis, it only further amplifies the fact that, fifty years on, the concerns of the Kerner Commission report remain relevant.

## DATA

Our data are drawn from three sources. The Neighborhood Change Database (NCDB), the linchpin of our analysis, consists of census tracts harmonized to the 2010 boundaries spanning five census decades since 1970. Originally constructed by the Urban Institute and sold commercially by Geolytics, Inc., the NCDB helps overcome changes in the boundaries and definitions of census tracts over time that limit longitudinal analyses in which tracts are the unit of analysis. Hence, the NCDB allow us to study how specific places have changed over time.

To the NCDB data, we match tract-level information denoting the location of riots occurring in 1967 for our representative cities: Detroit, Los Angeles, Newark, New Jersey, and Washington, D.C.[1] These cities experienced particularly deadly and destructive episodes of rioting that were featured in major news outlets, providing some of the impetus for President Johnson to establish the Kerner Commission. Finally, we augment these NCDB files with additional information from the decennial census (1970 through 2010) and the American Community Survey (for 2006 through 2010) to better characterize neighborhood environments.

Table 1 presents a descriptive breakdown of the neighborhoods used in the final analysis dataset. Our data include 2,978 tracts located within our representative cities. We then separately examine tracts nationwide to assess the contemporary status of black neighborhoods.[2] We define a black neighborhood as a tract whose population was 40 percent black or higher in any census year. Admittedly, this cutoff is somewhat arbitrary, but we believe, given the size of the black population and degree of segregation in most cities, that neighborhoods near this threshold likely would have been characterized as black in past decades. In addition, before 2000 almost all neighborhood transitions are one way and complete (Card, Mas, and Rothstein 2008; Casey 2018). Therefore, it is reasonable to assume that neighborhoods with such high proportions of blacks were

---

1. Census tract-level information on riot events for the four cities is provided by William Collins.

2. We focus on riots within these four major cities during 1967, but acknowledge, as mentioned, that hundreds of riots occurred in cities across the nation during the late 1960s.

**Table 1.** Breakdown by Neighborhood Type

|  | 1970 | 1980 | 1990 | 2000 | 2010 |
| --- | --- | --- | --- | --- | --- |
| Riot-affected cities, tracts in sample | 2,978 | 2,978 | 2,978 | 2,978 | 2,978 |
| Proportion black | 19 | 23 | 23 | 21 | 20 |

*Source:* Author's tabulations based on the Neighborhood Change Database, 2010, and the American Community Survey, 2006–2010 (U.S. Census Bureau 2010a).
*Note:* Riot tracts correspond to those identified by Collins and Margo (2004). Neighborhood characteristics are estimated at the census tract using the decennial census for 1970, 1980, 1990, 2000, 2010, as well as the 2006–2010 American Community Survey.

likely to continue to trend in that direction. Our organizing frame of characterizing a black neighborhood is motivated by well-established historical and contemporary patterns of racial and socioeconomic sorting and the range of observable inequities that arise from such sorting (Massey and Denton 1993; Cutler and Glaeser 1997).

Our riot cities generally had a high percentage of neighborhoods, on average, classified as black between 1970 and 1990: in 1970, approximately 19 percent and approximately 23 percent in 1980 and 1990. However, in the most recent census, this figure decreased to around 20 percent. This pattern is consistent with reports elsewhere suggesting that many of the former industrial cities affected by riots are losing their black population and becoming more integrated through gentrification and immigration.

For this study, we focus on the areas within four cities affected by the major riots that led to the establishment of the Kerner Commission report and remain among the most prominent examples in the late 1960s. Because the Kerner Commission was also concerned with the conditions facing black Americans nationwide and the potential for civil unrest to spread to a broader set of cities, we close by considering the twenty-first century outlook. Specifically, we compare contemporary conditions within the neighborhoods of America's one hundred largest cities to those within riot-affected cities.

## HOW FAR HAVE WE COME? THE EVOLUTION OF BLACK AND RIOT-AFFECTED NEIGHBORHOODS

Figures 1 and 2 present population trends for several comparisons of neighborhoods within riot cities, those that directly experienced riots versus neighborhoods overall within riot cities, and black neighborhoods that experience rioting and those that did not.

As figure 1 shows, neighborhoods in our riot cities that experienced rioting depopulated, on average, after 1970. The most pronounced drop occurred between 1970 and 1980, from roughly 4,500 to less than 4,000, declining more gradually thereafter. This depopulation does not occur when looking over the pooled set of neighborhoods in the riot-city metro areas overall. After a relatively constant population of approximately 3,250 between 1970 and 1980, these neighborhoods grow over time to almost four thousand people per tract, on average, by 2010. Figure 2 compares the same population trends restricted to black neighborhoods that directly experienced riots and those that did not within these cities. The similarities are striking, in that the depopulation of riot-affected neighborhoods mirrors that of unaffected black neighborhoods.

In tables 2 through 5, we summarize changes in the racial and ethnic composition of neighborhoods in our riot-affected cities since 1970. Riot-affected neighborhoods transitioned from being overwhelmingly black in 1970 to later being almost evenly split across black and nonblack residents (table 2), including a rising share of foreign-born and Hispanic residents. Neighborhoods also become increasingly racially and ethnically diverse (table 3). This shift holds for the full set of black neighborhoods, including those affected by riots (table 4) and those simply in riot-affected cities (table 5).

Table 6 examines transitions among black neighborhoods since 1970. Specifically, among neighborhoods classified as black in 1970, what

**Figure 1.** Population Trends, Overall and Riot-Affected Neighborhoods

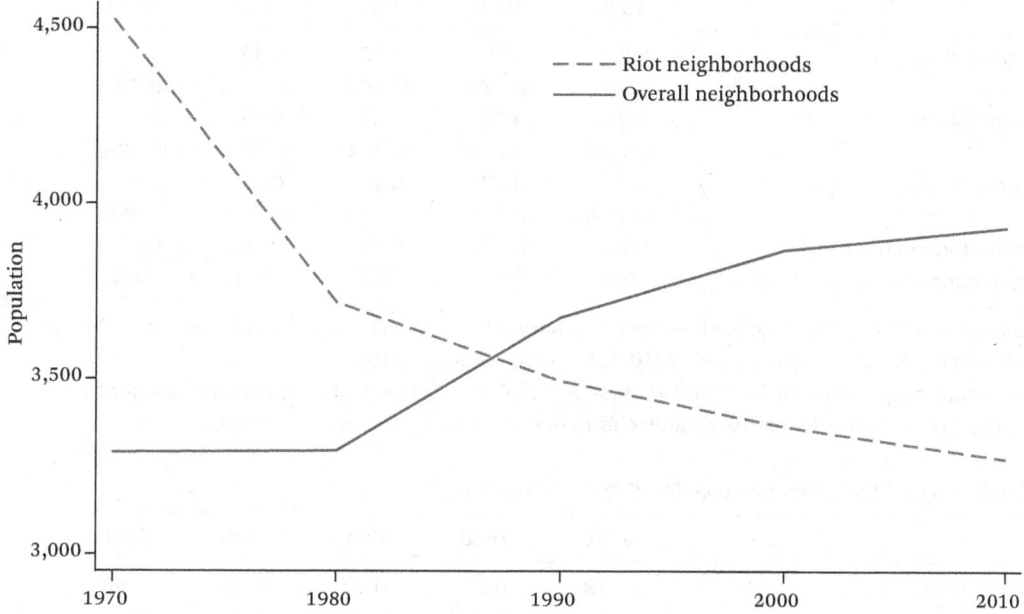

*Source:* Authors' calculations based on the Neighborhood Change Database, 2010, and the 2010 U.S. census (2010b).
*Note:* Riot tracts correspond to those identified by Collins and Margo (2004).

**Figure 2.** Population Trends, Overall and Riot-Affected Black Neighborhoods

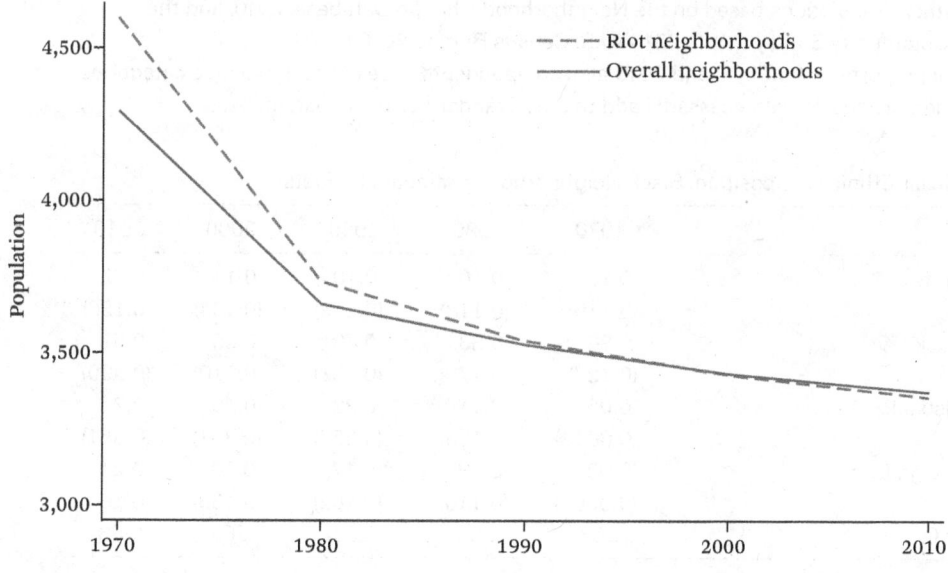

*Source:* Authors' calculations based on the Neighborhood Change Database, 2010, and the 2010 U.S. census (2010b).
*Note:* Riot tracts correspond to those identified by Collins and Margo (2004).

**Table 2.** Racial-Ethnic Composition, Riot-Affected Neighborhoods

|  | 1970 | 1980 | 1990 | 2000 | 2010 |
|---|---|---|---|---|---|
| Percent white | 0.22 | 0.15 | 0.13 | 0.17 | 0.23 |
|  | (0.264) | (0.179) | (0.160) | (0.162) | (0.207) |
| Percent black | 0.76 | 0.77 | 0.69 | 0.63 | 0.56 |
|  | (0.273) | (0.249) | (0.284) | (0.323) | (0.325) |
| Percent Hispanic | 0.07 | 0.13 | 0.23 | 0.29 | 0.34 |
|  | (0.117) | (0.194) | (0.274) | (0.321) | (0.356) |
| Percent foreign born | 0.05 | 0.11 | 0.18 | 0.20 | 0.21 |
| Observations | 309 | 309 | 309 | 309 | 309 |

*Source:* Author's tabulations based on the Neighborhood Change Database, 2010, and the American Community Survey, 2006–2010 (U.S. Census Bureau 2010a).
*Note:* Racial proportions for 2000 and 2010 allow respondents to select multiple race categories and, thus, proportions do not necessarily add to one. Standard errors in parentheses.

**Table 3.** Racial-Ethnic Composition, Neighborhoods Overall

|  | 1970 | 1980 | 1990 | 2000 | 2010 |
|---|---|---|---|---|---|
| Percent white | 0.79 | 0.63 | 0.52 | 0.46 | 0.48 |
|  | (0.32) | (0.3) | (0.29) | (0.26) | (0.25) |
| Percent black | 0.18 | 0.22 | 0.23 | 0.23 | 0.22 |
|  | (0.32) | (0.33) | (0.32) | (0.32) | (0.31) |
| Percent Hispanic | 0.15 | 0.23 | 0.31 | 0.37 | 0.40 |
|  | (0.17) | (0.24) | (0.27) | (0.30) | (0.31) |
| Percent foreign born | 0.11 | 0.19 | 0.27 | 0.31 | 0.30 |
|  | (0.08) | (0.15) | (0.18) | (0.18) | (0.18) |
| Observations | 2,978 | 2,978 | 2,978 | 2,978 | 2,978 |

*Source:* Author's tabulations based on the Neighborhood Change Database, 2010, and the American Community Survey, 2006–2010 (U.S. Census Bureau 2010a).
*Note:* Racial proportions for 2000 and 2010 allow respondents to select multiple race categories and, thus, proportions do not necessarily add to one. Standard errors in parentheses.

**Table 4.** Racial-Ethnic Composition, Black Neighborhoods Affected by Riots

|  | 1970 | 1980 | 1990 | 2000 | 2010 |
|---|---|---|---|---|---|
| Percent white | 0.13 | 0.10 | 0.10 | 0.14 | 0.22 |
|  | (0.119) | (0.118) | (0.112) | (0.134) | (0.186) |
| Percent black | 0.86 | 0.83 | 0.73 | 0.65 | 0.57 |
|  | (0.127) | (0.179) | (0.252) | (0.310) | (0.320) |
| Percent Hispanic | 0.05 | 0.11 | 0.23 | 0.30 | 0.35 |
|  | (0.0613) | (0.153) | (0.257) | (0.311) | (0.351) |
| Percent foreign born | 0.03 | 0.09 | 0.17 | 0.20 | 0.21 |
|  | (0.0369) | (0.110) | (0.182) | (0.189) | (0.184) |
| Observations | 263 | 263 | 263 | 263 | 263 |

*Source:* Author's tabulations based on the Neighborhood Change Database, 2010, and the American Community Survey, 2006–2010 (U.S. Census Bureau 2010a).
*Note:* Racial proportions for 2000 and 2010 allow respondents to select multiple race categories and, thus, proportions do not necessarily add to one. Standard errors in parentheses.

**Table 5.** Racial-Ethnic Composition, Black Neighborhoods Overall

|  | 1970 | 1980 | 1990 | 2000 | 2010 |
|---|---|---|---|---|---|
| Percent white | 0.17 | 0.12 | 0.11 | 0.15 | 0.21 |
|  | (0.161) | (0.147) | (0.140) | (0.154) | (0.195) |
| Percent black | 0.81 | 0.81 | 0.73 | 0.67 | 0.59 |
|  | (0.160) | (0.191) | (0.258) | (0.308) | (0.319) |
| Percent Hispanic | 0.06 | 0.11 | 0.20 | 0.27 | 0.31 |
|  | (0.0958) | (0.160) | (0.243) | (0.293) | (0.326) |
| Percent foreign born | 0.04 | 0.09 | 0.16 | 0.19 | 0.20 |
|  | (0.0398) | (0.104) | (0.172) | (0.179) | (0.175) |
| Observations | 566 | 566 | 566 | 566 | 566 |

*Source:* Author's tabulations based on the Neighborhood Change Database, 2010, and the American Community Survey, 2006–2010 (U.S. Census Bureau 2010a).
*Note:* Racial proportions for 2000 and 2010 allow respondents to select multiple race categories and, thus, proportions do not necessarily add to one. Standard errors in parentheses.

was their classification in 2010? The first panel presents these statistics for the riot-affected areas we study and the second for neighborhoods not directly affected. By contrast, of the areas classified as white in 1970, 64 percent transitioned to black by 2010. Nearly 60 percent of neighborhoods classified as black in 1970 remained as black neighborhoods in 2010. Among those black neighborhoods that transitioned away, almost none became a white neighborhood: 2 percent of neighborhoods classified as black became white neighborhoods whereas 40 percent became Hispanic. Among neighborhoods not directly affected by riots and those in comparison cities, racial compositions were even more stable: 67 percent of black tracts in 1970 remained black in 2010. Only 1 percent transitioned to white over the period. Compared with riot-affected neighborhoods, only 7 percent of neighborhoods initially classified as white transitioned to black over the period.

Although the differing population trends across neighborhood types are interesting, the Kerner Commission was specifically concerned with neighborhood quality experienced by blacks who lived in these neighborhoods. Figure 3 presents educational attainment levels within the neighborhoods of riot-affected cities. At baseline in 1970, levels are higher in neighborhoods overall than in riot-affected neighborhoods. College attainment in riot-affected neighborhoods rises at a rate similar to that of neighborhoods overall but fails to catch up to the higher attainment within the average neighborhood—roughly 25 percent of residents in the average neighborhood of a city that experienced rioting had a college degree by 2010, versus fewer than 15 percent in riot-

**Table 6.** Neighborhood Transitions

|  | Percentage |
|---|---|
| **Riot-affected neighborhoods** |  |
| Stable black | 58 |
| Black to white | 2 |
| Black to Hispanic | 40 |
| Black to other nonwhite | 0 |
| White to black | 64 |
| **Unaffected neighborhoods in riot-affected cities** |  |
| Stable black | 67 |
| Black to white | 1 |
| Black to Hispanic | 32 |
| Black to other nonwhite | 0 |
| White to black | 7 |
| **Overall neighborhoods** |  |
| Stable black | 84 |
| Black to white | 2 |
| Black to Hispanic | 12 |
| Black to other nonwhite | 0 |
| White to black | 15 |

*Source:* Author's tabulations based on the Neighborhood Change Database, 2010, and the 2010 U.S. census (2010b).

**Figure 3.** Education Trends, Overall and Riot-Affected Neighborhoods

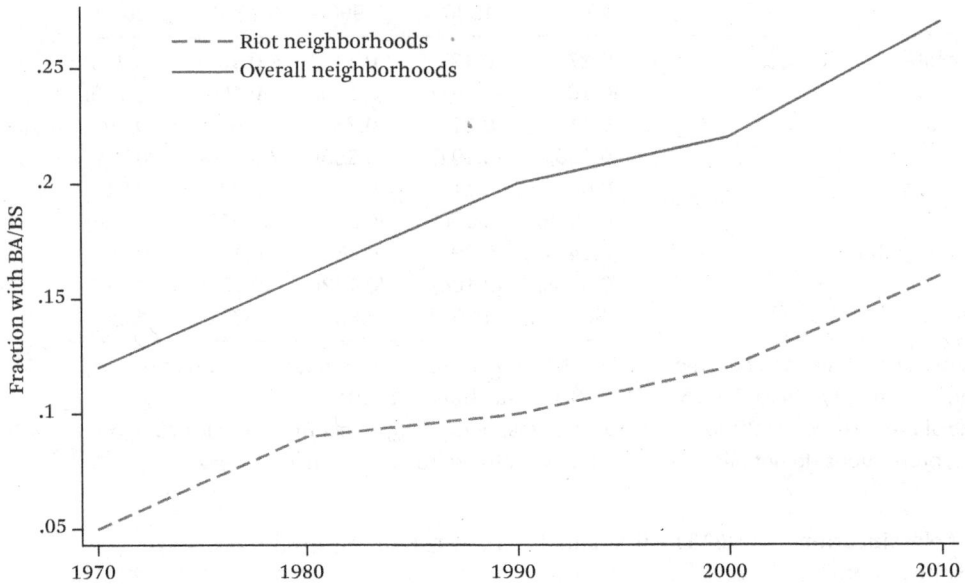

*Source:* Authors' calculations based on the Neighborhood Change Database, 2010, and the 2010 U.S. census (2010b).
*Note:* Riot tracts correspond to those identified by Collins and Margo (2004).

**Figure 4.** Black Education Trends, Overall and Riot-Affected Black Neighborhoods

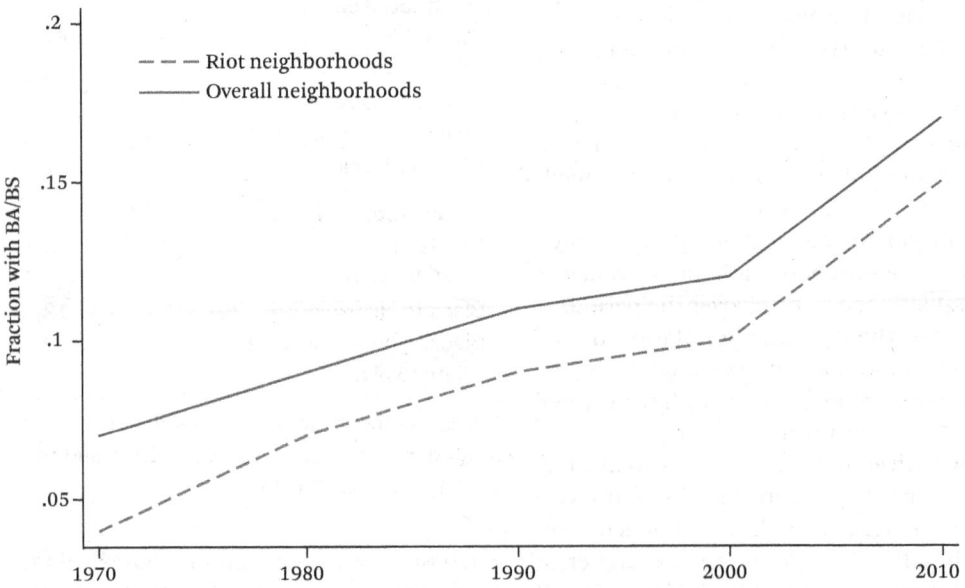

*Source:* Authors' calculations based on the Neighborhood Change Database, 2010, and the 2010 U.S. census (2010b).
*Note:* Riot tracts correspond to those identified by Collins and Margo (2004).

**Figure 5.** Income Trends, Overall and Riot-Affected Neighborhoods

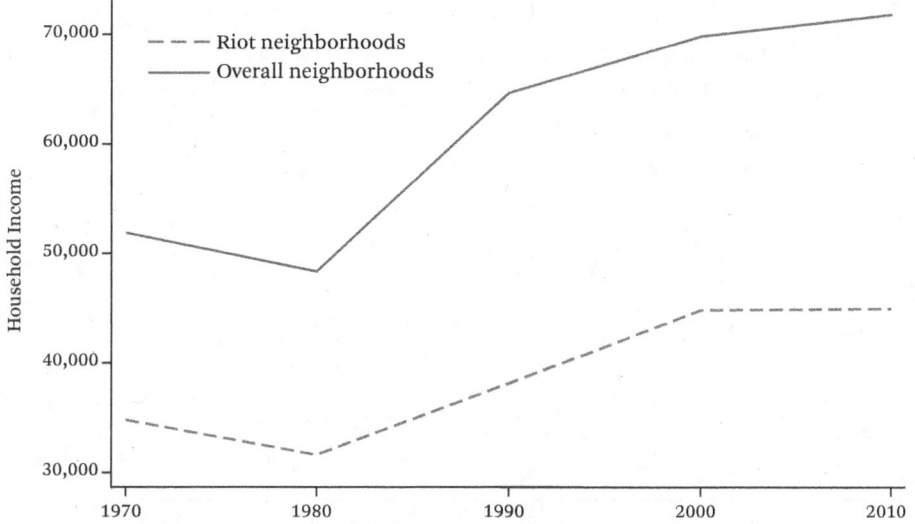

*Source:* Authors' calculations based on the Neighborhood Change Database, 2010, and the 2010 U.S. census (2010b).
*Note:* Average tract-level household income is adjusted for inflation using the personal consumption expenditure deflator for 2010. Riot tracts correspond to those identified by Collins and Margo (2004).

affected neighborhoods. In figure 4, restricting our view to black neighborhoods within our representative cities, we see a similar pattern for college attainment. Black neighborhoods generally look slightly better than riot-affected neighborhoods with respect to the proportion of residents with college degrees, though both follow the same trend over time—mirroring individual-level shifts in educational attainment concurrent with the changing structure of the economy favoring higher level skills (see, for example, Autor 2014).

We next examine household income within neighborhoods (figure 5). Within the four cities, riot and nonriot neighborhoods follow a similar trend in regard to income growth, but show large, persistent gaps. In 1970, the gap is roughly $20,000. By 2000, it is $25,000. By 2010, the average nonriot neighborhood residents had incomes over $70,000, versus approximately $45,000 in riot-affected neighborhoods. The riot-affected neighborhoods experience only $10,000 of real income growth over a forty-year period. When we examine differences between black and riot-affected neighborhoods, black neighborhoods overall fare only slightly better (figure 6). A modest $3,000 to $4,000 advantage persists for black neighborhoods relative to riot-affected neighborhoods, and the trends are almost identical over time.

Unemployment is a primary driver of income statistics; therefore, we next trace unemployment trends in our neighborhoods of interest. In figure 7, we show that riot neighborhoods begin with slightly higher unemployment rates in 1970, though both riot and nonriot neighborhoods have, on average, unemployment rates below 10 percent. However, between 1970 and 1990, a sizable neighborhood unemployment gap emerges—roughly 10 percentage points—before closing somewhat thereafter. Accordingly, this pattern mirrors the income trends shown previously. Black neighborhood unemployment trends in riot cities (figure 8) track similarly to neighborhood trends generally for riot-affected neighborhoods, which again is borne out in the previous series of income-based trends (figures 5 and 6).

We close our discussion of neighborhood economic and amenity trends by examining poverty and public assistance receipt within these neighborhoods. As figure 9 shows, within

**Figure 6.** Income Trends, Overall and Riot-Affected Black Neighborhoods

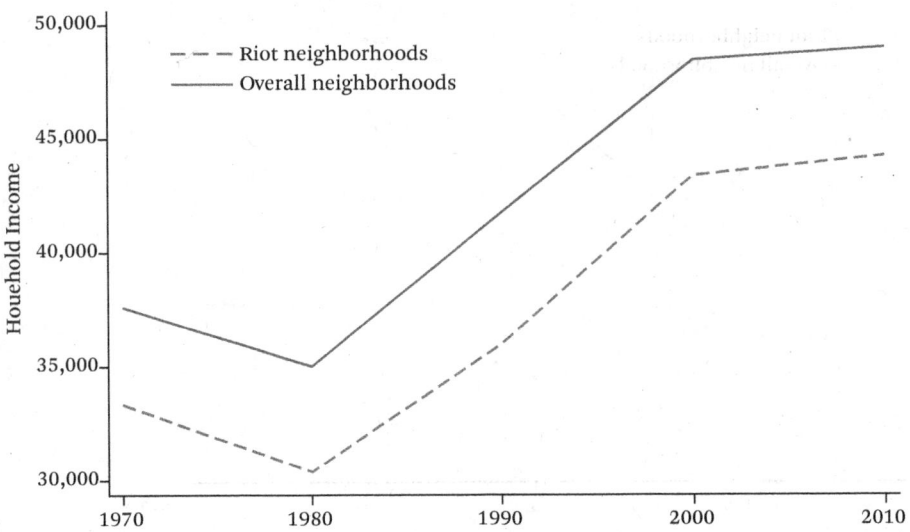

*Source:* Authors' calculations based on the Neighborhood Change Database, 2010, and the 2010 U.S. census (2010b).
*Note:* Average tract-level household income is adjusted for inflation using the personal consumption expenditure deflator for 2010. Riot tracts correspond to those identified by Collins and Margo (2004).

**Figure 7.** Unemployment Trends, Overall and Riot-Affected Neighborhoods

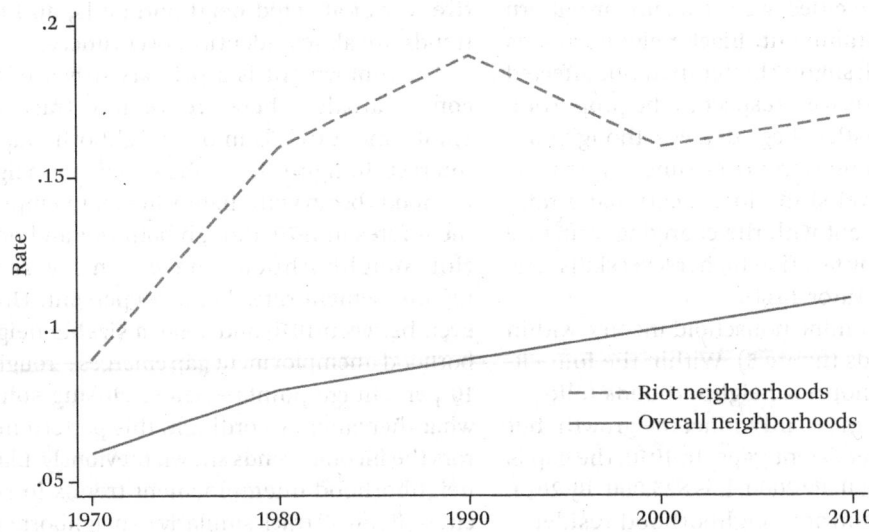

*Source:* Authors' calculations based on the Neighborhood Change Database, 2010, and the 2010 U.S. census (2010b).
*Note:* Average tract-level household income is adjusted for inflation using the personal consumption expenditure deflator for 2010. Riot tracts correspond to those identified by Collins and Margo (2004).

**Figure 8.** Unemployment Trends, Overall and Riot-Affected Black Neighborhoods

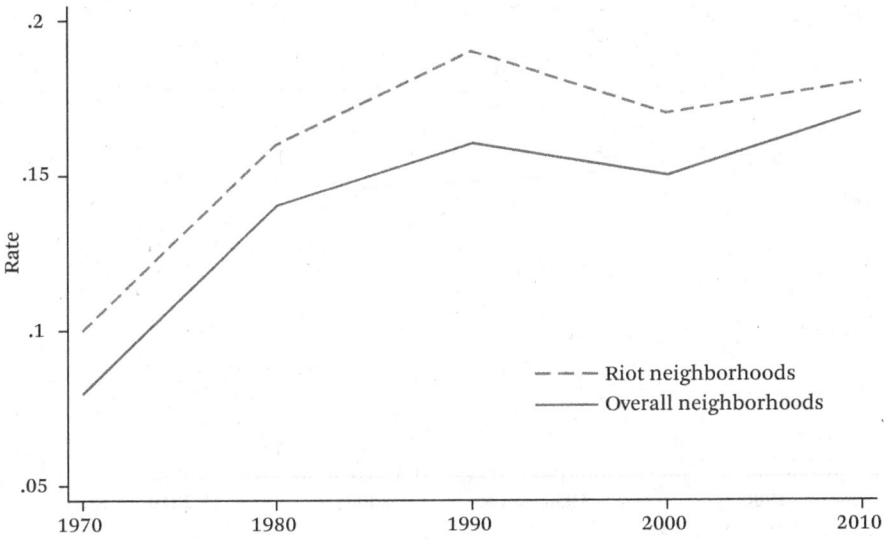

*Source:* Authors' calculations based on the Neighborhood Change Database, 2010, and the 2010 U.S. census (2010b).
*Note:* Riot tracts correspond to those identified by Collins and Margo (2004).

our sample, poverty rates in riot-affected neighborhoods are roughly 15 percentage points higher than in neighborhoods overall. Riot neighborhoods see a growth trend in poverty from 1970 through 1990 and a leveling off thereafter, whereas average neighborhoods (neighborhoods overall) within these cities experience very gradual growth in poverty over time, and from a much lower baseline. A sharp decrease in public assistance use occurs between 2000 and 2010 for both riot neighborhoods and neighborhoods overall, with public assistance use between both types of neighborhoods converging to less than 10 percent.

In figure 10, among the black neighborhoods, we observe that riot-affected neighborhoods have even higher poverty rates than the already-elevated levels generally, by approximately 3 to 5 percentage points. These rates, above 30 percent after 1970, are higher than national averages. For black neighborhoods, these levels roughly mirror trends at the individual and family level for black Americans, for whom poverty has held steady at between approximately one in four for individuals and one in three for families (Semega, Fontenot, and Kolla 2017). Meanwhile, public assistance use again falls and converges between 2000 and 2010 to under 10 percent. As shown in figure 9, public assistance falls dramatically, a divergence from poverty trends between 2000 and 2010. Given that no comparable, large reduction in poverty, the divergence in contemporary poverty-welfare assistance trends shown in figures 9 and 10 is broadly consistent with major policy changes to the nation's cash welfare program for the poor in 1996 that, by many accounts, have led to poverty without welfare benefits (Blank 2009; Ziliak 2016; Shaefer, Edin, and Talbert 2015).

## What Worked and Did Not Work: Neighborhood Policy Since Kerner

Aside from its ostensibly controversial assignment of blame, the Kerner report is notable for proposing a broad set investments—"enrichment" in its language—in the areas of housing, education, employment, and general welfare, coupled with "integration." The commission members believed investments in these areas would satisfy the dual aims of reducing the likelihood of additional violence and improving the life conditions and future prospects of black families and their children.

**Figure 9.** Poverty and Welfare Trends, Overall and Riot-Affected Neighborhoods

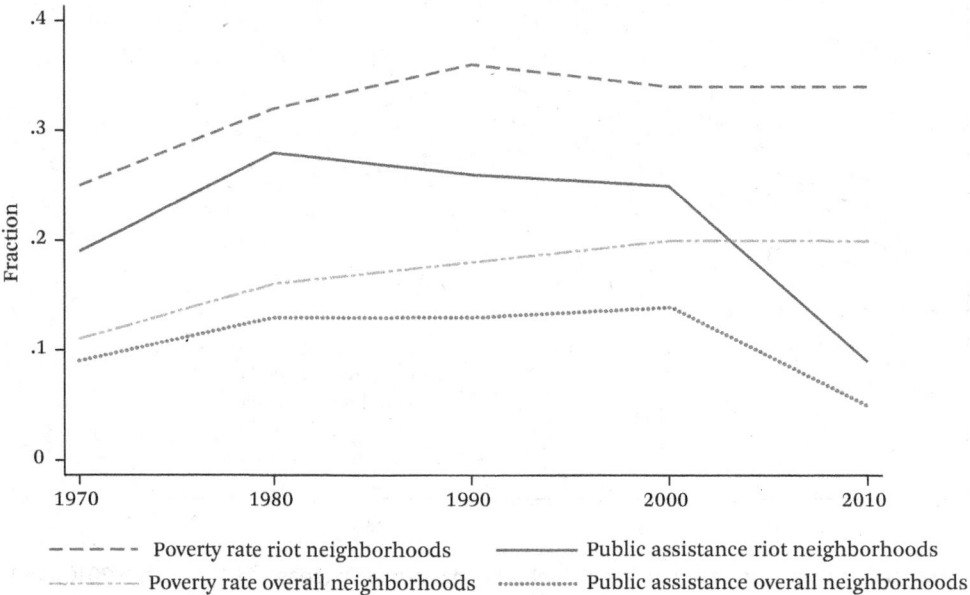

*Source:* Authors' calculations based on the Neighborhood Change Database, 2010, and the 2010 U.S. census (2010b).
*Note:* Percent poor is calculated as the proportion of families under sixty-five living below the poverty line. Riot tracts correspond to those identified by Collins and Margo (2004).

**Figure 10.** Poverty and Welfare Trends, Overall and Riot-Affected Black Neighborhoods

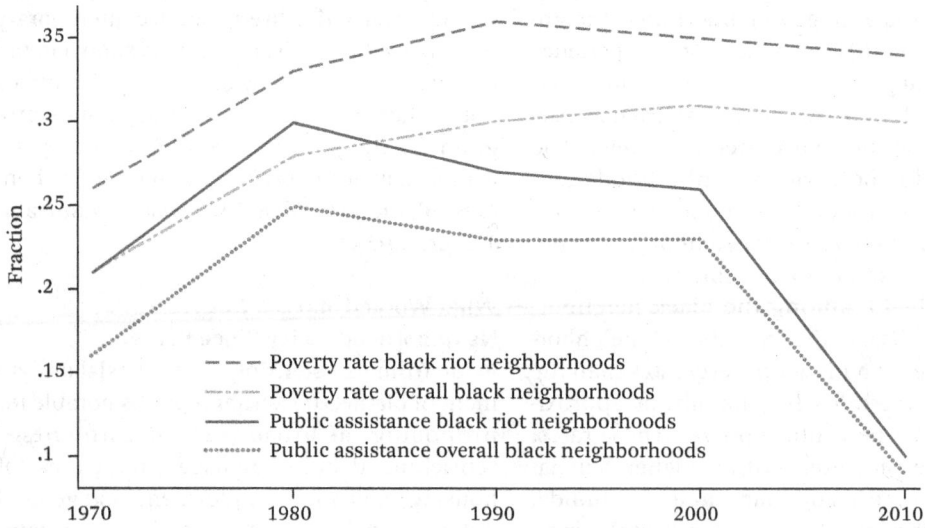

*Source:* Authors' calculations based on the Neighborhood Change Database, 2010, and the 2010 U.S. census (2010b).
*Note:* Percent poor is calculated as the proportion of families under sixty-five living below the poverty line.

The recommendations and observations of Kerner, many of which Rick Loessberg and John Koskinen summarize in this volume (2018), turned out to be especially prescient, given the link between neighborhood-level conditions and long-term individual-level socioeconomic outcomes. Almost none of these proposals, however, were directly implemented in the immediate aftermath of publication. Although a comprehensive review is beyond the scope of this article, we briefly discuss several of these programs that have had impacts on black (and other) neighborhoods and comment on their progress relative to the goals outlined in the Kerner Commission report.

A range of federally funded place-based policies, whether focused directly on people or indirectly by facilitating business growth to address poverty, high unemployment, and urban blight, have been implemented since the late 1960s. Though these policies were not necessarily as ambitious and targeted as those described in the report, they were similar in spirit, particularly in terms of promoting integration of neighborhoods, encouraging neighborhood economic development, and improving access to quality education in desegregated schools. In addition, though not place-based, research suggests that several key transfer programs such as SNAP (food stamps) had substantial positive impacts on economically disadvantaged communities including improved long-term outcomes for recipient children (see, for example, Hoynes, Schanzenbach, and Almond 2016).

The passage of legislation such as the Fair Housing Act (FHA) of 1968 and the Equal Credit Opportunity Act (ECOA) of 1974 were key steps toward the comprehensive federal framework for combating discrimination in the housing market and promoting desegregation that the commission considered of paramount importance. The FHA prohibited discrimination in both rental and owner-occupied housing and, at the time, many hoped it would help promote integration of blacks into higher quality, white neighborhoods (Massey 2015). However, it included no provisions prohibiting discrimination in mortgage lending markets, an omission corrected by the ECOA. Despite the symbolic power of this and related legislation, segregation between blacks and whites has declined nationally only slightly, though with some variation across cities (Rugh and Massey 2014). Moreover, audit studies suggest that discrimination in housing markets as well as in mortgage lending continue to affect black households.

Likewise, the Housing and Urban Development Acts of 1968 that provided funding for integrated developments outside central cities, the Community Reinvestment Act of 1974 that prohibited redlining of black neighborhoods, and the Housing and Community Development Act of 1974 that established a block grant program to support community development in the decade subsequent to the Kerner Commission report's publication represent important attempts to improve the quality and stability of black neighborhoods (see, for example, Massey 2015). Since this early legislation, much neighborhood development policy has come in the form of place-based economic development initiatives, some of which Jamein Cunningham and Rob Gillezeau also discuss in this volume (2018).

Among the most ambitious of these policies that are in the spirit, if not in the implementation, of the Kerner Commission report have been the establishment of enterprise and empowerment zones to promote economic development and private investment, primarily beginning by federal initiative in the 1980s and 1990s and later by states (Neumark and Simpson 2014). These strategies, which vary in intensity and size across jurisdictions, are often organized as tax incentives to promote hiring local workers, firm location, and investment within distressed areas (see, for example, Ladd 1994).

Evaluations of the net benefits of establishing such zones, however, are somewhat controversial (see Neumark and Simpson 2014). David Neumark and Jed Kolko, for example, argue in an evaluation of California's enterprise zones that the program was largely ineffective (2010). Like a number of studies published earlier, they find little evidence of an impact from designating a place as an enterprise zone on economic activity. In contrast, recent evidence on empowerment zones suggests that, in areas they were instituted, place-based policies substantially increase jobs and wages relative to places considered for status but rejected (Busso, Gregory, and Kline 2013). Even if the establishment of such zones were beneficial, additional concerns are that such policies help spur gentrification forces that raise rents and other costs in recipient neighborhoods, leading to fears of displacement of typically poorer, nonwhite incumbent residents. As a consequence, potential benefits accruing to existing black residents may be limited. This can occur when, for example, tax incentives to promote development are financed by diminished educational investments—which themselves promote economic development, and when incentives are targeted neither toward firms with a strong propensity to hire nor toward adults who wish to reenter the workforce (Bartik 2018).

Education policies implemented since Kerner include expansion of the federally funded Head Start prekindergarten program, enacted in 1965 to provide educational programming, meals, and other developmental activities to three- and four-year-old children living in poor families. The program was part of President Johnson's war on poverty and expanded in generosity throughout the 1960s and early 1970s with the goal of improving child development and subsequent outcomes during school-age years and into adulthood. Today, several states supplement Head Start with their own pre-K and early pre-K programs (Garces, Thomas, and Currie 2002; Currie 2006).

Within the domain of secondary education, policy responses to the racial stratification inherent in many cities sought to both integrate schools and improve school quality experienced by blacks. Policies adopted in this context include school district-level efforts to equalize educational opportunities across neighborhoods via the busing and transfer of students into higher quality schools and neighborhoods, often based on race and economic status. Frequently the result of court-mandated intervention to desegregate schools, such efforts have borne positive results for students yet at times met with resistance from families who fall within the school boundary (see, for example, Billings, Deming, and Rockoff 2014); many of these programs were abandoned throughout the 1990s and 2000s.

As a result of the pushback stemming, in part, from the altered racial composition of schools and removal of students from their neighborhoods, decentralized school choice mechanisms to improve educational opportunities among black students became increasingly attractive. School choice approaches to improving educational quality among low-income children in disadvantaged neighborhoods introduce competitive market principles into the K–12 educational space by providing vouchers for low- and moderate-income families to attend private or parochial schools or via the introduction of charter schools, privately run public schools. Although proponents laud competition and accountability by giving low-income students and families increased market power, the evidence on school choice and academic achievement is mixed at best and in some instances negative (Angrist, Pathak, and Walters 2013; Baude et al. 2018; Dynarski and Nichols 2017).

## IMPLICATIONS FOR THE TWENTY-FIRST CENTURY: BLACK NEIGHBORHOODS IN THE CHANGING CITY

As we approach the third decade of the twenty-first century, it is important to recognize that the neighborhoods where blacks live are much more variable than they were when the Kerner report was issued. In addition to suburbanization in many of the larger metropolitan areas, the last two to three decades have seen many blacks return to the South as well as move to other regions of the country—the Southwest, for example (Frazier, Tettey-Fio, and Henry 2016). Thus, in this final section we highlight 2010 socioeconomic statistics for black neighborhoods from a set of comparison cities not directly affected by the riots but generally areas where blacks live. Specifically, these are defined as the one hundred largest metropolitan areas in the 2010 census.[3] A number of these cities were affected by riots—in some cases much earlier in the decade or in the aftermath of the assassination of Martin Luther King Jr. in 1968.

---

3. For a list of the comparison cities, see table A1.

**Table 7.** National Neighborhood Characteristics, 2010

|  | Black | All |
|---|---|---|
| Tract population | 3,263 | 3,956 |
|  | (2,069.7) | (2,038.3) |
| Percent white | 0.28 | 0.58 |
|  | (0.304) | (0.294) |
| Percent black | 0.64 | 0.26 |
|  | (0.325) | (0.303) |
| Percent Hispanic | 0.18 | 0.26 |
|  | (0.240) | (0.277) |
| Percent foreign born | 0.14 | 0.20 |
|  | (0.142) | (0.169) |
| Percent poor | 0.31 | 0.21 |
|  | (0.214) | (0.176) |
| Percent of families receiving public assistance | 0.06 | 0.04 |
|  | (0.0680) | (0.0681) |
| Unemployment rate | 0.16 | 0.10 |
|  | (0.0977) | (0.0715) |
| Percent college graduate | 0.23 | 0.30 |
|  | (0.220) | (0.221) |
| Average household income (2010 dollars) | 49,504 | 63,875 |
|  | (29,767.4) | (41,383.7) |
| Number of observations | 2,066 | 12,718 |

*Source:* Author's tabulations based on the Neighborhood Change Database, 2010, the 2010 U.S. census (2010b), and the American Community Survey, 2006–2010 (U.S. Census Bureau 2010a).
*Note:* Standard errors in parentheses.

We begin by comparing black neighborhoods in these municipalities to the average neighborhood nationwide (see table 7). Similar to the riot-affected areas we focused on initially, these black neighborhoods generally lag the average U.S. neighborhood in 2010 across several socioeconomic indicators. Specifically, poverty and unemployment are generally higher, roughly 10 and 6 percentage points, respectively. Moreover, we observe a nearly $15,000 household income gap. Perhaps unsurprising as well, college attainment of those living in these neighborhoods lags that of the average national neighborhood by 7 percentage points. Overall, this fits a pattern that emerges across the indicators presented: riot-affected neighborhoods—and black neighborhoods more generally—lag the nation as a whole on a broad range of amenity and socioeconomic indicators.

## RACIAL SORTING AND ACCESS TO HIGH AMENITY NEIGHBORHOODS

Central to the Kerner Commission's concerns was desegregation and improving the quality of living conditions for black citizens. Given that black neighborhoods in riot-affected cities remain largely stable and persistently segregated, it is of interest to explore the degree to which blacks have access to higher amenity neighborhoods. As noted, most neighborhood diversity outside the core black neighborhoods in 1970 has been driven by growth in the Hispanic population. Neighborhood changes involving black migration into former white neighborhoods have largely been one way and complete (Card, Mas, and Rothstein 2008). In an era of gentrification, however, there remains the possibility that desegregation will occur through the mechanism of white entry into black neighborhoods.

**Table 8.** Evolution of Neighborhoods

|  | 1970 | 1980 | 1990 | 2000 | 2010 |
|---|---|---|---|---|---|
| **Population at least 20 percent black** | | | | | |
| At least 20 percent college graduates | 0.05 | 0.13 | 0.16 | 0.19 | 0.29 |
| At least 40 percent college graduates | 0.02 | 0.04 | 0.05 | 0.06 | 0.11 |
| At least 60 percent college graduates | 0.01 | 0.02 | 0.02 | 0.02 | 0.05 |
| Observations | 683 | 828 | 847 | 852 | 839 |
| **Population at least 60 percent black** | | | | | |
| At least 20 percent college graduates | 0.02 | 0.10 | 0.15 | 0.20 | 0.28 |
| At least 40 percent college graduates | 0.01 | 0.02 | 0.03 | 0.05 | 0.10 |
| At least 60 percent college graduates | 0.01 | 0.02 | 0.02 | 0.01 | 0.05 |
| Observations | 481 | 584 | 537 | 502 | 486 |

*Source:* Author's tabulations based on the Neighborhood Change Database, 2010, the 2010 U.S. census (2010b), and the American Community Survey, 2006–2010 (U.S. Census Bureau 2010a).

Table 8 explores how such access to amenities has evolved over time by exploring the joint distribution of average educational attainment and percentage black. While not a perfect proxy, the educational level of residents is usually correlated with a whole host of related components of neighborhood quality. In particular, highly educated neighborhoods typically have higher quality schools, more diversity in food and grocery options, and lower crime. Scholars have speculated that the prevalence of socioeconomically stratified neighborhoods is contributing to social inequality (see, for example, Putnam 2015). Studying how this joint distribution changes over time should provide some insight into how the neighborhoods where blacks live have changed.

We begin by exploring black neighborhoods overall, focusing on neighborhoods that are at least 20 percent or more (plus) black and those 50 percent or more black, respectively. The first panel of table 8, 20 percent or more black, reflects the rise in the number of people holding a college degree nationwide. In 1970, only 5 percent of the 683 neighborhoods that were at least 20 percent black had a population in which at least 20 percent held a college degree; roughly 1 percent of these neighborhoods featured a population in which 60 percent of the population held a college degree. By 2010, the number of neighborhoods where the population was at least 20 percent black had grown to 839. The fraction of these neighborhoods where at least 20 percent of the residents held a college degree had grown to 29 percent, the fraction in which 40 percent held a college degree was around 11 percent, while the fraction of these neighborhoods where the majority of the population held a college degree had grown to roughly 5 percent.

The lower panel of table 8 focuses on neighborhoods where blacks made up at least 60 percent of the population. Reflecting the broader trends in the United States, we observe steady growth in the share of these neighborhoods with relatively well-educated populations. In 1970, only 2 percent of neighborhoods had a population that was at least 60 percent black in which 20 percent of the population held a college degree; only 1 percent had a population where 60 percent of the population held a college degree. By contrast, in 2010 the fraction of neighborhoods with these characteristics had grown to 28 percent and 5 percent respectively. It's clear that recent concerns surrounding the societal implications of class-based segregation, driven by differences in income and education, very clearly have a racial component as well (see, for example, Putnam 2015). Tracts with large shares of highly educated residents rarely contain large shares of black residents.

Table 9 presents these statistics concentrating only on the riot-affected neighborhoods in the data. These neighborhoods generally lag behind on the share of the population that is

**Table 9.** Evolution of Riot-Affected Neighborhoods

|  | 1970 | 1980 | 1990 | 2000 | 2010 |
|---|---|---|---|---|---|
| **Population at least 20 percent black** | | | | | |
| At least 20 percent college graduates | 0.014 | 0.08 | 0.12 | 0.15 | 0.24 |
| At least 40 percent college graduates | 0.007 | 0.02 | 0.0458 | 0.06 | 0.11 |
| At least 60 percent college graduates | < 0.01 | 0.01 | 0.01 | 0.03 | 0.04 |
| Observations | 283 | 293 | 284 | 270 | 254 |
| **Population at least 60 percent black** | | | | | |
| At least 20 percent college graduates | 0 | 0.05 | 0.10 | 0.16 | 0.24 |
| At least 40 percent college graduates | 0 | 0.008 | 0.02 | 0.02 | 0.07 |
| At least 60 percent college graduates | 0 | < 0.01 | 0 | 0.01 | 0.01 |
| Observations | 243 | 251 | 199 | 169 | 149 |

*Source:* Author's tabulations based on the Neighborhood Change Database, 2010, the 2010 U.S. census (2010b), and the American Community Survey, 2006–2010 (U.S. Census Bureau 2010a).

college educated. For example, in 1970, just over 1 percent of these riot-affected neighborhoods in our data had a population that was at least 20 percent black and had a population where at least 20 percent held college degrees; almost none had populations where at least 50 percent held college degrees. By contrast, in 1970 majority black riot-affected neighborhoods where at least 20 percent of the population held a college degree were nonexistent. By 2010, however, roughly 20 percent of neighborhoods that were at least 20 percent black had a population with 20 percent of their population holding degrees; 11 percent had populations where 40 percent of the population held college degrees; 5 percent of these neighborhoods had populations where 60 percent of the population held degrees.

Turning to the riot-affected neighborhoods that were at least 60 percent black, by 2010, 24 percent had a population that was 20 percent college educated. However, very few of these heavily black riot-affected neighborhoods featured high fractions of college-educated residents: only 7 percent of these neighborhoods had 40 percent or more of their populations that held a college degree, whereas roughly 1 percent featured more than 60 percent of their populations with college degrees. In sum, despite the growth in educational attainment, residents of these neighborhoods typically continue to lag that of black neighborhoods pooled nationally.

## DISCUSSION AND CONCLUSION

This article studies the evolution of black neighborhoods in the decades after the publication of the Kerner Commission report. Focusing on Detroit, Los Angeles, Newark (New Jersey), and Washington, D.C., we match riot locations in these cities with tract-level census data harmonized over five censuses. We use these data to assess how neighborhoods in these areas changed over the period, focusing on a descriptive comparison of the evolution of a set of neighborhoods directly affected by rioting and others not directly affected.

We document a number of interesting stylized facts. First, in the years after the riots, in all riot neighborhoods, especially those that were heavily black, declines on a number of quality-of-life indicators were substantial. Second, the riot-affected neighborhoods in our sample remain among the most economically challenged. In our twenty-first-century look ahead, which is perhaps most pressing, black neighborhoods across cities have tended to appear comparable to riot-affected neighborhoods in these riot-affected cities despite improvements in education among people living in these neighborhoods.

A number of caveats, however, apply to the analysis. The study is descriptive and thus limited in its prescription. In addition, many of the 2010 economic measures potentially reflect the residual effects of the Great Recession and slow recovery thereafter. Because black communities are historically among the most vulnerable, they may have been disproportionately affected.

Nevertheless, the differences in socioeconomic evolution across neighborhood types are present prior to 2010 and illustrate an important conundrum. In the fifty years since the Kerner Commission issued its report, the United States has seen tremendous advancements in educational achievement, access to elite employment, income, and wealth for some blacks—it has even elected a black president. Yet, black neighborhoods, especially those directly affected by the period of rioting studied here, persistently lag the nation as a whole on a number of key dimensions. These neighborhoods typically face greater poverty and unemployment, have lower household income, and have relatively few college graduates. Perhaps more important, convergence across neighborhoods on these measures over the five decades since the Kerner report has been minimal. Within the context of current research, the importance of these findings is clear. A growing body of work shows that place matters for individual economic well-being in large part due to the amenities available in more socioeconomically elite neighborhoods (Chetty and Hendron 2018a, 2018b; Chetty et al. 2014, 2018; Andrews et al. 2017; Islam, Minier, and Ziliak 2015). Improvement of black neighborhoods therefore remains an important policy problem for the nation into the twenty-first century.

In sum, the Kerner Commission report issued a clarion call concerning the disparity in life quality experiences and life chances facing black people as a consequence of institutionalized features of American life. Although many of its fundamental suggestions were never adopted, its lasting legacy remains that it succeeded in making the forceful case that the government indeed had a responsibility and a role to play in mitigating the social and economic harm imposed on blacks by racism and discrimination. The persistent challenges that black neighborhoods face suggest that this argument remains relevant.

**Table A1.** Comparison Cities, by 2010 Population

| City | Population | City | Population |
|---|---|---|---|
| New York | 8,17,5133 | Santa Ana | 316,426 |
| Houston | 3,083,754 | Stockton | 313,180 |
| Chicago | 2,695,249 | Cincinnati | 310,278 |
| Philadelphia | 1,526,006 | Corpus Christi | 308,649 |
| San Antonio | 1,474,691 | Pittsburgh | 305,704 |
| Phoenix | 1,462,370 | Toledo | 302,664 |
| San Diego | 1,335,861 | Riverside | 301,887 |
| Dallas | 1,199,898 | Fort Wayne | 286,137 |
| San Jose | 972,437 | St. Paul | 285,068 |
| Jacksonville | 822,856 | Durham | 267,929 |
| Columbus | 820,334 | Lincoln | 263,313 |
| San Francisco | 805,235 | Buffalo | 261,310 |
| Fort Worth | 767,724 | Plano | 259,753 |
| Charlotte | 763,485 | Henderson | 258,843 |
| Memphis | 714,804 | Lubbock | 255,443 |
| El Paso | 659,098 | Reno | 253,633 |
| Seattle | 608,506 | Madison | 253,089 |
| Las Vegas | 604,364 | Glendale | 248,704 |
| Portland | 601,629 | Chula Vista | 247,101 |
| Denver | 600,158 | St. Petersburg | 246,865 |
| Milwaukee | 594,786 | Tallahassee | 246,698 |
| Oklahoma City | 573,116 | Norfolk | 242,803 |
| Tucson | 545,957 | Chandler | 241,278 |
| Fresno | 533,551 | San Bernardino | 238,536 |
| Omaha | 494,951 | Laredo | 238,152 |
| Mesa | 487,165 | Spokane | 237,577 |
| Kansas City | 472,632 | Winston-Salem | 236,395 |
| Sacramento | 463,193 | Fayetteville | 236,343 |
| Colorado Springs | 438,677 | Garland | 229,252 |
| Virginia Beach | 437,994 | Mobile | 229,085 |
| Raleigh | 430,546 | Shreveport | 227,213 |
| Tulsa | 407,595 | Fontana | 224,883 |
| Miami | 406,587 | Chesapeake | 222,209 |
| Wichita | 399,947 | Hialeah | 222,047 |
| Cleveland | 396,994 | Huntsville | 221,402 |
| Oakland | 390,733 | North Las Vegas | 220,933 |
| Minneapolis | 382,583 | Scottsdale | 218,095 |
| Tampa | 345,751 | Irvine | 217,577 |
| New Orleans | 343,829 | Irving | 216,290 |
| Knoxville | 332,156 | Rochester | 215,084 |
| Greensboro | 328,824 | Fremont | 214,089 |
| Orlando | 320,121 | Brownsville | 212,758 |
| St. Louis | 319,294 | Des Moines | 212,526 |

*Source:* Authors' tabulation based on the 2010 U.S. census (2010b).

## REFERENCES

Andrews, Rodney, Marcus Casey, Bradley Hardy, and Trevon Logan. 2017. "Location Matters: Historical Racial Segregation and Intergenerational Mobility." *Economics Letters* 158 (September): 67–72.

Angrist, Joshua, Parag Pathak, and Christopher Walters. 2013. "Explaining Charter School Effectiveness." *American Economic Journal: Applied Economics* 5(4): 1–27.

Autor, David. 2014. "Skills, Education and the Rise of Earnings Inequality Among the 'Other 99 Percent.'" *Science* 344(6168): 843–51.

Bartik, Timothy J. 2018. "Economic Development Incentives: Who Benefits? Who Pays the Costs? How Can They Be Improved?" *W. E. Upjohn Institute* Technical Report no. 18-034. Kalamazoo, Mich.: W. E. Upjohn Institute for Employment Research. Accessed May 9, 2018. http://research.upjohn.org/cgi/viewcontent.cgi?article=1037&context=up_technicalreports.

Baude, Patrick, Marcus Casey, Eric Hanushek, Gregory Phelan, and Steven Rivkin. 2018. "The Evolution of Charter School Quality." *NBER* working paper no. 20645. Cambridge, Mass. National Bureau of Economic Research.

Billings, Stephen. B., David. J. Deming, and Jonah Rockoff. 2014. "School Segregation, Educational Attainment, and Crime: Evidence from the End of Busing in Charlotte Mecklenburg." *Quarterly Journal of Economics* 129(1): 435–76.

Blank, Rebecca. 2009. "What We Know and Need to Know About Welfare Reform." In *Welfare Reform and Its Long-Term Consequences for America's Poor*, edited by James P. Ziliak. New York: Cambridge University Press.

Busso, Matias, Jesse Gregory, and Patrick Kline. 2013. "Assessing the Incidence and Efficiency of a Prominent Place-Based Policy." *American Economic Review* 103(2): 897–947.

Card, David, Alexandre Mas, and Jesse Rothstein. 2008. "Tipping and the Dynamics of Segregation." *Quarterly Journal of Economics* 123(1): 177–218.

Casey, Marcus. 2018. "The Microdynamics of Racial Transition." Working Paper. Chicago: University of Illinois.

Chetty, Raj, and Nathaniel Hendren. 2018a. "The Impacts of Neighborhoods on Intergenerational Mobility I: Childhood Exposure Effects." *Quarterly Journal of Economics*. Published online February 10. Accessed May 9, 2018. DOI: 10.1093/qje/qjy007.

———. 2018b. "The Impacts of Neighborhoods on Intergenerational Mobility II: County-Level Estimates." *Quarterly Journal of Economics*. Published online February 10. Accessed May 9, 2018. DOI: 10.1093/qje/qjy007.

Chetty, Raj, Nathaniel Hendren, Maggie R. Jones, and Sonya R. Porter. 2018. "Race and Economic Opportunity in the United States: An Intergenerational Perspective." *NBER* working paper no. 24441. Cambridge, Mass. National Bureau of Economic Research.

Chetty, Raj, Nathaniel Hendren, Patrick Kline, and Emmanuel Saez. 2014. "Where Is the Land of Opportunity? The Geography in the United States." *Quarterly Journal of Economics* 129(4): 1553–623.

Collins, William J., and Robert A. Margo. 2004. "The Labor Market Effects of the 1960s Riots." *Brookings-Wharton Papers on Urban Affairs*. Washington, D.C.: Brookings Institution.

Cunningham, Jamein P., and Rob Gillezeau. 2018. "The Effects of the Neighborhood Legal Services Program on Riots and the Wealth of African Americans." *RSF: The Russell Sage Foundation Journal of the Social Sciences* 4(6): 144–57. DOI: 10.7758/RSF.2018.4.6.07.

Currie, Janet. 2006. *The Invisible Safety Net: Protecting Poor Women and Children*. Princeton, N.J.: Princeton University Press.

Cutler, David M., and Edward L. Glaeser. 1997. "Are Ghettos Good or Bad?" *Quarterly Journal of Economics* 112(3): 827–72.

Dynarski, Mark, and Austin Nichols. 2017. "More Findings About School Vouchers and Test Scores, and They Are Still Negative." *Evidence Speaks* report 2, no. 18. Washington, D.C.: Brookings Institution. Accessed May 9, 2018. https://www.brookings.edu/research/more-findings-about-school-vouchers-and-test-scores-and-they-are-still-negative.

Farley, Reynolds. 2018. "Detroit Fifty Years After the Kerner Report: What Has Changed, What Has Not, and Why?" *RSF: The Russell Sage Foundation Journal of the Social Sciences* 4(6): 206–41. DOI: 10.7758/RSF.2018.4.6.10.

Frazier, John W., Eugene L. Tettey-Fio, and Norah F. Henry, eds. 2016. *Race, Ethnicity, and Place in a*

*Changing America*, 3rd ed. Albany: State University of New York Press.

Garces, Eliana, Duncan Thomas, and Janet Currie. 2002. "Longer-Term Effects of Head Start." *American Economic Review* 92(4): 999–1012.

Hoynes, Hillary, Diane Schanzenbach, and Douglas Almond. 2016. "Long-Run Impacts of Childhood Access to the Safety Net." *American Economic Review* 106(4): 903–34.

Hyra, Derek. 2012. "Conceptualizing the New Urban Renewal: Comparing the Past to the Present." *Urban Affairs Review* 48(4): 498–512.

Islam, Tonmoy, Jenny Minier, and James P. Ziliak. 2015. "On Persistent Poverty in a Rich Country." *Southern Economic Journal* 8(3): 653–78.

Kerner Commission. 1968. *Report of the National Advisory Commission on Civil Disorders*. Washington: Government Printing Office.

Ladd, Helen. 1994. "Spacially Targeted Economic Development Strategies: Do They Work?" *Cityscape* 1(1): 193–218.

Loessberg, Rick, and John Koskinen. 2018. "Measuring the Distance: The Legacy of the Kerner Report." *RSF: The Russell Sage Foundation Journal of the Social Sciences* 4(6): 99–119. DOI: 10.7758/RSF.2018.4.6.05.

Massey, Douglas S. 2015. "The Legacy of the 1968 Fair Housing Act." *Sociological Forum* 30(S1): 571–88.

Massey, Douglas S., and Nany A. Denton. 1993. *American Apartheid: Segregation and the Making of the Underclass*. Cambridge, Mass.: Harvard University Press.

Neumark, David, and Jed Kolko. 2010. "Do Enterprise Zones Create Jobs? Evidence from California's Enterprise Zone Program." *Journal of Urban Economics* 68(1): 1–19.

Neumark, David, and Helen Simpson. 2014. "Place-Based Policies." *NBER* working paper no. 20049. Cambridge, Masss.: National Bureau of Economic Research.

Olzak, Susan, Suzanne Shanahan, and Elizabeth H. McEneaney. 1996. "Poverty, Segregation, and Race Riots: 1960 to 1993." *American Sociological Review* 61 (August): 590–613.

Putnam, Robert. 2015. *Our Kids: The American Dream in Crisis*. New York: Simon and Schuster.

Rugh, Jacob S., and Douglas S. Massey. 2014. "Segregation in Post-Civil Rights: Stalled Integration or End of the Segregated Century?" *The DuBois Review: Social Science Research on Race* 11 (2): 205–32.

Russell, Judith. 2004. *Economics, Bureaucracy, and Race: How Keynesians Misguided the War on Poverty*. New York: Columbia University Press.

Semega, Jessica L., Kayla R. Fontenot, and Melissa A. Kollar. 2017. "Income and Poverty in the United States: 2016." *Current Population Reports* no. P60–259. Washington: Government Printing Office.

Shaefer, H. Luke, Kathryn Edin, and Elizabeth Talbert. 2015. "Understanding the Dynamics of $2-a-Day Poverty in the United States." *RSF: The Russell Sage Journal of the Social Sciences* 1(1): 120–38.

U.S. Census Bureau. 2010a. "Summary File, 2006–2010, American Community Survey." American Factfinder. Accessed August 1, 2017. http://factfinder.census.gov.

———. 2010b. "2010 Census Summary File 1." American Factfinder. Accessed August 1, 2017. http://factfinder.census.gov.

Ziliak, James P. 2016. "Temporary Assistance for Needy Families." In *Economics of Means-Tested Transfer Programs in the United States*, vol. 1, edited by Robert A. Moffitt, Chicago: University of Chicago Press.

# Detroit Fifty Years After the Kerner Report: What Has Changed, What Has Not, and Why?

REYNOLDS FARLEY

*Immediately after the Detroit violence of July 1967, President Johnson appointed the Kerner Commission and ordered it to determine what had happened, why, and what could be done to prevent urban riots. This analysis focuses on racial change in metropolitan Detroit. Progress has been made in racially integrating the suburban ring closed to African Americans at the time of the violence. Evidence indicates social integration in that interracial marriage is more common and blacks are more represented in prestigious occupations. However, on key economic measures, African Americans are now further behind whites than they were in 1967. This can be attributed to fundamental changes in employment and the failure of the educational system to provide the training needed for jobs in the new economy.*

**Keywords:** Kerner Commission, racial segregation, Detroit, racial gaps, civil rights movement

No city has played a larger role in the struggle for civil rights than Detroit. As soon as President Thomas Jefferson appointed the first federal judge for the Michigan territory in the early nineteenth century, litigation began about whether slaves held in the British era could be kept in bondage. Shortly after Judge Augustus Woodward arrived in 1805, he ruled that a Michigan slave who had lived in Canada and then returned to Detroit was a free person (Miles 2017, 177–83). When Michigan became a state, it enacted Black Code legislation that required African Americans to post $500 and demonstrate their freedom before entering the state, a law that was not enforced. When the public schools were established in the state, they were restricted to white children, but Detroit activists challenged this in the courts as early as 1840. Detroit is the nation's only city where the federal military has been deployed on the streets four times to prevent whites and blacks from killing each other, twice in both the nineteenth and the twentieth centuries.

The U.S. Supreme Court overturned the use of restrictive covenants in property deeds based on litigation initiated by the McGhee family who sought to remain in their home on Detroit's Seabalt Street.[1] Key organizational and

---

Reynolds Farley is research scientist at the Population Studies Center and Otis Dudley Duncan Professor Emeritus at the University of Michigan.

© 2018 Russell Sage Foundation. Farley, Reynolds. 2018. "Detroit Fifty Years After the Kerner Report: What Has Changed, What Has Not, and Why?" *RSF: The Russell Sage Foundation Journal of the Social Sciences* 4(6): 206–41. DOI: 10.7758/RSF.2018.4.6.10. Direct correspondence to: Reynolds Farley at renf@umich.edu, University of Michigan, Institute for Social Research, 426 Thompson St., Ann Arbor, MI 48105.

Open Access Policy: *RSF: The Russell Sage Foundation Journal of the Social Sciences* is an open access journal. This article is published under a Creative Commons Attribution-NonCommercial-NoDerivs 3.0 Unported License.

1. *Shelley et ux. v. Kraemer et ux. McGhee et ux. v. Sipes et al.*, 334 U.S. 1 (1948).

financial support for the August 1963 March on Washington came largely from the Detroit's United Auto Workers Union. Both Dr. Martin Luther King Jr. and Malcolm X gave their most famous orations in Detroit, King's "I Have a Dream" speech in June 1963 and Malcolm X's "Message to the Masses" that November. It is no surprise that the Kerner report came about in response to events in Detroit.

## THE BEGINNING OF THE DETROIT VIOLENCE

Early on Sunday morning, July 23, 1967, Detroit police entered an illegal after-hours drinking place know as a "blind pig" at the corner of Twelfth Street and Clairmount expecting to find a few patrons who could then easily be arrested for violating liquor laws, booked, and quickly released. Instead, they found eighty-two people celebrating the return of a soldier from Vietnam. The arrestees were held on Twelfth Street until police located enough vans to take them away. A crowd quickly gathered and taunted the officers. Looting started shortly thereafter. By late that Sunday, Michigan Governor George Romney ordered 1,200 Michigan National Guardsmen—later increased to eight thousand—to the streets of Detroit.

After the violence escalated on Monday, President Lyndon Johnson dispatched federal paratroopers, who arrived on the streets just after midnight Tuesday morning—the first time since the Detroit riot of 1943 that federal troops had been marshaled to put down urban racial violence (Zelizer 2016, xv). By Wednesday, July 26, the violence had ended but forty-three Detroit residents were dead—thirty-three blacks and ten whites (Kerner Report 1968, 84–103; McGraw 2017b, 2017c; Fine 1989, chapter 7). A month earlier, similar rioting in Newark resulted in twenty-three deaths. The previous summer, National Guardsmen had been called to African American neighborhoods in Chicago and Cleveland to curtail racial violence. A pattern of summer urban riots appeared to be emerging.

On July 28, 1967—just two days after the Detroit violence ended—President Johnson issued Executive Order 11365, establishing the National Advisory Commission on Civil Disorders, with Illinois Governor Otto Kerner as chair and Mayor John Lindsay of New York as vice chair (hence the more familiar Kerner Commission and Kerner report). Johnson asked the commissioners to determine what happened, why it happened, and what could be done to prevent it from occurring again. Moving with alacrity, the commission released its final report on February 29, 1968—one of the most provocative, far-reaching, and unexpected reports ever issued by a federal commission.

Commissioners devoted exceptional attention to Detroit for a variety of reasons. The largest of the World War II racial riots occurred in Detroit in June 1943 and culminated in the deaths of thirty-four residents (Capeci and Wilkerson 1991; Baime 2014, 245–48). By the 1960s, it was becoming obvious that the invasion of the "crabgrass frontier" (Jackson 1985)—that is, the development of suburban rings—provoked a tremendous migration of whites away from neighborhoods in older cities. This created increasingly African American cities surrounded by white suburbs. Democrats depended on both urban and suburban votes to sustain their national power. They realized the possibility for racial violence but hoped that federal investments might improve older cities and keep their voters in the Democrat column. In Detroit, they found an opportunity in 1961 when the city elected Jerry Cavanaugh its mayor, a seemingly talented young liberal who resembled Jack Kennedy. In the Kennedy and Johnson years, generous federal funds flowed to Motown with the expectation that it would become the model city for racial harmony and economic prosperity (Fine 1989, chap. 4; McGraw 2017a).

The Kerner Commission stressed the denial of equal treatment as the fundamental cause of urban violence. African Americans were targeted for abuse by the police, denied opportunities for education, and unable to compete fairly in the labor market because of discrimination. Underlying these racial inequities was the denial of opportunities in the housing market. Racial residential segregation, imposed largely by discriminatory practices and abetted consistently by federal and local government policies, allowed police to target African Americans, kept blacks out of areas where the new jobs were emerging and ensured that black children went to inferior and less well-financed schools. The Kerner commissioners viewed residential segregation as a linchpin maintaining the racial dominance of whites.

This essay describes what has happened in metropolitan Detroit regarding the key issues raised by the Kerner report:

> How far have we come?
>
> What worked and what did not work?
>
> What are the implications for the twenty-first century?

## RESIDENTIAL SEGREGATION AND THE INTEGRATION OF DETROIT'S SUBURBS

The most frequently cited conclusion of the Kerner Commission report was the statement that, if current trends continued, the nation would within two decades be riven by race, whites in suburbs and smaller cities and blacks concentrated in large central cities (Kerner Report 1968, 407). The commissioners were likely thinking about metropolitan Detroit when they drafted that warning. The Detroit suburban ring in 1970 was home to 2.7 million residents and included ten African American suburban enclaves. Beyond those segregated areas, African Americans made up only 0.5 percent of the suburban population.[2] The most influential book on racial residential segregation is Douglas Massey and Nancy Denton's *American Apartheid* (1993). That title appropriately describes metropolitan Detroit at the time of the violence.

Detroit was not racially segregated until after World War I. A few prosperous African Americans lived where they wished, but a larger number of low-income blacks lived east of downtown alongside immigrants from Eastern Europe (Katzman 1973). After the massive in-migration of Southerners to fill defense industry jobs during World War I, a pervasive system of Jim Crow segregation emerged for the first time (Zunz 1982). Many whites feared that if blacks came to their neighborhoods, property values would plummet, women and daughters would be at risk of violence, and school quality would decline. Detroit's real estate practices and restrictive covenants created an American apartheid residential pattern across the city. The most famous civil rights trial of the 1920s concerned Dr. Ossian Sweet—an African American physician who had purchased a home on the East Side. When hostile crowds attacked it in 1925 and the police did not protect it, Sweet and his brother defended the residence. A shot came from the home and one person in the crowd died. Sweet and his companions were immediately arrested and charged with murder. The NAACP recognized the importance of upholding the principal that a homeowner has the right to defend his property against mayhem. With the help of Clarence Darrow, Sweet was eventually exonerated, but his victory was Pyrrhic. African Americans were reminded that moving into a white neighborhood was possible but dangerous (Boyle 2004; Vine 2004; Boyd 2017, 109–11).

During the 1920s, restrictive covenants were written into the deeds of most new housing in the city and federal agencies, in the next decade, introduced redlining, isolating whites from blacks. By World War II, most of Detroit's 172,000 blacks lived in an East Side ghetto along Hastings Street, a West Side ghetto, and a small pocket in northwest Detroit separated from white neighbors by a quarter-mile six-foot wall built for the purpose of maintaining segregation (Rothstein 2017, 58; Schwartz 2017). Real estate broker guidelines stated that it was unethical to introduce a minority family to a white neighborhood. The first racial riot of World War II broke out in Detroit in February 1942. The federal government had erected housing for defense workers on a segregated basis and designated the Sojourner Truth Homes in northern Detroit for African Americans. Those homes, however, were close to white neighborhoods, whose residents fiercely opposed the housing and used force to keep African Ameri-

---

2. Demographic and economic data cited were, unless otherwise noted, obtained from public use files of data from the Census Bureau's American Community Survey, Current Population Survey, and decennial censuses accessed at the University of Minnesota Integrated Public Use Microdata Series (Ruggles et al. 2017) and at Queens University's Social Explorer (https://www.socialexplorer.com, accessed May 21, 2018).

cans out. After a six-week standoff, the federal and state governments mobilized police forces to allow blacks to enter their homes (Thomas 1992, 143–48; Jenkins 1991, 408–17).

Thomas Sugrue explains the battles for racial dominance in Detroit neighborhoods after World War II (1996). Because the defense industries paid high wages, Detroit's blacks, by national standards, were affluent. In Detroit, unlike in many other cities, African Americans had the resources to purchase homes commensurate with their prosperous economic status. During the war, workers were forced to save because durable goods and new homes were unavailable, setting the stage for racial contention throughout the city. With the ending of restrictive covenants, blacks bought homes in white neighborhoods. In a few locations, such as Sherwood Forest, Palmer Woods, Boston Edison, and Indian Village, integration occurred, and those neighborhoods remain peacefully integrated (Rodwan 2017). These were the exceptions. More frequently, whites fought diligently to preserve the racial purity of their neighborhoods. More than two hundred acts of violence were recorded against blacks moving into white Detroit neighborhoods after World War II. In 1958, the Michigan Civil Rights Commission concluded that almost all blacks who attempted to move into Detroit's white suburbs had been harassed or threatened (Rothstein 2017, 146).

By the mid-1950s, whites realized an attractive alternative to defending their neighborhoods from racial invasion. After World War II, the federal government developed housing policies to stimulate the economy, enabling moderate- and low-income households to purchase new homes for small down payments and modest monthly fees using government-insured loans. Veterans could do so for even smaller cash outlays. These programs, however, ended up maximizing segregation. In no other metropolis were suburban officials and residents as diligent and thorough when it came to blatantly telling African Americans that they were not welcome in the crabgrass frontier. Orville Hubbard, mayor of Dearborn for thirty years, became a well-known national symbol of suburban resistance to African Americans, thwarting government attempts to build defense-worker housing in Dearborn during World War II and preventing Metropolitan Life from constructing a large development because he feared they would be "soft" on segregation (Good 1989; Freund 2007, chap. 7). For decades, he kept Dearborn "lily white" but had no objection to blacks who were live-in servants. The Grosse Pointes became nationally known for their effective and highly organized point system. Anyone seeking to live in those five prosperous suburbs was required to apply to the Grosse Pointe Brokers Association, to be evaluated, and to have a certain minimum ranking on a point system. A detective investigated the candidate, after which a secret committee from the Brokers Association assigned points (Thomas 1966). Asians, blacks, and Mexicans were excluded without consideration.

Just a month before the July 1967 violence, Carado Bailey, a black Vietnam veteran and his white wife moved into the suburb of Warren. For three nights, hostile crowds surrounded the home. On the fourth night, the police sealed the area. The white press barely covered the incident. The African American media did, however, and the black community consensus was that the Warren police, rather than controlling the hostile white protestors, abetted them (Killeen 2018; Fine 1989, chap. 4).

August Comte is credited with the phrase "demography is destiny." Figures 1 through 4 illustrate the population trends that influenced the Kerner Commission and report what has unfolded more recently. Figure 1 describes the rapid growth of metropolitan Detroit as it became known, in then President Franklin Roosevelt's words in a 1940 speech, as the "Arsenal of Democracy." The area's overall population reached a high in 1980 but since then has stagnated. Its white population had peaked in 1970 but declined as a consequence of much lower birth rates and out-migration until, by 2016, it was one million smaller than at the time of the violence. The black population peaked about 2000, then declined, and is now about 5 percent smaller.

Figure 2 reports population trends for the city of Detroit, a municipality that has annexed no new area since 1926. Its peak census count was tallied in 1950, when, with just fewer than

**Figure 1.** Population of the Three-County Detroit Metro Area (in Thousands)

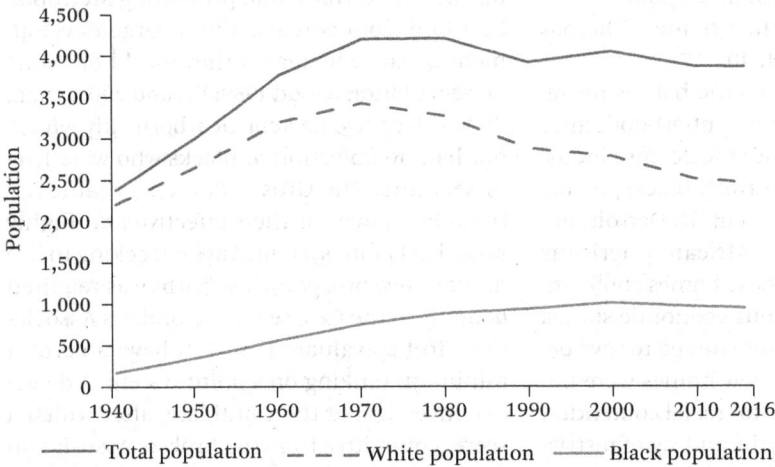

*Source:* Author's calculations based on public use data from the Census Bureau's decennial censuses and the American Community Survey. Data accessed at University of Minnesota Integrated Public Use Microdata Samples (Ruggles et al. 2017) and at Queens University's Social Explorer (www.social explorer.com, accessed May 21, 2018).

**Figure 2.** Population of the City of Detroit (in Thousands)

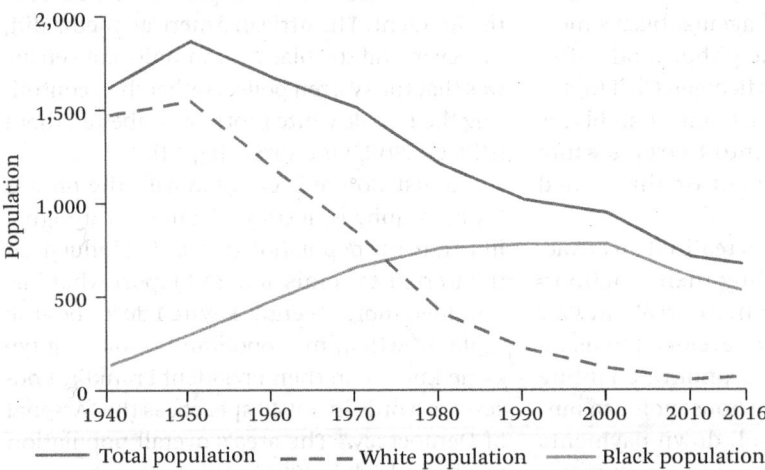

*Source:* Author's calculations based on public use data from the Census Bureau's decennial censuses and the American Community Survey. Data accessed at University of Minnesota Integrated Public Use Microdata Samples (Ruggles et al. 2017) and at Queens University's Social Explorer (www.social explorer.com, accessed May 21, 2018).

two million residents, it was the nation's fourth largest city. Only New York, Chicago, and Philadelphia were larger. The government's housing policies and the National Defense Highway system encouraged an out-migration of whites and, by 2016, the city's white population was only 3 percent what it had been in 1950. The black population, meanwhile, grew rapidly until 1970 and then slowly peaked in the mid-1990s. After that, black out-migration acceler-

**Figure 3.** Population of the Three-County Detroit Suburban Ring (in Thousands)

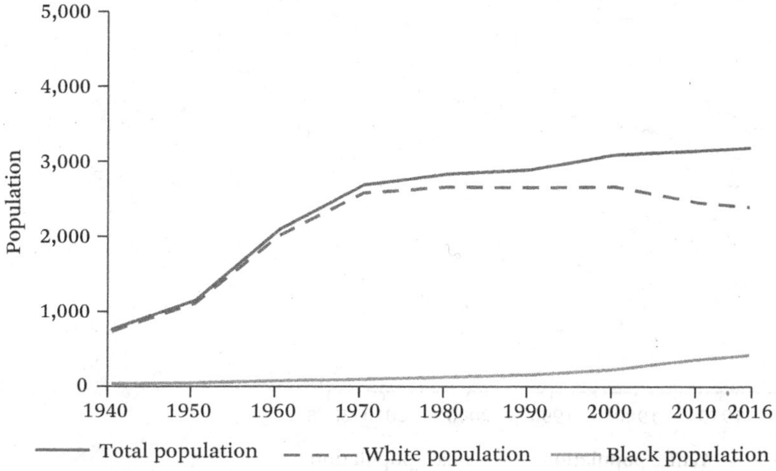

*Source:* Author's calculations based on public use data from the Census Bureau's decennial censuses and the American Community Survey. Data accessed at University of Minnesota Integrated Public Use Microdata Samples (Ruggles et al. 2017) and at Queens University's Social Explorer (www.socialexplorer.com, accessed May 21, 2018).

ated and, by 2016, the number of black city residents had dropped by a quarter million.

Figure 3 graphs the suburban population's rapid growth from 1950 to 1980 and subsequent slow growth or stagnation. Most significant in terms of the Kerner Commission warning is the opening of Detroit's suburbs to African Americans. The suburban black population had seen some growth before 1990 but it was concentrated in ten segregated suburban pockets. Since 1990, it has grown rapidly. Indeed, the total suburban population would now be declining rather rapidly were it not for the in-migration of African Americans, primarily from the city of Detroit.

Anthony Downs drafted the component of the Kerner report describing the future of cities (Gillon 2018, 217). Five years later, he published *Opening the Suburbs*, a widely cited and influential volume that reiterated many ideas of the Kerner report (Downs 1973). Ending the barriers that kept blacks out of suburbs, he argued, would facilitate their economic and social mobility. Figure 4 shows the proportion of the metropolitan population living in the suburbs. At the outset of World War II, that was one in three residents. By the time of the Kerner report, it was two in three. The proportion continues to rise, albeit slowly. The pattern of suburbanization differs greatly by race, however. By 1970, 75 percent of whites were in the suburbs. By 2010, 98 percent were. At the time of the Detroit violence, about one metropolitan black in eight lived in a suburban African American enclave. This changed little until 1990. Then the suburbs opened, and African Americans moved from the city to the ring in substantial numbers just as whites did in earlier decades. By 2016, 44 percent of metropolitan African Americans were suburban residents. Detroit's suburban ring now has a larger black population—420,000—than the black population of all but four central cities: New York, Chicago, Philadelphia, and Detroit.

### Traditional Measures of Racial Residential Segregation

For six decades, demographers have assessed racial segregation using the index of dissimilarity. This measures whether blacks and whites are living in the same neighborhoods, but it does not assess social contacts. Figure 5 displays indexes measuring the segregation of whites from blacks from 1940 to the present for the entire three-county metropolis for the city of Detroit and for its suburban ring. A score of

**Figure 4.** Percent of the Metro Detroit Population Living in Suburban Ring

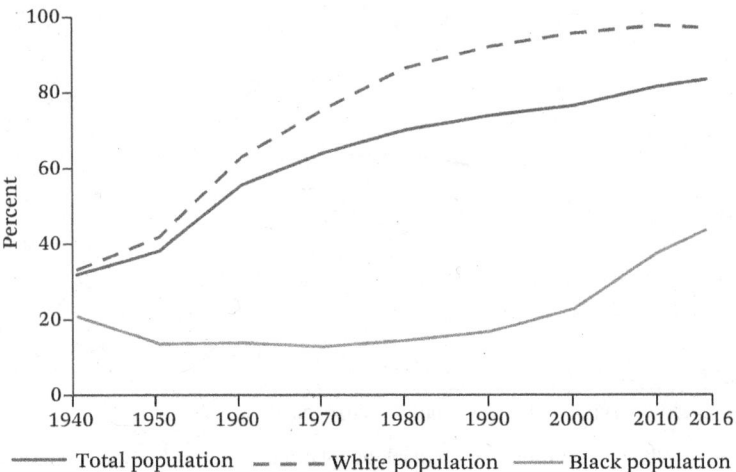

*Source:* Author's calculations based on public use data from the Census Bureau's decennial censuses and the American Community Survey. Data accessed at University of Minnesota Integrated Public Use Microdata Samples (Ruggles et al. 2017) and at Queens University's Social Explorer (www.social explorer.com, accessed May 21, 2018).

**Figure 5.** Residential Segregation of Whites from Blacks, Index of Dissimilarity

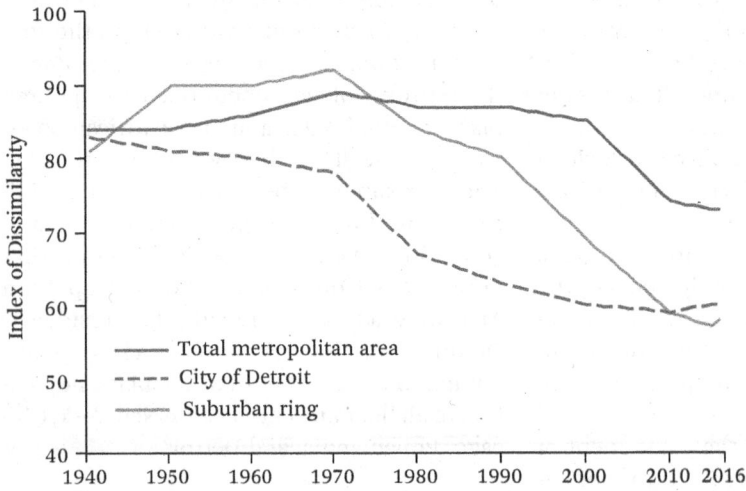

*Source:* Author's calculations based on public use data from the Census Bureau's decennial censuses and the American Community Survey. Data accessed at University of Minnesota Integrated Public Use Microdata Samples (Ruggles et al. 2017) and at Queens University's Social Explorer (www.social explorer.com, accessed May 21, 2018).

100 would indicate that every neighborhood was either exclusively white or exclusively black—that is, total apartheid. These data refer to blacks and whites from 1940 to 1970 and non-Hispanic whites and non-Hispanic blacks since then. The most recent data for census tracts were gathered by the Census Bureau in the 2012 to 2016 interval. Census tracts are generally considered neighborhoods in urban research.

Residential segregation peaked in 1970, when

**Figure 6.** Average Percentage Black Residents in Census Tract of Typical White

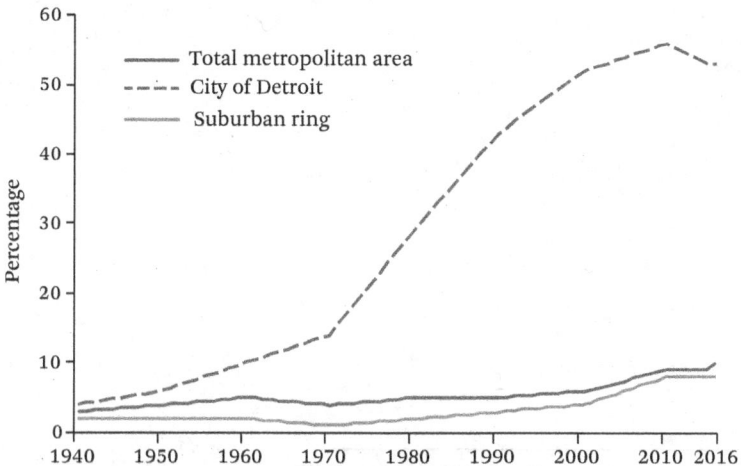

*Source:* Author's calculations based on public use data from the Census Bureau's decennial censuses and the American Community Survey. Data accessed at University of Minnesota Integrated Public Use Microdata Samples (Ruggles et al. 2017) and at Queens University's Social Explorer (www.social explorer.com, accessed May 21, 2018).

the score for the Detroit metropolitan area was 89. That is, either 89 percent of whites or 89 percent of blacks would have to move from one neighborhood to another to bring about an even residential distribution of the races. Segregation in the metropolis declined moderately after 1970. The city was most segregated in 1940 and has slowly become more integrated. As blacks moved into formerly white neighborhoods following the demise of restrictive covenants, the city's segregation score dropped. The long-term trend toward more integration continued and the score fell to 60 in 2016.

Segregation in the suburban ring peaked in 1970 with a score of 92, but then declined, especially after 1990, as middle-class blacks migrated to the suburbs. By 2016, the suburban segregation score declined to 57. Douglas Massey and Nancy Denton describe scores of lower than 60 as indicating moderate segregation (1993). Detroit's suburban ring has gone from hyper to moderate segregation in the decades since the Kerner report. The segregation score for the entire metropolitan area is higher than the score for either the city or the suburban ring because of the substantial racial differences in the composition of these different areas.

Figure 6 reports the average percentage of black residents living in the census tract of the typical white and suggests that segregation has by no means disappeared. Indeed, the segregation score for the entire metropolitan area remains high. Since the 1970s, African Americans have made up one-quarter of the metropolitan population. Whites who remained in the city saw sharp rises in the proportion of black neighbors, but the suburbs have also changed. In 1970, the typical suburban white lived in a neighborhood where only 1 percent of the residents were black. Forty-six years later, that number was 8 percent.

Figure 7 shows the average percentage white in the neighborhood of the typical black for the city of Detroit and the suburban ring. In the city in 1940, African Americans resided in census tracts where, on average, 40 percent of the residents were white. This changed rapidly as whites moved away from the city, and in 2010, African Americans in Detroit lived in neighborhoods where, on average, only 5 percent of the residents were white.

The suburbanization of African Americans in recent decades produced a large city-suburban difference on this index of racial mixing at the neighborhood level. In the city, blacks have few white neighbors, but the 44 percent

**Figure 7.** Average Percentage White Residents in Census Tract of Typical Black

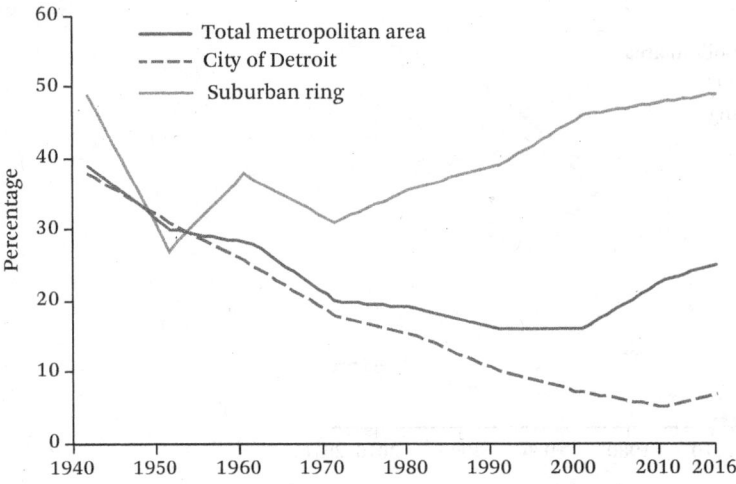

*Source:* Author's calculations based on public use data from the Census Bureau's decennial censuses and the American Community Survey. Data accessed at University of Minnesota Integrated Public Use Microdata Samples (Ruggles et al. 2017) and at Queens University's Social Explorer (www.social explorer.com, accessed May 21, 2018).

of metropolitan blacks who live in the suburban ring are typically residents of neighborhoods where half the residents are white (for an analysis of neighborhood changes in other cities with 1967 era violence, see Casey and Hardy 2018).

**The Suburban Migration of Middle-Class African Americans**

The exodus of whites from Detroit occurred on a selective basis: the most prosperous moved to the suburbs first, followed later by those with middle or lower incomes. The same economic selectivity characterizes African American suburbanization. Figures 8 and 9 sort white and black households into six economic groups from impoverished to comfortable (household incomes five or more times the poverty line). The poverty line, in 2017, was $24,900 for a family of four, so an income of $125,000 qualified a family of four for the comfortable status. Figures 8 and 9 show the percentage of households in each economic category living in the suburbs rather than in the city. Data are shown for 1980 and 2016.

By 1980, virtually all economically successful white households were in the suburbs. Among whites below the poverty line, however, more than one in four lived in the city. A generation later, in 2016, almost all whites—98 percent—lived in the ring regardless of their economic well-being. In 1980, the American apartheid system closed suburbs to African Americans, so most blacks lived in the city regardless of income. That changed over time. By 2016, most middle-income and economically comfortable African Americans had suburban addresses. This out-migration will likely continue as Detroit blacks seek to live in places that are perceived to have more effective schools, to be safer, and to have better city services and much lower property tax rates (Williams 2015).

The relatively low segregation score for the Detroit suburban ring in 2016 is surprising given the long history of extreme racial hostility. Just after the 1967 violence, suburban Dearborn Mayor Hubbard called the participants "mad dogs" and offered advice to his constituents: "learn to shoot, shoot straight and learn to be a dead shot." He then had his suburb fund courses for housewives in how to use shotguns, handguns, and rifles (Serrin 1969). Following passage of the Fair Housing Act, Dearborn voters approved an ordinance that limited use of their parks to city residents (Barrow 1986) and Grosse Pointe Park proposed building a wall at

**Figure 8.** Percent of Detroit Metropolitan-Area Whites Living in Suburban Ring

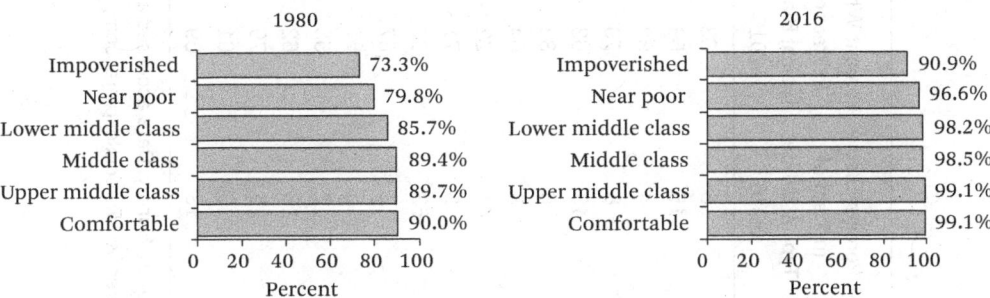

*Source:* Author's calculations based on public use data from the Census Bureau's decennial censuses and the American Community Survey. Data accessed at University of Minnesota Integrated Public Use Microdata Samples (Ruggles et al. 2017) and at Queens University's Social Explorer (www.social explorer.com, accessed May 21, 2018).
*Note:* Impoverished: incomes below the poverty line. Near poor: incomes 100 to 199 percent of poverty line. Lower middle class: incomes 200 to 299 percent of poverty line. Middle class: incomes 300 to 399 percent of poverty line. Upper middle class: incomes 400 to 499 percent of poverty line. Comfortable: at least five times the poverty line.

**Figure 9.** Percent of Detroit Metropolitan-Area Blacks Living in Suburban Ring

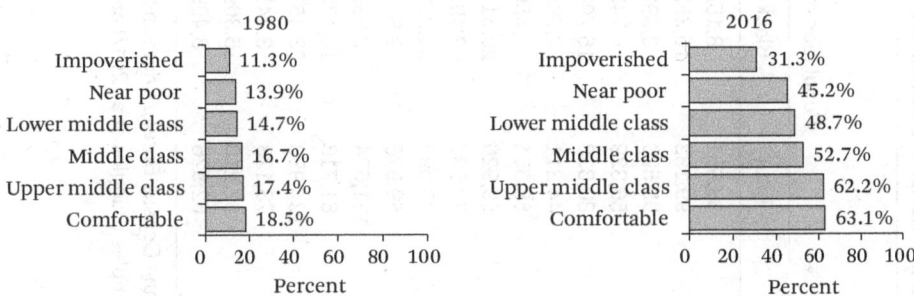

*Source:* Author's calculations based on public use data from the Census Bureau's decennial censuses and the American Community Survey. Data accessed at University of Minnesota Integrated Public Use Microdata Samples (Ruggles et al. 2017) and at Queens University's Social Explorer (www.social explorer.com, accessed May 21, 2018).
*Note:* Impoverished: incomes below the poverty line. Near poor: incomes 100 to 199 percent of poverty line. Lower middle class: incomes 200 to 299 percent of poverty line. Middle class: incomes 300 to 399 percent of poverty line. Upper middle class: incomes 400 to 499 percent of poverty line. Comfortable: at least five times the poverty line.

their border with Detroit, ostensibly for flood control (Wilkinson 1986).

It is important to determine whether suburbs with substantial African American populations at present are residentially integrated or are pockets of largely black neighborhoods surrounded by exclusively white neighborhoods. I calculated segregation scores for those thirteen suburbs of Detroit with fifty thousand or more residents where in 2016 at least 5 percent of the residents were black (see table 1). Two suburbs notorious for their strenuous efforts to bar blacks—Dearborn and the Grosse Pointes—were included.

The strategies that kept blacks out were highly effective, as shown in the population figures for 1970: Dearborn had more than 100,000 residents but only 13 African Ameri-

**Table 1.** Racial Change in Large Detroit Suburbs 1970 to 2016 and Racial Residential Segregation Scores for 2016

| Suburb | Population in 1970 Total | Population in 1970 Black | Population in 2016 Total | Population in 2016 Black | Percent Black | Index of Dissimilarity | Percent Black in Tract of Typical White, 2016 | Percent White in Tract of Typical Black, 2016 |
|---|---|---|---|---|---|---|---|---|
| Canton Township | 48,616 | 64 | 89,651 | 8,150 | 9 | 32 | 8 | 63 |
| Clinton Township | 72,400 | 163 | 99,193 | 16,353 | 16 | 32 | 15 | 69 |
| Dearborn | 104,137 | 13 | 95,520 | 3,693 | 4 | 44 | 4 | 82 |
| Dearborn Heights | 80,083 | 12 | 56,329 | 4,748 | 8 | 31 | 8 | 79 |
| Farmington Hills | 62,270 | 84 | 80,338 | 15,708 | 20 | 19 | 19 | 63 |
| The 5 Grosse Pointes | 58,708 | 96 | 44,311 | 2,585 | 5 | 47 | 6 | 83 |
| Novi | 9,668 | 7 | 58,351 | 4,558 | 8 | 29 | 8 | 64 |
| Pontiac | 76,715 | 22760 | 59,920 | 29,511 | 49 | 35 | 41 | 22 |
| Rochester Hills | NA | | 72,987 | 3,495 | 5 | 34 | 5 | 71 |
| Southfield | 69,129 | 64 | 73,093 | 51,283 | 70 | 28 | 63 | 22 |
| St. Clair Shores | 88,083 | 167 | 59,976 | 2,843 | 5 | 39 | 5 | 87 |
| Sterling Heights | 61,530 | 69 | 131,674 | 6,835 | 5 | 27 | 5 | 81 |
| Taylor | 70,082 | 63 | 61,716 | 10,470 | 17 | 47 | 12 | 55 |
| Warren | 178,234 | 129 | 134,998 | 23,455 | 17 | 37 | 15 | 62 |
| Waterford Township | 59,123 | 33 | 73,123 | 3,745 | 5 | 32 | 5 | 79 |
| Westland | 86,655 | 2255 | 82,218 | 15,309 | 19 | 37 | 16 | 61 |
| West Bloomfield Township | 41,962 | 100 | 62,926 | 8,499 | 14 | 32 | 13 | 69 |

*Source:* Author's calculations based on public use data from the Census Bureau's decennial censuses and the American Community Survey. Data accessed at University of Minnesota Integrated Public Use Microdata Samples (Ruggles et al. 2017) and at Queens University's Social Explorer (www.socialexplorer.com, accessed May 21, 2018).

cans; Farmington Hills' 62,000 residents was also home to 84 blacks; in Warren only 129 of the 178,000 residents were African American. That changed. Dearborn now has almost 4,000 black residents, Farmington Hills has 15,000, and Warren has 23,000. Southfield, a prosperous suburb contiguous to Detroit, underwent the change some demographers predicted would happen with African American suburbanization. Its black population rose to 51,000 and African Americans now make up 70 percent of the total residents.

The suburban white population has been declining since the 1970s due to both the aging of the population and declining economic opportunities. The black population has grown, however. This demographic shift had the unexpected consequences of promoting the residential integration that Kerner commissioners advocated. The indexes of black-white residential segregation shown in table 1 for Detroit suburbs for 2016 are revealing. All of them are relatively low, indeed, very low in the Detroit context where, for decades segregation scores of 85 to 90 were the norm (Massey and Denton 1989). Southfield, which has the largest African American population, is relatively integrated, having a segregation score of 28, a score that Massey and Denton would consider low. Warren, which lies in the heart of Macomb Country where the Reagan Democrats propelled Ronald Reagan to the presidency in 1980, has a score of 37. Farmington Hills' score is 22. Even Dearborn and the Grosse Pointes have scores under 50. Table 1 reports that, by 2016, whether African Americans made up a large proportion of a suburb's population, as in Pontiac and Southfield, or a small percent as in Dearborn and Sterling Heights, the suburbs are not highly racially segregated.

Given the history of racial exclusion and hostility, could the suburbs now be only moderately segregated? Could there be so much racial change in one generation? Are the moderate and low segregation scores misleading? Perhaps within these suburbs, many block or block groups are exclusively African American but scattered within the larger census tracts. If so, using smaller geographic units such as block groups will produce much higher segregation scores.[3] Block groups in the Detroit ring average 1,300 residents. For the entirety of Oakland County, the segregation score computed from census tract data for 2012 to 2016 was 64; when computed from the smaller block groups, it was 68. For Macomb County, the census tract index of segregation was 48; the block group index was 57. Apparently no "Dalmatian" pattern of segregation is found within these suburban counties.

Are Detroit's suburbs becoming racially integrated? Does that mean that the eighty-one thousand school-age African American children who live in the ring attend integrated schools? That is a more challenging question to answer because the boundaries of Michigan school districts seldom correspond to municipal boundaries. The three-county Detroit metropolis includes eighty-two public school districts. I considered the twelve largest suburban districts as well as Grosse Pointe and their enrollment data by race from the Common Core of School Data for the 2015–2016 academic year (National Center for Education Statistics 2018). The index of dissimilarity was used to assess racial segregation with individual public schools as units. The findings are shown in table 2.

Since 1990, middle-class blacks have moved into Detroit's traditionally white suburbs and now live in what most would define as racially integrated neighborhoods. Many of them, it appears, enroll their children in racially integrated public schools, quite unlike the situation in the city, where the schools enroll very few white students. In the large suburban school districts considered here, the segregation scores range from a low of 12 in the Farmington and Troy districts to a high of 45 in Dearborn.

This does not mean that all suburban school districts are thoroughly integrated. Many of the smaller school districts enroll few African Americans, and the indexes reported here do not measure possible segregation within individual schools. Race is still a salient issue in suburban schools and two suburban school districts: East Detroit and Southfield lost many

---

3. Data reporting the racial composition of city blocks provide the most precise assessment of residential segregation. They are available only from decennial censuses.

**Table 2.** Large Suburban Detroit School Districts: Enrollment by Race in 2015 and Racial Segregation Scores

| School District | Total Enrollment | Percent African American | Index of School Segregation | Percent Black in School of Typical White | Percent White in School of Typical Black |
|---|---|---|---|---|---|
| Utica | 27,758 | 5 | 26 | 5 | 85 |
| Dearborn | 19,757 | 3 | 45 | 3 | 87 |
| Plymouth Canton | 17,177 | 10 | 24 | 9 | 67 |
| Chippewa Valley | 16,658 | 10 | 24 | 9 | 76 |
| Rochester | 14,796 | 4 | 26 | 4 | 72 |
| Warren | 14,484 | 13 | 17 | 12 | 71 |
| Livonia | 14,215 | 9 | 31 | 8 | 72 |
| Walled Lake | 14,174 | 9 | 19 | 9 | 74 |
| Troy | 12,117 | 5 | 12 | 5 | 58 |
| L'Anse Creuse | 10,641 | 13 | 23 | 12 | 73 |
| Farmington | 9,205 | 25 | 12 | 25 | 55 |
| Grosse Pointe | 7,249 | 18 | 38 | 15 | 62 |

*Source:* Author's calculations based on data for the Common Core of School Data for the 2015–2016 year (National Center for Educational Statistics 2018).
*Note:* This table provides information for the dozen largest public school districts in the three-county Detroit suburban ring and for the Grosse Pointe district where there has been controversy about integration. Data pertain to enrollment in the 2015–2016 academic year.

white students due to Michigan's freedom of school choice law that permits students to enroll in public schools outside their district. It is important to stress that some progress has been made in reducing school segregation in the metropolis: middle-class African American parents now have school integration options for their children that they did not in 1967. Forty-eight percent of metropolitan Detroit's school-age black children now reside in the suburbs, where the schools are more racially mixed and diverse than in the city. Integration trends in suburban Detroit are components of a similar change across the state. In 2000, 58 percent of the state's African American students attended schools that were at least 90 percent black; by 2015, 40 percent did (Chambers and MacDonald 2017).

### What Explains Suburban Residential Integration?

What worked to open the suburbs and thwart the Kerner Commission's chocolate city, vanilla suburbs prediction? The racial attitudes of whites liberalized. Along with colleagues, I conducted studies of the causes of residential segregation in metropolitan Detroit three times. The last, unfortunately, was fourteen years ago. Nevertheless, the proportion of a random selection of whites who said they would try to move out if a single black family moved into their neighborhood declined from 24 percent in 1976 to 8 percent in 2004. The proportion of whites who said that if they were searching for a new home and found an attractive, affordable one in a neighborhood where one-third of the residents were black they would consider buying it increased from 50 percent in 1976 to 79 percent in the most recent study (Farley 2011). This may be linked to a changing white perception of black migration. In the 1960s, Chicago Alderman Lawler gave a succinct definition for integration, namely, that short span between the time the first Negro moved in and the time the last white moved out. That describes what happened in many Detroit neighborhoods. But suburban residents may now realize that such change is seldom occurring in their suburbs and that the African Americans who purchase or rent homes in their neighborhoods will be their economic and social peers. The Census Bureau's annual surveys support this claim since they report that the characteristics of African Americans and whites in the larger suburbs are roughly comparable. In Sterling Heights, the per capita income of adult blacks was 92 percent of that of whites, in Westland 90 percent, and in Warren 85 percent.

Second, the attitudes of African Americans also changed. Our studies found that Detroit-area blacks strongly preferred racially integrated neighborhoods, but many were reluctant to pioneer in a white neighborhood. In 1992, 31 percent said they would be willing to pioneer if they found an attractive, affordable home in an all-white neighborhood. By 2004, that had increased to 40 percent (Farley, Couper, and Krysan 2006, 37). In the wake of the rapid suburbanization of African Americans, many more suburban neighborhoods have large enough black populations to make them appealing, perhaps, to those who are hesitant to pioneer. In 2016, the number of census tracts in the Detroit suburbs numbered 860. Fifty-four percent of them had populations at least 5 percent African American, presumably signaling to blacks that they could move there and not face the violence that Dr. Sweet did in 1925.

Third, the Kerner report hastened passage of the Fair Housing Act of 1968. A federal law to ban racial discrimination in the housing market had been introduced in early 1967 but languished because many in Congress believed that the government should not tell property owners whom to sell to or rent to (Loessberg and Koskinen 2018). The Kerner Commission issued its clarion call for integration on February 29, 1968. The congressional log jam ended on March 11 when the measure was reported out of committee (Mathias and Morris 1999; Zasloff 2016). Debate about the effectiveness of this law aside, I believe it had an impact by changing standard operating procedures in the real estate industry. Brokers gradually came to appreciate that they could be punished for blatant racial discrimination. Fair housing groups spread across the country and filed suit when they saw violations. Studies of discrimination in the Detroit and twenty-seven other real estate markets were conducted by the Department of Housing and Urban Development in 1977, 1989, 2000, and 2012. They confirm not the disappearance but instead a consistent and substantial decline in racial discrimination by brokers involving the rental or sale of advertised properties. The 2012 analysis in Detroit used paired testers to measure thirty-nine possible types of discrimination against blacks who sought to rent advertised units. The racial difference was not significant on thirty-three of the thirty-nine dimensions (Turner et al. 2013, appendix F).[4]

Finally, market forces greatly abetted the suburban migration of African Americans. After the 1970s, the demand for housing in the suburbs fell sharply; that is, the white population of the ring fell by two hundred thousand from 1970 to 2016. This led suburban officials and real estate brokers to appreciate the influx of new residents from the city who had the funds to purchase or rent suburban homes, apartments, and condos. That in-migration helped to stave off the many problems resulting from falling populations and declining tax bases including the painful process of laying off police and fire officers and closing schools. In many suburbs, African Americans are replacing whites, thereby reducing segregation.

The gradual trend toward less segregation seems likely to continue. The Kerner Commission report played some role in popularizing the norm that racial discrimination in the housing market is wrong and illegal. And the now increasing white population of the city of Detroit may lead to more racially mixed neighborhoods in the city. However, at this point there are few policies or programs to hasten the residential integration trend.

---

4. The 2012 HUD study tested for discrimination against home buyers using a large enough sample to show a decline over time at the national level. However, their sample in metropolitan Detroit was small, so data are not specifically shown (Margery Turner, lead author, personal communication, May 2018).

## EVIDENCE OF NO RACIAL PROGRESS: THE INCREASING ECONOMIC GAP THAT SEPARATES WHITES FROM BLACKS

Kerner commissioners focused on employment and emphasized that African Americans, especially men, were much more likely to be unemployed than whites and that blacks who held jobs were concentrated in low-paying occupations. The commissioners accurately predicted that, in the short run, most job creation would be in the largely white suburban rings and the chronically unemployed would continue to be concentrated in central cities. Observing Detroit, they commented about the loss of more than one hundred thousand auto industry jobs in the city in the years before the violence (Kerner Report 1968, 406). To minimize the chances for future "hot summers," the commissioners called for the creation of one million new jobs in the public sector and one million in the private sector within the next three years, jobs that would pay at least the minimum or prevailing wage (421–30).

When it comes to key economic indicators, all standard measures show that blacks fell further behind whites following the 1967 violence. Whites in the Detroit area, as a group, were better off economically than blacks at the time of the Kerner report but blacks lost much more income and wealth than whites as industrial jobs disappeared.

As table 3 reveals, these decades since 1970 have been challenging for metropolitan Detroit. The median income of Detroit-area white households, in constant dollars, dropped by $10,200 (17 percent) from 1970 to 2016. But for black households, the decline was $15,500 (32 percent). The racial gap in median household income had been $25,300 (in 2016 dollars) when the Kerner commissioners penned the report. It grew to $30,600. Black households have less and less to spend relative to whites.

The economic status of adults is assessed by the median earnings of adults who reported earnings. In 1970, African American men reported earnings 75 percent those of white men; by 2016, it was down to 56 percent as much. The Detroit Urban League for decades struggled to eradicate Jim Crow practices that kept blacks out of many occupations. By the 1960s, African American women in Detroit could work at an array of jobs other than domestic service. Indeed, they were more likely to be employed than white women and their median earnings were 89 percent those of white women. This changed as white women joined the labor force, completed college in large numbers, and moved into prestigious occupations, leading to a much larger racial gap in the earnings of women. The racial gap in earnings remains smaller among women than among men, however.

The decline in income and earnings helps explain the substantial rise in poverty. Both whites and blacks in metropolitan Detroit were much more likely to be impoverished in 2016 than when the violence occurred. In 1970, 6 percent of white children and 28 percent of black children lived in impoverished households. Forty-six years later, the numbers rose to 14 percent for whites and 41 percent for blacks. The racial gap in poverty rate grew larger, although the rate of poverty rate increase was greater among whites.

As Susan Gooden and Samuel Myers show in their introductory essay to this issue, changes in Detroit differ from national trends (2018). Black families across the nation have certainly not narrowed the economic gap that distinguishes them from white families, but neither has the gap grown much larger, as it has in metropolitan Detroit.

### Economic Changes Since the Kerner Report

Detroit-area residents have lower incomes now than fifty years ago and the poverty rate is higher. Why? The lucid answer to this question, given by William Julius Wilson, is the disappearance of work (1996). Wilson describes inner-city minority neighborhoods, but his observations also apply to most residents of metropolitan Detroit. Henry Ford perfected the modern assembly line in 1914, thereby supplying the nation with low-priced, reliable vehicles. Because of a booming vehicle industry, Detroit was the nation's fastest growing metropolis in the early decades of the last century. Detroit prospered economically and demographically through the World War II years. For a quarter-century afterward, consumer demand for new cars and a powerful labor movement maintained Detroit's status. For example, in

**Table 3.** Indicators of the Economic Status of Whites and African Americans in Metropolitan Detroit: 1970 and 2016

|  | White | Black | Race Difference | Black as Percent of White |
|---|---|---|---|---|
| **Median household income** | | | | |
| 1970 | $74,400 | $49,100 | −$25,300 | 66 |
| 2016 | 64,200 | 33,600 | −30,600 | 52 |
| **Median earnings of men reporting earnings** | | | | |
| 1970 | $60,300 | $45,200 | −$15,100 | 75 |
| 2016 | 46,200 | 25,900 | −20,300 | 56 |
| **Median earnings of women reporting earnings** | | | | |
| 1970 | $22,800 | $20,300 | −$2,500 | 89 |
| 2016 | 29,200 | 23,600 | −5,500 | 82 |
| **Percent of total population impoverished** | | | | |
| 1970 | 5.3 | 21.2 | +15.9 points | 400 |
| 2016 | 10.4 | 27.7 | +17.3 points | 266 |
| **Percent of children under age eighteen impoverished** | | | | |
| 1970 | 5.8 | 28.2 | +22.4 points | 486 |
| 2016 | 14.0 | 40.9 | +26.9 points | 292 |

*Source:* Author's calculations based on public use data from the Census Bureau's decennial censuses and the American Community Survey. Data accessed at University of Minnesota Integrated Public Use Microdata Samples (Ruggles et al. 2017) and at Queens University's Social Explorer (www.socialexplorer.com, accessed May 21, 2018).
*Note:* Amounts in constant 2016 dollars.

1970 the per capita income of adults in metropolitan Detroit was 21 percent above the national average and considerably greater than in metropolitan Boston, Chicago, Los Angeles, New York, or San Francisco. Detroit's African American community at the time of the violence was, on economic indicators, the most prosperous African American community in the nation.

In 1972, the Organization of Petroleum Exporting Nations (OPEC) embargoed the sale of oil to Western nations. The price of gasoline skyrocketed, and consumers switched to buying small, fuel-efficient cars. Detroit's Big Three were not prepared to profitably assemble the efficient cars consumers sought. They came under great pressure to reduce costs, but while trying to do so, lost market shares to European and Asian manufacturers. The result was a dramatic reduction in Detroit-area employment. The 1967 Census of Manufacturers counted 2,900 manufacturing firms in the city of Detroit and 210,000 employees. The most recent census, in 2012, enumerated just 382 firms and 18,000 employees.

The Kerner Commission remarked on the rapid growth of suburban manufacturing jobs, but that trend ended shortly after the report got to bookstores. The 1967 Censuses of Manufacturing counted 375,000 men and women working at production in the suburban ring. By 2012, that number was down to 160,000.

Blue-collar jobs in manufacturing industries in metropolitan Detroit declined sharply; from 591,000 in 1970 to 191,000 in 2016, a 68 percent decrease. The average earnings of these workers, in constant dollars, dropped 25 percent for a variety of reasons, including the declining clout of unions. Earnings have fallen substantially even for those blue-collar occupations that have grown rapidly. The number of truck drivers in metropolitan Detroit increased by 81 percent in this period but their average annual earnings fell 33 percent in constant dollars.

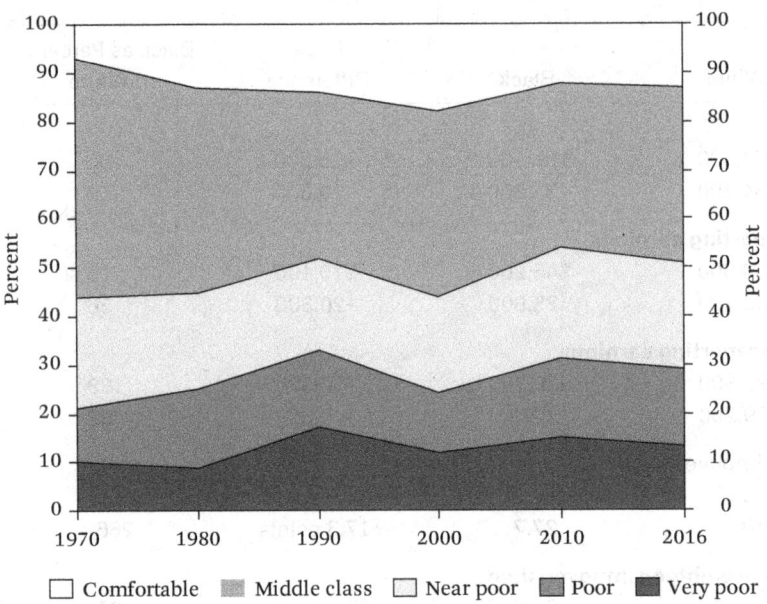

**Figure 10.** Economic Status of Blacks in Metropolitan Detroit, 1970 to 2016

*Source:* Author's calculations based on public use data from the Census Bureau's decennial censuses and the American Community Survey. Data accessed at University of Minnesota Integrated Public Use Microdata Samples (Ruggles et al. 2017) and at Queens University's Social Explorer (www.social explorer.com, accessed May 21, 2018).
*Note:* Comfortable: household income 500 percent or more of the poverty threshold. Middle class: 200 to 499 percent of the poverty threshold. Near poor: 100 to 199 percent of the poverty threshold. Poor: 50 to 99 percent of the poverty threshold. Very poor: less than 50 percent of the poverty threshold.

Estimates from the federal statistical system show that total employment in metropolitan Detroit grew slowly after 1970 and peaked at about 2.1 million jobs at the end of the twentieth century. The number of jobs declined slowly at first but then sharply in the 2008 recession. Since then, a post-recession rise put total employment in early 2018 at about 10 percent below what it had been twenty years earlier (Bureau of Labor Statistics 2018). However, employment has shifted substantially: assembly line jobs are far fewer than previously, and more jobs fall at the extremes of the pay scale, service workers in retail trade on the one end and highly skilled jobs in health services, finance, and technology on the other. These shifts help explain declines in earnings and population stagnation.

The vehicle industry remains the backbone of metropolitan Detroit's economy and will not disappear. The share of North American production in the greater Detroit area may increase. After emerging from bankruptcy, vehicle sales boomed. There was no labor-management bargaining while the federal government supervised the bankruptcies of General Motors and Chrysler, but a new contract was signed in late 2015. The three large producers promised to invest $21 billion dollars in new plants and equipment in the United States. Those investments are being made as the industry prepares to produce self-driving and electric vehicles, but this does not mean that assembly line jobs will grow. The Bureau of Labor Statistics since the 1980s has carefully measured labor productivity in vehicle manufacturing. The rise has been a consistent 4 percent per annum (Bureau of Labor Statistics 2015). Year after year, manufacturers are turning out 4 percent more vehicles than in previous years with no increase in labor.

Some employment sectors have grown, es-

**Figure 11.** Economic Status of Whites in Metropolitan Detroit, 1970 to 2016

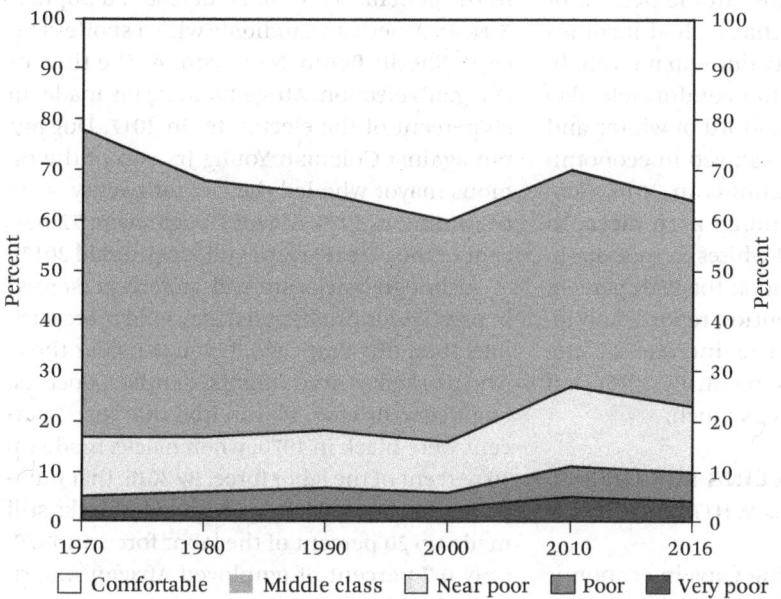

*Source:* Author's calculations based on public use data from the Census Bureau's decennial censuses and the American Community Survey. Data accessed at University of Minnesota Integrated Public Use Microdata Samples (Ruggles et al. 2017) and at Queens University's Social Explorer (www.socialexplorer.com, accessed May 21, 2018).
*Note:* Comfortable: household income 500 percent or more of the poverty threshold. Middle class: 200 to 499 percent of the poverty threshold. Near poor: 100 to 199 percent of the poverty threshold. Poor: 50 to 99 percent of the poverty threshold. Very poor: less than 50 percent of the poverty threshold.

pecially medical services and education. The employment of many women in these sectors explains why women have fared better than men in this era of industrial restructuring and declining wages for blue-collar workers. But no new industrial sectors have emerged or are emerging in the Detroit area that would make up for the tremendous loss of jobs and earnings in vehicle manufacturing.

Figures 10 and 11 concisely illustrate the economic changes that occurred in metropolitan Detroit since the violence. Residents are classified according to their household income: *very poor* for those in households with incomes below one-half the poverty line, *poor* for those with incomes 50 to 99 percent of the poverty line, *near poor* for 100 to 199 percent of the poverty line, *middle class* for those with incomes 200 to 499 percent, and *comfortable* for those in households with incomes five or more times the poverty line.

Commenting on the Kerner report, William Wilson argued that the commissioners overlooked a substantial African American middle class and went on to contend that, in economic terms, the black community could be divided into a thriving economically successful group, a struggling working class, and an underclass that was falling further and further behind (1978). His observations describe trends in Detroit very accurately but apply to the white as well as the African American community.

The size of the middle class has been reduced. There are, proportionally, more poor and more comfortable people among both races. Poverty increased as high-paying jobs disappeared and programs in support of the poor became more parsimonious. As Kathryn Edin and Luke Schaefer demonstrate, the proportion whose incomes fall below one-half the poverty line increased sharply after the Personal Responsibility and Work Opportunity Act of 1996 terminated traditional welfare (2016). By 2016, 4 percent of whites and 13 percent of blacks were very poor—that is, had incomes below one-half the poverty line—in metropolitan Detroit. The proportion comfortable also increased: more than one-third of whites and about one-eighth of blacks lived in economically comfortable households in 2016. Economic inequality rose among both races. In 1970, for both blacks and whites in metropolitan Detroit, the household at the 95th percentile of the income distribution reported an income fourteen times the income of the household at the 20th percent. By 2016, that grew to twenty-one times as much.

## WHY ARE BLACKS FALLING FURTHER AND FURTHER BEHIND WHITES IN ECONOMIC STATUS?

What explains the growing gaps in economic status?

### The Changing Labor Market

Numerous suburbs have peacefully integrated without incidents of violence. Although residential integration does not necessarily mean social integration, indications are that it is occurring. Consider the increase in interracial marriage. If we consider recently married young persons—those age twenty-five to thirty-nine—we find that in 1980, in metropolitan Detroit, only 0.7 percent of African American husbands were married to a white spouse. In 2010, the figure was 4.5 percent. Correspondingly, 2.5 percent of young married black women had a white husband in 1980. By 2010, 9.2 percent did. Not surprisingly, the mixed-race population is growing. By 2016, 4 percent of children under age ten who were identified by their parents as white by race were also identified as black. And 10 percent of children under ten identified by their parents as black were also identified as white. Interracial marriage leads to a larger mixed-race population (Livingston and Brown 2017).

Another indicator demonstrates changing racial attitudes. A white candidate for mayor, Michael Duggan, grew up in the city, moved to the suburbs, and then bought a home in the city's Palmer Woods neighborhood just a year before the 2013 contest. For him to win the primary election, voters had to write in his name. In the general election, he defeated a popular African American candidate with a spotless record, Sheriff Benny Napoleon. At the time of Duggan's election, African Americans made up 80 percent of the electorate. In 2017, Duggan ran against Coleman Young Jr., son of the famous mayor who led the city for twenty years beginning in 1974. Mayor Duggan won 72 percent of the vote (Ferretti and MacDonald 2017).

Although blacks are still underrepresented in prestigious professions, they hold more such jobs than fifty years ago. If you consider those who worked as accountants, dentists, doctors, engineers, or lawyers, you find that just 4 percent were black in 1970, when blacks made up 20 percent of the labor force. By 2016, that number had increased to 10 percent and blacks still made up 20 percent of the labor force. In 1970, only 0.7 percent of employed African Americans in metro Detroit earned more than $100,000 (constant 2016 dollars). In 2016, 3.7 percent did so. Despite the deteriorating economic status of most Detroit-area African Americans, a modest growth of those with professional jobs and substantial earnings is undeniable.

Although affirmative action has all but disappeared as a strategy, a norm of diversity is widely accepted and espoused. Boards of directors are scrutinized for diversity, advertisements for consumer products prominently show women and minorities, and it is now de rigueur for the coaching staff of sports teams to include minorities. It appears that racial discrimination in the Detroit area labor market may have declined, but I did not test any specific hypotheses about that topic and discrimination may still influence employment. Several studies using paired testers report that white applicants for jobs are more likely to be called for interviews than African Americans with identical credentials. A recent synthesis of these studies reports that such racial discrimination declined only moderately since the 1980s (Quillian et al. 2017).

Changes in the labor market explain much of the growing economic gap that separates blacks from whites. At the time of the Kerner analysis, blacks were much more likely than whites to be in the occupations and industries

**Table 4.** Indicators of the Housing Status of African Americans and Whites in Metropolitan Detroit

| Year | White | Black | Racial Difference | Black as Percent of White |
|---|---|---|---|---|
| **Percent of households owning or purchasing their residence** | | | | |
| 1970 | 76 | 53 | −23 points | 70 |
| 2008 | 81 | 49 | −32 points | 60 |
| 2016 | 77 | 40 | −37 points | 52 |
| **Median value of owner-occupied residences (constant 2016 dollars)** | | | | |
| 1970 | $146,300 | $105,600 | −$40,700 | 72 |
| 2008 | $195,600 | $109,800 | −$85,800 | 56 |
| 2016 | $154,600 | $57,000 | −$97,600 | 37 |
| **Percent of residents living in concentrated poverty (census tracts poverty rates 40 percent or higher)** | | | | |
| 1970 | 0.10 | 1.70 | +1.6 points | 1700 |
| 2008 | 0.20 | 21.90 | +21.7 points | 1095 |
| 2016 | 4.00 | 33.40 | +29.4 points | 835 |

*Source*: Author's calculations based on public use data from the Census Bureau's decennial censuses and the American Community Survey. Data accessed at University of Minnesota Integrated Public Use Microdata Samples (Ruggles et al. 2017) and at Queens University's Social Explorer (www.socialexplorer.com, accessed May 21, 2018).

that lost employment and saw wages decline. In 1970, just under five hundred thousand whites and about a hundred thousand African Americans were employed in manufacturing in the metropolis. Among whites in manufacturing at the time of the violence, 36 percent held white-collar jobs; the rest labored in blue-collar occupations. Among African Americans, just 8 percent held white-collar jobs and the other 92 percent blue-collar positions. From 1970 to 2016, blue-collar jobs in manufacturing declined 69 percent and white-collar jobs increased 8 percent.

## Subprime Lending and Its Consequence for Economic Status and Wealth Holdings

The Kerner commissioners focused on the housing challenges of minorities, but they did not emphasize the role that home ownership played in the accumulation of wealth. The commission called for a new federal program that would pay a portion of the mortgage payments for low-income families seeking to buy a home. It is important to examine homeownership because it is the primary source of wealth for most households. Changes have been unfavorable for whites since the Kerner years but more so for African Americans in metropolitan Detroit, as shown in table 4.

At the time of the violence, more than half of African American householders in metropolitan Detroit owned their residence, reflecting the prosperity of the area. Stable black middle-class neighborhoods and a few stable racially mixed neighborhoods had emerged. The number of African Americans owning their homes in metropolitan Detroit, 53 percent, was much higher than Chicago's 26 percent, Washington's 30 percent, or Los Angeles' 38 percent. Since then, the proportion owning their home declined by 13 percentage points for Detroit-area blacks but increased by 1 percentage point for whites. If you consider the racial gap in the median value of residences in metropolitan Detroit in 1970, you find the racial gap was $41,000 (in 2016 dollars). Forty-six years later, the median value of residences owned by whites had increased little but the median value for blacks had been just about cut in half and the racial gap rose to $97,000. African Americans are falling further and further behind whites in wealth holdings.

In the 1980s, William Wilson introduced the concept of concentrated poverty (1987). These are census tracts in which 40 percent or more of the residents live in impoverished households. Wilson links concentrated poverty to numerous social and economic problems. Subsequent research demonstrates that growing up in impoverished neighborhoods truncates opportunities for upward economic mobility (Chetty, Hendren, and Katz 2016; Chetty and Hendren 2017). Concentrated poverty in metropolitan Detroit was rare at the time of the 1967 violence. Only four of the area's 1,014 census tracts had poverty rates high enough to qualify for Wilson's definition. The final array of numbers in table 4 shows that almost no whites and fewer than 2 percent of blacks lived in concentrated poverty neighborhoods at the time of the violence. Economic trends shifted dramatically, and, by 2016, 4 percent of whites and 33 percent of blacks did.

While there are federal programs to assist first-time home buyers, they are modest and not well known. In brief, Congress did not respond to the Kerner Commission's call to initiate a major new program to promote home ownership for moderate-income families like the home ownership stimulation Congress enacted followed World War II. Those programs exacerbated segregation and made Detroit the nation's most prominent chocolate city, vanilla suburbs metropolis (Rothstein 2017).

More important in explaining the changes in tenure and value is the subprime crisis and how it interacted with tax policies in Michigan. Detroit homeowners were particularly challenged: declining home values, extremely high property tax rates, and sharp increases in unemployment along with declines in earnings after the recession began in 2008. As a result, many homeowners could not pay their property taxes or mortgages. The Citizens Research Council of Michigan determined that, by 2011, taxes were paid only on 53 percent of the taxable parcels in the city of Detroit (2013). As housing values sank, many owners found they owed more in unpaid property taxes and interest than their home was worth, giving them an incentive not to pay. Many homeowners found they could neither afford their high property taxes nor their mortgages, so foreclosure became extremely common. Between 2005 and 2016, 36 percent of the residential properties in the city of Detroit went into foreclosure (Kurth and MacDonald 2015).

Subprime lending and foreclosures hastened the impoverishment of many white households, but the effects were greater among blacks (Dewar, Seymour, and Druță 2015; Deng et al. 2017). In 2000, 76 percent of the African American homeowners in metropolitan Detroit resided in the city, where subprime lending was common. Among white homeowners, only 3 percent lived in the city. As Jacob Rugh and Douglas Massey demonstrate, racial residential segregation was a powerful predictor of the foreclosure rate (2010). Analyses of subprime lending found that African Americans and Hispanics were much more likely than comparable white applicants to end up with subprime financing (Ghent, Hernandez-Murillo, and Ouyang 2014; Badger 2013; for an analysis of similar issues in Los Angeles, see De La Cruz-Viesca et al. 2018). As table 4 makes clear, most of the decline in home ownership and all the decline in the median value of owner-occupied homes in metropolitan Detroit occurred after subprime lending became common.

## RACIAL DISPARITIES IN EDUCATIONAL ATTAINMENT

If jobs disappear, it is wise for individuals—and for their children—to gain the skills needed for the growing occupations. In metropolitan Detroit, jobs in manufacturing, transportation, and utilities declined 32 percent between 1970 and 2016 but jobs grew in other industrial sectors. Growth was particularly rapid in the medical sector and hospitals—an increase of 149 percent; in financial services, it was up 67 percent, and in education 32 percent.

Federal statistical agencies collect few data about how many adults successfully enroll in and complete training programs that allow them to get a rewarding new job after their old one disappears. High school and college completion rates are collected annually, however. These have limitations and the count of young college graduates in a metropolis is influenced by selective migration. Nevertheless, educational trends in the post-Kerner years suggest that whites have been more successful than African Americans in earning the degrees often

**Figure 12.** Education in Metropolitan Detroit, High School Diplomas Among Those Age Twenty to Twenty-Nine

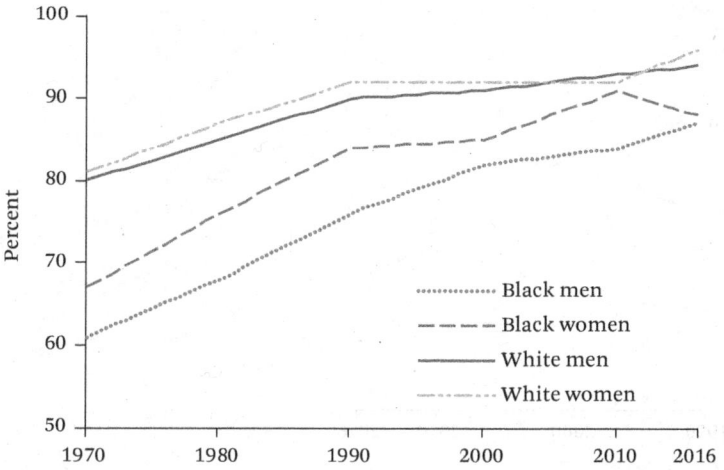

*Source:* Author's calculations based on public use data from the Census Bureau's decennial censuses and the American Community Survey. Data accessed at University of Minnesota Integrated Public Use Microdata Samples (Ruggles et al. 2017) and at Queens University's Social Explorer (www.social explorer.com, accessed May 21, 2018).

needed for career success in the growing industries.

In parallel with the national trend, progress has been made in reducing racial gaps in high school graduation, at least as reported by Detroit residents. Just after the Kerner report, about 80 percent of whites in their twenties and 67 percent of blacks in their twenties reported they earned a high school diploma (see figure 12). By 2016, the proportion with high school degrees was well over 90 percent for whites and for black women; black men lagged not far behind (for the national trend toward a racial convergence in high school completion, see Gooden and Myers 2018, figure 4).

A trend emerges when data about four-year college degrees are examined. As Walter Allen and his colleagues report, only modest progress has been made across the nation in narrowing the substantial racial gap in college completion (2018). Like the national trend, the rate of college completion in the Detroit area increased much more among women than men and very much more among whites than among African Americans. Figure 13 shows the proportion of those age twenty-five to thirty-nine who reported earning a four-year college degree since the era of the Kerner report. Among white men, the change was from 21 percent to 36 percent with a college diploma but among white women, the increase was much shaper: 12 percent to 42 percent. Increases were very much greater for whites than for blacks and thus the racial gap widened substantially. The change among African American men was remarkably small. At present, among Detroit-area black men in the early years of their careers, just one in ten earned a college diploma—a lower rate than among white men five decades ago. African American women graduate from college at a higher rate than in the past, but their college completion rate is well below that of their white peers.

Racial differences in educational attainment help explain why the economic status of Detroit-area blacks declined both in absolute terms and relative to whites. In 2014, employed adult black men in metropolitan Detroit earned 56 percent as much as their white counterparts. At all educational levels, blacks reported lower earnings than similarly educated whites. However, if black men had the same education as white men but their own earnings at each level of education, they would have reported earn-

**Figure 13.** Education in Metropolitan Detroit, Bachelor's Degrees Among Those Age Twenty-Five to Thirty-Nine

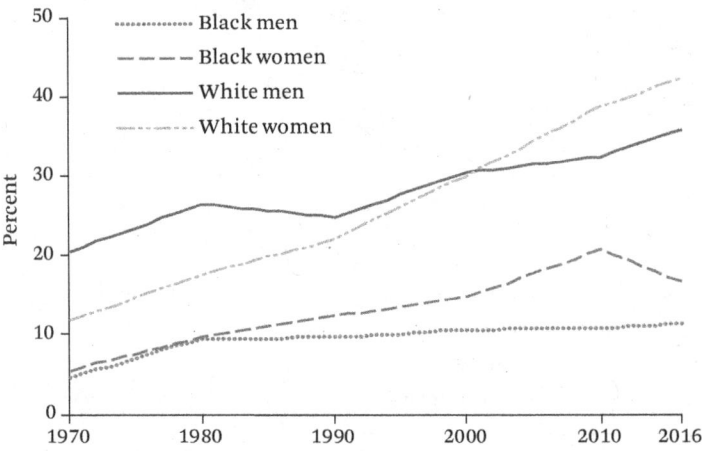

*Source:* Author's calculations based on public use data from the Census Bureau's decennial censuses and the American Community Survey. Data accessed at University of Minnesota Integrated Public Use Microdata Samples (Ruggles et al. 2017) and at Queens University's Social Explorer (www.social explorer.com, accessed May 21, 2018).

ings at 66 percent that of white men. In 2014, employed African American women earned 75 percent as much as white women. If black women had education similar to that of white women, they would have earned 84 percent as much. Racial differences in education account for a share of the racial gap in earnings.

The consensus that public schools in Michigan have been poorly financed and ineffective is well established. The Kerner Commission observed that spending per pupil in Detroit suburbs was 27 percent greater than in the city and that spending since World War II had risen more in the suburbs than in the city (Kerner Report 1968, 435). Two major changes were made to resolve the state's educational problems. In 1993, public schools in rural Kalkaska County ran out of funds and closed in early March. Within a short time, Michigan voters approved an encompassing proposal that decoupled the funding of public schools from the local property tax. Sales and tobacco taxes were raised, and local property taxes for school operation were eliminated. A new uniform statewide property tax was imposed. The state collects those taxes and now distributes school funds to districts on the basis of their enrollment. Michigan annually provides about $7,600 for each pupil enrolled in every school district. This supports teachers and the day-to-day operation of schools although voters in a district may tax themselves for special programs and capital improvement (Bessette 2006). The new policy moved the state toward more equity in school funding but does not recognize that it is much costlier to educate some children than others (Courant and Loeb 1997).

Detroit's schools, in the past, enrolled the majority of the state's African American children. Those schools were viewed as so underperforming and poorly run that the state took them over in 1999. Then, in 2008, after many protested, the schools were returned to local control. Problems persisted, however, and in 2011 the state of Michigan took over again. The takeover did not improve achievement levels and generated new debts of about a half billion dollars. The state paid off those debts in 2016 and funded the creation of a new locally run school district (Gray 2016).

In the last dozen years, a powerful and well-funded movement to replace public schools with state-funded charter schools was led by Betsy DeVos, who subsequently was appointed secretary of education in the Trump administration. The rationale for charter schools had a prominent and specific racial focus. Advocates argued that African American children in Detroit, Flint, Benton Harbor, and other segregated cities were forced to enroll in underperforming public schools. Prosperous parents had the flexibility to move to suburbs with excellent schools or to enroll their children in private schools. The solution was for the state to fund privately operated schools that would, presumably, provide much better education than the failing public schools. Michigan adopted the nation's most liberal laws regarding charter schools and now provides about $7,600 per year for each student enrolling in charter schools, funds that in the past would have gone to public schools.

One change in education was positive. State-equalized support for all students ended the situation in which the funding for a student's instruction was directly linked to the tax base of the student's district. With the second experiment, Detroit and a half-dozen other districts became the national experiment to see whether loosely regulated, state-funded charter schools could boost the achievement scores and attainment of low-income black students. So far, the results are mixed at best, and many believe the charter school experiment greatly damaged Michigan's public schools by withdrawing students and financial support (Benelli 2017). Detroit's public schools enrolled 290,000 at the time of the Kerner report. In 2017, the city's new public school system enrolled 48,000, and charter or suburban public schools another 60,000 Detroit children (Citizens Research Council of Michigan 2016; Van Buren 2016).

## The Police in Detroit, Urban Violence, and the Kerner Report

Forty-five years after the Kerner report, the Black Lives Matter movement emerged after a white Florida resident, George Zimmerman, was acquitted in the shooting death of a black teenager, Trayvon Martin. The movement grew and gained national prominence after the police killings of unarmed African American males—Eric Garner in New York City, Michael Brown in Ferguson, Missouri, and Tamir Rice in Cleveland. This suggests that little progress has been made in addressing how policing and prosecution is or is not accomplished when African Americans are involved.

The Kerner Commission would never have been established had there not been police violence against African Americans. The proximate cause of the July 1967 Newark violence was the brutal and highly visible mistreatment of black taxi driver John Smith. Sidney Fine, author of the definitive history of the Detroit violence, stressed the importance of police brutality as a cause (1989, 105–107). He described three incidents that, he believed, helped incite the violence, incidents that were well known in Detroit's black community in the summer of 1967 but ignored by most whites. In the 1960s, professional sex workers congregated on Detroit's John R Street seeking customers who completed their shifts in nearby plants. Cynthia Scott, a tall and impressive black woman, was well known in her profession. In July 1963, officers saw money in her hand, presumed she had stolen it from a customer, and put her into their cruiser. She was shot in the back and killed as she exited the vehicle (Boyd 2017, 194). The officers were known in the black community for their exceptional racial hostility. The issue quickly became a cause célèbre. Officers contended that they had shot in self-defense and were exonerated.

A vibrant and influential black media, especially the *Michigan Chronicle*, covered racial issues in Detroit at the time. Many in the black community claimed that the real story was different from what the police asserted and that Scott had been shot for refusing the advances of the officers. Controversy persisted throughout the summer, numerous protests demanding that the officers who killed Scott be fired and charged with murder. Detroit Representatives Diggs and Conyers, who made up half of all African Americans serving in Congress at the time, sought to bring national attention to the Scott killing but failed to secure a federal investigation (Fine 1989, 105–107).

In June 1967—just weeks before violence broke out—an African American Vietnam veteran, Danny Thomas, picnicked with his pregnant wife in Rouge Park on Detroit's West Side. He was told by a gang of hostile whites that "niggers" were not allowed in the park after dark. He departed, but shortly after, realized that he had left equipment in the park. He returned to pick it up and was again confronted by the gang, who killed Thomas and injured his wife so seriously that she lost the baby. Police arrested several members of the group but released them shortly thereafter. Police officials asked the city's two major newspapers to print nothing about the murder for fear of generating a riot. One complied. The other buried the story on a back page without mentioning its racial components. The active black press, however, publicized the murder and stressed their view that the Detroit police never seriously investigated the murders of African Americans by whites, thereby automatically exonerating any whites who killed blacks.

On July 1, 1967, an African American professional sex worker, Vivian Williams, was shot and killed on Twelfth Street, three blocks from the starting point of the Detroit violence. The police issued two conflicting explanations of the killing and arrested no one. The consensus in Detroit's black community was that a white police officer tried to arrest Williams on June 29, but she pulled a knife and he backed off. Two nights later, in the opinion of many African Americans, the white police officer returned and shot her to death (Fine 1989, chap. 4).

Has the situation changed in Detroit? The consensus is that the harsh treatment of blacks in Detroit increased in the years immediately following the violence. Many intellectuals argued that disturbances in urban centers in the 1960s were rebellions. They contended that whites and municipal power structures had, for decades, oppressed blacks, respected none of their rights, and confined them to ghettos, thereby denying opportunities for education, employment, and financial security. Inevitably, the oppressed rose up and used force to end the racial domination in American cities just as people in Asian and African colonies rose up to forcefully end domination by European empires. Thus, the urban violence was like the successful decolonization movement that swept the globe in the decades after World War II.

How urban violence was defined had great implications for policy. The press and many politicians saw the racial violence of the 1960s very differently than the Kerner commissioners did. The popular view defined the violence as commodity riots. This had significant consequences for federal urban policies. The police, many argued, were weak in enforcing laws protecting property. Given an opportunity to loot and steal, many would do so. Indeed, the descriptions of the Detroit violence suggest that this happened (McGraw 2017b). On Sunday, July 23, 1967, Detroit police did not attempt to end the looting. Rather, they sought to prevent people from entering the Twelfth Street area while allowing people to leave riot neighborhoods even if they were transporting television sets, liquor, and other apparently stolen goods. During that Sunday, Detroit police were under order to use no firearms (Fine 1989, chap.7). In describing the white underclass in Detroit's Briggs neighborhood, John Hartigan recounts how blacks and whites cooperated to loot local stores in their integrated neighborhood during the violence (1999).

Patrick Gillon convincingly argues that President Johnson thoroughly disagreed with the causal explanation offered by the Kerner Commission (2018, 33). He never publicly accepted their report or thanked the commissioners. He was not alone. West Virginia Senator Robert Byrd argued that rioting should be put down with brutal force and that looters should be shot. Illinois Senator Everett Dirksen claimed that national planning went into organizing the riots and that a factory in New York produced Molotov cocktails for the participants. South Carolina Senator Strom Thurmond attributed the violence to communism and to the criminal instincts of the rioters. Georgia Governor Lester Maddox said that communists had started the violence and Richard Nixon asserted the Kerner commissioners blamed everybody for the riots except the actual perpetrators of the violence.

Around the country, demand was growing to strengthen polices forces so that they could promptly and sternly thwart riots before they started. Responding to such demands, Detroit Police Commissioner John Nichols used federal crime control funds to establish a STRESS unit (Stop Robberies, Enjoy Safe Streets). Four-man crews with heavy armaments patrolled low-income neighborhoods to prevent crime, using whatever force they found necessary

(Thompson 2001, 80–81). In Detroit's African American community, this became known as a reign of terror. Detroit's blacks viewed STRESS as an all-white vigilante group run by the police but answering to no one. At this time, Detroit police used "investigative arrests," picking up an individual, holding them for up to twenty-four hours and then releasing them without charge. This was widely seen as a strategy to harass black men. Michigan law, at that time, had a no-knock provision allowing police, including the STRESS unit, to break into homes without a warrant if they had reasonable cause to think that the law had been violated in any way. Detroit police also conducted many "tip over" raids, that is, entering a place where they believed illegal activities were occurring such as after-hours drinking or gambling and destroying the property there without making an arrest (Locke 1969, 59). Within two years, STRESS officers had killed seventeen, all but two of them black men (Hinton 2016, 191–203). Abetting the action of the STRESS unit was the Supreme Court's 1968 *Terry v. Ohio* ruling, giving police wide latitude to "stop and frisk" even if there was little evidence of crime.[5]

Coleman Young, in 1973, campaigned for mayor with a promise to disband the STRESS unit. Young defeated his opponent, Police Commissioner Nichols, and terminated STRESS his first day in office. He made efforts to racially integrate the police and change their mode of operation. This proved challenging. Protests were numerous and litigation from groups representing both African American and white officers was frequent. By the end of Young's second term, some progress had been made in racially integrating the department, but the Young years witnessed a spike in the homicide rate, perhaps because of the racial conflict within the police department (for a description of the evolution of police efforts to control potential urban violence, see Gillham and Marx 2018).

Unfortunately, the integration of the police department and its demographic shift from primarily white to primarily black did not end the brutality in Detroit. Between 1994 and 2000, Detroit police officers shot forty-seven to death—including six who were unarmed. Another nineteen died in police custody. Mayor Dennis Archer was concerned about the alarming rise in the police killings of Detroit residents but realized that he could not rectify the institutionalized problems of police violence (Boyd 2017, 300). He requested that the U.S. Department of Justice investigate the city's force. In 2003, the Justice Department charged the Detroit police with excessive use of lethal force and consistent abrogation of civil rights.[6] The Department of Justice document is an extremely harsh indictment of the types of abuse carried out by the Detroit police in the post–riot era. The district federal court ordered federal oversight. In the five years after that order, the police killed seventeen—far fewer than in the pre-supervision span. After numerous consent decrees, negotiations, and fine payments, the Detroit police department was freed from federal supervision in 2014. A consent decree remains in force, however (Burns 2014).

Police brutality calls to mind the killing of unarmed blacks. Another aspect of policing in the decades after the riots, however, may contribute directly to the continued high poverty rate of African Americans in Detroit and similar cities. Heather Thompson, a Detroit native, won the Pulitzer and Bancroft prizes for her book *Blood in the Water* (2016). In this essay, I argue that the declining economic status of African Americans in metropolitan Detroit is a result, primarily, of the disappearance of blue-collar jobs and the failure to alter the educational system so that it would prepare the next generation for available employment. Thompson does not dispute that view but contends that it is seriously flawed because it omits how the criminal justice system treated African American men in the decades after the Kerner report (Thompson 2013). She observes that financially rewarding jobs in manufacturing had by the 1960s created a large, secure and home-owning black middle class in Detroit. They had economic power, lived in middle-class neighborhoods, were active in numerous social jus-

---

5. *Terry v. Ohio*. 392 U.S. 1 (1968).

6. *U.S. v. City of Detroit, Michigan*, 2003. 2:03-cv-72258 (E.D. Michigan).

tice movements, and were gaining considerable political influence (Castle 2018; Hamlin 2012).

Responding to the call for more and harsher policing in African American neighborhoods, Congress funded its "war on crime." President Johnson, in 1965, signed the Law Enforcement Assistance Act, which for the first time made substantial federal funds available to local police departments. They bought high power weapons and military-style vehicles in hopes of ending summers of violence. Just three months after the Kerner report, President Johnson signed the Omnibus Crime Control and Safe Streets Act, providing more federal assistance to local police. This was a clear congressional rejection of the ideas of the Kerner Commission because that law was a turning point in the militarization of urban police. In many cities, including Detroit, the new resources were used to purchase equipment and weapons that were deployed frequently in African American neighborhoods. Shortly thereafter, the federal government established its war on drugs, which was—intentionally or not—often targeted against African Americans. In Thompson's view, these strategies reinforced the stereotype that black neighborhoods were unsafe areas populated by threatening criminals. Furthermore, the public schools in those neighborhoods also became subject to police control. Police were not assigned to Detroit schools until 1969. After the war on crime was announced, almost every school was assigned one or more officers. Once they were, they helped define schools as unsafe and dangerous places. The police arrested youths who were then charged as adults. By 2011, Michigan had the second highest number of juveniles serving life sentences without parole—366, some as young as fourteen. Elizabeth Hinton points out that the federal government's Public Housing Security Act provided generous funds for policing and security hardware in the nations' public housing projects including the Jefferies and Douglas Homes in Detroit (2016, 296). She describes congressional debate about funding either job training or security in public housing. Congress devoted the lion's share of money to more policing rather than devoting federal funds to urban education or job training. A clear conclusion is that Congress and the federal government unambiguously rejected the Kerner Commission's calls for both promoting residential integration and improving employment and educational opportunities. Instead, they presumed that a strategy of militarizing the urban police would thwart riots.

Thompson contends the post-Kerner war on crime had disastrous consequences for the middle-class neighborhoods emerging in Detroit (2010, 2013). Those who had the resources to do so moved away, depleting the neighborhoods of potential community leaders. When the war on crime evolved into the war on drugs, it targeted the offenses of African American men, who were arrested, charged, and convicted in massive numbers. Just after the Kerner report, Michigan prisons housed 7,800 inmates. By 2011, some 42,900 were incarcerated in forty-two state prisons and numerous halfway houses. Thompson attributes some of the decline of marriage among African Americans and the rise of unemployment among men to the policy of incarcerating a substantial proportion of Detroit's black men, thereby reducing their chances for educational attainment, employment, and marriage. She also cites the implications of mass incarceration for the political power of Detroit's African Americans. Prisoners in Michigan may not vote but they are counted for purposes of reapportionment. Many of those arrested in Detroit were imprisoned in the overwhelmingly white counties of Chippewa, Ionia, and Jackson. Detroit lost representation in the state legislature and rural counties gained it based on people who could not vote. Almost all indicators of the status of black men show that they fell further and further behind white men in employment, earnings, and income. This finding is certainly consistent with Thompson's powerful arguments about the consequences of the racialized wars on crime and drugs (Bobo and Thompson 2010). A contrasting view is offered by Johannes Spreen, who served as Detroit police commissioner from 1968 to 1970. He argues that the persistent criminal behavior of Detroit residents and numerous constraints put on police when they sought to suppress crime were leading causes of the city's decline (Spreen and Holloway 2005).

## GROWING RACIAL GAPS: CHANGES IN HOUSEHOLD LIVING ARRANGEMENTS

The Kerner commissioners were influenced by Daniel Patrick Moynihan's controversial report about the black family (Kerner Report 1968, 252). Moynihan argued that the absence of good jobs for African American men in large cities was responsible for destabilizing the traditional two-parent family system. Because of the lack of employment for men, blacks were foregoing marriages and African American children were increasingly raised by a woman without a husband (Moynihan 1965). The Kerner commissioners described the unemployment rates of black men and also cited them as a cause of female-headed families and high rates of illegitimacy. They also cited illegitimacy and excessive childbearing as a cause of African American poverty. Indeed, the commissioners, apparently influenced by Moynihan's ideas, considered but then rejected a proposal that would have required single mothers to live in YMCA-style dormitories (Gillon 2018, 201).

Fertility rates declined sharply among both races. From 1970 to 2016, the birth rate per thousand women age fifteen to forty-four in Michigan fell by 46 percent for blacks and by 34 percent for whites. The races now have roughly similar low birth rates (Michigan Department of Health and Human Services 2017). The Kerner Commission's recommendation for reduced fertility has been accomplished.

Family living arrangements also shifted rapidly for both races, a change that contributes to persistent poverty and increasing racial gaps in economic status. In metropolitan Detroit in 1970, 72 percent of white households included a married couple; in 2016, 51 percent did. Among African Americans, the decrease was from 51 percent to 20 percent: only one in five black households included a married couple. The number of children under age eighteen living in a two-parent household also declined. In 2016, 82 percent of white children but only 29 percent of black children lived with two parents. Two-thirds of black children in the Detroit area lived in a household headed by an unmarried woman.

Children and women in husband-wife households are better off economically than those in households headed by a woman. For example, in metropolitan Detroit in 2016, white children in two-parent households had a poverty rate of 9 percent; those in households headed by a white woman had a 34 percent poverty rate. Among African American children, 20 percent of those in two-parent households were impoverished, but 52 percent of those in households headed by their mother were.

Across the nation, the proportion of children born to an unmarried woman increased, while the share of children living with two parents decreased steadily (Haskins 2009). When Moynihan drafted his report in the 1960s, 4 percent of white and 26 percent of African American births were to unmarried women. By 2015, those numbers increased to 36 percent for whites and 71 percent for blacks. Many analysts present evidence that the dearth of good jobs for men who lack advanced educations or highly valued skills is an important, perhaps the primary, reason for changes in family structure (Sawhill and Haskins 2016). Others argue that young adults increasingly judge that the benefits of marriage are modest and the loss of independence it entails is important, leading them to postpone or eschew marriage (Pew Research Center 2010). Isabel Sawhill and Jonna Venator describe those causes but also present strong evidence that the massive incarceration of black men diminished the pool of desirable potential husbands (2015). Whatever the reason, the rapid change in family structure and the shift of childrearing from married couples to single parents account for some increase in poverty and growing racial gaps in economic welfare in metropolitan Detroit.

## WHAT WORKED, WHAT DID NOT, AND IMPLICATIONS FOR THE TWENTY-FIRST CENTURY

The Kerner Commission warned that a continuation of the trends that provoked the 1967 violence would result in a greater geographic separation of the races and increasing racial economic gaps, especially in larger, older metropolises such as Detroit (1968, 407). In the fifty years since then, several dozen studies demonstrated that residential segregation is linked to racial disparities in employment, school quality and educational attainment, accrual of wealth, exposure to environmental pollutants, and criminal victimization (Krysan and Crowder 2017, 27–33). Racial residential segregation has slowly declined, especially since 1990 (Farley and Frey 1994; Glaeser, Cutler, and Vigdor 1999; Logan, Stilts, and Farley 2004). To be sure, Detroit and many other metropolises remain highly segregated; soon, however, more suburban than central-city African Americans are likely to be found in the metropolitan Detroit population. Whites and blacks in numerous southern and western metropolises, particularly those that grew rapidly thanks to the in-migration of Hispanics and Asians, were by 2010 no more than moderately segregated (Logan and Stilts 2011).

Other concerns were emphasized in the Kerner report, specifically black-white differences in employment, earnings, and educational achievement. Regarding these, the Detroit area has seen anything but progress. Although Detroit-area whites are less economically secure than they were at the time of the violence, blacks are, on average, much less well off. The urban underclass has grown in metropolitan Detroit. In 1970, only 13,000 Detroit-area African Americans lived in census tracts of concentrated poverty; in 2016, 218,000 did.

The Kerner commissioners could not foresee two fundamental and pervasive changes that have contributed to substantial increases in inequality both within and between racial groups. First were changes in the labor market as the number of highly rewarding blue-collar jobs in manufacturing declined. If the Detroit-area manufacturing firms needed as many strong backs and arms as they did before the OPEC crisis, racial gaps in economic status in Detroit would be more modest and inner-city neighborhoods that are now largely abandoned might be stable and prosperous (Wilson 1996). Although, given the change in racial attitudes, the suburban African American population would also likely be larger than at present. Changes in labor demand presented great challenges for both whites and blacks desiring to either hold on to their middle-class economic status or move up from poverty (Hanna-Attisha 2018).

Second, the Kerner commissioners did not foresee that the elections of Margaret Thatcher in 1979 and Ronald Reagan in 1980 would basically shift the role of government and the views of many about whether the government should fund programs to encourage the upward mobility of those who lack economic resources or are victims of Jim Crow and sexist policies.

Eduardo Bonilla-Silva popularized the concept of "racism without racists" (2017). That is, a policy may be adopted by a governmental body without the specific intent of harming a racial group, but the consequences of that policy may differ greatly by race and by economic status. In this era of neoliberal government, such policies seem common. After 1980, Congress increased funding for programs to militarize the police and to strictly enforce drug laws. Their aim may have been to reduce crime but, as Thompson and Hinton contend, those laws greatly impede the upward mobility of urban African American men.

As the Detroit suburb of Hamtramck approached insolvency in 1988, the state enacted an emergency financial manager law. If a Michigan city or school district came to the cusp of bankruptcy, local governance would be suspended, and the governor would appoint an emergency manager obligated to balance the books while paying the bond holders. Perhaps this law had no racial intent. But nine of the eleven cities with a financial manager, including the city of Detroit, had a majority African American population and the three school districts with emergency managers were overwhelming black in their enrollments (Lewis 2013). In the past decade, about 80 percent of Michigan's black population lived in municipalities where their elected officials had no power; only about 4 percent of whites did. The suspension of local governance and the appointment of an emergency financial manager in Flint played a role in the decision to balance that city's books by using polluted water (Bridge Magazine Staff 2016).

The legislature, in 2013, made Michigan a right-to-work state. Perhaps the intent was to attract employers. But an effort to reduce the power of the state's unions appears to have a differential racial consequence given that the African American middle class was more dependent than the white middle class on high-paying unionized jobs in manufacturing and civil service.

Facing a financial crisis in 2003, the state of Michigan drastically increased fines for driving without a license, driving without insurance, reckless driving, or driving under the influence of alcohol. If the fines were not paid promptly, a person could not obtain or renew his or her driver's license. The fines generated much revenue for the state but had the consequence of further immiserating the poor and making it more difficult for them to get to work.

At the time of the Detroit violence, the University of Michigan undergraduate full-year tuition was $368—about $2,700 in 2016 dollars. The university's website informed in-state students enrolling in the fall of 2017 that they should expect to pay $14,800 in tuition and incur total expenses of $30,000 for a year's education (University of Michigan 2017). Presumably, the nation's universities did not raise their costs to exclude students from middle- and low-income families, but their strategy may have accomplished exactly that.

A quick reading of the Kerner report leads to the observation that the commissioners considered an enrichment strategy as a possible way to end the urban violence. Presumably, federal programs could have financed an extensive rebuilding of ghettos including new schools, social service centers, parks, shopping centers, and amenities. The commissioners rejected the "Enrichment Strategy," also known as "Gilding the Ghetto," because, in their view, disadvantaged blacks could never achieve equality of opportunity with whites if nearly complete residential segregation were in place (Kerner Report 1968, 404). A more thorough reading, however, reveals that throughout the report are calls for numerous federal programs to improve inner-city schools and neighborhoods. Chapter 17, "Recommendations for National Action," is a long list of proposed federal government programs to assist the underclass living in ghettos, such as job training, improving schools including higher salaries to attract skilled teachers, making capital available for business formation, programs to foster better school-community relations, removal of abandoned properties, and new programs to make higher education affordable. Some of these calls were, to a degree, heeded in the 1970s. President Nixon, during his 1972 reelection campaign, proudly announced and then enacted a national program of federal revenue sharing that sent funds, with few strings, to all local governments. Presumably they could and were used to address the ghetto conditions the Kerner Commission found troubling. President Ford implemented the Community Development Block Grant program that specifically provided funds to private nonprofits that served low-income areas by providing social services and fostering economic development. During Ford's term, the Earned Income Tax Credit became law, sending a federal cash supplement to the working poor. Albeit modest, they are overlooked consequences of the Kerner report.

What about the future? In his inaugural address, President Reagan repeated the phrase "Government is not the solution to our problems, government is the problem." A neoliberal philosophy has influenced governmental decisions for almost four decades, a philosophy that differs greatly from the more liberal policies adopted from the Roosevelt through Ford administrations. When Reagan came to office, revenue sharing was terminated and, though the Community Block Development Grant program survives, it is a shadow of its former self. It seems unlikely that governmental funds will be available to either promote residential integration or to fund the numerous urban improvements the Kerner Commission advocated.

These changes in governmental policies have great implications for cities and localities, especially those where little if any growth is evident in jobs and population, including metropolitan Detroit and Michigan. Few federal or local dollars are available to make the investments that the Kerner Commission recommended. Funding must come from the investments of corporations that have a strong interest in the economic prosperity of where they are located as well as from large foundations that may be willing to address economic and racial inequity. Fortunately, the Detroit area is well positioned. The nation's three largest vehicle firms continue to invest heavily in the area. Seven well-endowed foundations with links to the city—Davidson, Ford, Hudson-Weber, Kellogg, Kresge, Skillman, and Wilson—now spend generously to improve the quality of life, often funding endeavors once funded by the government.

It is informative to consider recent developments in the Detroit area in light of the many specific recommendations the Kerner Commission delineated in chapter 17 of its report. The problems of joblessness and education are well understood in Michigan. Further, an awareness is prevalent that African Americans are especially challenged. Every recent governor has sought to boost employment in the state, generally by reducing taxes. In 2017, the state adopted a Good Jobs Michigan program that substantially cuts taxes for firms that create new jobs that pay the local wage (Snyder 2017). Firms also get even more tax abatements if those jobs pay 25 percent above the local average.

The city of Detroit has been at the center of employment creation activities since it exited bankruptcy in 2014. Entrepreneur Dan Gilbert of Quicken Loans purchased or leased more than a hundred downtown buildings in his quest to cooperate with the vehicle firms to make Detroit the *axis mundi* for the development of the information technology that will transform automobiles to make them safer and more efficient. The Ford Motor Company purchased a long-abandoned hosiery mill in the city's Corktown neighborhood to provide office space for two hundred specialists who will focus on autonomous and electric vehicles. In deciding to locate in an historic neighborhood near downtown Detroit, Ford stressed its desire to recruit the best talent, stating that many of those they sought desired a modern urban life style. In spring 2018, the Ford Motor Company purchased the nearby but long-empty 500,000 square foot Michigan Central Depot and office building to provide more space for their work on the next generation of vehicles. The Illich family, owners of Little Caesar's Pizza, not only built a new baseball park for their Detroit Tigers team, but also created a Detroit district in the center of the city, a project of more than one billion dollars with an arena for the Detroit Red Wings and Detroit Pistons, apartments, condos, offices, a new Wayne State business school, and numerous shops. Between 2017 and 2021, $5.4 billion in private investment will be spent in downtown Detroit to build or renovate 2.1 million square feet of office space, six thousand residential units, and 1,200 hotel rooms (Blitcock 2017).

Private foundations funded a New Economic Initiative for Southeast Michigan that seeks to recruit entrepreneurs, provide them with what they need to establish their firms, and educate Detroit-area residents for jobs in the new labor market. Skillman Foundation invested millions in six large Detroit neighborhoods with the aim of encouraging the organizational skills and facilities that residents need to secure the social services they need, especially improved schooling (Allen-Meares et al. 2017). A modern light rail line opened in 2017 linking downtown and Midtown Detroit, three-quarters of the funding coming from Detroit foundations and entrepreneurs.

Following bankruptcy, Detroit residents elected a mayor who argued that every Detroit neighborhood—not just downtown—had a future and asked to be judged on whether he could reverse the seventy-year decline in the city's population. Renewal is evident in dynamic downtown Detroit, the east waterfront, and Midtown. Coming out of bankruptcy, federal bankruptcy judge Steven Rhodes reserved about $1.7 billion for capital expenditures that the city could spend over a decade. Those funds and monies obtained from foundations allowed the city to resume the street lights that had been turned off in bankruptcy, to improve the bus service, to raze thousands of abandoned homes, to rebuild and revitalize many of the city's three hundred parks, and to once again sweep detritus off the streets. The state of Michigan rented Belle Isle from the city and made the requisite capital investments to restore that international park toward the top of the list of the nations' most impressive urban parks.

The mayor and Detroit's city planner, Maurice Cox, in 2016 announced that $42 million, largely from philanthropies, would be devoted to revitalizing neighborhoods far from downtown. Dilapidated homes were razed, abandoned residences and apartment buildings improved and resold, playgrounds refurbished, vacant lots turned into mini-parks or community gardens, and walking paths laid out to link residential areas to schools and shopping. In 2018, another $130 million in quasi-public funds, that is, monies from foundations and businesses but administered by the city, became available to revitalize ten additional neighborhoods (Edwards 2018). Consistent with Kerner Commission recommendations, the city has been promoting home ownership through the sale of foreclosed homes owned by the city's Land Bank, a program that aids new owners in securing financing and assistance in bringing the home up to code. Kerner commissioners argued that it was important to encourage business ownership in ghetto neighborhoods. The city now administers a public-private Detroit Micro Enterprise Fund that has loaned $27 million to start-ups and small firms (City of Detroit 2018).

There may be some evidence of success. From 2011 to 2016, the number of metropolitan Detroit African Americans employed increased by 23 percent and per capita income (in constant dollars) went up by 14 percent. Consistent with Sharkey's finding about trends in large cities, crime has steadily decreased in the city of Detroit, with the number of murders sinking to a fifty-year low in 2017 (Sharkey 2018; Hunter 2017). Although numerous problems in the education system remain, Detroit has a new public school system with dynamic leadership. The most recent scores from the National Assessment of Educational Progress found that children in the Detroit public schools scored lower than those of children in all other large cities on tests of reading and mathematics but the new superintendent, Nicolai Vitti, vowed to change that (Higgins 2018). The A. Philip Randolph High School was established to specifically train students for jobs in the new labor market. Consistent with the Kerner Commission's call for easier access to college education, a Detroit Promise program was established, funded by foundations and the city, providing qualified students who graduate from Detroit high schools with free tuition at community colleges. If they are successful there, they may qualify for two more years of college tuition (Smith 2017). It is impressive to read the litany of recommendations the Kerner Commission offered and then to observe that many of them are now being implemented, to some degree, in Detroit due to the capital investments of private firms and foundations.

Positive development is under way that will please those who endorse the ideas of Jane Jacobs about the importance of public spaces for urban vitality and safety (2011). From the first warm days of spring until autumn, Detroit's Campus Martius, Hart Plaza, the Eastern Market area, the east waterfront, and Belle Isle are busy on weekends—and sometimes on week days—with racially diverse crowds shopping, picnicking, eating at cafes, bicycling, running, or demonstrating at protest events. This was unthinkable at the time of the Kerner report.

These are positive steps, and metropolitan Detroit could become the poster child illustrating that a location devastated by jobs loss and riven by race can rise from the ashes. However, it will be necessary to recognize the legacy of decades of racial conflict and hostility that made Detroit the quintessential American apartheid metropolis. Additionally, many governmental program and policies that were implemented recently or will be put into operation soon may have severe adverse consequences for the upward economic mobility of racial minorities and those with limited educations.

## REFERENCES

Allen, Walter R., Channel McLewis, Chantal Jones, and Daniel Harris. 2018. "From Bakke to Fisher: African American Students in U.S. Higher Education over Forty Years." *RSF: The Russell Sage Foundation Journal of the Social Sciences* 4(6): 41–72. DOI: 10.7758/RSF.2018.4.6.03.

Allen-Meares, Paula G., Trina R. Shanks, Larry M. Gant, Leslie Doty Hollingsworth, and Patricia L. Miller. 2017. *A Twenty-First Century Approach to Community Change: Partnering to Improve Life Outcomes for Youth and Families in Under-Served Neighborhoods*. New York: Oxford University Press.

Badger, Emily. 2013. "The Dramatic Racial Bias of Subprime Lending During the Housing Boom." *City Lab*, August 16.

Baime, Albert J. 2014. *The Arsenal of Democracy: FDR, Detroit, and a Quest to Arm an America at War*. New York: Houghton Mifflin Harcourt.

Barrow, James. 1986. "Parks New Racial Issue in Dearborn." *New York Times*, January 19.

Benelli, Mike. 2017. "Michigan Gambled on Charter Schools. Its Children Lost." *New York Times Magazine*, September 5.

Bessette, Anne-Marie. 2006. "Evaluating Public School Funding in Michigan and the Impact of Proposal A." *SPNA Review* 3(1): 22–39.

Blitcock, Dustin. 2017. "CBRE: Downtown Detroit Will See $5.4 Billion Investment Between Now and 2020." Benzinga, July 25. Accessed May 21, 2018. www.benzinga.com/news/17/07/9813519/cbre-downtown-detroit-will-see-5-4-billion-investment-between-now-and-2020.

Bobo, Lawrence D., and Victor Thompson. 2010. "Racialized Mass Incarceration: Poverty, Prejudice, and Punishment." In *Doing Race: 21 Essays for the 21st Century*, edited by Hazel R. Markus and Paula Moya. New York: W. W. Norton.

Bonilla-Silva, Eduardo. 2017. *Racism Without Racists*, 5th ed. Lanham, Md.: Rowman & Littlefield.

Boyd, Herb. 2017. *Black Detroit: A People's History of Self Determination*. New York: Harper Collins.

Boyle, Kevin. 2004. *Arc of Justice: A Saga of Race, Civil Rights, and Murder in the Jazz Age*. New York: Henry Holt.

Bridge Magazine Staff. 2016. *Poison on Tap: How Government Failed Flint and the Heroes who Fought Back*. Traverse City, Mich.: Mission Point Press.

Bureau of Labor Statistics. 2015. "Databases, Tables, and Calculators by Subject: Productivity." Accessed December 1, 2017. http://data.bls.gov/pdq/SurveyOutputServlet.

——. 2018. "Databases, Tables, and Calculators by Subject: Employment." Accessed May 1, 2018. http://data.bls.gov/cgi-bin/dsrv.

Burns, Gus. 2014. "Court Removes Federal Oversight of Detroit Department Stemming from Past Unconstitutional Activities." *Detroit Free Press*, August 25.

Capeci, Dominic J., Jr., and Martha Wilkerson. 1991. *Layered Violence: The Detroit Rioters of 1943*. Jackson: University of Mississippi Press.

Casey, Marcus D., and Bradley L. Hardy. 2018. "The Evolution of Black Neighborhoods Since Kerner." *RSF: The Russell Sage Foundation Journal of the Social Sciences* 4(6): 185–205. DOI: 10.7758/RSF.2018.4.6.09.

Castle, Joann. 2018. *What My Left Hand Was Doing: Lessons from a Grassroots Activist*. Detroit, Mich.: Against the Tide Books.

Chambers, Jennifer, and Christine MacDonald. 2017. "Despite Gains Michigan Schools Are Among Most Segregated." *Detroit News*, December 4.

Chetty, Ray, and Nathaniel Hendren. 2017. "The Impacts of Neighborhoods on Intergenerational Mobility II: County Level Estimates." *NBER* working paper no. 23002. Cambridge, Mass.: National Bureau of Economic Research.

Chetty, Raj, Nathaniel Hendren, and Lawrence F. Katz. 2016. "The Effects of Exposure to Better Neighborhoods on Children: New Evidence from the Moving to Opportunity Experiment." *American Economic Review* 106(4): 855–902.

Citizens Research Council of Michigan. 2013. "Detroit City Government Revenues." Report No. 382. Lansing: Citizens Research Council of Michigan. Accessed May 21, 2018. http://www.crcmich.org/PUBLICAT/2010s/2013/rpt382.pdf.

——. 2016. "Public School Enrollment Trends in Detroit." Memorandum No. 1141. Lansing: Citizens Research Council of Michigan. Accessed May 21, 2018. http://www.crcmich.org/PUBLICAT/2010s/2016/enrollment_trends_in_detroit-2016.pdf.

City of Detroit. 2018. "Start or Grow Your Business." Accessed May 21, 2018. http://www.detroitmi.gov/Detroit-Opportunities/Start-or-Grow-Your-Business/faqid/1616.

Courant, Paul, and Susanna Loeb. 1997. "Centralization of School Financing in Michigan." *Journal of Policy Analysis and Management* 16(1): 114–36.

De La Cruz-Viesca, Melany, Paul M. Ong, Andre Comandon, William A. Darity Jr., and Darrick Hamilton. 2018. "Fifty Years After the Kerner Commission Report: Place, Housing, and Racial Wealth Inequality in Los Angeles." *RSF: The Russell Sage Foundation Journal of the Social Sciences* 4(6): 160–84. DOI: 10.7758/RSF.2018.4.6.08.

Deng, Lan, Eric Seymour, Margaret Dewar, and June Manning Thomas. 2017. "Saving Strong Neighborhoods from the Destruction of Mortgage Foreclosures. The Impact of Community Based Efforts in Detroit." *Housing Policy Debate* 28(2): 1–27.

Dewar, Margaret, Eric Seymour, and Oana Druță. 2015. "Disinvesting in the City: The Role of Tax Foreclosure in Detroit, Michigan." *Urban Affairs Review* 51(5): 587–615.

Downs, Anthony. 1973. *Opening the Suburbs: An Urban Strategy for America*. New Haven, Conn.: Yale University Press.

Edin, Kathryn, and H. Luke Shaeffer. 2016. *$2.00 a Day: Living on Almost Nothing in America*. Boston, Mass.: Mariner Books.

Edwards, Roz. 2018. "City to Expand Strategic

Neighborhood Fund by $130 Million." *Michigan Chronicle*, May 6.

Farley, Reynolds. 2011. "Black-White Residential Segregation: The Waning of American Apartheid." *Contexts* 10(3): 36–43.

Farley, Reynolds, Mick Couper, and Maria Krysan. 2006. "Race and Revitalization in Detroit: A Motor City Story: A Report of Findings from the University of Michigan's 2004 Detroit Area Study." Unpublished paper, University of Michigan, Ann Arbor, Population Studies Center.

Farley, Reynolds, and William H. Frey. 1994. "Changes in the Segregation of Whites from Blacks During the 1980s: Small Steps Toward a More Integrated Society." *American Sociological Review* 59(1): 23–45.

Ferretti, Christine, and Christine MacDonald. 2017. "Victorious Duggan: 'One Detroit for All of Us.'" *Detroit News*, November 7.

Fine, Sidney. 1989. *Violence in the Model City: The Cavanaugh Administration, Race Relations, and the Detroit Riot of 1967*. Ann Arbor: University of Michigan Press.

Freund, David M. P. 2007. *Colored Property: State Policy & White Racial Politics in Suburban America*. Chicago: University of Chicago Press.

Ghent, Andre C., Ruben Hernandez-Murillo, and Michael T. Ouyang. 2014. "Differences in Subprime Loan Pricing Across Races and Neighborhoods." Working Paper No. 2011–022C. St. Louis: Federal Reserve Bank of St. Louis.

Gillham, Patrick F., and Gary T. Marx. 2018. "Changes in the Policing of Civil Disorders Since the Kerner Report: The Police Response to Ferguson, August 2014, and Some Implications for the Twenty-First Century." *RSF: The Russell Sage Foundation Journal of the Social Sciences* 4(6): 122–43. DOI: 10.7758/RSF.2018.4.6.06.

Gillon, Steven M. 2018. *Separate and Unequal: The Kerner Commission and the Unraveling of American Liberalism*. New York: Basic Books.

Glaeser, Edward, David Cutler, and Jacob Vigdor. 1999. "The Rise and Decline of the American Ghetto." *Journal of Political Economy* 107(3): 455–560.

Good, David L. 1989. *Orvie: The Dictator of Dearborn: The Rise and Reign of Orville L. Hubbard*. Detroit, Mich.: Wayne State University Press.

Gooden, Susan T., and Samuel L. Myers Jr. 2018. "The Kerner Commission Report Fifty Years Later: Revisiting the American Dream." *RSF: The Russell Sage Foundation Journal of the Social Sciences* 4(6): 1–17. DOI: 10.7758/RSF.2018.4.6.01.

Gray, Kathleen. 2016. "Legislature Oks $617M Detroit Public Schools Rescue Plan." *Detroit Free Press*, June 9.

Hamlin, Michael. 2012. *A Black Revolutionary's Life in Labor: Black Workers Power in Detroit*. Detroit, Mich.: Against the Tide Books.

Hanna-Attisha, Mona. 2018. *What the Eyes Don't See: A Story of Crisis, Persistence, and Hope in an American City*. New York: Penguin Random House.

Hartigan, John. 1999. *Racial Situations: Class Predicaments of Whiteness in Detroit*. Princeton, N.J.: Princeton University Press.

Haskins, Ron. 2009. "Moynihan Was Right: Now What?" *Annals of the American Academy of Political and Social Science* 621(1): 281–314.

Higgins, Lori. 2018. "Detroit Schools Score Worst in Nation Again but Vitti Vows That Will Change." *Detroit Free Press*, April 10.

Hinton, Elizabeth. 2016. *From the War on Poverty to the War on Crime: The Making of Mass Incarceration in America*. Cambridge, Mass.: Harvard University Press.

Hunter, George. 2017. "Detroit on Pace for Fewest Homicides Since '66." *Detroit News*, December 29.

Jackson, Kenneth T. 1985. *Crabgrass Frontier: The Suburbanization of the United States*. New York: Oxford University Press.

Jacobs, Jane. 2011. *The Death and Life of Great American Cities*. Reprint, New York: Modern Library.

Jenkins, Bette Smith. 1991. "Sojourner Truth Housing Riots." In *Detroit Perspectives: Crosswords and Turning Points*, edited by Wilma Wood Hendrickson. Detroit, Mich.: Wayne State University Press.

Katzman, David M. 1973. *Before the Ghetto: Black Detroit in the Nineteenth Century*. Urbana: University of Illinois Press.

Kerner Commission. 1968. *Report of the National Advisory Commission on Civil Disorders*. Washington: Government Printing Office.

Killeen, Mary B. 2018. "The Incident on Buster Drive: A Precursor to the 1967 Detroit Rebellion." *Michigan History* 102(1): 56–57.

Krysan, Maria, and Kyle Crowder. 2017. *Cycle of Segregation: Social Processes and Residential Stratification*. New York: Russell Sage Foundation.

Kurth, Joel, and Christine MacDonald. 2015. "Volume of Abandoned Homes 'Absolutely Terrifying.'" *Detroit News*, May 14.

Lewis, Chris. 2013. "Does Michigan's Emergency Manager Law Disenfranchise Black Children?" *The Atlantic*, May 13. Accessed May 21, 2018. https://www.theatlantic.com/politics/archive/2013/05/does-michigans-emergency-manager-law-disenfranchise-black-citizens/275639/.

Livingston, Gretchen, and Anna Brown. 2017. *Intermarriage in the U.S. 50 Years After Loving v. Virginia*. Washington, D.C.: Pew Research Center.

Locke, Hubert G. 1969. *The Detroit Riot of 1967*. Detroit, Mich.: Wayne State University Press.

Loessberg, Rick, and John Koskinen. 2018. "Measuring the Distance: The Legacy of the Kerner Report." *RSF: The Russell Sage Foundation Journal of the Social Sciences* 4(6): 99–119. DOI: 10.7758/RSF.2018.4.6.05.

Logan, John, and Brian Stilts. 2011. "The Persistence of Segregation in the Metropolis: New Findings from the 2010 Census." *US2010 Project* Census Brief. Providence, R.I.: Brown University. Accessed May 21, 2018. https://s4.ad.brown.edu/Projects/Diversity/Data/Report/report2.pdf.

Logan, John, Brian Stilts, and Reynolds Farley. 2004. "Segregation of Minorities in the Metropolis." *Demography* 41(1): 1–22.

Massey, Douglas S., and Nancy A. Denton. 1989. "Hypersegregation in U.S. Metropolitan Areas: Black and Hispanic Segregation Along Five Dimensions." *Demography* 26(3): 373–91.

———. 1993. *American Apartheid: Segregation and the Making of the Underclass*. Cambridge, Mass.: Harvard University Press.

Mathias, Charles, and Marion Morris. 1999. "Fair Housing Legislation: Not an Easy Row to Hoe." *Cityspace* 4(3): 21–33.

McGraw, Bill. 2017a. "Before '67 Riot Detroit Thought It Could Avoid Civil Unrest." *Detroit Free Press*, July 15.

———. 2017b. "Riot or Rebellion? What to Call Detroit '67." *Detroit Free Press*, July 17.

———. 2017c. "He Helped Start the 1967 Detroit Riot, Now His Son Struggles with the Legacy." *Detroit Free Press*, July 20.

Michigan Department of Health and Human Services. 2017. "Fertility Rates by Race of Mother, Michigan Residents, Selected Years, 1970–2016." Natality, Pregnancy, and Abortion Statistics. Last updated November 15, 2017. Accessed May 21, 2018. http://www.mdch.state.mi.us/pha/osr/natality/tab1.4.asp.

Miles, Tiya. 2017. *The Dawn of Detroit: A Chronicle of Slavery and Freedom in the City of the Straits*. New York: The New Press.

Moynihan, Daniel Patrick. 1965. *The Negro Family: The Case for National Action*. Washington: U.S. Department of Labor.

National Center for Education Statistics. 2018. "Common Core of Data: America's Public Schools." Accessed May 21, 2018. https://nces.ed.gov/ccd/.

Pew Research Center. 2010. *The Decline of Marriage and Rise of New Families*. Social and Demographic Trends Report. Washington, D.C.: Pew Research Center.

Quillian, Lincoln, Devah Pager, Ole Hexel, and Arnfinn H. Midtbøen. 2017. "Meta-Analysis of Field Experiments Shows No Change in Racial Discrimination in Hiring Over Time." *Proceedings of the National Academy of Sciences* 114(4): 10870–75.

Rodwan, Gail. 2017. *The Story of Sherwood Forest: One Hundred Years in a Detroit Neighborhood*. Detroit, Mich.: Wayne State University Press.

Rothstein, Richard. 2017. *The Color of Law: A Forgotten History of How Our Government Segregated America*. New York: W. W. Norton.

Ruggles, Steven, Ronald Goeken, Josiah Grover, and Matthew Suber. 2017. "Integrated Public Use Microdata Series: Version 7.0" [dataset]. Minneapolis: University of Minnesota. DOI: 10.18128/D010.V7.0.

Rugh, Jacob S., and Douglas S. Massey. 2010. "Racial Segregation and the American Foreclosure Crisis." *American Sociological Review* 75(5): 629–51.

Sawhill, Isabel, and Ron Haskins. 2016. "The Decline of the American Family: Can Anything be Done to Stop the Damage?" *Annals of the American Academy of Political and Social Science* 667(1): 8–34.

Sawhill, Isabel, and Jonna Venator. 2015. "Is There a Shortage of Marriageable Men?" *Center on Children and Families* Brief No. 56. Washington, D.C.: Brookings Institution.

Schwartz, Robin. 2017. "Detroit's Wailing Wall." In *The Intersection: What Detroit Has Gained, and Lost, 50 Years After the Uprising of 1967*, edited by Bridge Magazine and The Detroit Journalism Cooperative. Traverse City: Mission Point Press.

Serrin, William. 1969. "Mayor Hubbard Gives Dearborn What It Wants—and Then Some." *New York Times*, January 12.

Sharkey, Patrick. 2018. *Uneasy Peace: The Great Crime Decline, the Renewal of City Life, and the Next War on Poverty*. New York: W. W. Norton.

Smith, Ashley. 2017. "Early Success in Detroit Promise Program." *Inside Higher Education*, July 27. Accessed May 21, 2018. https://www.insidehighered.com/quicktakes/2017/07/27/early-success-detroit-promise-program.

Snyder, Rick. 2017. "Gov. Rick Snyder: Michigan Now More Competitive for New Jobs, Diverse Industries." Press Release, July 26. Lansing: Office of Governor Rick Snyder, State of Michigan. Accessed May 21, 2018. https://www.michigan.gov/snyder/0,4668,7-277-57577_57657-427329--,00.html.

Spreen, Johannes, and Diane Holloway. 2005. *Who Killed Detroit? Other Cities Beware*. Lincoln, Neb.: iUniverse.

Sugrue, Thomas J. 1996. The *Origins of the Urban Crisis: Race and Inequality in Postwar Detroit*. Princeton, N.J.: Princeton University Press.

Thomas, Norman C. 1966. *Rule 9: Politics, Administration and Civil Rights*. New York: Random House.

Thomas, Richard W. 1992. *Life for Us Is What We Make It: Building Black Community in Detroit: 1915–1945*. Bloomington: Indiana University Press.

Thompson, Heather Ann. 2001. *Whose Detroit? Politics, Labor and Race in a Modern American City*. Ithaca, N.Y.: Cornell University Press.

———. 2010. "Why Mass Incarceration Matters: Rethinking Crisis, Decline, and Transformation in Postwar American History." *Journal of American History* 97(3): 703–34.

———. 2013. "Unmaking the Motor City in the Age of Mass Incarceration." *Journal of Law and Society* 41(5): 41–61.

———. 2016. *Blood in the Water: The Attica Prison Uprising of 1971 and Its Legacy*. New York: Pantheon.

Turner, Margery Austin, Diane K. Levy, Doug Wissoker, Claudia L. Aranda, Rob Pitingolo, and Rob Santos. 2013. *Housing Discrimination Against Racial and Ethnic Minorities 2012*. Washington, D.C.: The Urban Institute.

U.S. Census Bureau. 2016. "American Community Survey." Washington: Government Printing Office. Accessed May 21, 2018. https://www.census.gov/programs-surveys/acs/news/data-releases.html.

University of Michigan. 2017. "Cost of Attendance: Estimated Fall/Winter, Michigan Residents (In-State)." Accessed December 1, 2017. https://finaid.umich.edu/cost-of-attendance.

Van Buren, April. 2016. "The Decline of Detroit's Neighborhood Schools," Michigan Public Radio, August 16. Accessed December 1, 2017. http://stateofopportunity.michiganradio.org/post/decline-detroits-neighborhood-schools.

Vine, Phyllis. 2004. *One Man's Castle: Clarence Darrow in Defense of the American Dream*. New York: Harper Collins.

Wilkinson, Isabel. 1986. "Race Raised as Issue in Variety of Disputes at Detroit's Borders." *New York Times*, October 10.

Williams, Corey. 2015. "Whites Moving into Detroit, Blacks Moving Out as City Shrinks," *Crain's Business Detroit*, May 15.

Wilson, William Julius. 1978. *The Declining Significance of Race: Blacks and Changing American Institutions*. Chicago: University of Chicago Press.

———. 1987. *The Truly Disadvantaged: The Inner City, The Underclass and Public Policy*. Chicago: University of Chicago Press.

———. 1996. *When Work Disappears: The World of the Urban Poor*. New York: Alfred A. Knopf.

Zasloff, Jonathan. 2016. "The Secret History of the Fair Housing Act." *Harvard Journal on Legislation* 53(247): 247–77.

Zelizer, Julian E. 2016. "Introduction to the 2016 Edition." In *The Kerner Report: The National Advisory Commission on Civil Disorders*, edited by Sean Wilenz. Princeton, N.J.: Princeton University Press.

Zunz, Olivier. 1982. The *Changing Face of Inequality: Urbanization, Industrial Development and Immigration in Detroit: 1880–1920*. Chicago: University of Chicago Press.